THE NOVEL OF FEMALE ADULTERY

Also by Bill Overton

THE MERCHANT OF VENICE: Text and Performance
THE UNOFFICIAL TROLLOPE
THE WINTER'S TALE: The Critics Debate

The Novel of Female Adultery

Love and Gender in Continental European Fiction, 1830–1900

Bill Overton
Senior Lecturer in English
Loughborough University

First published in Great Britain 1996 by
MACMILLAN PRESS LTD
Houndmills, Basingstoke, Hampshire RG21 6XS
and London
Companies and representatives
throughout the world

A catalogue record for this book is available
from the British Library.

ISBN 0–333–61451–8

First published in the United States of America 1996 by
ST. MARTIN'S PRESS, INC.,
Scholarly and Reference Division,
175 Fifth Avenue,
New York, N.Y. 10010

ISBN 0–312–16500–5

Library of Congress Cataloging-in-Publication Data
Overton, Bill.
The novel of female adultery : love and gender in continental
European fiction, 1830–1900 / Bill Overton.
p.   cm.
Includes bibliographical references and index.
ISBN 0–312–16500–5 (cloth)
1. Fiction—19th century—History and criticism.   2. Adultery in
literature.   I. Title.
PN3352.A38O84   1996
809.3'9353—dc20   96–27423
                                                             CIP

10   9   8   7   6   5   4   3   2   1
05   04   03   02   01   00   99   98   97   96

Printed and bound in Great Britain by
Antony Rowe Ltd, Chippenham, Wiltshire

Produced as camera-ready copy by the author using
Impression Publisher on an Acorn Archimedes

Contents

Preface

During the second two-thirds of the nineteenth century a distinct type of novel, dealing with female adultery, was widely produced and widely read in Continental Europe. The leading features of novels of this type are strikingly similar. With minor variations, each is based on a plot in which a married woman from the middle or upper classes is seduced by an unmarried man and comes to grief. The examples discussed in this book, which originate from France, Russia, Denmark, Germany, Portugal and Spain, not only achieved large circulation in their own day, in translation as well as in their original languages, but most have also become known as classics of European writing. The type is further characterized by an impersonal narrative voice, and by male authorship.

In his book *Adultery in the Novel: Contract and Transgression*, Tony Tanner puts forward several far-reaching claims about the relationship between adultery and the novel, and indeed between adultery and Western literature in general.[1] The aims of this study are less sweeping, for it is confined to the particular kind of novel, centred on female adultery, identified above. Nevertheless, the topic is still of sufficient breadth and complexity to demand much. First, it requires an attempt to understand the nineteenth-century novel of adultery in history. This means both offering a history of this type of fiction and placing it within its various cultural contexts. Second, and as a corollary, it calls for analysis of the specific forms taken by novels of adultery in different national traditions and within different ideological frameworks. Although works belonging to the tradition have much in common, each comes out of a distinct cultural and historical formation, and the story told in each is by no means the same. Third, and perhaps most important, this book aims to demonstrate the crucial role played in nineteenth-century adultery fiction by questions of gender.

All the writers of the novels of adultery to be discussed came from countries in which adultery was understood as a crime which husbands as well as wives could commit. Nevertheless, a double standard operated in each of these countries, and in most cases this was vested both in law and in social practice. It is not by accident, then, that the novel of adultery is specifically a novel of female adultery. Yet, though it is well established that there existed a tradition of novels of adultery in the nineteenth century,[2] the term itself conceals the fact which is most specific to it and which indeed chiefly defines it as a tradition. No classic novel, let alone any fictional tradition, is based on male adultery. The widely used term 'novel of adultery' is therefore a misnomer which masks a gender bias both in the novels themselves and in the critical discourses within which they have been interpreted. This is why I employ the term 'novel of female adultery' instead.

The failure to recognize sufficiently the gender bias of nineteenth-century adultery fiction is the single most important limitation of previous critical treatments of the subject. The most interesting and ambitious of such treatments, Tony Tanner's, provides an example. Tanner remarks in his Introduction that 'it is almost inevitably the adulterous *woman* on which [sic] many nineteenth-century novels focus' (p. 13). Yet, although he adds that this is 'a matter for later comment', he spends comparatively little time in the rest of his long book addressing its implications. The rather limited priority he gives to gender is probably connected with the fact that all of the philosophical literature he considers concerning marriage and adultery – including work by Locke, Maine, Rousseau and Vico – is written from a perspective which is patriarchal if not also, as in the case of Vico, misogynist. The generalizations which result therefore apply to particular philosophical or, better, ideological traditions; they are not universally valid. Tanner does not recognize that the view that 'adultery threatens all social bonds' (p. 29) is no absolute, but the product of a way of thinking which is culturally and historically produced. His assertion that 'society depends' on the 'interfamilial exchange of the daughter in marriage' (pp. 28–9) is not true of all societies, whether possible, historical or existing. No one could guess from his book that the significance of adultery might have been controversial, even in the nineteenth century. For instance, as I will show, female novelists such as George Sand and Emilia Pardo Bazán challenged orthodox thinking about marriage and adultery; and not all of their male counterparts constructed adultery in conventional ways. A case in point is the relationship between attitudes to adultery and the availability or otherwise of divorce, which varied across Europe. When Tanner remarks that divorce is not an issue in the novels he considers, he fails to take into account whether it was obtainable or not, and he refrains from examining the assumptions which could allow it to be dismissed so easily. Yet, as Chapter 7 will demonstrate, the novel of female adultery took a different form in the few countries in which divorce was both legal and, though not without difficulty, acceptable.

This book offers, then, a comparative approach to the history of the novel of adultery from the perspective of gender. The opening chapter defines the terms 'adultery' and 'novel of adultery', and discusses how the form arose in Continental Europe, but failed to appear in Britain. The next three chapters show how the novel of female adultery developed in France from the traditions of the libertine text and the Romantic confession during a period of political reaction and of bourgeois consolidation; and the fifth illustrates some alternatives, including the challenges mounted by George Sand and other Frenchwomen. The final three chapters deal with examples of the novel of female adultery from Russia, Denmark, Germany, Portugal and Spain, demonstrating how it functioned within various national traditions and ideologies.

To compare examples of the form from different cultures is to put in question the common assumption that the novel of adultery is all of a piece. Each writer whose work is discussed here used the form in his own way and for his own purposes; each text is inflected by the particular culture and history within which it was written. But there is no canonical novel of female adultery written by a woman. The agenda of the form is intrinsically male.

Acknowledgements

No study of any scope can be completed without incurring many debts, and this is no exception. However, it is difficult to obtain funding for so heterodox a project as mine has been, especially within the prevailing climate of higher education in Britain. I therefore have no grant-awarding bodies to thank for their support; but I am very grateful to Loughborough University for allowing me a year's study leave during which I could work on the project almost uninterruptedly. I also wish to express my very great appreciation of the help given by staff at the Pilkington Library, Loughborough University, and at the other libraries I have used, especially the British Library and the libraries of Nottingham, Leicester and Cambridge Universities.

Most of my debts, however, are to individuals. I am grateful to Professors Malcolm Jones and Richard Stites for their kindness and courtesy in answering queries arising from Chapter 6; to Bill Leatherbarrow, Michael Robinson and Hilary Owen for their help in reading and commenting on drafts of Chapters 6, 7 and 8 respectively; to John Lucas and Marion Shaw for reading through and commenting on the completed book in draft; to Chris White for her suggestions of reading for Chapter 1 and of the drawing by Gustav Klimt for the cover illustration; to Grace Overton, Susan Overton and Helen Peberdy for encouragement and support; and to colleagues in the Department of English and Drama at Loughborough University for their backing and forbearance. Finally, I wish to express special thanks for the help I have received from two people who have read through and commented on the book while I have been drafting it: Elaine Hobby, who also advised on questions of translation from the Russian; and Keith Overton, who also advised on questions of translation from the German. The book has benefited greatly from all the help I have received; responsibility for the failings which remain is mine.

Chronology

1840   Birth of Zola

1841   Balzac, 'La Femme de province', and Lucas, 'La Femme adultère', in *Les Français peints par eux-mêmes*

1842   Balzac, *A Woman of Thirty* and Preface to *Human Comedy*

1843   Balzac, *The Muse of the Department*; births of Pérez Galdós and Eça de Queirós; death of Tristan

1844   Mérimée, *Arsène Guillot*

1847   Baudelaire, *La Fanfarlo*; d'Agoult ('Daniel Stern'), *Valentia*; Herzen, *Who Is to Blame?*; Charlotte Brontë, *Jane Eyre*; Emily Brontë, *Wuthering Heights*; birth of Jacobsen

1848   Revolutions across most of Europe; Dumas, *La Dame aux camélias*; Dickens, *Dombey and Son*; Thackeray, *Vanity Fair*; deaths of Chateaubriand and Blicher

1850   Death of Balzac; Hawthorne, *The Scarlet Letter*

1851   Birth of Pardo Bazán

1852   Napoleon III becomes Emperor of France; birth of Alas

1853   Outbreak of hostilities between Russia and Turkey

1854   Start of Crimean War

1855   Champfleury, *Les Bourgeois de Molinchart*

1856   End of Crimean War

1857   Flaubert, *Madame Bovary*; acquittal on charges of obscenity; death of Musset

1858   Feydeau, *Fanny*; Michelet, *L'Amour*; Proudhon, *De la Justice dans la Révolution et dans l'Église*

1859   Tolstoy, *Family Happiness*

1860   Michelet, *La Femme*; birth of Chekhov

1861   Emancipation of serfs in Russia

1863   Fromentin, *Dominique*; Chernyshevsky, *What Is to Be Done?*

1864   Defeat of Denmark by Austria and Prussia over Schleswig-Holstein; Chernyshevsky exiled for life

1866   Defeat of Austria by Prussia; Dumas, *L'Affaire Clémenceau*; first volume of Larousse, *Grand dictionnaire universel du dix-neuvième siècle* (completed 1886)

1867   Sand, *Le Dernier amour*; Zola, *Thérèse Raquin*; death of Baudelaire

1868   Revolution in Spain and abdication of Isabella II

1869   Flaubert, *Sentimental Education*; Trollope, *He Knew He Was Right*; Mill, *The Subjection of Women*

1870   Franco-Prussian War, leading to fall of Second Empire in France; Amadeo of Savoy becomes King of Spain; Andersen, 'The Family of Hen-Grethe'; death of Mérimée

1871	Paris Commune; unification of Germany and foundation of Second Reich under Prussian hegemony
1872	Dumas, *La Question de la femme* and *L'Homme-femme*; George Eliot, *Middlemarch*
1873	Abdication of Amadeo and proclamation of First Republic in Spain; death of Feydeau
1874	First Republic in Spain overthrown
1875	Restoration of Spanish monarchy; Eça de Queirós, *The Sin of Father Amaro*; Zola, *The Abbé Mouret's Sin*; Proudhon, *La Pornocratie ou les Femmes dans les Temps Modernes*
1876	Jacobsen, *Marie Grubbe*; deaths of d'Agoult, Fromentin, and George Sand
1878	Tolstoy, *Anna Karenina*; Eça de Queirós, *Cousin Bazilio*
1879	Ibsen, *A Doll's House*
1880	Jacobsen, *Niels Lyhne*; Zola, *The Experimental Novel*; death of Flaubert
1881	Pardo Bazán, *A Wedding Journey*
1882	Fontane, *L'Adultera*
1884	Reintroduction of divorce in France; Galdós, *La de Bringas*; Alas ('Clarín'), *La Regenta* (Part I)
1885	Alas, *La Regenta* (Part 2); death of Jacobsen
1886	Chekhov, 'Agafya' and 'Misfortune'; Pardo Bazán, *The House of Ulloa*; Ibsen, *Rosmersholm*
1887	Galdós, *Fortunata and Jacinta*
1888	Strindberg, *Miss Julie*
1889	Deaths of Champfleury and Chernyshevsky
1891	Tolstoy, *The Kreutzer Sonata*; Fontane, *Beyond Recall*
1893	Chekhov, 'An Anonymous Story'
1895	Chekhov, 'Three Years'; Fontane, *Effi Briest*; death of Dumas *fils*
1898	Chekhov, 'A Case History'; death of Fontane
1899	Chekhov, 'A Lady with a Dog'
1900	Tolstoy, *Resurrection*; death of Eça de Queirós
1901	Death of Alas
1902	Death of Zola
1903	Chekhov, 'A Marriageable Girl'
1904	Death of Chekhov
1910	Death of Tolstoy
1911	Tolstoy, 'The Devil' (written 1891)
1920	Death of Pérez Galdós
1921	Death of Pardo Bazán

Editions Used and References

References to all texts discussed are given in parentheses immediately after the quotation or citation; an endnote after the first reference identifies the edition or editions used.

The form of the references is: part number (where applicable), in upper-case Roman; chapter number (where applicable), again in Roman, lower-case if preceded by part number; and page number in Arabic. In the second half of the first chapter, and in the following four chapters, all of which deal with writing in French, the page number of the English translation (where available) is followed by a semi-colon, and then the page number of the French edition I have used. Where I have modified the translation, this is indicated by the abbreviation 'TM'.

Where more than one English translation exists, I have normally chosen the one most likely to be accessible. Where no translation into English exists, and in the three cases where the only such translations are rare (George Sand's *Jacques*, Mérimée's *Arsène Guillot* and Feydeau's *Fanny*), all translation of material quoted is my own. As in the cases where I have modified an existing translation, I have aimed for an accurate equivalent, though the result may be more literal than literary.

In the remaining three chapters, which deal with the novel of female adultery in a variety of cultures from Russian, Danish and German to Portuguese and Spanish, references are to the English translation only, except where this is unsatisfactory.

The date of first publication in book form for each literary work cited is given in parentheses after its title on the first occasion when it is mentioned. The title is normally cited in English where there is a translation, but otherwise in the original language followed by an English translation of the title in parentheses. Details of serial publication, if any, are given in discussion or in the notes where this is relevant. Publication dates in the Chronology follow the same convention.

1

Female Adultery, Ideology and Nineteenth-Century Fiction

At the end of the nineteenth century, while denouncing the art of his time, Leo Tolstoy declared that 'Adultery is not only the favourite, but almost the only theme of all the novels.'[1] As he was only too well aware, adultery had figured largely in his own fiction, although he could not be accused of the erotic preoccupations which he was attacking. What Tolstoy did not say, and might not necessarily have recognized, is that the novel of adultery is in effect the novel of female adultery. This is all the more surprising in that he did not support the double standard of sexual morality which has long been entrenched in Western as in most other cultures.[2] He had already written *The Devil* (1911), centred on male adulterous desire and published after his death, and he was already working on *Resurrection* (1899), which condemns male fornication. Yet his most famous achievement is his own novel of female adultery, *Anna Karenina* (1878), and his most notorious work, *The Kreutzer Sonata* (1891), is based on a husband's suspicion of his wife's infidelity.

With the partial exception of a few works by Tolstoy and a small number of other writers whose fiction is also discussed in this book, male sexual transgression plays only a minor role in the Western novelistic tradition. Indeed, almost the only nineteenth-century novels in the literary canon to centre on such transgression concern fornication by a priest. Even then, however, as in *The Abbé Mouret's Sin*, by Émile Zola, or *The Sin of Father Amaro*, by the Portuguese José Maria Eça de Queirós, both first published in 1875, the issue is not disapproval of male sexual misconduct. Instead, while Zola challenges the sexual repressiveness of Catholic doctrine, Eça attacks the corruption of priests, Church and state.[3]

The relationship between literary texts, ideology, and the canon is extremely complex, but the fact that novels of female adultery have

1

stood for so long as the novel of adultery suggests how large a part ideology plays in deciding meanings. For this reason it is necessary to begin with definitions – both of adultery and of the novel of adultery. Then, as this type of novel is specific to nineteenth-century Continental Europe, the next step is to consider not only how and why it developed where it did, but why it never became established in the English-speaking world during that period.

It is essential to recognize from the start that there is no single, universally applicable definition of adultery. Instead, the concept of adultery varies, in some respects critically, across different cultures and different historical periods. For instance, Jack Goody points out that,

> although in European law adultery is defined as sexual intercourse where one of the partners is married, in most other societies it is only considered adultery when the woman is married. This is the case in Roman law. The reason for this is that in general marriage confers relatively exclusive rights on a man over the sexual services of a woman. It is most unusual to find that the woman acquires similar rights over the male, even in matrilineal societies.[4]

The gender bias highlighted by this observation is self-evident in the novel of female adultery, though it goes unremarked in the definition given by the *OED*: 'Violation of the marriage bed; the voluntary sexual intercourse of a married person with one of the opposite sex, whether unmarried, or married to another (the former case being technically designated *single*, the latter *double adultery*).' Such formal definitions are, then, of interest not only for what they contain, but also for what they omit. For example, it is worth comparing the *OED* definition with Annette Lawson's in her sociological study of adultery: 'In both church and law, adultery is technically sexual intercourse between a married woman or man and someone who is not at that time their spouse.'[5] Unlike the *OED* definition, Lawson's takes consent for granted, though in some societies a married woman is considered to have committed adultery even if she has been raped. But in two other respects Lawson goes beyond the *OED* definition. She remarks that sexual intimacy between a married man or woman and another person of the same sex can also be considered as adultery, and has indeed been prosecuted on the same terms in one North American state.

She further notes that over 40 per cent of the participants in her study 'reported a relationship as adulterous even though they and their partners had "never made love"'.[6]

This latter finding has parallels in literary-critical discussions of adultery. Of the three main examples analysed by Tony Tanner in the best-known study of the subject, *Adultery in the Novel*, two, Rousseau's *Julie, or The New Eloise* (1761) and Goethe's *Elective Affinities* (1809), centre on relationships which are not in fact adulterous. Similarly, two recent psychoanalytical studies present as novels of adultery various texts in which adultery is absent or marginal. Naomi Segal remarks that the ten examples of the French Romantic confession which she discusses are also, 'in most cases, novels of adultery', although adultery takes place in only two of them and is crucial to none; and Alison Sinclair treats as novels of adultery Madame de Lafayette's *The Princesse de Clèves* (1678) and Dickens's *Dombey and Son* (1848), in both of which the main female character rejects adultery.[7]

The trouble with such terminological promiscuity is that it risks obscuring what is at issue. On the one hand, there is a case for extending the definition of adultery to include adulterous desire. This would be in keeping with Christ's remark that 'whosoever looketh on a woman to lust after her hath committed adultery with her already in his heart' (Matthew 5: 28); and it would support Tanner's analysis of structures of power, desire and taboo in the bourgeois family, as well as Segal's and Sinclair's psychoanalytical interpretations of family and sexual conflict. On the other hand, the question whether or not adultery actually occurs is fraught with consequence in fiction as in life itself. In nineteenth-century novels, for example, a common result for a woman who commits adultery is death. By contrast, as Chapter 5 will show, novels of the period in which illicit love stops short of adultery present a range of different outcomes, and these have different implications again. The present study therefore confines itself to the *OED* definition of adultery. It does so not out of literal-mindedness, but because its primary focus is adultery as a social, an ideological and a legal fact.

However, what should already be clear, as a fact of almost equal consequence to whether or not adultery takes place, is the double standard of morality which is so deeply rooted in attitudes to sexual transgression. Although this passes without comment in almost all dictionary definitions, its importance in the fiction of adultery is fundamental.

The *OED* definition begins 'Violation of the marriage bed', and this requires a further though perhaps obvious stipulation. Simply, although lovers can be unfaithful, there can be no adultery without marriage. Intercourse between unmarried persons is not adultery but fornication; it is on that ground only of marginal interest here. In his history of divorce in Western society, Roderick Phillips clarifies the significance of the distinction:

> Adultery usually fell between the extremes of illicit sexual activity. It was not an offense against nature itself, but it was readily viewed as an offense against the nature of marriage, and it was this that made adultery more serious an offense than premarital sex. With fornication there was not necessarily any victim or deception, and it could even be a preliminary to marriage; in many cultures sexual intercourse was socially acceptable after betrothal but before marriage. Adultery was quite a different matter in that it usually involved deception and that it had a victim: the adulterer's spouse. Moreover it necessarily involved a breach of the contract of sexual exclusivity that marriage entailed.[8]

No discussion of adultery can be adequate without taking fully into account the institution of marriage, and especially the specific functions which marriage serves.

Like the definition of adultery, such functions vary in different societies and in different periods, and even in different classes within the same society and period. The social and historical context of the novel of female adultery is principally a number of bourgeois societies in nineteenth-century Continental Europe. In those societies, as in some others at different times and in different places, marriage is linked very closely to the transmission of property, to the idea of the family, and to the role of motherhood. These above all are the factors, absent from dictionary definitions, which dominate novels of adultery, and which have led to the representation of adultery in Western fiction almost as an offence peculiar to females. Perhaps that bias is not surprising, allowing for the fact noted by Jack Goody that in many societies adultery is defined as sexual intercourse involving a married woman. Nevertheless, in light of the distinction between single and double adultery, it is significant that the great majority of novels of adultery deal with single adultery on the part of the female. It is important to appreciate this point because, thanks to the double standard, the participation of a female in sex outside marriage has been and to a large extent still is regarded more seriously than that of a male. The fact that the adultery of males, whether married or not, is considered to be of little or no consequence helps explain why, in the novel of female adultery, double adultery is of no special concern. But only such additional factors as the importance of property, family and motherhood can explain why the same tradition virtually ignores the adultery of unmarried women, despite the powerful stigmas attached to female unchastity.

The focus of the novel of adultery is indeed highly selective. Though – or rather because – this kind of fiction is fraught with social and ideological meaning, it has limited itself to only a few of the possible categories of adultery identified by dictionaries, sociologists and the law. Such selectiveness, when once discerned, makes it easier to recognize the assumptions behind the literary tradition. What complicates definition of the novel of adultery is, instead, the nature of the attention given to the issue in fiction. Although, as Tolstoy complained, adultery is a frequent fictional theme, those novels in which it is the leading theme compose a select group. In this way the novel of adultery may be defined as any novel in which one or more adulterous liaisons are central to its concerns as identified by its action, themes and structure. On such a definition *Madame Bovary* (1857) is very plainly a novel of adultery, while, if a little less plainly, *The Red and the Black* (1830) is not; for Flaubert gives adultery a prominence and a focus which Stendhal applies to a variety of topics, only one of which is adultery. *The Red and the Black* is not a novel of adultery, but a novel in which adultery features. As I have already suggested, the main factor in this difference is to be found in attitudes to gender. For Stendhal, as with other male writers until very recently, a novel about the career of a young man could not centre on the theme of adultery, though its action might well include one or more adulterous episodes. Instead, novels centred on male sexual experience almost always place that experience outside marriage altogether. Examples in the French literary canon include Prévost's *Manon Lescaut* (1731), Constant's *Adolphe* (1816), and Musset's *Confession of a Child of the Century* (1836), in none of which are the principal male or female characters married. In *The Red and the Black*, Julien Sorel has two extra-marital affairs, one of which is adulterous, but these are not the novel's main business. Had Stendhal focused on the experience of Madame de Rênal, Julien's married lover, he would have written a novel of adultery within the tradition I am addressing. It was that kind of novel, centred almost exclusively on the experience of a married woman, which Flaubert produced in *Madame Bovary*. Yet this was precisely the kind of novel which could not be accepted during the same period in Britain. Before going any further, it is important to consider what conditions might account for the absence from Britain of a tradition which became so firmly established across Continental Europe.

Donald Thomas's history of literary censorship in England makes very clear why adultery could not become more than a marginal theme in nineteenth-century British fiction. Paradoxically, during a period in which it became much more difficult to secure convictions for seditious libel or blasphemous libel, the law of obscene libel was applied with increasing strictness. In 1888 and 1889 Henry Vizetelly was first fined and then imprisoned for publishing translations of novels by Zola and Maupassant among others; and as late as 1909 the National Vigilance Association succeeded in obtaining 'a triumphal destruction order for Balzac's *Contes Drolatiques*'.[9] However, as Thomas indicates,

> the most important form of moral censorship was one with which the law was not directly concerned. It was a censorship exercised ultimately by booksellers and libraries, penultimately by publishers or editors, and in the first place by authors themselves. And when all this was done there still remained the individual censorship of the buyer or the borrower.[10]

Perhaps the most effective material control was exercised by the lending libraries, with their powerful Evangelical influence. As Guinevere L. Griest has pointed out, the largest of the libraries, Mudie's, was for nearly 50 years 'the single most important distributor of fiction'.[11] Not for nothing did the library boast the word 'Select' in its title. Mudie watchfully controlled what he published, and works he believed unsuitable, such as Meredith's *The Ordeal of Richard Feverel* (1859), were banned or withdrawn. Fiction published serially in magazines was subject to even tighter constraints, because of the requirement that it be suitable for family reading. Thackeray, who, in the Preface to *Pendennis* (1850), had famously chafed at the influence of Mrs Grundy, found himself having to enforce even tighter restrictions when he edited the *Cornhill*, one of the most successful magazines of the period.[12] Where the curbs imposed by the lending libraries and magazines did not apply, as in the publication of verse, authors exercised their own restraint. It is striking that the two most successful long narrative poems of the period, *Idylls of the King* (1859–86) and *The Ring and the Book* (1869), both turn on the question of adultery. But it is equally striking that Tennyson makes adultery both symptom and cause of social disintegration, and that Browning has the virtue of his heroine Pompilia proved immaculate.

The same ideological constraints ruled the visual arts as well as fiction. In her study of representations of women in Victorian Britain, Lynda Nead has pointed out that, 'in comparison with images of the feminine ideal and the prostitute, there are very few visual representations of the adulteress', and that, 'as far as it is possible to tell, Augustus Egg's trilogy *Past and Present*, which was shown in 1858, was the only modern-life depiction of adultery exhibited at the Royal Academy during the middle decades of the nineteenth century'.[13] Details in two of the panels of Egg's triptych signify baneful influence from France, for, as Nead also indicates, 'French society was regarded as unstable and dangerous; its literature was believed to be a source of corruption and immorality and many contemporaries were concerned about the harmful reverberations of French morality in England.'[14] Such were the attitudes which galvanized the National Vigilance Association in its campaign against French novels with sexual themes, and which sharply constrained the treatment of parallel themes in Britain.

Again, it is important to remember that these constraints were widely supported. In 1890, at the high-water mark of Victorian prudery, *The New Review* published essays by Walter Besant, Eliza Lynn Linton and Thomas Hardy on 'Candour in English Fiction'. The first of the three, which is the most conservative, not only defends censorship but suggests that it is best exercised by writers themselves. In the conclusion to his essay, Besant declares:

Can any writer demand greater freedom than has been taken by the authors of *Adam Bede*, *A Terrible Temptation*, *Ruth*, or *The Scarlet Letter*? With these examples before him, no one, surely, ought to complain that he is not permitted to treat of Love free and disobedient. The author, however, must recognise in his work the fact that such Love is outside the social pale and is destructive of the very basis of society. He *must*. This is not a law laid down by the great authority, Average Opinion, but by Art herself, who will not allow the creation of impossible figures moving in an unnatural atmosphere. Those writers who yearn to treat of the adulteress and the courtesan because they love to dwell on images of lust are best kept in check by existing discouragements.[15]

This judgement from a distinguished and by no means illiberal Victorian man of letters acknowledges only the motive of salacity for fiction about adultery or prostitution, and fully accepts what he euphemistically terms 'discouragements' for such fiction. But the novels cited by Besant as if they were examples of British literary freedom are even more revealing. First, Besant was presumably unaware, or had forgotten, that *A Terrible Temptation* (1871) was one of the several novels by Charles Reade which Mudie banned. The entry in John Sutherland's *Longman Companion to Victorian Fiction* indicates that one of the characters, a discarded mistress, 'provoked extreme critical hostility and *The Times* advised mothers to keep the first volume away from unmarried daughters'.[16] Second, though both Elizabeth Gaskell's *Ruth* (1853) and George Eliot's *Adam Bede* (1859) were stocked by Mudie's, neither was published without protest. More significantly, both were written within conventions which did not threaten but rather endorsed accepted Christian morality.

The most important of those conventions was that the so-called fallen woman be sexually innocent: she owes her seduction not to sexual desire on her own part, which was inadmissible in British novels of this period, but to male importunity and her own ignorance (also, in the case of Eliot's Hetty Sorrel, to vanity and ambition). Next, and almost equally important, fornication cannot lead to pleasure or benefit. Instead the liaison is brief, and its effects are not only unhappy but often fatal. Ruth is persecuted for passing as a widow, and she dies from the typhus she catches from nursing her seducer; Hetty is convicted of infanticide, and, though her sentence of death is commuted, she dies while returning from transportation. In such ways the figure of the so-called fallen woman was moralized and made acceptable. Indeed, Ruth is not only a pure but a redemptive character.

In Besant's fourth example, Hawthorne's *The Scarlet Letter* (1850), the sin is adultery rather than fornication, but again the focus is on its impact and consequences. The novel sets the act of adultery in the past; it punishes the mother in part through the daughter she has by her lover; it requires the mother to redeem herself through good works; and, most of all, because her lover is a minister, it is concerned with him as well as with her, and also with her avenging husband. In this way *The Scarlet Letter* is a novel not of adultery but of post-adultery, half historical, half allegorical, dealing with spiritual crime and punishment. Hawthorne wrote within and about a specifically North American culture, and few British novels of the period went even as far as he. Instead, writers exercised their ingenuity by devising plots which enabled matrimonial irregularity to be depicted without undue compromise to moral convention. One common device, especially in the 1860s, was bigamy; another was the bogus wedding. As Tom Winnifrith says, the former allowed the heroine to be 'technically guilty but morally innocent', and the latter 'to have the cake of rectitude and eat the fruit of sin'.[17] However, the most interesting way in which novels of the period dealt with sexual sin was to refract or displace it. This suggests not only the self-censorship which Besant would later commend, but an internalized repression of taboo subjects.

The theme of adultery arrived early in the history of the novel in Britain, in the work of writers of bourgeois fiction such as Aphra Behn and Daniel Defoe. Yet, as the British novel developed, the focus shifted from adultery: to marriage on the one hand and seduction on the other. That pivotal text, Samuel Richardson's *Pamela* (1740–1), celebrates the one after first threatening the other; and Richardson went on to develop each theme in *Sir Charles Grandison* (1753–4) and *Clarissa* (1747–8) respectively. By virtue of the increasing prudery of British society after the middle of the eighteenth century, the theme of adultery in fiction became submerged. According to Judith Armstrong, 'Even cheap fiction, of second-rate but non-pornographic quality, avoided adultery like the plague.'[18] The same is true of politer forms. In Jane Austen's *Mansfield Park* (1814) adultery happens offstage, to the accompaniment of much deprecation from narrator and characters, and exemplary fictive punishment. Elsewhere the subject is more often displaced than given even this kind of marginal treatment. Jane Eyre recoils from Rochester; in *Vanity Fair* (1848) Thackeray leaves ambiguous how far Becky Sharp really goes with Lord Steyne; and Lady Glencora, in Trollope's Palliser series, backs off from Burgo Fitzgerald. More interesting still are those texts in which a surrogate for or a spectre of adultery has its impact: *Wuthering Heights* (1847), in the relation between Cathy and Heathcliff; *Dombey and Son* (1848), where Edith runs off with Carker only to repudiate him; *Bleak House* (1853), in Lady Dedlock's guilty past; Trollope's *He Knew He Was Right* (1869), in which a husband goes mad from mere suspicion of his wife; or *Middlemarch* (1872), in which Casaubon responds to Dorothea's relation with Ladislaw as if it threatened a kind of adultery beyond the grave. These are novels in which the disturbing power even of sub-adulterous liaisons highlights one of the main taboos governing fiction aimed at general readers. Victorian fiction therefore makes it possible to distinguish a type of novel in which adultery is neither the main theme nor one of a number of themes, but appears in repressed or transferred forms. Not until Meredith, Hardy, James and Moore established themselves as novelists did it begin to assume the explicit importance it had on the Continent; and even then, if not veiled by art, under a barrage of protest.

It is important to distinguish between the various ways in which adultery has been represented in fiction, because the differences reflect crucial distinctions both in ideological attitudes and in fictional practices. The restriction of the canon of the novel of adultery to novels of female adultery is one example of ideological determination; the displacement of the theme of adultery in nineteenth-century British fiction is another. A third example consists in pointed avoidance of the theme. For instance, George Sand and Emilia Pardo Bazán were probably the two best-known Continental European women novelists of the nineteenth century. It is significant that Pardo Bazán never produced a novel of female adultery; and that even Sand, out of all her prolific fictional output, wrote only one novel which may be placed within the tradition – although, as the discussion in Chapter 5 will show, it does not fit there easily. It was not because of the constraints, powerful though these were, against women writers portraying sexual relationships that the two avoided the theme. Sand was notorious for writing about sexual love, but she was much more interested in the problems of marriage than in adultery. As she saw very clearly, what impaired marriage was the wife's inequality with her husband. This made adultery the only way, however hollow, in which wives might gain a kind of freedom. So, like her few female contemporaries who portrayed adultery in their fiction, and whose work is also discussed in Chapter 5, Sand represented it in different ways from those which characterize the tradition. Pardo Bazán took up a similar position. Her views on the emancipation of women were close to Sand's; and although she, no more than Sand, refrained from portraying sexual relationships, she never wrote a novel of female adultery. Indeed, Alison Sinclair has pointed out that in Pardo Bazán's second novel, *A Wedding Journey* (1881),

> the commission of adultery would have more than sufficient justification in the form of the husband's infidelity and poor marital behaviour, but, in a rare moment of social verisimilitude, adultery as a solution to marital distress (rather than as the cause of marital distress) is eschewed by the authoress for her heroine, who returns to her paternal home, leaving both husband and lover behind.[19]

In the light of Pardo Bazán's debt to the Naturalist movement, which was at its height during most of her career and which scarcely discouraged the representation of adultery, her refusal of the theme in such circumstances is almost ostentatious. It is all the more striking because, as Judith Drinkwater has argued, the novel's ending 'exposes the weaknesses of a cliched genre: virtue is not rewarded, and adherence to social norms in Lucía's case brings the censure of society upon her as harshly as if in fact she had chosen to leave Spain with Artegui'.[20]

The novel of female adultery was born in France in the 1830s. Though the most famous French example did not appear until the serialization in 1856–7 of *Madame Bovary*, the theme which Flaubert chose for his novel, and which was to attract so many other Continental European writers during the next half century, was by then already hackneyed. Indeed, not the least of its attractions for Flaubert was precisely that in France it had become a fictional cliché. In discussing the rise of the novel of female adultery, it is therefore necessary to consider why it arose in France and how it developed initially.

The factors which favoured the emergence of this kind of novel in the France of the 1830s are multiple and complex, but it is possible to group them under four main headings. First, the years of Revolution, Empire and Restoration had produced vast social changes, which included improvements, quickly reversed, in the position of women; second, behind those changes was the rise of the bourgeoisie, which by 1830 had achieved more social power and influence in France than anywhere else in Europe; third, the libertine literature of the previous century had already established a tradition and an acceptance of writing about sex; fourth, all these conditions were reinforced by economic, social and technological developments, including increased literacy and a massive expansion in the output of printed writings of all kinds, which further assisted the bourgeoisie in achieving hegemony.

The changes which occurred in France between the Revolutions of 1789 and 1848 mixed public and private spheres, national and domestic politics, in especially complicated ways. Demography shows one massive shift which took place. As Claire Goldberg Moses has recognized,

In most European countries, fertility did not diminish until after 1880. France, however, was unique. There the decline in fertility rates began before the end of the eighteenth century. By the mid-nineteenth century, the two-child household was commonplace throughout France. This may have been the most important change in the lives of women in the nineteenth century as compared to those of the *ancien régime*.[21]

Moses draws two crucial inferences from demographic evidence. One main reason for the early decline in the French birth rate was, she notes, that

by the first decades of the 1800s family limitation was already widely practiced. The result was to split sexuality from reproduction and to transform the meaning of motherhood, which opened up a far-ranging debate on sexual behaviour, family structure, and the nature of mothering.[22]

What Moses calls the splitting of sexuality from reproduction had especially far-reaching effects. Not only were large numbers of women able for the first time to avoid repeated confinements and child-bearing. At the same time, the possibility of sex for its own sake, without risking pregnancy, could only heighten male fears of female sexuality. Such an influence should not be over-emphasized, as the main method of contraception was withdrawal – not always satisfactory either in avoiding pregnancy or in enabling pleasure. Nevertheless, the ability to limit reproduction unquestionably affected both the practice and the perception of sex. It is important to recognize, however, that the meaning of motherhood was probably transformed less radically than Moses' phrasing suggests. Indeed, from one point of view it is possible to understand the exaltation of motherhood as a way of channelling female energies away from sex. In the absence of frequent child-bearing, and, for many women, of other non-domestic employment inside or outside the home, motherhood was represented as offering the paramount role for female fulfilment.

The idealization of motherhood was also part of an increasingly gendered separation of the private from the public sphere. As Joan Landes declares, 'It is not enough to say [. . .] that we owe the origin of a new family ideology in the West to the rise of the bourgeoisie, and to the corresponding decline of an older code of aristocratic sociability.'[23] Men both on the political right and left feared the participation of women in public life, and they reacted accordingly. This was not only an outcome of the Revolution, although, as Landes observes, 'the militant participation of women provoked a violent and fearful response on the part of most men'.[24] It also sprang from an already established and powerful suspicion of the influence imputed to women in the salons of the Old Regime. On the one hand, Landes points out, 'In the eyes of male radicals, "impudent" revolutionary women were often indistinguishable from the queen, aristocratic emigrés, or Girondin intriguers.' Thus, she continues, 'the revolt against the father was also a revolt against women as free and equal public and private beings', and 'liberty and equality came to be overshadowed by fraternity'.[25] On the other hand, as Moses has shown,

> Conservative thinkers such as Louis de Bonald and Joseph de Maistre had come to believe that it was the family lifestyle of eighteenth-century aristocrats that had brought down the *ancien régime* and that the strength of the restored monarchy depended on 'the authority of the husband, the subordination of the wife, and the dependency of the children.' No less so than those republicans who had advocated a 'republicanized' family, conservatives also saw themselves as reformers: the subjugation of wives to husbands and the confinement of wives to the domestic sphere – practices that we might call 'traditional' – were

espoused as reforms to an aristocratic way of life that, according to Bonald and Maistre, had permitted the undue prominence of women in public life.[26]

As Linda M. Shires has succinctly put it, middle and upper class women were consigned 'to domestic space'.[27] That space was at the same time the domain of repression and a vacuum seeking to be filled. The ideological prescription was that women should become, in the words of Estelle B. Freedman and Erna Olafson Hellerstein, 'specialists in emotional and spiritual life, protecting traditions and providing a stable refuge from the harsh, impersonal public sphere that men now entered in increasing numbers'. Furthermore, the same two commentators add, as life expectancy increased, and the marriages of many couples lasted longer, nineteenth-century women 'may well have looked for greater emotional satisfaction from these lengthy marriages than their ancestors had, for a new emphasis on romantic love as a basis for union raised expectations for marital happiness'.[28] Such expectations created obvious dangers when marriage failed to meet them, even or especially when it was based on romantic love.

The novel of female adultery is a form stemming from social tensions concerning the role of women in marriage, motherhood, the family and the transmission of property. The form first developed in France not only because of the historical factors outlined above, but because French culture of the period enabled a freedom of thought and expression, at least on sexual matters, impossible elsewhere in Europe. Claire Goldberg Moses suggests that 'the collapse of the power and influence of religion – also unique in France at this time – explains the special French experience'.[29] While this probably exaggerates the extent to which Church power in France declined, a strong anticlerical tradition inhibited censorship on grounds of morality, though it could not wholly prevent it.[30] Moses goes on to remark that 'French Romantic literature makes clear that the French, unlike the English or the Americans of the same period, continued to recognize women's innate sexuality and to fear its potential for social disruption.'[31] Although this statement is too sweeping – and although the phrase 'innate sexuality' is misleading – it calls attention to a fact which was critical to the development of the novel of female adultery. For there could be no such form without both an explicit recognition of female sexuality, and at least a qualified licence to represent it.

Furthermore, it is likely that there would have been no novel of female adultery at all if men had not responded to an acute sense of female sexuality as disruptive.

The significance of most of the factors behind the emergence in France of the novel of female adultery is illustrated by a work which itself influenced the form strongly, Balzac's *Physiology of Marriage*. Balzac had begun work on the *Physiology* by 1824, during his literary apprenticeship before *The Human Comedy* started to take shape. Although it was not published until December 1829, he had completed and even printed an earlier version in 1826.[32] The work is neither a novel nor a scientific study, though it owes debts to both genres. Instead, a physiology was a kind of book which offered a pseudo- or quasi-scientific account of a social type or phenomenon. Popular in France in the earlier nineteenth century, its purpose was to instruct and entertain the reader about leading features of contemporary social life. An early and famous example, which Balzac mentions and which he was certainly attempting to emulate, was Brillat-Savarin's gastronomical treatise, *The Physiology of Taste* (1825). The form developed as the growth in numbers and power of the middle classes produced a market for information not only about the world around them but also about how best to negotiate it. Balzac's *Physiology* is at least as much conduct book as social study. This is what makes it so revealing about contemporary attitudes to marriage and adultery.

Though the physiology is now ranked as sub-literary, at this period it was the novel which was considered the inferior form. Novels were usually published in duodecimo, and works thought yet more ephemeral in thirty-twomo. *The Physiology of Marriage* first appeared in the prestigious format of octavo, reflecting Balzac's sense of its importance.[33] While it owes much to his early philosophical ambitions, the *Physiology* turned out to both herald and found the fiction which would make his name. It anticipates *The Human Comedy* in its observation and anecdotes of social life, and especially in its portrayal of marriage. It is the earliest work to join *The Human Comedy* without substantial revision; and it is the sole example which Balzac was able to complete of the 'Analytical Studies' which he intended to crown the 'Studies of Manners' and 'Philosophical Studies' of its first two sections.[34] Because the aim of this final class of works was to explain the principles behind the behaviour shown in the first two, there is a case for reading *The Physiology of Marriage* as the keystone of his design.[35]

The *Physiology* also heralds, and helps explain, the rise in France of the novel of female adultery. Balzac often depicts adultery, male and female, in *The Human Comedy*; and the *Physiology* offers the analysis by which he intended that female adultery might be glossed. But the work's importance consists much more in the evidence it provides of contemporary bourgeois thinking about marriage and adultery, and in its role as one of the sources of the novel of female adultery in the work of other writers as well as of Balzac himself. Most of all, the *Physiology* illustrates the factors which, I would suggest, help account for the emergence of this kind of novel in France around 1830.

First, there is the impact of the Revolution of 1789 and of the ensuing period of social and political reaction. This is figured in *The Physiology of Marriage* by repeated analogies between husband and king, or state, and between wife and people. For instance, Balzac asks rhetorically whether 'the political methods of husbands should not be more or less those of kings' (X.111, TM; 1016);[36] conversely, he has one of his husbands observe that 'A married woman behaves with us as the citizens of a constitutional monarchy do with a king' (XVI.147–8, TM; 1051). More sinister is his remark that 'all husbands should be in a position to produce the Terror in their households, and should prepare long in advance a matrimonial 2nd of September' (XXII.216, TM; 1115). Balzac entitles one of his sections 'The Wife's Charter', and in it he refers to 'the liberty of the subject' and 'the liberty of the Press' (Meditation XVI, ibid.). But these parallels have a significance beyond their attempted wit. As Sandra Dijkstra has remarked, 'If the Revolution marked the culmination of a period dominated by feminist energies, so the period which followed marked their repression.'[37] Balzac's analogy suggests a need on the part of the established male order to suppress all but the most marginal rights for women. It points to masculinist anxiety stemming from what had been briefly achieved by women during the Revolution. What was at stake in monarchy and marriage, and what is at stake in the novel of female adultery, is the rule of the fathers – especially that model of patriarchy developed for its own interests by the newly dominant class of the bourgeoisie.

Balzac's analogy between monarchy and family was scarcely original. Peter McPhee quotes, for instance, from what Louis de Bonald had to say at the peak of royalist reaction in 1816, during the debates which led to the abolition of divorce. He warned that, just as political democracy 'allows the people, the weak part of political society, to rise against the established power', so divorce, 'veritable domestic democracy', allows the wife, 'the weak part, to rebel against marital authority'. Thus, 'in order to keep the state out of the hands of the people, it is necessary to keep the family out of the hands of wives and children'.[38]

Divorce had been first introduced in 1792. It was available equally to women and to men – not surprisingly, more of the former than of the latter took advantage of the new law – and the grounds for legal action which it specified included notorious immorality but not adultery. The suppression of divorce after the Revolutionary period is a leading example of the resurgence of patriarchal power. It was first restricted by Napoleon in a decree of 1803 incorporated into the Civil Code of the following year, and then abolished altogether under the Restoration in 1816.[39] One of the questions with which Balzac opens the *Physiology* is whether 'divorce, that admirable palliative to the ills of marriage, will be demanded once more by all' (I.13, TM; 913). However, though repeated attempts were made to restore divorce, both in the early years of the July monarchy, between 1831 and 1834, and later, these were unsuccessful until 1884. Antony Copley comments that 'in the age of the double standard the French male had alternative outlets for his sexuality in adultery and prostitution', and asks: 'Have we explanations here for why France was able to survive without divorce between 1816 and 1884?'[40] Conversely, it may not be by coincidence that the 50 or so years between 1830 and 1884 mark the heyday in France of narratives of female adultery.

But it was the Civil Code itself which constituted the husband as king of the family. The Code's provisions were powerful and oppressive. They influenced strongly the nature of married life in France not only as portrayed by Balzac in the *Physiology* but for long afterwards – some of them remaining law long into the present century. Jill Harsin has summarized the main provisions:

The virtual civil nonexistence of women under the law had been confirmed by the Napoleonic Code of 1804. Because of Napoleon's determination to protect his notion of the family, the most serious prohibitions fell upon married women. Without her husband's permission, a wife could not maintain a separate residence, attend school, or hold a job; her husband had unconditional control over family property, as he did over any wages or royalties her work might bring. The Civil Code included women in the category of unfit persons, along with minors and ex-convicts; women were declared incompetent to witness certificates of marriage, birth, or death.

Probably the best known provisions of the Civil Code were those involving sexual relations. The code prohibited the filing of paternity suits, for fear that some men might be falsely accused. In cases of adultery, an erring wife was liable to imprisonment for three months to two years, while a guilty husband was subject only to a fine; this was fairly consistent, since those without sufficient independent financial resources – wives, the poor, members of the working class – were always punished by imprisonment. A husband, moreover, could be charged with adultery only if he brought his mistress into the family home.[41]

The context of this summary is a history of the policing of prostitution in nineteenth-century Paris. As Harsin suggests, it is revealing that the treatment of prostitutes should provide graphic evidence of the position of women in general in France at that time. No wonder that the novel of adultery which arose in such a society was a novel of female adultery.

The hegemony achieved by the bourgeoisie, and consolidated by the Revolution of 1830, is the second factor in the rise of the novel of female adultery indicated by Balzac's *Physiology of Marriage*. Balzac addressed his book to men in what he termed 'the privileged classes' (XVII.162; 1064), and he confined his discussion of women to those he considered as 'respectable' (*honnête*). His criteria include 'an income of at least six thousand francs in the provinces, or of twenty thousand in Paris' (III.32; 933). These were substantial sums at the period. André Jardin and André-Jean Tudesq quote statistics compiled by Adeline Daumard indicating that in Paris 'the bourgeoisie accounted for 16.2 per cent of the population in 1820 and 14.6 per cent in 1847'. They add, however, that 'those who had fortunes between 2,000 and 20,000 francs represented 8.4 per cent of the total population in 1820 and 6.9 per cent in 1847'.[42] The levels of income cited by Balzac therefore show that the type of household to which he refers belongs to the upper bourgeoisie. According to

Jardin and Tudesq, the bourgeoisie had achieved 'undisputed preponderance after 1830', but, 'even before the end of the Restoration, the struggle for predominance between the aristocracy and the bourgeoisie was won by the latter, although this group too was composed largely of landowners'.[43]

What is more significant for the novel of female adultery is Balzac's account of the kind of marriage supported by such incomes. In several ways the *Physiology* amounts to an early and detailed study of what is now known as bourgeois marriage. In such a marriage, the wife's main functions are to enhance the status of her husband and to produce legitimate children as heirs. Balzac points to the first requirement when he observes that 'in France a private man has much less influence on society than his wife; it is only from her that ridicule comes to him' (XXIII.227, TM; 1124). It is therefore up to the fashionable husband to ensure that his wife creates a suitably distinguished style of living. In Peter McPhee's words, the July Monarchy, between 1830 and 1848, saw 'the expression of a distinctive bourgeois culture in the nature of personal relations, the place of women and children, the style and function of clothing, furniture and food, and the practice of leisure and manners'. This became still more important as 'bourgeois culture melded into a lifestyle of "notability"'.[44] As I will suggest, not the least of the problems resulting from the wife's role was the combination of enforced leisure and limited opportunities for its enjoyment.

Balzac flatters the class aspirations of his bourgeois reader by appealing to aristocratic values. He refers to 'the superior man to whom this book is dedicated' (III.34; 935), quoting the same words unctuously in the dedication proper. The manners he commends are nonchalant. To a husband discovering his wife with her lover he advises 'an air of superiority', and he underlines the point with giveaway insistence by observing: 'men in high social spheres have nothing in common with ordinary folk, who do not know how to lose a fork without raising a hue and cry' (XXII.218, TM; 1117). Later he comments approvingly on examples of husbandly grace in extremity: 'This is truly genial', 'Greatness of soul is there', 'There is nobility for you' (XXVII.283, TM; 1179). He adds further class appeal by presenting as his main informants a Duchess who 'had been one of the most accomplished and witty ladies of Napoleon's court', and her young and beautiful friend who 'was already playing, in Paris, the role of a fashionable woman' (Introduction, 6,

TM; 908–9). In this way Balzac aims to finesse the old libertine trick of pretending not only that the ladies are on his side but that they were there before him. He implies prestigious female approval both for the marital policy he recommends to husbands and for tolerance of male sexual licence.

This is, thirdly, one of the ways in which the *Physiology* draws attention to the importance, in the rise of the novel of female adultery, of the French tradition of libertine writing. As Nancy K. Miller has shown, that tradition still dominates the received canon of eighteenth-century French fiction.[45] If it had not been so firmly established in the earlier nineteenth century, it is doubtful whether so scandalous a topic as adultery would have gained acceptance as a leading fictional theme. It achieved such acceptance in no other Western country until after the example of *Madame Bovary*, and to only a limited extent in Britain and North America even then. Balzac borrowed from the libertine tradition in several of the anecdotes with which he garnished the *Physiology*, including the longest – though, in the more prudish climate of the 1820s, he bowdlerized this carefully.[46] But, despite the scandal it caused on its first publication,[47] the *Physiology* is both more and less than a libertine work. What makes the difference is marriage. The spicy anecdotes, and the headnote declaring 'Ladies not admitted', are merely sauces for what is actually a guide to marital management. Balzac's fundamental aim is 'to show how a wife may be prevented from deceiving her husband' (I.19; 919).

He pursues that aim to obsessive lengths. The *Physiology* is a comprehensive manual to help bourgeois men guard against their wives' infidelity. Its devices and strategies include domestic architecture and furniture designed to deny secret entry or concealment; a regime of enfeebling diet and demanding exercise to keep the wife's energy to a minimum; and 'Police Methods' (the title of Meditation XX) such as surveillance, interception of letters, and censorship. The work implies a husband whose fear of being cuckolded is nothing less than paranoid. This fear may be explained in part by social and economic tensions fostered by the growth of the bourgeoisie. Peter McPhee identifies a key concern when he remarks: 'Central to the gender stereotyping elaborated by bourgeois men was anxiety about the male line: if noblemen had ancient codes which guaranteed "honour", how was a bourgeois eminence based on work and wealth to be protected from filial deviation?'[48] This anxiety bore especially hard on three intersecting social categories: homosexuals, prostitutes and women. So, for instance, the *Physiology* declares of a wife's adultery: 'it is for her the greatest social crime, since for her it implies all others' (XXVI.277, TM; 1173); and the Pléiade editor points out that for Balzac the greatest evil of adultery was 'the introduction of a bastard into a family'.[49] Nevertheless, even allowing for pressures and convictions such as these, it is not easy to explain the fixation betrayed by *The Physiology of Marriage* with cuckoldom.

Balzac accounts for that fixation in part by a battery of 'Conjugal Statistics' (Meditation II). But, though these place the risk of a wife's infidelity very high, it is the assumptions behind them that reveal most. For instance, because bourgeois marriage requires an income few men can command until they are 30, the husband will be older than his wife. Not only is the age difference likely to favour younger rivals, but the later age at which men marry produces a large standing army of sex-hungry bachelors. The odds worsen yet further on the assumption that women are sexually available for a much shorter period than that during which men are sexually active. On Balzac's alarming estimates, a population of 400,000 'respectable women' is exposed to a total of three million liaisons. Well might husbands feel paranoia. Yet, thanks to what now seems an even stranger assumption, these estimates confine male adultery to bachelors. Though Balzac mentions once, very briefly, the 'secret adventures' of husbands (IV.41; 942), and though he confides that a wife's maid, or an intimate friend, may 'help her discharge marital love' (XXV.260, TM; 1156), male infidelity is simply not an issue in his work. This is to assert with a vengeance a double standard of sexual morality. Not only does Balzac express male paranoia about female infidelity within marriage, but he ignores male infidelity almost completely, whether in marriage or not.

What helps explain this paradox is, again, the institution of bourgeois marriage. The basic principle of such a marriage is to keep everything in the family. This means control of money and property, but also, because these are transmitted through women, of female sexuality. One reason why it was important for the bourgeoisie to claim aristocratic values was to mask actual dependence on money. With characteristic bluntness, Balzac points out to husbands: 'the men who desire your money are much more numerous than those who desire your wife' (IV.46; 948). But this offers little consolation, for, if the lover fathers a child, at the same time he threatens the husband's property. No such threat is posed to the family by an unfaithful husband; and even then the husband who confines his attentions to the maid also confines them to the home. Balzac emphasizes the link between money, marriage and female sexuality in four related proposals. He argues, first, that women should be allowed sexual liberty while they remain unmarried but, second, that their fidelity within marriage should be sternly enforced. The third and fourth proposals are economic: that daughters should be 'disqualified from inheriting beyond a carefully judged limit', and that they should be married 'without dowry' (IX.101; 1006). Balzac presents such proposals elsewhere as favouring women by excluding financial motives for marriage on the part of men.[50] What they do instead is to minimize still further the chances of female independence.

I have suggested that the fear of female independence stemmed in part from memories of the Revolutionary period. That period had seen the introduction of divorce and of new property rights for women – the latter rescinded even more quickly than the former. Many women had been active in challenging for more equitable legal and civil positions, although in other ways these hardly showed even temporary improvement. An equally powerful source of male anxiety was probably the vacuum created for women by the enforced idleness of bourgeois marriage. The rise of the nuclear family reduced the responsibilities of the wife and gave her more privacy. Such a wife, whose role was to a large extent the narrowly social one of enhancing the reputation of her husband, would also have time for activities which might endanger both that reputation and the husband's property. Balzac, however, leaves no doubt as to where the power lies. Should any husband shrink from careful supervision and, if necessary, determined action, he points out that 'a wife is a chattel acquired by contract', and that 'nature made her for our use, made her to bear everything: children, sorrows, even blows and punishments from man' (XII.125, TM; 1030).

It is this kind of brutal clarity which renders Balzac's *Physiology of Marriage* so revealing an introduction to the novel of female adultery. Even so, it still leaves a lot to be inferred. One possible deduction, for instance, is that there were much stronger grounds for concern over prostitution than over female adultery. Instead, Balzac takes the opposite course of proposing legalized prostitution on the grounds of physical benefit for men and as a safeguard to marriage and wifely purity (IV.43–5; 945–7). Such arguments in favour of tolerating or licensing prostitution were common in the period; yet, in default of commercial sex, there are the intimate friend and the obliging maid whom he suggests as boons for the harassed wife, or indeed the unmarried women whose sexual liberation he advocates so kindly. Balzac could not solve, or indeed perhaps fully recognize, the contradiction he produced in trying to give both marriage and sexual desire their due – especially male sexual desire. This contradiction haunts the novel of female adultery.

The *Physiology* thus prefigures a great deal, and often in detail, in the form which it helped to inaugurate: the relative ages of husband and wife, the unmarried status of the lover, the silence over possible infidelity on the part of the husband, the boredom to which the vacuum of the wife's social role consigns her. For example, the *Physiology* anticipates *Madame Bovary* in all these respects and in others still more specific, including the folly of the obtuse husband (VII.74; 978–9), and the dangers of boarding schools (VI.63–71; 967–76), religiosity (VIII.87; 992), and, of course, reading novels (XI.114–15; 1019–20).[51]

2

Towards the Novel of Female Adultery: Chateaubriand, Constant, Musset, Mérimée

The main forerunners of the novel of female adultery in France are the Romantic confession and the narrative of seduction. In a key respect these two forms are inversely related. While the narrative of seduction tells how a man obtains illicit sex with a woman, the confessional narrative presents the troubles and the ending of an intimate relationship which is illicit or which threatens to become so. This chapter begins by discussing the two founding confessional narratives of the French Romantic tradition, Chateaubriand's *Atala* (1801) and *René* (1802; 1805). It goes on to consider a further two examples of the confession, Benjamin Constant's *Adolphe* (1816) and Alfred de Musset's *Confession of a Child of the Century* (1836); then, finally, two examples of the seduction narrative, both by Prosper Mérimée, *The Double Mistake* (*La Double Méprise*, 1833) and *Arsène Guillot* (1844). The contrast between the seduction narratives and the later two of the confessional narratives is particularly sharp, for, while the two stories by Mérimée show how a woman succumbs to seduction, those by Constant and Musset show the difficulties the lover undergoes in sustaining and then ending a liaison.

In her book *The Adulteress's Child*, Naomi Segal considers *Atala*, *René*, *Adolphe* and *Confession of a Child of the Century* along with six other French narratives from the eighteenth to the twentieth century. She brings out several convincing similarities between them, although, as comparison will reveal, her summary elides some prominent differences and is, especially, much less adequate to Musset's *Confession* than to the two works by Chateaubriand and to *Adolphe*. Segal further claims that her ten examples of confessional narrative 'are also, in most cases, novels of adultery',[1] but, as I have suggested above in Chapter 1, this is to be prodigal with the truth. If the term is used strictly, not one can be properly so called. Adultery does not occur in *Atala*, *René*, *Adolphe* or in Musset's *Confession*; indeed the only example of illicit sex in Chateaubriand's two stories takes place before the action of either starts, and it consists not in adultery but in fornication. Such distinctions are essential to a clear understanding of the fictional and ideological structures at work. This chapter will argue both that the confessional narrative anticipates the novel of female adultery, and that, nevertheless, it should be recognized as a different form.

In summarizing a number of important resemblances between French confessional narratives, Segal declares that in almost all

the woman dies and the man tells the tale. She is usually older than he (though this trait is less insisted upon in the *femme fatale* versions) and always treats him maternally. The hero has generally lost his mother in childbirth, has a worldly, powerful father, and tells his story to a sympathetic older man. He adores the woman but contrives to murder her, more or less literally, closing the account of anger and guilt that began with the childbed death.[2]

Atala and *René* largely bear out this analysis. Both turn on the death of a woman who perishes as a result of a sexual taboo, and in both cases the role of mothers is significant. Atala is the offspring of a pre-marital liaison between her Indian mother and the Spaniard Lopez. Passionately in love with the Indian Chactas, she kills herself rather than break the vow of virginity her mother had imposed on her in contrition for her own sin. René's mother has died giving birth to him, and he is subject to the incestuous passion of his older sister Amélie – doubly incestuous, in effect, as he shows by calling her 'nearly a mother' when she comforts him (83, TM; 132).[3] Amélie enters a convent when she cannot repress a love which she believes unreciprocated, and she dies nursing others in an epidemic. *Atala* and *René* also exemplify the narrative situation which, as Segal indicates, is a common feature of the Romantic confession. Both stories are told by a man speaking to one or more other men: the first by Chactas in old age to his adoptive son René, the second by René to Chactas and an elderly Catholic priest.

The end towards which the Romantic confession drives is a young man's redemption from a woman. *Atala* and *René*, like

Adolphe and Musset's *Confession*, present this as supremely painful but necessary. In the first two stories, the agent of separation is religion. Writing about *Atala*, Naomi Schor has suggested that

> in the guise of rehabilitating Christianity in the wake of the secularizing trends of eighteenth-century philosophy and the dechristianization promoted by the revolution, Chateaubriand fuses to stunning effect the categories of gender with those of religion. The coupling of the two is mutually beneficent and reinforcing: a threatened Christianity draws renewed strength from being mapped onto sexual difference while a threatening breakdown of sexual hierarchies is averted by sanctifying the cultural construction of femininity.[4]

Indeed, one of the roles of the confessional narrative is to put women in the place ordained for them by patriarchal ideology, and to do so all the more effectively by co-opting religion. The whole manoeuvre is even more powerful ideologically in that the outcome is presented less as a tragedy for the dead women than for the bereaved men.

The location chosen by Chateaubriand for his stories is also significant. *Atala* and key parts of *René* are set in eighteenth-century North America. Chactas loses his father in battle, is captured by the enemy tribe to which Atala belongs, and is finally killed, along with René, in a massacre of his tribe by the French. The narrator learns how the tribe has been wiped out from René's granddaughter, one of the last survivors. He ends the Epilogue to *Atala* by drawing a parallel with his own position: 'like you, I wander at the mercy of men; and, less fortunate in my exile, I have not borne the bones of my fathers with me' (65, TM; 99). Given Chateaubriand's position as a returned émigré from a family whose members had suffered imprisonment during the Revolution, and whose elder brother had been guillotined, this parallel aligns the wars between Indian tribes, and between Indian tribes and Europeans, with French civil strife and Revolutionary war in the 1790s. The parallel is sentimental in that it occludes the fact of European imperialism, equates civil war with genocide, and implies that the customs and ceremonies of Indian culture correspond to Old Regime tradition. What makes it of interest to the sexual politics displayed by the two narratives is that it helps account not only for their tragic tenor, but for the sacrificial role they allot to women.

If *Atala* and *René* refract a young male aristocrat's experience of civil war, emigration and dispossession during the Revolution, at the same time they confine, even as they consecrate, the figure of woman. In her study of the representation of dead and dying women in visual and literary art during the Revolutionary and Napoleonic periods, Madelyn Gutwirth finds 'a persistent male anxiety around the issues of masculinity as dominance and of sexual fidelity'. She goes on to suggest that, to most men of the time,

the wresting of sexual order out of its chaos seemed [. . .] to demand the redomestication of women and their departure from the public space. [. . .] As the claims of women were swept aside, first Jacobin and then Napoleonic politics would finally embody those lovingly fashioned, seductive visions of sacrificial female goodness in their legislation. The long evolution from monarchical society's dominant conceptualization of women as man's lively and energetic opposite, even when defeated or despised, had given way to the new paradigm: the feeble subordinate.[5]

The new paradigm, as Gutwirth terms it, is based in part on a glorification of motherhood. If, as with other French confessional narratives, the action both of *Atala* and of *René* springs from an errant or an absent mother, *Atala* makes amends with an array of images displaying maternal delight in babies and grief for babies who die. Its opening chapter contains several figures of this kind, and in the Epilogue, when the narrator stumbles upon René's granddaughter, she is nursing a dead child. In this way the story idealizes the bond between child and nursing mother while elegizing the Indian society which it constructs as natural.

The ideological work performed by *Atala* and *René* in redefining images of women complements the legal and constitutional restrictions on the role of women, summarized in Chapter 1, which were being enacted at the time of their first publication. What links the two stories to the novel of female adultery is on the one hand the function of bourgeois wife and mother to which they point, and on the other the fear of female sexuality which lies behind it. That fear is evoked in three of Chateaubriand's characters. In the first of the two stories, Atala's mother is guilty not only of pre-marital but of exogamous sex; and Atala kills herself rather than give in to the sexual passion prohibited by her vow. This suicide is particularly significant because it dramatizes the fact and the power of female sexual desire. As Margaret Waller has pointed out, the highlighting of that desire presents 'an audacious exception to eighteenth-century codes of feminine virtue', even though, at the same time, the story 'makes the woman bear the whole weight of sexual guilt and exonerates the man'.[6] Similarly, in *René*, Amélie is led by the strength of her passion for her brother first to flee to a convent and then to virtual suicide through nursing victims of the epidemic.

The two stories foreshadow the novel of female adultery in the ideological pressure they place on the role of women; at the same time, they point to the social and historical frame of reference for that pressure. However, what sets them categorically apart from the novel of female adultery is their image of the male. The contemporary reception of each text marks the distinction clearly. Margaret Waller has observed that, while *Atala* was enormously popular from the time of its first appearance in 1801, *René* 'did not reach the height of its success until long after its first publication'. It was only in the 1820s that, through René,

> the figure of the aristocrat, outmoded by the revolution, became a model for postrevolutionary man. Through his identification with a disenfranchised upper class, the bourgeois reader allied himself with the margins as a way of denying his connections to a society increasingly organized to promote the interests of his own sex and class. Unlike the aristocratic Chateaubriand, however, these Romantic readers had not been shunted aside by the French Revolution. Instead, it was the subsequent restoration of the monarchy as well as the rise of industrial capitalism that had made them strangers in their own land. When bourgeois male readers of the 1820s looked into the mirror that was *René*, they saw a portrait that transformed their social and economic marginalization into an aesthetic aristocracy of the spirit in the newly Romantic age.[7]

This is a convincing analysis, even though Waller presses it too far in applying it to all bourgeois male readers. It helps account not only for the huge popularity and influence of *René* from the 1820s, but also for a paradox in the story's ideological message. For there is an apparent contradiction in *René* between the endorsement of a woman's role as wife and mother, and the hero's inability to co-operate. Although René has married an Indian bride, he is not living with her at the time of the story, and the penultimate sentence reads: 'It is said that, urged by the two old men, he returned to his wife, but found no happiness with her' (96; 146). Chateaubriand thus strikes a double attitude: one of conventional morality through the main female figures, and of fascinating despair through the male. It was a combination that would prove highly successful, especially as later novelists developed it. Waller has pointed out how they did so in an important remark on later examples of the French Romantic confession. Because, she suggests,

> these antisocial texts offer few public outlets for the hero's ambitious wish, the heroine plays a crucial compensatory role. She provides him with one of the few remaining arenas at his disposal for exercising and displaying the powers and prerogatives he still possesses as a man.[8]

This is the pattern followed by Constant in *Adolphe* and by Musset in *Confession of a Child of the Century*. At the same time, however, both texts raise the psychological and the ideological stakes by bringing together the heroine's role and the mother's.

The presentation of the mother in *Adolphe* and *Confession of a Child of the Century* differs from that in *Atala* and *René*. This difference is bound up with the fact that, unlike Chactas and René, the narrators of the later two stories have their own sexual sins to confess (though not, as it happens, the sin of adultery). In both texts, and crucially, the role of beloved is joined, even confounded, with the role of mother. Again this invites an interpretation which combines psychoanalysis and history.

The central liaison in both narratives is between the young male narrator and an older woman who is unmarried but sexually experienced. Adolphe's lover, Ellénore, is at first the established mistress of a Count who had begun an affair with her when she was left alone and without resources following the death of her mother.[9] She comes from an illustrious Polish family, but her father has been ruined during troubles – arising presumably from Partition – in the 1790s. Ellénore lives as the acknowledged partner of the Count, by whom she has had two children. She has gained social acceptance with much difficulty, but her unmarried status renders her hopelessly vulnerable. When she leaves Count P*** after he forbids her to see Adolphe, she finds, as Adolphe puts it, that she is 'sunk down for ever into the position she had spent her life trying to rise out of' (V.73; 75).[10] Because she is unmarried, her standing is insecure even after she gains possession of her father's estates, which are restored to him before he dies. Not only do her relatives use the scandal against her to dispute her inheritance, but when she attempts to regain an honourable place in society she is humiliated (VIII.101–2; 97–8).

The difference between the position of an unfaithful wife and an unfaithful mistress is also displayed by Ellénore's relationship with Adolphe. He accounts for her passionate love for him by pointing out that this is her first relationship in which she has not been dependent, so that she has 'recovered her self-respect by a love free from all calculation and self-interest' (IV.65; 68). Yet she is no better placed after her father's death has given her provisional economic independence. When she takes Adolphe back with her to Poland, he is stung by his father's remark that instead of acting as her protector he has become her dependant (VII.90; 88). This is to imply that the unfaithful mistress can only keep her new lover by paying for him, a slur which would be as intolerable to Ellénore as it is to Adolphe. He has already observed that her principles are high, as befits her birth, and that the contrast 'between her sentiments and the place she occupied in society had made her emotionally unstable' (II.47; 55). The fact that she has even more to lose than a wife intensifies her insecurity and possessiveness.

In *Confession of a Child of the Century* it is the narrator, Octave, who is insecure, but his insecurity results from sexual betrayal. The action begins with his discovery that his lover is having an affair with one of his best friends. The fact that the lover is never given a name may suggest, as Jeanne Fuchs has claimed, that for Octave 'she becomes the incarnation of the unfaithful and capricious female'.[11] His sense of betrayal is all the sharper because he cannot attribute her behaviour to dependence; she is neither his wife nor his paid mistress. He declares: 'I did not understand the reason why a woman, who was forced neither by duty nor interest, could lie to one man when she loved another' (I.iii.25; 83).[12] Octave's responses make it important to distinguish between the social and emotional processes at work in Musset's *Confession* and those in *Adolphe*, on the one hand, and in the novel of female adultery on the other. The motifs which dominate the *Confession* are the man's sense of betrayal and his frantic jealousy; whereas *Adolphe* centres on the woman's insecurity and the man's lack of commitment; and the novel of female adultery on the woman's desire and suffering.

Octave's lover, who is a widow, turns out to be involved with three men simultaneously, deceiving Octave's friend as well as himself. When Octave meets one of her confidantes, she first tells him of her unhappy marriage and her own betrayal by her lover, and then tries to seduce him. Later Octave meets a prostitute who resembles his former lover; he torments himself after taking her home by having her degrade the image of the woman he loved by briefly taking her place. In another episode his friend Desgenais sends him his own mistress whom Octave has admired, but Octave recoils and returns her.

Octave's account of betrayal and debauchery helps motivate his jealousy in the subsequent affair with Brigitte which is the novel's main focus. As in *Adolphe*, the woman is older, sexually experienced and unmarried. Like his first lover, she is a widow; but she had been seduced and abandoned before her marriage by the man to whom she had been betrothed. Octave has thus been anticipated by two sexual rivals. Just as, in Constant's novel, Adolphe has no sooner won his mistress than he begins to tire of her, so, in Musset's, Octave has no sooner won Brigitte than he begins to become jealous. He flares up arbitrarily when she innocently pretends that a musical piece of her own creation is by the composer Stradella; and soon he suspects her with her dead husband's friend who has paid court to her unsuccessfully. The crises which follow, in which he repeatedly torments her with groundless suspicions, are reverse images of those in *Adolphe*, in which Ellénore is tormented by fears that Adolphe will leave her.

Yet the two novels end in the same place, with each narrator free of his mistress. After Adolphe tries and fails several times to leave Ellénore, she breaks down and dies when she receives two letters sent by a friend of his father who has been urging him to end the relationship; one is in Adolphe's own hand, promising that he will leave her. Musset ends the *Confession* by having Octave's suspicions come true. Brigitte keeps reassuring Octave that she loves him, but she has fallen in love with another man. At Octave's insistence they part as friends when he realizes that she is staying with him only out of pity. In both texts, as in other confessional narratives, what is of interest in the portrayal of women gives way to male concerns dramatized through the position of the narrator.

Naomi Segal has rightly argued that there are strong Oedipal elements in *Adolphe* and *Confession of a Child of the Century*, as in other French confessional narratives. In both novels the narrator is an only son whose mother is dead; Adolphe never mentions his mother, Octave mentions his only once. Adolphe has a strong but distant father, abetted by the friend who acts on his behalf while Adolphe is in Poland; Octave's father dies suddenly during the course of the novel, and for a while afterwards Octave tries to model himself upon him. Segal suggests that the main character's behaviour in the confessional narrative may be understood as a reaction to his having been deprived of his mother:

> The traumatic moment of the childbed death is the premise from which his history proceeds: the infant hero has both murdered and been abandoned by the mother, and his consequent attitude to the mother's surrogate is a complex of resentment and guilt. The beloved functions as a substitute mother upon whom a vengeful repetition of the childbed death will be practised.[13]

This interpretation fits *Adolphe* convincingly, especially if account is also taken of the father's role, and not least because Constant was himself an only child whose father was distant and whose mother had died soon after his birth. Adolphe speaks at the start of his 'passionate desire for independence and at the same time complete impatience with ties holding [him] down and an insurmountable terror of forming new ones' (I.38; 48). In his relationship with Ellénore, he oscillates continually between fear and renewal of emotional commitment. His interest in her is only kindled fiercely when at first she rebuffs him; then, having flagged, it is powerfully though temporarily reawakened when his father has her sent away. After Ellénore's death, Adolphe mourns for the loss of the care he has previously resented, though he has himself been instrumental in her destruction.

On the face of it, Musset's *Confession* readily sustains a similar interpretation. Whereas Brigitte shows care and forgiveness to Octave, he behaves towards her with irrational resentment and suspicion. He reports her as having told him: 'many days when I am your mistress I want to be your mother', and he addresses her as: 'my mistress, my mother and my sister' (IV.iii.199–200; 212–13). But the main theme of *Confession of a Child of the Century* is betrayal by the mother rather than, as in *Adolphe*, her rejection. Octave's despair reaches its crisis when, having decided to kill himself, he sees Brigitte's breast uncovered while she is sleeping. He immediately feels violent jealousy, exclaiming: 'shall another hand than mine be placed upon that fine, transparent skin, another mouth upon those lips, another love in that heart, or another man's head upon this pillow?' (IV.vi.286; 278). What is at issue here is not the same as the adult's reaction to deprivation of the mother in childhood. One possible interpretation is Oedipal conflict with the father; another, the adult's memory of sibling rivalry (although, as pointed out above, Octave is an only child – unlike Musset). However, the fact that it is the woman's breast which excites Octave's jealousy may invite a Kleinian reading. The object-relations psychology of Melanie Klein and others gives special emphasis to the child's relation to the mother. Alison Sinclair outlines part of the theory as follows:

> faced with what he experiences as bad (as when basic needs are not met) the child's response is of distress, anger, fear. Those feelings, however, are themselves too terrifying and distressing to be contained within him, so he projects them out, and comes to the belief that the part of his external world which is causing him distress is also the sole possessor of all the badness in the situation.[14]

This figure on whom the child projects negative feelings is, of course, the mother who is also the source of food and comfort. In Kleinian theory, the resulting conflict is not simply a stage passed through on the way to maturity, but one which may easily return under stress or in trauma. An unresolved relationship with the mother will be even more likely to produce feelings of rage and rejection. On a Kleinian reading, Octave experiences such feelings when he is seized by jealousy at the sight of the sleeping Brigitte's breast. Having decided to kill her as well as himself, he refrains only when he sees 'between her two white breasts a little ebony crucifix' (IV.vi.291; 282).

The endings of the two novels give further weight to a psychoanalytical interpretation. Both close with the narrator in bleak emancipation from the woman who, in the terms of this approach, has figured for him as his mother. Adolphe writes: 'I was already alone in the world and no longer living in that atmosphere of love with which she had surrounded me' (X.118; 110–11). Even more expressive of such a sense of separation is Octave's switch from personal to impersonal narrative for his last chapter. Describing himself as if he were another, he remarks: 'Any one of experience would have recognized the child become a man, whose confident gaze was beginning to harden his heart' (IV.vii.295–6; 285). Each novel may therefore be read as a young man's sentimental education, though in both cases the result is dysphoric. Adolphe, the reader is told, 'made no use of the liberty regained at the cost of so much grief and so many tears' (124; 116), and Octave writes his *Confession* still in the grip of misery.

In their focus on male emotional and sexual experience, male rites of passage, both texts differ fundamentally from the novel of female adultery. Yet both also point to some of the historical and ideological factors which contributed to the emergence of the new form. First, there is a distinctly moral undertow in both texts. When Constant prepared his story for publication in 1816, ten years after having written it, he supplied a narrative frame which criticizes Adolphe, and he later supplemented this with two prefaces. The writer of the 'Letter to the Publisher' which follows Adolphe's narrative declares: 'Ellénore's tragedy proves that even the most intense emotion cannot struggle against the accepted order of things' (123; 115); and the Publisher responds: 'If it has any instructive lesson, that lesson is for men' (125; 116). Though these views may seem inconsistent with each other, they are in fact complementary in that both construct women as prey to emotion and place on men the obligation of avoiding irregular liaisons. As Margaret Waller has argued, 'Constant's remarks stress women's dependency and vulnerability to such a degree that he ends up reessentializing women as the weaker sex,' so that the text suggests that 'the problem of the individual's liberty and responsibility is a problem for and about men'.[15] Even some of Adolphe's own comments carry a similar message. In a phrase worthy of his father, he observes: 'the fetters with which I had been hampered for so long made me a thousand times more dependent than an official, accepted union could ever have done' (VII.94; 91). Later he adumbrates the course Constant himself was to take, and which Chateaubriand had recommended, when he speaks of the need for religion (X.119; 111–12).

Such themes are much more explicit in *Confession of a Child of the Century*, written nearly 30 years later. Musset begins his novel with two rhetorical chapters about the state of mind of men of his generation, 'sons of the Empire, and grandsons of the Revolution' (I.ii.8; 69). He states: 'All the malady of the present century arises from two causes: the nation which has lived through '93 and 1814 carries wounds in its heart. All that used to be is no more; all that will be does not yet exist' (I.ii.19, TM; 78). What is striking, however, is that after evoking so passionately the accumulated impact of Revolution, war and Restoration, Octave turns almost immediately to personal life in order to demonstrate his own experience of 'the malady of the century' (I.iii.21; 79). He draws no direct connection between historical and personal events, but his betrayal by his lover functions ideologically as an instance of moral chaos produced by massive social changes. An important sign of the link between the historical and the personal is his view of the sceptical writers of the previous century. After his betrayal Octave reads the libertine novelists avidly, addressing them in his despair: 'you alone know the secrets of life; you alone dare to say that debauchery, hypocrisy and corruption are the only real things' (I.vii.51; 103). He reverses this view at the novel's climax, when he sees Brigitte's crucifix between her breasts and undergoes a conversion. Now, instead, he blames his irreligion in part on his reading from the same period: 'Poisoned as my mind had been from my youth by all the works of the previous century, I had quite early drunk the sterile milk of impiety' (IV.vi.292; 283). Previously Octave has quoted St Augustine, one of the obvious sources for his own *Confession* (II.iv.91; 132). He ends the novel by looking forward to his cure 'by God' (IV.vii.297; 286), through the 'one love only which does not trouble, which penetrates, and that [. . .] only dies with the being in which it has taken root' (IV.vii.298; 287).[16]

In Musset's *Confession*, more than in *Adolphe*, ideological and psychological themes coalesce. At the same time as the novel depicts a conflict between son and mother, re-enacted in the son's sexual relationships with women, it points to anxiety about female emancipation. In his rhetorical introduction Octave imagines 'the angel forerunner of future societies, who was already sowing in women's hearts the seeds of human independence, to which some day they will lay claim' (I.ii.12, TM; 72); yet he is far from at ease with women who act for themselves in the present. Both of his most important liaisons are with women whose widowhood gives them a greater degree of freedom, and he mentions without criticizing Brigitte's penchant for wearing men's clothing, for riding, and for all-night walks in the forest. On the other hand, however, he shows disquiet about the independence not only of his first lover, who in his eyes deceived him quite arbitrarily, but also of his second, who has had a previous lover as well as a husband, and who later leaves him by agreement for still another man. The episode with the Italian woman Marco gives further evidence of Octave's anxiety about female autonomy. He is possessed with desire for Marco after a single waltz, and his friend Desgenais arranges for him to spend the same night with her although she is 'almost married to' her protector (II.iv.103; 142). Nonetheless, once Octave is alone with her, all his desire vanishes. He leaves after seeing on her desk a letter reporting a woman's death, and, before she goes back to sleep, receiving from her the reply that the woman was her mother (II.iv.109–10; 146–7). Octave does not comment on the episode, but what it implies is that he cannot brook the woman's claim to freedom: from himself, for whom she shows no emotion; from her protector, whom she is willing to betray in order to oblige another; and, to cap it all, from the mother whom she has just lost.

Atala, René, Adolphe and Musset's *Confession* are part of the social and religious reaction which followed the immense upheavals stemming from the French Revolution. Written and narrated by men, all four texts betray a fear of female independence and female sexuality. They also betray nostalgia for what to many males in this period represented psychological and social safety: the woman's confinement to the role of a mother. In response they free the hero from female ties, even at the cost of bereaving him (for that is their emphasis); and they prepare the way for a bourgeois reinforcement of patriarchal gender roles. It is entirely relevant, as Naomi Segal indicates, that Constant and Musset wrote these novels in the shadow of women writers who at the time were much better known and more successful than themselves.[17] Indeed, it may not be too far-fetched to speculate that Constant's fictionalization of aspects of his relationship with Madame de Staël, and Musset's of his relationship with George Sand, represent an attempt on the part of both writers to expunge a female power and influence by which they felt threatened.

The French Romantic confessional narrative overlaps historically with the dominant tradition in the previous century of libertine novels. However, although *Adolphe* tells the story of one liaison, and *Confession of a Child of the Century* the story of several, neither narrative owes much to the libertine tradition. Neither focuses on the male's achievement of sexual experience, any more than do *Atala* and *René* with heroes who are wholly chaste. Yet, although the confession was the emerging form at this period, in the first third of the nineteenth century, the libertine tradition remained influential. Chapter 1 has suggested how much Balzac owed to that tradition in *The Physiology of Marriage*; Chapter 3 will give further evidence of his debt, while demonstrating how it affected his contribution to the novel of female adultery. But it is two novellas by his contemporary, Prosper Mérimée, which illustrate most clearly how the new form began to emerge from the libertine tradition. These are *The Double Mistake* and *Arsène Guillot*.

Nancy K. Miller has suggested that libertine texts are typically structured by 'the recollections of a man's life as organized and narrated through his sexual experience'.[18] They are also defined not only by their preoccupation with sex and, especially, with seduction, but above all by their appeal to a masculinist point of view. Examples include Crébillon's *The Wayward Head and Heart* (1736–8),[19] Duclos's *Les Confessions du Comte de **** (1741), Laclos's *Les Liaisons dangereuses* (1782), and also, in a more complex way, Prévost's *Manon Lescaut*. Most of these novels – Laclos's is an exception – take the form of a memoir in which a man addresses other men. For instance, *Manon Lescaut*, which began as part of a much longer work entitled *Mémoires d'un homme de qualité*, and was at first entitled *Histoire du chevalier des Grieux et de Manon Lescaut*, is narrated by des Grieux to the man of quality, Renoncour, and his pupil. The story is described by Renoncour as 'a moral treatise entertainingly put into practice',[20] but it nowhere presents a female point of view, least of all that of Manon herself, and such teaching as it offers is effectively for men alone.

The novel of female adultery did not come into existence until bourgeois values were widely established and accepted, especially in relation to marriage. It is an essentially bourgeois form, although, as Chapter 6 will show, *Anna Karenina* is a distinguished exception. The libertine text, which originated and flourished under the Old Regime, is in contrast essentially an aristocratic form – even though, paradoxically, it developed in France during a period in which the structures of aristocratic society had already begun to dissolve. Like *Manon Lescaut*, libertine texts usually attempt to justify themselves as guides to the ways of the world. The world in question is often socially exclusive, offering an outwardly refined arena for the display of social and sexual prowess. Such an arena no longer existed after the Revolution, though some of its practices, such as the taking of lovers, and at least one of its institutions, the literary or artistic salon, still lived on in Paris.[21] The novel of female adultery is centred instead in marriage and the family, and the image of society it presents is mainly composed not of like-minded potential admirers but of a diversity of ready censors.

Changes in artistic form rarely follow neat lines of innovation and development, and it is the later of Mérimée's two novellas which is closer to the libertine text, and the earlier which is closer to the novel of female adultery. *Arsène Guillot* is fundamentally a narrative of seduction. Its three main characters form a triangle which differs in a cardinal respect from the one familiar in the novel of female adultery: the excluded partner is not the wife's husband, but the lover's former mistress. Moreover, it is through the mistress, whose name Mérimée took for his story's title, that the liaison begins.

A worldly irony is the hallmark of the libertine text, and *Arsène Guillot* is ironic in both its structure and tone. The central irony is that an attempt on the part of Madame de Piennes to redeem first Arsène, and then also her friend Max de Salligny, ends in her own seduction. This irreverent reversal partly explains the scandal the novella caused when it was first published, the day after Mérimée's election to the French Academy.[22] Not only does it show how a virtuous woman is seduced in an office of charity, but the chief object of her care is a women of easy virtue who acts as the catalyst for her seduction. Worse still, from the viewpoint of orthodox morality, much of the story's irony is at the expense both of the virtuous woman and of religion. The two women first encounter each other in a church. Mérimée suggests that Arsène's appearance and costume signal her 'social position' (I.892),[23] but Madame de Piennes prefers to believe her a model of devotion until Arsène tells her the obvious truth. This she does when Madame de Piennes goes to visit her after she has attempted suicide in a state of poverty and despair, following her lover's desertion and her mother's death. At the same time she explains that the devotional candle she had bought in the church had not been for her mother, as Madame de Piennes had assumed. Instead its motive had been secular and practical: to bring her a new lover. There are other local ironies against Madame de Piennes too. When she terms Max Arsène's 'seducer', the courtesan almost smiles through her tears (II.919); and Mérimée absurdly applies military metaphors normally used for campaigns of seduction to her attempt to convert the two (II.924).

Arsène Guillot recalls the libertine tradition not only through its sceptical wit, its ironies and its plot of seduction, but also through its disregard for the deceived husband. Indeed, it is the fact that the story gives the husband no importance whatsoever – not even as an obstacle, let alone as a potential victim – that most distinguishes it from the emerging form of the novel of female adultery. Madame de Piennes's marriage is one of convenience. Her husband is highly respectable but dull, and he is absent on his estates for nine months of the year, the period of the action included.

However, in several respects *Arsène Guillot* diverges from the libertine tradition. First, it is significant that the action is not presented from the seducer's point of view. Although the narrator plays a prominent role, and although much of the story is told through dialogue, the central figure is Madame de Piennes. It is her thoughts and feelings which are represented, not those of Max or Arsène. Furthermore, the story does not simply ironize her piety as naive or self-deluded. Mérimée states that Madame de Piennes has no interested motive for going to church (I.891–2), and he leaves it to be inferred that her devotions constitute an attempt to curb needs and emotions unsatisfied by her marriage. Indeed, her reluctance to recognize Arsène's position, and her dogged endeavour to save first Arsène, then also Max, suggest that she is attempting to repress her own sexuality. Mérimée observes that, like many a virtuous woman, Madame de Piennes experiences a sensation of curiosity at meeting 'a woman of another kind' (I.905). But he also pays tribute to her 'humanity' in not deserting Arsène once she knows what kind of woman she is (I.903); and the care she gives to Arsène shows kindness as well as a rather artificial piety.

Second, there is another side to the seduction narrative. The story not only indicates that Max and Madame de Piennes had been attracted to each other before the latter's marriage, but suggests that this effectively justifies their liaison. Though the two had known each other since they were children, Max had been rejected as a possible husband because of his reputation for fast living, and a safer man had been found instead. In implying that love had been pushed aside for the sake of a conventional marriage, the story shifts from irony into sentiment. Max, who has been travelling for over two years, implicitly to escape his sorrows, says there is no one it would now suit him to marry (II.911); Madame de Piennes finds that he has a picture of her and carries it in his wallet (II.914); he explains his relation to Arsène by calling her 'a distraction from a more serious affection which had to be struggled with' (II.922); and this is borne out when Arsène relates a quarrel over a camellia which Madame de Piennes had given him (II.927–8). All this suggests that Max's relation to Madame de Piennes is romantic and not merely sexual. By the same token, it detaches the story from the libertine tradition, in which the main object is sex rather than love.

The story's climax mixes ironic wit with romantic sentiment. For all Madame de Piennes's efforts, Arsène's interests stay stubbornly carnal. Still in love with her former keeper, but recognizing that she is dying, she brings the two lovers together over her deathbed. When the abbé asks her if she forgives all those who have done her wrong, her reply, 'Yes, let them be happy!' (III.933), tacitly sidesteps the liturgy and gives the couple a profane blessing. Her dying words and gesture implicitly prompt the beginning of the liaison. Replying to Max's rhetorical question, 'What happiness has she had in this world?', she simply declares, 'I have loved!', motions to each of them to take one of her hands, and repeats her phrase 'with a sad smile' (III.934). Mérimée leaves the reader to infer that the couple then begin an affair. Having prefaced the story cryptically with an epigraph from Homer predicting the defeat of the brave (in other words, Madame de Piennes), he ends it with a vignette of Arsène's tombstone and its pencilled inscription, '*Poor Arsène! she is praying for us*' (IV.935).

All the same, with the exception of these words, which conclude the story, *Arsène Guillot* does not look beyond the beginning of the affair. What distinguishes the novel of female adultery, in contrast, is that it presents consequences, particularly those arising from husband, family and social milieu. Mérimée's novella romantically implies that its two lovers may properly flout an empty arranged marriage, and even, perhaps, that they would have been happy together if they had been allowed to marry each other. Yet the romance is possible not only because of the husband's exclusion, and the absence of children and any concerns of family or property. It also depends on the mediation, and then removal, of the kept woman. The most decisive moment in the action is Madame de Piennes's shocked meeting with Max at Arsène's sickbed when, having lost contact with his former mistress, and then having heard of her troubles, he goes to visit her. It is this which encourages Madame de Piennes to reform Max through her reform of Arsène, and which results instead in her own seduction. Furthermore, one of the story's crueller ironies is the doctor's comment that Arsène need not have hurried to kill herself, as she is consumptive (I.898). Mérimée's story anticipates *The Lady of the Camélias* (1848) in more respects than its reference to camellias, and the courtesan's death from tuberculosis.[24] Like Dumas's novel, in which Marguerite is required to sacrifice herself for the good of Armand's respectable family, *Arsène Guillot* may further be read to suggest that the courtesan is a necessary but disposable element in the sexual functioning of this patriarchal society. Arsène not only meets the sexual needs of the privileged man, but enables, though involuntarily, his liaison with a woman of his own class.

To this there is an autobiographical link. Mérimée wrote *Arsène Guillot* for his long-time lover Valentine Delessert, who is the unidentified 'madame' addressed at intervals during the narrative. The original for Arsène was an opera-singer called Céline Cayot, who was his regular mistress until his affair with Valentine began. As Jean Mallion and Pierre Salomon have pointed out, in *Arsène Guillot* Mérimée 'explains and justifies himself concerning his liaison with Céline Cayot'.[25] Though Mérimée was prepared to sacrifice Céline in this way, she did not, happily, meet the early end of her fictional counterpart; and, according to A. W. Raitt, 'he remained vaguely in touch with her almost until his death'.[26]

This difference between fiction and reality is particularly significant because, like *Arsène Guillot*, *The Double Mistake* also ends with a woman's death. In the latter story, first published 11 years before *Arsène Guillot*, the woman who dies is the adulteress, and she does so from shame and shock in the aftermath of her seduction. Such an ending is only one of the ways in which *The Double Mistake* is closer than *Arsène Guillot* to the developing novel of female adultery. Nevertheless, *The Double Mistake* first introduces itself as a libertine tale, and it retains clear links with the older tradition.

The novella's opening chapter is headed by a verse in Spanish which may be translated as follows: 'Young girl, whiter than the flowers, blonde and with green eyes, if you think of falling in love, lose yourself well, because lose yourself you will' (I.11, my translation; 605).[27] But *The Double Mistake* aligns itself most with the libertine tradition by addressing a sophisticated masculinist readership. It constructs a reader whose interests and values are those of a man of the world, or who is capable of assuming those interests and values imaginatively. The narrator appeals to such a reader's connoisseurship when Julie's husband interrupts her while she is undressing: 'Chaverny was eyeing his wife whose dress was in that state of slight disorder which is so attractive. He found her rather "piquant" (if I may use an expression I detest)' (II.18; 610). Here the narrator assumes not only a voyeuristic taste for female beauty on the reader's part, but also a way of describing it which is itself, for the connoisseur, tasteful. He implies that his own sensibility is more refined than Chaverny's, and he invites the reader's collusive agreement. This imaginative conspiracy against the husband suggests that he is being set up as that butt of libertine writing, the cuckold. The story begins by remarking drily that, out of six years of married life, the first six months sufficed to end any regard his wife may have held for him. Its tone is ironic from the start, as when the narrator comments that, for Julie de Chaverny, dining with her husband several times a week was 'quite enough to keep her aversion alive' (I.11; 605).

Such an idea of marriage is characteristic of the libertine text, where it is taken for granted that dissatisfaction will be mutual and may be relieved by discreet affairs. The joke, indeed, is against marriage, as when the narrator observes that, although Chaverny rarely looks at his wife, 'even a husband could hardly remain unmoved' when she pouts as he arranges her shawl (II.16; 608). The narrator attempts to implicate the reader in the joke more directly still when he describes Chaverny's would-be cuckolder as 'aiding and abetting him with that single-minded devotion that you may yourself be lucky enough to experience if you happen to have a pretty wife' (V.32–3; 619).

The Double Mistake also draws on the libertine tradition by displaying a kind of structural wit. This is perhaps more sophisticated than in *Arsène Guillot*, especially in its play with reversals of expectation. For instance, after the introduction of husband and discontented wife in the first two chapters, an alert reader might expect a transition to the would-be lover. Such a transition does occur, but only after Mérimée has wrong-footed the reader by abruptly introducing Major Perrin, a ludicrous candidate as lover and a comic figure even in the role he turns out to play, that of confidant. Further, a key structural irony is that the story gives much more attention to preliminaries than to the expected seduction and its results. It is not until two thirds of the way through that the carriage journey begins which is to result in Julie's seduction. This teasing delay, along with the nature of the textual foreplay, again points to the affinity between *The Double Mistake* and the libertine tale. The narrative holds back in two main ways, the first of which plays further with the reader's expectations. Julie is courted by Châteaufort, her would-be lover, only to be set up more effectively for seduction by Darcy. Ironically, not only the husband is to be cuckolded, but also, as if by anticipation, the would-be lover. The second delay is Darcy's story-within-the-story about a Turkishwoman saved by his English friend and himself from her husband's attempt to have her drowned. This offers Julie a melodramatic parallel for her own position. It also indulges the same dry irony as the surrounding narrative, for instance in the cynical ending when the rescued woman, far from devoting herself either to Darcy or to religious conversion, runs off with the cook.

The similarity between Darcy's tone in telling his story and that of the narrator is significant. The libertine tradition invites engagement with the seducer's point of view, and so, up to a point, does *The Double Mistake*. When Julie expresses her unhappiness in the carriage, the narrator comments that Darcy is touched by her tears but also that 'he felt six years younger' (XI.84; 655). It is his response which Mérimée presents first, after the space between two chapters in which the couple have sex. The tone is sardonic, as when the narrator remarks that assiduous hand-kissing saves Darcy quite a few words, and that Julie's dejection made his position 'rather difficult and even, if one may be allowed to say so, somewhat tiresome' (XII.88; 657). Mérimée goes so far to have Darcy reflect that to have brought back a concubine from Turkey 'would have been like taking figs to Damascus' (XIII.92; 660).

Nevertheless, the space which Mérimée gives to Julie's response is more significant – particularly because of the light it casts on the development of the novel of female adultery. The beginning of the story already hints at a more serious engagement with the experience of the unhappily married woman than is characteristic of the libertine tale. In describing Julie's revulsion from her husband, Mérimée even briefly anticipates *Madame Bovary*: 'She found everything about him repellent: the way he ate, the way he drank his coffee, the way he spoke, set her nerves on edge' (I.11; 605). But he goes much further than Flaubert in presenting Julie's state of mind after her seduction. The length and intensity of the passages in which he conveys her confusion and anguish offer a sharp contrast with Darcy's detached satisfaction. It is left for the reader, however, to decide what to make of this. On the one hand, it is easy to infer from the text a tacit critique of Darcy's complacent unconcern. On the other hand, there is more than a hint that what is in question is also Julie's naivety. In her shame at having yielded so quickly, and to a man she hardly knows, she assumes that she is already 'a social outcast, that her family would cast her off' (XII.90; 659). Yet the story has indicated long before then not only that Julie is aware of, and tolerates, her husband's infidelity (II.17–18; 609–10), but that he would tolerate hers: 'As he left his wife completely free in her actions, it would never have occurred to him to imagine that she might not want to allow him the liberties that he was prepared, if need be, to allow her' (VI.39; 623). The double misunderstanding of Mérimée's title is on Julie's part that Darcy is in love with her, and on Darcy's part that Julie is offering him the chance of a casual affair. Yet the deeper issue is radical uncertainty about the social codes surrounding marriage and adultery.

Mérimée wrote his story in 1833, three years into the reign of Louis-Philippe, but set it, like *Arsène Guillot*, in the last years of the Restoration.[28] *The Double Mistake* straddles aristocratic and bourgeois models of marriage as well as the transition from absolute to bourgeois monarchy. In accordance with the aristocratic model, the Chaverny marriage is largely the result of relatives settling 'the business side' (I.12; 606), and the discreet infidelity of either partner can be tolerated. But Julie, as Mérimée's French editors say, is 'solicitous of respectability and bourgeois virtue'.[29] She has no wish to be unfaithful; she cares for her reputation; and she wants a husband she can love. This is why what decides her seduction is Darcy's implied rebuke that, in rejecting him for his lack of money several years before, she had followed the Parisian preference for marriage over love (XI.87; 657). She is trying to find the loving partner she has missed in Chaverny. In turn, Mérimée suggests that Darcy is callous as a result of that rejection. Ironically, the story ends with him marrying for advantage. This is only, however, after Julie has died from a fever she contracts as she journeys to her mother in shame and despair. Again, the event may be read in more than one way. At the sentimental end of the spectrum, the woman's death and the man's empty marriage might convey a hint of tragically disappointed love; at the cynical end, so extreme a response on a woman's part to seduction might be taken to imply a perverse and heartless tribute to the conquering male. Nevertheless, in the tradition that was to develop, few novels of female adultery end without the death of the heroine; and, despite the contrived effect of Mérimée's ending, it is in keeping with a legal and social intolerance of the adulterous woman which was already strengthening under the Restoration.

Novels of adultery can only come into being when marriage is understood, as it is in bourgeois society, as a binding legal and, ideally, emotional contract. In bourgeois marriage, the husband's role is to provide a social and an economic position which it is the wife's role to help sustain, and advertize, through a display of possessions, acquirements and moral probity; each partner is further supposed entitled to the undivided erotic affections of the other. If the libertine text depends on not taking seriously an institution which the social if not the legal arrangements of the day tended to devalue, the novel of female adultery takes marriage very seriously indeed. Part of the interest of *The Double Mistake* is that it demonstrates a shift from one form to the other. If, as I have suggested, Mérimée's delaying tactics come out of a tradition of libertine wit, they also lend psychological plausibility to the wife's behaviour. Julie yields very quickly to a man she hardly knows, but whom she suddenly comes to believe she should have married. This is more probable in light of the details of her unhappy marriage; especially as her courting by Châteaufort has already led her to begin thinking of another partner.

The final sentence of *The Double Mistake* may be translated literally as follows: 'These two souls [*coeurs*] who had so misunderstood each other were perhaps made for one another' (XVI.104; 668). Again the story faces two ways: the remark can be read ironically, in keeping with the libertine tradition, or sentimentally, at odds with it. The ambivalence may be traced not only to the social and historical changes which I have indicated, but also to Mérimée's private life. His commentators claim that the story represents his revenge on George Sand for his sexual fiasco with her earlier in the same year; yet Sand also supplied details which he put into his account of the unhappy wife, some of them verbatim.[30] Perhaps there also lies behind the story the collapse in 1830 of his hopes for marriage to Mélanie Double.[31] However, leaving biographical determinations aside, the story illustrates with striking clarity how the novel of female adultery began to emerge from the libertine text, casts light on the social and historical context of the new form, and helps distinguish more sharply what identifies it.

3
The Formation of the Novel of Female Adultery: Balzac

While Mérimée adopts the form of the novella for *The Double Mistake* and *Arsène Guillot*, and has each turn on a wife's seduction, Balzac represents adultery in a variety of situations and forms in the *Human Comedy*. No reader of *The Physiology of Marriage* is likely to find it surprising that its author would go on to produce a large number of narratives involving female adultery. However, it is debatable whether more than one or two of these constitute an adultery text in the sense defined in Chapter 1, that is, a narrative in which one or more adulterous liaisons are central to its concerns as identified by its action, themes and structure. Instead, a number of different ways of construing and representing adultery may be traced in the extraordinary mass of writing which Balzac shaped into *The Human Comedy*.

There are various possible explanations for the complex and even contradictory patterns that emerge. First, the range of attitudes which is evident probably owes much to Balzac's personal life. It is relevant, for instance, that he resented his mother for bearing a son by one of her lovers and for favouring him over himself; that he had a series of adulterous liaisons, especially with older women; and that, when Madame de Castries refused to become his lover, he put some of his animus against her into his story *The Duchesse de Langeais* (1834).[1] Second, there is the impact of Balzac's direct and indirect responses to the social and political changes of his time. The relation between writing and history is even more difficult to interpret than that between the work and the life of an author, but Balzac's novels clearly show his reactions to the July Revolution of 1830 and how it marked the eclipse of an aristocratic by a bourgeois social order. Since there were key differences between aristocratic and bourgeois social conventions governing marriage, this fundamental shift had its own impact on the representation of adultery. Third, Balzac wrote in a number of different genres, including journalism as well as fiction. He experimented with a variety of forms, and he often revised and remoulded his writing. Even before he devised the massive framework of *The Human Comedy*, he was given to moving texts from one matrix to another in the various editions of his work. At a period when the political, social and cultural life of France was itself in flux, especially around the critical year of 1830, this practice of revision, reconstruction and rearrangement encouraged a diversity of forms and perspectives.

The two novels by Balzac which most nearly meet the definition given above of the novel of adultery are, though for different reasons, *A Woman of Thirty* (1834–42) and *The Muse of the Department* (1843). Before discussing these, I will consider a number of narratives featuring the theme of adultery and written during the early 1830s. These draw on a variety of traditions, ranging from the libertine tale and the physiology to the cautionary tale and the story of tragic love. They help to show how the novel of female adultery emerged, and they also help to distinguish this new type of fiction from the traditions out of which it developed.

These texts may be placed loosely in three groups. First, there are the narratives which make up *History of the Thirteen* (1839): *Ferragus* (1834), *The Duchesse de Langeais* (1834), and *The Girl with the Golden Eyes* (1835). These owe most to the libertine tradition, although, in their accounts of such phenomena as the *grisette*, the Faubourg Saint-Germain and the social classes of Paris, they also reflect the genre of the physiology. In contrast, the narratives in the second group are, at least ostensibly, cautionary tales. In each one a character relates an anecdote which presents a warning to women of 'the dangers of misconduct'. That phrase, which was the original title of the earliest story in this group, later to be called *Gobseck* (1830), supplies a convenient heading for them all.[2] The others in the group are *Le Conseil* (*Advice*, 1832), a composite text including *The Message* and *La Grande Bretèche*, later broken up for the repositioning of both stories; and *La Maîtresse de notre colonel* (*Our Colonel's Mistress*, also 1832). Finally, there are two stories on the theme of the abandoned woman, one with that title, *La Femme abandonnée* (1833), the other entitled *La Grenadière* (1832 once more).

The main features which connect *History of the Thirteen* to the libertine tradition are clear. Balzac acknowledges his debt to that tradition when he alludes to Laclos's *Les Liaisons dangereuses* and the Marquis de Sade's *Justine* (377–8; 1097),[3] or to the conventional role of the crafty servant in eighteenth-century comedy (68–9;

826–7, and 342; 1066). More important, each plot begins from an Old Regime idea of adultery. The Duchesse de Langeais is in a marriage of convenience, living apart from her husband 'both factually and sentimentally' (194; 937); and she is informed by a *grande dame* from the previous century that 'marriage is an imperfect institution which has to be tempered with love', so long as this is done discreetly (283; 1017). Similarly, in *Ferragus* Auguste de Maulincour pursues a married woman according to 'the eighteenth-century doctrine of *galanterie*' instilled into him by a former accomplished seducer, the Vidame de Pamiers (41; 802). The action of *Ferragus* begins from a libertine perspective as the narrator muses about following pretty women in the streets by night (34–9; 796–800); while in the third story, *The Girl with the Golden Eyes*, Henri de Marsay assumes that he is 'about to act the eternally old, eternally new comedy' of cuckolding (346–7; 1071).

The Thirteen are a group of superior men pledged to promote each other's aims regardless of law or morality. They represent a fantasy of collective male power. In *Ferragus* they are able after several attempts to have Maulincour killed; in *The Duchesse de Langeais* they raid a Majorcan convent in an attempt at abduction; and in *The Girl with the Golden Eyes* they break into a well-guarded Parisian mansion with the same object. In his Preface to the *History*, Balzac credits the Thirteen with almost unlimited power. Yet all three stories show that power failing. *Ferragus* ends with its eponymous hero broken and bereaved of his daughter; the Duchesse de Langeais never becomes Armand de Montriveau's lover; and Henri de Marsay succeeds in becoming Paquita's lover only for her to be killed – not by a cuckolded husband, but by a rival who is a lesbian and, moreover, his half-sister.

Drawing on comments by Naomi Schor on the persistent 'questioning of sexual roles' in nineteenth-century French literature, Margaret Waller has called attention to two opposing patterns in fiction of the 1830s: 'While the first pattern would seem to represent a "breakdown of gender distinctions," the second reinforces these differences and the power relations they imply even though it seems to reverse them.'[4] Examples of the first type are Théophile Gautier's *Mademoiselle de Maupin* (1836), and Balzac's *Sarrasine* (1830), as well as *The Girl with the Golden Eyes*; of the second, Charles Augustin Sainte-Beuve's *Volupté* (1834), Balzac's *Lily of the Valley* and Musset's *Confession of a Child of the Century* (both 1836). In parallel with this, the period of the July Monarchy saw what

Peter McPhee has called an increasing 'sex-role differentiation' – in medicine, in cooking and most noticeably in dress:

At the same time that élite men were wearing simplified 'business suits' as a sign of serious activity, shunning the jewellery and lace of the Ancien Régime, women's dress was increasingly complicated and fussy, a 'language' with multiple meanings: their husband's wealth, the titillating modesty of narrow bodices and flounced skirts, and of women's inactivity in tight corsets and full dresses.[5]

Such pressure to reinforce gender distinctions suggests underlying uneasiness about them. The same tension appears in *History of the Thirteen*, for, as Shoshana Felman has demonstrated in her essay on *The Girl with the Golden Eyes*,[6] the whole bizarre compilation reflects male anxiety about the feminine.

It is that anxiety which differentiates the three stories from the libertine tradition. It takes a different shape in each one. In *The Girl with the Golden Eyes*, which comes closest to the tradition, it consists in the suspicion not only that a woman might prefer another woman as a sexual partner, but that, even if she accepts the man, it is because of his resemblance to his sister. Felman goes so far as to suggest that in this story femininity becomes '*that which subverts the very opposition of masculinity and femininity*'.[7] In *The Duchesse de Langeais*, more conventionally, the problem is female resistance to male importunity. This Balzac presents as aggravated coquetry: the Duchesse holds out for a long time, but, when her would-be lover's attempt at revenge makes her eager to yield completely, his failure to arrive on time for the assignation provokes her to flee for the rest of her life to a convent. But it is *Ferragus* which is separated from the libertine tradition most clearly by male anxiety about the female. Although the story begins from a libertine perspective, Maulincour has no hope of seducing Clémence, who is happily married. Instead he becomes convinced by a chance meeting that she has a lover. This suspicion he spreads to her husband Jules, who cannot accept her assurances and does all he can to find her out. Clémence ends by dying of grief, but only after Jules has established that the suspected lover is her father, an escaped convict whose identity she is sworn to protect. The bourgeois marriage of Clémence and Jules differs from the typical marriage in the novel of female adultery only in that the two are in love. That this is in one way a very small difference is shown by Jules's inability to trust his wife. He shows a level of suspicion concerning his wife's fidelity which rivals that of the mistrustful husband in *The Physiology of Marriage*. Indeed, the fact that both Maulincour and Ferragus also feel jealousy on her account points again to a general masculine anxiety about female sexuality.

Ferragus invites psychoanalytical interpretation as flagrantly as *The Girl with the Golden Eyes*. However, what is more relevant to the formation of the novel of female adultery is the social, political and ideological commentary which Balzac built into all three stories. Although *History of the Thirteen* is set during the early years of the Restoration, it was written after the Revolution of 1830. According to Balzac's analysis, foreshadowed in *Ferragus* and given at length in *The Duchesse de Langeais*, the restored aristocracy failed to consolidate its position and allowed the bourgeoisie to gain power. Balzac criticizes the aristocracy most directly in the figure of the Duchesse de Langeais, and to a lesser extent, in *Ferragus*, in that of Maulincour. He represents both characters as typical of their generation and their class in failing to give substance to the Old Regime roles they try to play. Maulincour's interest in Clémence is of necessity platonic; and the Duchesse enjoys the attentions of a suitor who will never become her lover. It is characteristic, and revealing, that Balzac should have fictionalized his political analysis in terms of sexual relationships. Part of the explanation is that, as in *The Physiology of Marriage*, he equated women with the people and men with the rulers. Thus, in *The Duchesse de Langeais*, he claims that 'the popular classes, like women, love to see strength in those who govern them' (181; 926–7). In the absence of strong Restoration government, the Thirteen offer an outlaw alternative. They stand for the rule of the fathers, asserting an arbitrary, masculine authority in which bourgeois values have no place.

But the *History* also suggests that at some level Balzac recognized this as a nostalgic fantasy. The three stories are set in the first years of the Restoration, though the opening and closing scenes of *The Duchesse de Langeais* occur in 1823. The story which is set earliest, though it comes last in the series, *The Girl with the Golden Eyes*, is both the closest of the three to the libertine tradition and the one in which the Thirteen are most nearly successful. Significantly, it is set during Napoleon's Hundred Days. In contrast, *Ferragus*, which is set latest, though it comes first, shows how the leader of the Thirteen comes to grief. This is not because of any action from law or police, but because of tensions within the family. The married couple at the centre of the story are pillars of the bourgeoisie, and what leads to Ferragus's ruin is his attempt to regain a socially acceptable identity, not least in the eyes of his son-in-law. In this way *Ferragus* acknowledges, and implicitly regrets, the rise of a respectable bourgeois social order. It was within that order, with its changing social and moral conventions, that the novel of female adultery was to form.

At the time when Balzac wrote *History of the Thirteen*, he had already produced several fictions with a quite different perspective on adultery. Herbert J. Hunt has suggested that he may have been 'desirous of atoning for the apparent levity of *La Physiologie de mariage*' in the two volumes of stories, first published in 1830, which included *The Dangers of Misconduct*.[8] As the later change of title to *Gobseck* indicates, Balzac came to decide that the story centred not on the wages of adultery but on the moneylender who profits from these and other sins and follies. But it would be truer still to say that the story's underlying theme is the displacement of aristocratic excess by emerging bourgeois values of prudence and decency. What makes it necessary to formulate the theme in that way is that *Gobseck* implies a more positive view of bourgeois life than does *History of the Thirteen*, though it conveys an equally jaundiced view of the aristocracy. The theme is embodied in the narrative structure, in which a self-made man, the lawyer Derville, 'seventh child of a small tradesman at Noyon' (330; 979),[9] tells the story at the house of the Vicomtesse de Grandlieu, 'one of the greatest ladies in the Faubourg Saint-Germain' (309; 962). Derville owes his success not only to hard work and good management, but to the help he has given the Grandlieu family, émigrés during the Revolution, in recovering their former property. His story is aimed at enabling Camille Grandlieu to marry the young Comte de Restaud. It tells how the Restaud fortunes have been saved from the mother's desperate attempts to keep her spendthrift aristocratic lover.

The nub of the story is that, rather as Derville has helped the Grandlieus recover their losses, so Derville, backed by Gobseck, prevents further losses for the Restaud property. Balzac shows the dangers of misconduct in portraying the bitterness, despair and near ruin to which the Comtesse's liaison reduces herself and the

Comte, not to mention the further risk of destitution for the children. To that extent Derville's story might point a warning to its youngest listener, Camille, as well as to its female readers. But Camille falls asleep before the story is ended, and it has a stronger application to her aristocratic parents – not just so that they know the young Comte's fortune is secure, but so that they receive an example of bourgeois virtues. It is an alliance based on hardheaded commercial and legal practice between Derville and Gobseck which saves the Restaud fortunes. The aim of the marriage, at least for Derville, is in keeping with a bourgeois conception of matrimony and of the family. In this way Derville not only helps the dying Comte save his elder son's inheritance, but insists that he also protect the interests of the other two children – even though, all but explicitly, it was not the Comte but his wife's lover who fathered them. Equally important, the marriage Derville encourages between Camille and the young Comte will be based on mutual love as well as on equivalence in wealth and rank.

Bourgeois ideals of social and moral self-help are built deep into the story. For instance, the improvidence of the Comte and Comtesse de Restaud is paralleled by that of Derville's employer, whose bankruptcy enables Derville to buy his practice with a loan from Gobseck. Then, after Gobseck has contrasted his visits to the Restaud household and to that of Fanny Malvaut, a poor but beautiful and virtuous seamstress, it turns out that Derville has subsequently married Fanny for love and been further rewarded by an unexpected legacy from her uncle. *Gobseck* centres, then, much more on the superiority of bourgeois values than on the theme of adultery. Indeed, it implies that the aristocracy will survive to the extent that it assimilates such values. Despite Derville's deference to the Grandlieus, and although the story was written before the Revolution of 1830, he is clearly their master.

Le Conseil is much more directly a warning against the dangers of misconduct. Again, however, the text turns out to have a different and in this case an ironic orientation. The advice of the title is offered to a young wife who is being wooed by an aspiring lover. It takes the form chiefly of the two stories *The Message* and *La Grande Bretèche*, on the principle that morality is better taught by example than by theory. The frame which Balzac's original text provided for these stories is notably self-reflexive. It begins with a discussion in a high-class salon of literature and morality, and of questions concerning social and theatrical decorum. But, more important, it also calls attention to the position and motives of the advisor. Since Villaines is jealous of Madame d'Esther's suitor, his words are scarcely disinterested. Indeed, although he tells his stories to the company, they are intended as much for her ears as the advice he confides to her personally. Yet Villaines's motives are not simply amorous. The story ironically leaves him 'passionately in love with Madame d'Esther' (1373).[10] But it has already suggested that his behaviour may be explained chiefly by his need to compensate, after the Revolution of 1830, for losing the consideration he formerly enjoyed as *'nephew of a peer of France'* (1369). In this way *Le Conseil* parallels *Gobseck* and *History of the Thirteen* in suggesting the decline of the aristocracy's importance.

Although Villaines's class position may seem of marginal interest, it is significant because it indicates a fundamental connection between literary form on the one hand, and social and ideological formation on the other. As I have suggested in Chapters 1 and 2, the novel of female adultery is an essentially bourgeois form, while the libertine text is rooted in social values and practices associated with the eighteenth-century French aristocracy. *Le Conseil* may be read as a libertine text to the extent that Villaines's role of moral advisor gives way to that of potential seducer; it begins to approach an adultery text to the extent that the advice may be taken seriously. Villaines's ambiguous role reflects his changed social position under the bourgeois monarchy. Beyond this, it points to shifting social attitudes about marriage and adultery.

The first cautionary tale told by Villaines, *The Message*, shows a parallel ambiguity. Its action is simple: following a coach accident, the narrator goes at the request of a dying fellow passenger to break the news to his mother and his married lover, and to return to the latter her letters. According to Villaines, the anecdote warns against adultery because it shows how chance strikes at 'criminal liaisons' and how 'this secret justice' works independently from that of society (1372). However, such a reading is at odds with the story's debts to the libertine tradition. Not only does it refer to the eighteenth-century *Amours du chevalier de Faublas*, in which the hero loves two mistresses equally,[11] but it sets up the deceived husband as a grotesque, much more interested in his gargantuan meal than in his wife's distress, and it adopts the viewpoint of 'an experienced man of pleasure' for its description of the bereaved mistress. The narrator goes so far as to exclaim: 'the sight of her awakened an irresistible desire of possession in the depths of the heart' (298; 401).

Indeed, as Nicole Mozet points out, under its moralistic cover the text leaves for divination 'the underlying theme of the impossible seduction'.[12] However, although the mistress visits the narrator late at night to hear what he cannot say in front of her husband, he takes no advantage of her but merely notes, ungallantly, how quickly and how totally her beauty has faded. This might be seen, cynically, as part of the cautionary element in the story, but the narrator ends by paying tribute to 'one of those beloved, loving, and self-sacrificing natures so rarely found upon this earth' (305; 407), and by presenting his mistress's reaction after he has told her what had happened: 'Oh, my dear, not you! *you* must not die!' (306; 407).

In view of the mixture of attitudes conveyed by *The Message*, it is not surprising that Villaines's hearers find it ineffectual as a cautionary tale. This gives a pretext for a much more violent story, *La Grande Bretèche*, and again it is the libertine tradition which is more in evidence. The story is about the punishment of a wife and her lover by a vengeful husband. Its affinities with libertine writing consist in the aristocratic status of the characters, the marriage of convenience from which the wife seeks relief, and, most of all, a tone of sardonic wit. The punishment devised by the husband is cleverly sadistic. Knowing that his wife's lover is in her closet, though she denies it, he trumps her lie by having the closet door immediately bricked up. He then keeps watch while the lover slowly dies, protecting his mistress's honour by doing his best to keep quiet. There is a further libertine twist in that the narrator of the story – Villaines in the original, Bianchon in the final version – finds out the crux of what has happened by seducing the wife's former maid. The emphasis of *La Grande Bretèche* is scarcely moral. It is a sophisticated literary performance, with its complex narrative structure, involving no fewer than three subordinate narrators, all rendered deftly, as well as the storyteller in the frame; and with the neat formal rhyme by which the opening description of the sealed house, the name of which gives the story its title, echoes the closet turned torture chamber and tomb.

Finally, *La Maîtresse de notre colonel* is another story of revenge. Here, the lover and his mistress are burned alive by the latter's Italian husband, who can no longer bear the openness of a liaison made all the more insulting by the makeshifts of retreat from Moscow. Balzac first published the story in his collection *Contes bruns* (*Dark Stories*) in 1832, and, thanks to its Napoleonic associations, it appeared two years later in a Bonapartist review.

But it was under the guise of a cautionary tale that he placed it in *Another Study of Woman* in the 1842 edition of *The Human Comedy* – to be joined by *La Grande Bretèche* in the 1845 edition.[13] There, introducing the story, its narrator says: 'I have always noticed the effects of some obscure chance, which you may call Providence, inevitably overwhelming those whom we name light women' (47, TM; 703). Once more, there is no attempt at pointing any moral to the adulterer, who also perishes.

The five stories I have been discussing under the loose heading of cautionary tales were all published and republished in a variety of settings. This is due partly to Balzac's ability to place them profitably in different journals or collections, and partly to his prolonged reshaping of the body of work which became *The Human Comedy*. At the same time, however, the different and sometimes conflicting implications of these texts, both in themselves and in their various incarnations, suggest an uncertainty both formal and ideological about the representation of female adultery. Another sign of that uncertainty is that, at the same time as Balzac was writing these stories, in the early 1830s, he also produced two stories of abandoned women, *La Grenadière* and *A Forsaken Lady*. Paradoxically, although both show grief and loss as a result of adultery, these do not encourage reading as cautionary tales.

While *La Grenadière* focuses on the decline and death of a woman bereaved of her lover, and on her care of her children, *A Forsaken Lady* shows a second love affair ending even more unhappily than the first.[14] One way of explaining why Balzac chose not to exploit the monitory possibilities these scenarios invite is to suggest that he was attempting to stir sympathy for women in loveless marriages. *La Grenadière* briefly lifts the veil it draws over its central character's past to reveal 'a careless childhood, a loveless marriage, a terrible passion' (279, TM; 434). After Madame de Willemsens's death, it calls her adultery 'the sweetest of crimes, a crime always expiated in this world, so that the pardoned spirit may enter heaven' (289; 442). Similarly, in *A Forsaken Lady* the narrator goes so far as to call the lover of a man in a loveless marriage 'his wife in truth, whom he forsook for a social chimera' (262; 503). Indeed, here the woman's position is doubly hard. Not only is it impossible for Madame de Beauséant to marry her lover, because her husband in a marriage of convenience will not, if he can help it, release her by dying (249; 493); but her lover, after living nine happy years with her, bows to propriety and enters a marriage of convenience himself.

On such a reading, the two stories might seem to bear out those who argue that Balzac was a feminist before the letter.[15] However, comparison with *Gobseck* suggests another possibility. The position of Madame de Beauséant in *A Forsaken Lady* differs from that of the Comtesse de Restaud in two material and related respects: first, she has no children; second, she risks no one's interests but her own. In yielding to her second lover's importunity, Madame de Beauséant commits herself to permanent social ostracism, and exposes herself to the misery of ultimate desertion, but she threatens neither family nor property. This allows Balzac to honour the passion of a woman who loves to the full, yet has the integrity to refuse her lover when he besieges her again after his marriage. *La Grenadière*, on the other hand, celebrates the woman's care for her children as she dies with little money and no legitimate name to leave them, the victim of her husband's vengeance, bereaved of her lover. The story emphasizes suffering, maternal love and the older son's preparation for the role of 'father' (its last word) to his brother. In this way, despite adultery, family (not to say patriarchal) values are affirmed.

A Woman of Thirty is one of only two full-length narratives by Balzac to centre on female adultery. Significantly, however, the work was neither conceived nor written as a whole, but assembled over a period of more than ten years from an assortment of stories and sketches. Although it acquired its definitive title only in the first edition of *The Human Comedy*, in 1842, nearly all of this material had first been written in the same years as the stories just discussed, between 1829 and 1834.[16] Balzac formed it into a single though episodic narrative chiefly by distilling the main characters from a series of prototypes. For instance, the woman of thirty, Julie d'Aiglemont, is compounded from no fewer than three such originals.

There are two main affinities between *A Woman of Thirty* and the other works involving plots of female adultery which Balzac composed during the same period. The more striking of these is the use of the cautionary tale. The last three of the novel's six episodes present melodramatic punishments of the adulterous woman, in each case through her children. In the first, 'The Finger of God', the favoured son Julie has had by her lover is drowned during a riverside assignation thanks to a push from her legitimate daughter, Hélène, whom she has slighted. The second episode, 'The

Two Meetings', set several years later, involves the same daughter, who elopes with an outlaw on the night when he takes refuge with her family. The result is still more bizarre: having accompanied her husband on a career of piracy, near the end of which he captures and releases her father, Hélène dies a destitute widow, bereaved of her own baby daughter, in her mother's arms. As if this were not enough, in the final episode, 'The Old Age of a Guilty Mother', Balzac adds the further retribution of incest. Julie dies, suffering from her surviving favourite child, Moïna, the daughter she has had by her lover, not only the same cold treatment she had given her legitimate daughter, but the knowledge that Moïna has unwittingly begun a liaison with her own half-brother, the same lover's legitimate son.

If this didacticism somewhat lacks subtlety, it jars even more after episodes which have struck a very different note. For the second main way in which *A Woman of Thirty* recalls Balzac's concurrent portrayals of female adultery is its debt to the libertine tradition. Julie d'Aiglemont has two love affairs, the first of which is never consummated. There is a libertine cynicism in the sardonic comedy of the sequence in which her first wooer has his fingers crushed in her closet door as he hides from her husband, and then catches a fatal dose of pneumonia from spending the night on her window sill. This Balzac caps by inviting the reader to infer how the episode ended from a conversation in which Julie's ignorant husband delivers the punchline. However, the episode entitled 'At Thirty Years' reveals further contradictions in the novel's representation of female adultery. This is the account of Julie's successful wooing by her second lover, which is linked in two main ways to the libertine tradition. First, not only is it written chiefly from the lover's point of view, but the values and attitudes it implies are those of a male connoisseur of the female. Second, Balzac's generalizations about women and wooing offer hints and tips for the suitor. He not only commends the woman of thirty to his male readers, claiming that she 'satisfies every requirement' (111; 1129), but explains how to seduce her: 'a woman only surrenders at the summons of a virtue' (122; 1139). It is not easy to reconcile this lover's manual with the moralistic melodrama of the following episodes, especially when Balzac explains how flattering it is to a man's vanity when for his sake a woman 'immolates the honour of a whole family' (110; 1129).

However, despite these egregious examples of the double standard, *A Woman of Thirty* also offers an alternative view to that of the cautionary tale or the libertine text in its treatment of female adultery. This view, which was to prove much more characteristic of the fictional tradition to be centred on that theme, comes from the character herself. At several points in the novel's first two episodes, Balzac portrays an unhappy wife's suffering and sense of injustice from her own perspective. For instance, he has her passionately denounce to a curé the inequality and oppression of a woman's lot:

> Marriage, the institution on which society today depends, makes us alone feel all its weight: freedom for the man, duties for the woman. We must give our whole lives to you; you are only bound to give us a few moments of yours. Indeed a man makes a choice, while we blindly submit. Oh, sir, to you I can speak freely. Ah dear, marriage as it is carried on today seems to me to be legal prostitution. (92, TM; 1114)

The curé's conventional answers do nothing to help. Instead, Julie has already decided to 'neither be a prostitute in [her] own eyes nor in those of the world' (64; 1091), by refusing not only her admirer's attentions but also her husband's. This is chastity with a vengeance, but the narrator underlines Julie's dilemma when he says that her decision will please the defenders neither of duty nor of passion, and that this shows 'either the misery which follows in the train of broken laws, or some truly unfortunate defects in the institutions upon which society in Europe is based' (68, TM; 1044–5). Although the novel's later episodes show the misery and not the defects, this is a telling admission.

That said, it would be wrong to underestimate the conflict in *A Woman of Thirty* between lurid caution against female adultery, encouragement to male licence, and sympathy for a wife trapped in a bad marriage. There are several possible ways of understanding that conflict. For instance, the novel's editors in the Pléiade series, Bernard Gagnebin and René Guise, attribute its inconsistencies to its piecemeal composition and to Balzac's change of role, in 1832, from the witty cynic of *The Physiology of Marriage* to that of a moral right-thinker and legitimist.[17] However, in revising the text ten years later for *The Human Comedy*, Balzac did not choose to remove or reduce the contradictions I have indicated. Indeed, he also allowed its narrative discontinuities to stand, as Christopher Prendergast has pointed out, although these are scarcely typical of his work in general.[18] I suggest that the irregularities of the work are themselves significant; that they cannot be explained only by its complicated textual history or by biographical detail; and that *A Woman of Thirty*, like the texts already discussed which were written in the same period, betrays radical tensions in its treatment of the theme of female adultery.

The contradictions of the work are such as to deny straightforward interpretive choices. Christopher Prendergast has claimed that it is possible to read *A Woman of Thirty* either as 'a moral tale', 'entirely didactic', or 'as surreptitiously criticising the paternalistic and reactionary ideology which it appears to be defending'.[19] But the paternalism runs very deep. For instance, in the opening episode, entitled 'Early Mistakes', Julie's first error is to ignore her father's advice and marry Victor d'Aiglemont, a dashing young colonel in the cavalry. Her unhappiness therefore does not result from an arranged marriage, but from her own choice. Then there is a double bind in the apparently radical idea that a wife prostitutes herself in having sex with a husband she does not love. When the narrator first introduces this idea, he suggests that the deception entailed by such unwilling surrender shows 'an already existing corruption, which had nothing yet on which to exercise itself' (57, TM; 1084). He goes on to say, magnanimously, that 'starving wretches, compelled to respect the laws of property, are not less to be pitied' than unhappy wives tempted by adultery (57; 1084–5); thanks to the Civil Code, with its guarantees for male control of property, the comparison is especially, though perhaps inadvertently, apposite. Finally, there is the repeated pattern according to which the sins of the mother are not only visited upon but punished by her daughters, even, in one case, to the third generation. From Julie d'Aiglemont, motherless herself, issue no fewer than three examples of that retributive figure in the novel of female adultery which Naomi Segal has called 'the adulteress's child'.[20]

As the Pléiade editors observe, 'What Balzac condemns in his heroine is the guilty mother, much more than the unfaithful wife.'[21] Yet, although this is a common pattern in the novel of female adultery, it has a quite different emphasis, and form, in *A Woman of Thirty*. The novel may seem to recall the libertine text in marginalizing the deceived husband, and to defer to nineteenth-century bourgeois values in idealizing motherhood. But, although it pays conventional tribute to the mother's role, what it really promotes is a masculinist idea of love. The reason why the mother suffers through her children is that she cannot love the children she has by the husband she does not love, and cannot help loving those she has by her lover. This contrasts very directly with, for instance, *Anna Karenina*, where Anna loves her legitimate son and cannot love her illegitimate daughter. Balzac celebrates the superiority of the lover, who alone can father children who will be loved. If, in so doing, he seems to give nature priority over society, he also redresses the balance sharply; for, without impugning the father, the natural children become the means of the mother's punishment.

What is also significant is the literary form in which Balzac shows the working out of that punishment. The novel's three retributive episodes are notorious for their melodrama. Indeed, it is probably this aspect of *A Woman of Thirty* which has attracted most criticism, including from Balzac himself.[22] Christopher Prendergast is unusual in defending the novel both for its melodrama and for its narrative discontinuity. Yet, in casting it as 'a powerful drama of the conflicts between kinship obligations and sexual desire, authority and individuality, repression and violence, enacted at various levels of familial relationships',[23] he fails to recognize its profoundly masculinist bias. The novel shifts into melodrama only when it shows female adultery being punished. Such shifts are at odds not only with the form and the tone of the narrative elsewhere, but also with what would become the dominant conventions of the novel of female adultery. It was not yet possible, in the 1830s, to present female adultery in an everyday setting, subject to the accepted codes of plausibility. The melodrama of *A Woman of Thirty* may be seen as resulting from contradictions which could not be assimilated between orthodox morality and male sexual demands.

A *Woman of Thirty* is the text which gives clearest evidence among Balzac's writings of formal and ideological tensions in the representation of female adultery. In *The Muse of the Department*, most of which was written ten to twelve years later,[24] the most prominent of these tensions disappear. The novel is accordingly much closer to *Madame Bovary* in its treatment of female adultery. Indeed, as Flaubert certainly knew *The Muse*, it figures among the sources of that work.[25]

The Muse of the Department addresses the theme of adultery both in its action and, self-reflexively, in much of its discourse. In one scene the main characters not only discuss adultery in literature, but three men tell stories about adultery to a group including the heroine, Dinah de La Baudraye, and all her admirers, in an attempt to find out whether she is having an affair with one of them. The stories are *L'Histoire du chevalier de Beauvoir*, *La Grande Bretèche*, and *Le Grand d'Espagne*. All had been first published by Balzac over ten years earlier, although, in three of the four versions of *The Muse of the Department* for which he was responsible, he did not even include the text of *La Grande Bretèche*; he claimed it was too well known for repetition, and in the final version he referred his readers to *Another Study of Woman*, to which he had transferred it.[26] The device of placing adultery texts within a framing narrative which is itself about adultery clearly recalls *Le Conseil*. But *The Muse of the Department* goes much further than the earlier work in reflecting on the representation of adultery. Not only does it often refer to the literature of illicit love, for instance to Constant's novel *Adolphe*, to Stendhal's *De l'Amour* and even to *A Woman of Thirty*, quoting the latter's title turned catchphrase with humorous self-assurance (139, 705; 236, 783). It also makes its heroine a writer who deals with the theme of adultery.

Dinah de La Baudraye differs in this and in two related respects from the central figures in Balzac's previous narratives of adultery. First, she is a 'woman from the provinces'; indeed, the novel originated in part from a description of that social type which Balzac contributed in 1841 to a collection entitled *Les Français peints par eux-mêmes* (*The French Portrayed by Themselves*).[27] Second, Dinah is an ambitious bourgeoise. Balzac constructs her as a woman of ability and purpose. Bred as a Protestant, 'at the age of seventeen she was a convert solely from ambition' (55; 635), and she marries for the same motive shortly afterwards. If, in the literature of adultery, she anticipates Madame Bovary as a woman of the provinces, her drive and ambition recall Stendhal's Julien Sorel. But the advantages of social class which she enjoys over Julien are more than offset by the constraints imposed by her gender.

Dinah's fundamental handicap is that Balzac allows her to advance herself only through men. At the start she commits herself to marriage much as Julien commits himself to the church; but she meets much tougher obstacles. The first of these is that her husband's motive for marriage is also ambition. Balzac embeds her story as adulterous woman in a framing story of her husband's self-aggrandizement. He describes with characteristic insight, precision and wit the steps by which La Baudraye rises in 40 years from the sickly son of a depleted émigré to a count and the richest proprietor of his region. Dinah soon finds that she cannot influence her husband, whose financial schemes long limit her expenditure very strictly. But she is allowed to play the role of a lady of fashion, and her salon draws admirers who offer consolation, not only through a love affair, but in part through the reflected social consequence of a successful man. This ambition also fails, thanks to the promotion of one suitor, who leaves the region, and to the defeat of another in the election for deputy. Her third attempt is to attach herself to a celebrity from Paris. In this she succeeds, to the extent of leaving her husband to live with Lousteau, her journalist lover, in the city. For a time she enjoys the life of a Parisienne, but she has two children by Lousteau, he tires of her, and she leaves him to return to her now ennobled and much wealthier husband.

Compared with the tradition to be epitomized by *Madame Bovary*, *The Muse of the Department* is both more and less a novel of female adultery. It is more in that it deals not just with the theme of adultery but with the ironic triumph of the heroine's husband and of the class of acquisitive landowners for which he stands; less, in that, unlike any other heroine in the tradition which was still in process of formation, Dinah de La Baudraye does not meet with disaster. (I use the words 'more' and 'less' in a formal and not in an evaluative sense; there is much to be said for a novel of adultery survived by its heroine.) Near the end of the novel, when Dinah's liaison with Lousteau has reached a crisis, the narrator declares:

In real life these violent situations are not closed as they are in books, by death or cleverly contrived catastrophes; they end far less poetically – in disgust, in the blighting of every flower of the soul, in the commonplace of habit, and very often too in another passion, which robs a wife of the interest which is traditionally ascribed to women. (228; 777)

As well as pointing a contrast between *The Muse* and the later novel of female adultery, this remark bears critically on all stories in which adultery comes to a violent end – as in the stories told earlier within the novel, and as in other adultery texts by Balzac himself. Dinah is not punished for her adultery, though Lousteau treats her badly; instead, after several years as his mistress, she returns to the provinces rehabilitated.

What makes such an ending possible is an ironic merging of her husband's impotence and his ambition. La Baudraye takes Dinah back, with the children she has had by Lousteau, because he himself cannot father children, and yet needs heirs for his title and property. In this way, no emotional conflicts are produced, as in *A Woman of Thirty*, by the wife's bearing of children with one man she loves and another she does not. At another level, the compromise represents a fusion of the aristocratic marriage of convenience with the bourgeois marriage of outwardly respectable advancement. La Baudraye is an aristocrat who adopts principles of bourgeois acquisition with great success. But it is important to distinguish his way of life from the new style of bourgeois life which was developing, which was to characterize the novel of female adultery, and which Balzac illustrates in the novel through a marriage almost contracted by Lousteau. Down on his luck, and just before Dinah's arrival, Lousteau accepts the proposal that he marry the daughter of a rich lawyer whose lover has died after getting her pregnant. His friend Bixiou advises him: 'We are struggling in an essentially *bourgeois* age, in which honour, virtue, high-mindedness, talent, learning – genius, in short – is summed up in paying your way, owing nobody anything, and conducting your affairs with judgment. Be steady, be respectable, have a wife and children, pay your rent and taxes . . . ' (191; 748). The ploy fails farcically, thanks to a mother who is as purposeful as she is proper, and who is examining Lousteau's bachelor apartment at the moment when Dinah comes to join him, pregnant and unannounced. But it gives a glimpse into the stiff, prudish and often hypocritical world of bourgeois marriage which Balzac saw as the norm after 1830.

The comic tone of the episode in which Lousteau almost gets married marks another contrast between *The Muse of the Department* and the novel of female adultery. That tone is sounded elsewhere in the text, for instance when the narrator observes that the jealousy of Dinah's three would-be lovers 'was a comedy to the lookers-on' (71; 648). Yet the next paragraph refers to Dinah's domestic life as 'one of those slow and monotonous conjugal tragedies' which is only revealed by nineteenth-century analysis (72; 649); and a few pages later Balzac invokes the term 'tragi-comedy' instead (82; 657). The novel of female adultery is an essentially tragic or, at the least, ironic form. *The Muse of the Department* can accommodate wide variations in tone partly because it has no tragic outcome, and also because of sudden changes in point of view. On several occasions its tone and angle of presentation recall the libertine tradition. For instance, Lousteau opens his campaign of seduction by arranging to travel alone with Dinah in her carriage, and then by making her appear compromised by deliberately crushing her dress.[28] Later, Balzac describes not only the arrangements for Lousteau's abortive marriage chiefly from the latter's perspective, but also the sequel, in which he tries to rescue his position by inducing Dinah to sacrifice herself. Indeed the advice given by Bixiou, quoted above, is heartlessly aimed for her to overhear so that she will deny herself for her lover's benefit; and the scheme only fails because the prospective bride's redoubtable mother produces a better match. Yet Balzac caps this display of masculinist conspiracy in two ways, and in doing so he strikes a very different note from that of the libertine tradition. He reverses the point of view, to present Dinah's often bitter experience of the liaison; and he has Lousteau finally come off worse. Not only does Dinah move in with her lover when his marriage plan misfires, but he fails to profit from what the narrator calls a 'senseless cohabitation' (196, TM; 751) because her husband does not make her a widow. Above all, Dinah turns the tables on Lousteau when he has comprehensively failed and betrayed her. Having secretly arranged to return to her husband on terms which restore her wealth and status, she treats the astonished Lousteau to a sumptuous dinner and then dismisses him.

Nevertheless, the novel carefully limits Dinah's freedom of action. Not only does it offer her the chance to realize herself solely through men, and restore her to an empty though now opulent marriage; it even takes away the single opportunity it gives her for independence. Dinah achieves success as a writer after her initial disappointment in her marriage, publishing under a pseudonym. Later, living with Lousteau, she both helps him in his writing and produces work which he passes off as his. Yet the novel is distinctly chary of literary aspirations in a woman. It concedes only grudgingly ('to do her justice') that Dinah is 'thirsty for knowledge' (66, TM; 644), as well as for emotional and material satisfactions. It presents her work first as therapy and then as offerings to her lover. It has her agree to stop writing when her husband is angered by the links, obvious to all who know her, between her work and her life. And, especially, it disparages women's writing and women's aspirations in general:

When, after the Revolution of 1830, the glory of George Sand was reflected on Le Berry, many a town envied La Châtre the privilege of having given birth to this rival of Madame de Staël and Camille Maupin, and were ready to do homage to minor feminine talent. Thus there arose in France a vast number of tenth Muses, young girls or young wives tempted from a silent life by the bait of glory. Very strange doctrines were proclaimed as to the part women should play in society. Though the sound common sense which lies at the root of the French nature was not perverted, women were suffered to express ideas and profess opinions which they would not have owned to a few years previously. (87; 662)

This is a revealing comment, not least because Balzac ekes out his list of women writers with a figure of his own invention, Camille Maupin.[29] It displays anxiety not only about women's writing but about the demands for greater freedom of thought and action which that writing implied. And, much in the spirit of the male ideologists of the Restoration, it links those demands with a bourgeois revolution. Yet, as even Balzac's own text suggests elsewhere, the life of a bourgeois woman was scarcely liberating. Reunited with her husband, Dinah is 'happy only through her children, on whom she lavished all her disappointed affection' (236–7, TM; 783–4); and she owes such social standing as she can attain to her work for charity (239; 786).

The Muse of the Department marks an important step in the formation of the novel of female adultery. It dispenses with the form of the cautionary tale and its attendant melodrama; and also, through presenting its heroine as more than a love interest, with that of the libertine text. These formal changes it foregrounds through its own self-reflexiveness. But it is especially significant that Balzac made his heroine a writer – of sorts, at least. What this suggests, especially in light of Balzac's depreciation of women's writing, is a built-in link, within patriarchal ideology, between female adultery and women's aspirations for freedom of thought and expression. In effect, through its ending, *The Muse* allows Dinah's adultery to be tolerated. But this requires the sacrifice of her writing, and of her other aspirations; and it is possible only because finally it neither injures nor endangers family or property.

4

From Old Paradigms to New: Champfleury, Feydeau, Flaubert

Before the novel of female adultery can come into its own, marriage must be given its orthodox bourgeois weight. This is in sharp contrast to the Romantic confession, in which marriage plays only a background role, and in which the focal relationships are between actual or virtual kin: siblings in the two works by Chateaubriand (René and Amélie, also Atala and Chactas, daughter and adoptive son of Lopez); son and mother-figure in *Adolphe* and *Confession of a Child of the Century*. Though all these texts except Musset's *Confession* suggest that to marry is a man's social duty, and though all, without exception, imply that female sexuality must be controlled, none of the four gives marriage more than a nominal role. Surprisingly, perhaps, Mérimée offers greater potential for marriage in his two rescensions of the seduction narrative. Although the marriages, each arranged, in both stories are wholly empty, in *The Double Mistake* Julie Chaverny dies from her adulterous encounter with the man she believes, too late, she should have married; and *Arsène Guillot* hints that the lovers who are united at the end might better have been partners in a marriage than in a liaison. In Balzac, as *The Physiology of Marriage* demonstrates plainly at the start of his career as a serious writer, marriage is much more significant. However, even in *A Woman of Thirty* and *The Muse of the Department*, the two works by Balzac which come closest to the novel of female adultery, marriage does not carry the same consequence as in later, canonical, examples of the genre. Crucially, in both novels the husband is aware of and prepared to tolerate his wife's affair: in the first case because of his own philandering, in the second because of his need for heirs. In the full-fledged novel of female adultery, the wife's liaison is intolerable – whether to her husband, the society around her, or both.

This intolerance is displayed very clearly by two non-fictional works which were widely circulated during the heyday of the novel of female adultery in France and to which Michael Riffaterre first drew attention.[1] First, in 1841 a 'physiology of the adulterous wife' appeared in the same series to which Balzac had contributed his physiology of the woman of the provinces.[2] According to its author, Hippolyte Lucas, 'adultery is before everything a child of laziness and boredom' (271). Lucas claims that adultery leads almost inevitably to prostitution and/or suicide (267), and he goes on to call it 'this scourge which devours families, like a secret leprosy, and against which the laws have no remedy' (271). As these examples imply, and as is explicit in the article's title, the word 'adultery' connotes, almost by definition, adulterous wife.[3] Needless to say, the eight volumes of the series contain no profile of an adulterous husband. Lucas paints a lurid picture of the angel of the house turning into a 'dishevelled Bacchante' while her husband is slaving day and night so that she can enjoy a decent standard of living (266). Although he concedes that arranged marriages and disagreeable husbands often motivate adultery, and although he recognizes the double standards imposed by French law in its punishment, the two main themes of his essay are an ideal of marriage – in his phrase, 'this faithful union which consoled our first parents for the loss of immortality' (272) – and a deep-seated suspicion of female independence. That suspicion is manifest in his view that of the three types of adulterous women he distinguishes – those who sin because of the heart, the mind, or the senses – the second is the most characteristic and the most dangerous.

A second key specimen of entrenched prejudices about female adultery appeared in 1866, in Pierre Larousse's *Grand dictionnaire universel du dix-neuvième siècle*, under the section for the noun '*Adultère*'. The entry is too long to quote in full, but the five citations heading it as examples include remarks by the abbé Louis Bautain that '*Adultery* is the ruin of the family and of society', and by the socialist Pierre-Joseph Proudhon that '*Adultery* is a crime which contains in itself all others.'[4] In the encyclopedic part of the entry it is stated that '*Adultery* introduces betrayal and division into the family; it takes from the mother the respect of her children, from the children the father's affection and care, and from the father the joys of paternity.' Explicit arguments are offered in an attempt to explain why, as the entry acknowledges, 'it is nearly always on the woman alone that the law has extended its rigours'. The first set of these is taken from Montesquieu's discussion in *The Spirit of the Laws* (1748),[5] but, before summarizing the provisions of the Penal Code, the entry ventures a lighter note:

> Let us add that the deceived wife may still be loved and above all be respected by her husband, while the adulterous wife generally has only contempt for the man whom she dooms to ridicule. This was the view of a lady of the court of Louis XIV. When a too officious friend took a malign pleasure in passing on to her the rumours which were going the rounds about her husband's flightiness, this woman of sense replied, 'What does it matter if he parades his heart abroad from morning till night, so long as he brings it back to me in the evening?'

In his discussion of the article by Lucas and the entry in Larousse's *Dictionary*, Michael Riffaterre suggests that both, and the latter especially, incarnate orthodox bourgeois attitudes of the period. This is probably too sweeping an inference, for the *Dictionary*'s entry on fornication expresses a more enlightened outlook on the double standard of sexual morality for men and women than those cited above;[6] and, as I will go on to show, other entries do not always advance the same uncomplicated view. Nevertheless, taken together, the essay by Lucas and the *Dictionary* entry register clearly the tenor of mainstream French opinion concerning adultery during the period when the novel of female adultery first came into prominence. This chapter discusses three novels of the 1850s in which the action turns on female adultery; and it considers what is distinctive about each, especially the one which has proved most influential, *Madame Bovary*. The three writers – Champfleury, Ernest Feydeau and Flaubert – were all, coincidentally, born in the same year, 1821; and the entry in Larousse's *Dictionary* for Feydeau's novel, *Fanny*, classes them together as realists.[7]

The first of the three novels to be published was Champfleury's *Les Bourgeois de Molinchart* (1855). Champfleury was the pen-name of Jules Husson, a writer on art – including a history of caricature – as well as of fiction, who is now most likely to be remembered as a minor theorist of realism. In some ways *Les Bourgeois de Molinchart* follows Balzac's *The Muse of the Department*, especially in taking up the figure of the woman of the provinces. But, as Champfleury's title suggests, the novel's main characters are from lower down the social scale than Balzac's, and its attitude towards them is satirical. Much of the novel consists of humorous sketches of the provincial bourgeoisie. The husband whose wife is seduced is a lawyer, who hardly practises but lives off the money his father has made in the coaching business. His main occupations in the novel are an absurd form of amateur meteorology and the social activities that go along with it. These allow Champfleury to introduce an assortment of eccentrics, including an archaeologist whose unit as well as his instrument of measurement is an umbrella. Each supposed savant indulges in the display of spurious knowledge, not only in the company of his neighbours but in that of fellow pseudo-scholars at, for instance, a conference of the Racinian Society. Champfleury devotes a chapter to the conference, and several other chapters also take the form of a set-piece which could almost stand on its own. These include a provincial dinner (Chapter IV), a prize-giving at a girls' school (VIII), and a trial scene at which rival advocates show off the wit they profess (XIV). Still other chapters are devoted to the description of provincial types: the young wife (Chapter III), the old maid (V), and the headmistress (XV).

These tableaus of provincial manners are in the tradition of literary genre pictures for which Champfleury was already making a name.[8] They seem to have little in common with a plot of female adultery; indeed Tony Williams, in the only discussion of *Les Bourgeois de Molinchart* which I have found in English, does not mention them, even though they make up the greater part of the novel.[9] This makes it all the more striking that, in the opening chapter, Champfleury has his adultery plot begin from, and within, a scene of small-town farce. The two main characters meet thanks to the chaos caused by the pursuit of a roe-deer which has escaped its hunters only to be chased by butchers, kitchen-boys and others through streets, a shop and a private house to be cornered finally in a wine-cellar. Their romance then takes its course through various ludicrous episodes. These include not only the lover's exposure to the husband's monologues, in all their banality and cod science, but also visits in his company to the Racinian conference and even to a non-existent meteorological society in Paris. The lover suffers further troubles from a trick-rider in a visiting circus whom he uses as a cover but who falls hopelessly in love with him.

This outline of *Les Bourgeois de Molinchart* suggests that Flaubert had no great reason to fear competition from Champfleury in a study of provincial adultery. Since the wife and her suitor only become lovers near the end, in the twentieth chapter of twenty-two, it seems as if the scenes of provincial comedy function so as to suspend consummation of the affair; or, alternatively, that the love-plot provides a frame on which to string humorous tableaus. Yet the tone of the novel changes decisively in Chapter XVIII, when, under her sister-in-law's surveillance, the wife is tricked into a meeting with her suitor. It is at this point that comparison with *Madame Bovary* begins to gain more pertinence.

Louise Creton du Coche is a woman of thirty in years but not in character. Already married for ten years to a man 20 years her senior, she has no living parents, no close relatives and no children. As she offered no dowry, she was married for her looks. Although she is virtuous, Champfleury's description implies latent passion and sensuality by emphasizing the darkness of her eyes and skin, and by suggesting the idea of Spanish ancestry (III.30–1).[10] She no longer shares a bed with her husband, who blandly takes her for granted and whose conversation is numbingly banal; and she has virtually given up going out because life in the town is so tedious. Louise's suitor is Julien de Vorges, a count in his mid-twenties who has returned to his mother's estate to recover from an unhappy love affair. He is helped partly by his cousin but much more by two spinsters from the town: Louise's sister-in-law, Ursule, and the new headmistress, Madame Chappe. Ursule is presented as a miserly, sanctimonious old maid. Embittered by her brother's marriage and determined to inherit his property, it is in her interests that Louise be discredited and the marriage broken up. Madame Chappe is a cunning schemer eager to get money by any means in order to live at her ease. After at first acting as an ill-rewarded spy on Ursule's behalf, she changes sides to cash in as Julien's confidante and go-between. She provides a room for him to meet Louise, while, in revenge, Ursule sets up the vantage-point from which her brother sees the two arrive and leave.

In several respects, and especially in contrast with *Madame Bovary*, the action of Champfleury's novel seems designed to minimize the significance of the adultery to which it leads. The reader is invited to laugh at the husband who is to be deceived, there are no children who might be harmed by the affair, and there are no money worries either for husband or wife or, least of all, for the wealthy suitor. Even more to the point, Louise is given little opportunity for choice. This is not so much because her husband, in his tedious self-absorption, has no time for her and is so blind to Julien's attentions that he all but encourages them; or even because Julien, superior to him in every respect, shows overwhelming persistence. What finally defeats Louise are the machinations of the two spinsters. Strongly attracted to Julien, and oppressed by Ursule, she does not resist when, manipulated unawares by Madame Chappe into escaping, she finds herself in his arms. Yet, if Champfleury does almost all he can to remove responsibility from Louise, he does not sidestep the consequences of the elopement.

First, thanks to Ursule's malice and her power over her brother, the couple are pursued and ultimately charged with adultery. The novel's last chapter takes the form of a letter from Julien to his cousin Jonquières which ends by revealing that he is in custody pending sentence. He does not say what is happening to Louise, who, under the Civil Code, faces imprisonment for a minimum of three and a maximum of 24 months, unless her husband asks for suspension of the punishment. However, the second consequence is in one way still worse, for the couple's happiness after their elopement has proved short-lived. Much of Julien's letter attempts to analyse his relationship with Louise. Although he insists that he loves her more than ever now they are parted, and although he says he will find her again, his and the novel's last words are: 'But then! . . .' (XXII.308). This doubt recalls his fear that she would tire of him – a fear which turns out to reflect, and perhaps to rationalize, the fact that he is tiring of her. In his previous affair he had driven the woman away by constant expressions of love, and he claims that he may do the same with Louise: 'she is a woman, she could tire of me [. . .] I feared satiety on her part' (XXII.304). It becomes clear, however, that the disenchantment is his: 'I feared so much that Louise would tire of me, and it was I who was tired of her; I dared not admit it to myself, finding myself cold and reserved when I went home, as Caroline used to be near the end of our affair' (XXII.307). He goes on to say that the suffering which results is worse even than that of being rejected.

One way of reading this ending is as the culmination of a cautionary tale. Before Julien begins his siege of Louise, Jonquières advises him against an affair with a married woman, especially in the provinces. In his letter Julien has to concede that his friend was right, and the outcome bears out, even more than might have been expected, Jonquières's warning that the woman will suffer most. It is difficult, however, to reconcile such a message either with the humorous tone which dominates the novel, or with the nature of the narrative focus. The main point of view is that of the impersonal narrator, but, although he admits the perspectives of various characters, including Louise, he allows the most space and invites the most sympathy for Julien. Much more likely than a moral dimension to the novel is the influence of the Romantic confession, discussed in Chapter 2 above. The form and the leading theme of the final chapter point strongly to such a connection. In the personal narrative of Julien's letter Champfleury adopts the same formal convention as that of the confession; and the letter betrays the same dominant theme of the sorrows, from a man's point of view, of living with and leaving a woman he no longer loves.

In this way *Les Bourgeois de Molinchart* draws incongruously on several different fictional traditions, ranging from the satirical genre-picture of the provincial bourgeoisie to the narrative of seduction (in Julien's pursuit of Louise), and its ideological foil, the Romantic confession. For all its attempted humour, the novel shows a fear of female power and independence. First, it gives the leading roles in the action not to the lover but to the two spinsters Ursule and Madame Chappe – aided by a further pair of spinsters in the shape of the sisters who lend their house for purposes of spying and who spread damaging scandal. Second, and conversely, it constructs the adulterous woman as almost wholly passive. Not only is Louise granted little freedom of action, but, despite the erotic hints in Champfleury's opening description, to judge by everything else the text has to show of her she could be innocent of sexual desire altogether. Indeed Champfleury ludicrously idealizes the elopement: 'they were souls who were meeting in celestial embraces' (XX.281).

When *Les Bourgeois de Molinchart* first appeared, the writing of *Madame Bovary* was already well advanced. As Tony Williams has shown, Flaubert's initial concern that parallels would be drawn between the two novels soon gave way to the recognition that they had little in common.[11] In 1858, however, a year after *Madame Bovary* was first published in book form, *Fanny*, a novel by Ernest Feydeau, achieved an immediate and a dazzling success. Within a few years it had run to 30 editions, and, though it quickly became notorious for its explicit treatment of sexual behaviour, it was praised by several leading critics, notably by Sainte-Beuve.[12]

Feydeau deals with little else in *Fanny* but relationships and themes derived from a woman's adultery. Yet it was *Madame Bovary* which later writers of novels of adultery took as their model, and it is *Madame Bovary* which later critics have considered as a supreme example of the genre. Because *Fanny* was rated so highly in its own time, and because it differs significantly both from *Madame Bovary* and from *Les Bourgeois de Molinchart*, comparison is especially important.

There are two main differences between Feydeau's novel on the one hand and those by Flaubert and Champfleury on the other. First, *Fanny* is a personal narrative, while both in *Madame Bovary* and in *Les Bourgeois de Molinchart* the dominant narrative voice is impersonal. This difference has further critical implications which will be discussed below. Second, and relatedly, in his intense focus on the situation of adultery, Feydeau provides only the slenderest indications of setting. While Champfleury offers a series of genre pictures of small-town bourgeois life, and while Flaubert more than justifies his subtitle of 'Life in the Provinces', Feydeau presents no scenes of social life at all, and he limits the action almost completely to his two main characters of lover and adulterous wife. These are also the only figures to have speaking parts in the narrative, which is related by the lover.

It is not only its use of personal narrative, and the abstraction of its action and setting, that link *Fanny* to the Romantic confession. Even more directly than *Atala*, *René*, *Adolphe*, and *Confession of a Child of the Century*, Feydeau's novel invites psychoanalytical interpretation. At 24 the narrator, Roger, is 11 years younger than Fanny, and the two often speak of each other as child and mother. Roger still mourns his biological mother, who died when he was 20, and at several points, especially at the novel's climax, he associates her with Fanny. He says almost nothing of his father, who has died before the action begins. Instead, it is Fanny's husband who takes the father's role in a transparently Oedipal drama. Obsessed by this unnamed figure even before he has met him, Roger presents him as terrifyingly powerful. Few writers can have anticipated so fully and so clearly Freud's conception of the son's fantasy, at the Oedipal stage, of the father.[13] In his description of his rival Roger repeatedly stresses the other's massive build, his indomitable will, his apparent omnicompetence and his inscrutability. He depicts him as 'a kind of bull with a human face' (XIV.35), 'a lion' (L.152), and even 'a kind of sun which illuminated, warmed and conveyed life to everything which surrounded him' (L.147).[14] Roger cannot help comparing himself with this powerful figure, who makes him feel like 'a frightened sylph contemplating the statue of a giant' (XIV.37).

Feydeau heightened the contrast between lover and husband by placing them in different social classes. While Roger is of genteel birth, and lives in effete leisure, his rival is a self-made man who has overcome the opposition of Fanny's parents in marrying her, and who, in the course of the narrative, restores his standing after the failure of his bankers. This disparity in class position between lover and husband parallels that between Julien and Creton du Coche in *Les Bourgeois de Molinchart*, and between Charles and Rodolphe in *Madame Bovary*. The fact that Feydeau did little to exploit it illustrates the much greater abstraction of his novel. The further and more surprising fact that he chose not to develop the jealousy of lover for husband points in a different direction. Despite the narrator's Oedipal imagery, the novel's action is driven by his mounting animus against his mistress. Hardly aware of the husband at first, and ready to believe that Fanny 'was free and did not share herself' (XI.26), Roger is soon fantasizing about the marital relationship. When he pictures their life together he torments himself by imagining, implicitly, that it includes sexual intercourse: Chapter XVII ends with the exclamation that they are spouses, and with ellipsis marks. Yet Roger declares soon after: 'In a short time I understood that from then on it was a duel to the death between Fanny and myself' (XXIII.61). He is furious to find that Fanny still has affection for her husband (XLIII.124), and outraged when she forgives his violence and despotism (LX.184–5). The riddle of Fanny's behaviour is finally answered as he watches an enactment of the primal scene at the novel's climax. But the crux of the scene is not so much the sexual relationship of husband and wife as the woman's own sexuality. What Roger finds shocking above all else is that she initiates the lovemaking; and his immediate impulse is to tear apart not her husband but Fanny herself (LXVII.214).

The subtitle of Feydeau's novel is *A Study* – expanded though not quite misrepresented in the contemporary English translation as *Revelations of a Woman's Heart*.[15] The subject of this *Study* is not female adultery, or even infidelity, but 'Woman' herself. Roger presents Fanny as an enigma, on the one hand degradedly sexual, on the other remote and dignified. In a familiar opposition, he supposes that two souls express themselves in her at the same time:

'a Phryne, absorbed and serious', and 'an immaculate angel' (XXVIII.80). He responds by oscillating between cursing and adoring her, as he puts it when attacking her for her infidelity – infidelity to him, as he sees it, rather than to her husband (LXXI.230). In the same scene he describes her as a Magdalene (LXXI.229). The essential riddle his narrative poses is that of female sexual desire, which Roger can acknowledge only in furious anguish and humiliation as 'the thirst of an abominable pleasure' (LXXI.231). In this way *Fanny* takes its place in the discourse of its time concerning women and female sexuality, along with Jules Michelet's *Love* (*L'Amour*, 1858) and *Woman* (*La Femme*, 1860), and sections of Proudhon's *De la justice dans la révolution et dans l'Église* (*On Justice in the Revolution and in the Church*, 1858), developed at length in his posthumous *La Pornocratie ou les femmes dans les temps modernes* (*Pornocracy, or Women in Modern Times*, 1875).[16]

Feydeau focused his *Study* sharply. Not only did he limit himself to the barest details of context and setting, but he gave neither of the main characters a surname, and the husband – referred to most often as 'he', sometimes in capitals – no name at all. The effect is to suggest that the characters have a representative status; in particular, Fanny is constructed implicitly and at times explicitly as a type of the female. The second chapter ends with the remark: 'She was a woman to the very ends of her fingernails' (II.10); and near the end Feydeau has Fanny tell Roger: 'I am only a woman. And you do not know women' (LXXI.231). There are three main respects, all interrelated, in which the novel produces Fanny as such a type. First, she is a creature of emotion. For example, she asks Roger: 'What wife would take a lover, if her husband gave her what a lover gives? Not only care, consideration, attention, friendship, but a little of that balm which is the essence of all our life: a little love!' (XXIV.66). Here the word 'our', linked as it is to the phrase 'What wife?', contains a generalization: the essence of life for all women, not only Fanny, is love. Second, Fanny is weak. Shortly after the question just quoted she exclaims: 'God has not given me strength, and, all my life, I will bear the affliction of my weakness. I have always lived differently from how I wanted to live; always been to one side of what I wanted to do' (XXVI.73–4). Third, because of her need for love, and because of her weakness, Fanny is compelled to deceive. After Roger has discovered that she has forgiven her husband, he observes: 'In fact Fanny certainly did not have a manly soul nor even perhaps a very noble soul at all, for she liked to scheme better than to fight, and she preferred to degrade herself by sharing herself rather than to disorder her life' (LXI.189).

Nevertheless, there are occasions when the text allows a different reading of Fanny's behaviour. This is not because it offers grounds for supposing that its narrator is unreliable; although Roger tells the story himself, and although his behaviour is often unreasonable (to put it mildly), there is no evidence that it is to be read as discrediting him. Instead, because it represents Fanny speaking, and because it shows Roger trying to understand her behaviour, it concedes some space to another point of view, however prejudged by the writer and even if aimed chiefly at adding plausibility. So, for instance, Roger records: 'She hung from my neck and looked me straight in the eye: "My poor children! so young! Do you think of them? You who are good, you who love me, can you ask me to leave them?"' (XXXVII.110). On a much more painful occasion, during the final scene between the two, this is how Feydeau has Fanny explain the lovemaking with her husband which Roger has witnessed:

> I have no love for him, since I love you, but I belong to him. Is that not natural? Divided between the desire of keeping his affection and the fear of being obliged to show him an equivalent affection, I want to keep him when he goes away, and, when he draws near, I try in vain to escape him. I gave way to duty. I feared that he would leave me. The thought of my children abandoned with me made me mad. Forgive me. (LXXI.230–1)

From this speech, and others like it, it is possible to imagine the woman's predicament: no longer in love with a cool, domineering husband, but still feeling affection for him and familiarity with him; no longer wishing to be married to him, but shrinking both from leaving her children and from being left alone with them; settled in a desirable and a respected way of life, but without the resources or the confidence to change it. Yet it is in the same speech that Fanny says she is only a woman; and Roger responds by denouncing what he sees as her lust, her inability to match with sacrifices the love she professes, and her corruption by luxury and social status. In the same way, although Fanny is allowed to speak of her children, they are granted almost no further presence in the text. Thus the point of view the novel implies ultimately has little room for the woman's position; indeed, it gives no reason for denying Roger's prediction: 'another man, some day, will come to take my place' (LXXII.238). In this respect, as in others, the idea of the adulterous woman constructed by *Fanny* is in keeping with those put forward by Hippolyte Lucas and by Larousse's *Dictionary*. Equally, no account is taken of male sexual licence, as when Fanny's husband flaunts a mistress, or when Roger tries to revenge himself through debauchery.

As Sainte-Beuve recognized in his review of *Fanny*, and Jules Janin in his Preface, Feydeau's novel has affinities with *Adolphe*.[17] Like the Romantic confession, it is both centred in a young man's experience and ended by his leaving the woman he has loved. The novel of female adultery depends not just on giving orthodox bourgeois weight to marriage, as is suggested at the start of this chapter, but on an attempt to present marriage from the point of view of women as well as of men. A personal narrative told by a young man is inherently inadequate to such a task. It is almost certainly in part for this reason that all canonical novels of female adultery are told by an impersonal narrator. Rhetorically, at least, these novels aim at greater objectivity. To what extent, if any, they achieve this is a different question, which needs to be faced with each one.

Among novels of adultery, *Madame Bovary* is the most famous for its impersonality. However, before questions relating to the novel's narrative form can be addressed properly, it is important to determine what was at issue in Flaubert's choice of the theme of adultery. In the article in which he considers the notions of adultery given currency by Hippolyte Lucas and by Larousse's *Dictionary*, Michael Riffaterre claims that the whole of *Madame Bovary* can be shown to derive from the 'descriptive system' exemplified by those texts regarding the figure of the adulteress in mid-nineteenth-century France.[18] Riffaterre goes even further in a second article, in which he maintains that 'no written historical evidence is needed to document an intertextual authority already monumentalized in the collective psyche of a nation: the key word and its semic system are quite sufficient'.[19] According to this view, what Flaubert did in *Madame Bovary* was to propagate an entire novel from the 'kernel' afforded by the word 'adulteress' and by the system of beliefs that went along with it. Riffaterre's advice that recourse to written historical evidence is unnecessary is all the more startling in light of his own instructive use of the discussions in Lucas and Larousse. So extreme an example of structuralist nonchalance about history would be of scant interest if it were not for the fact that adultery was, notoriously, one of the most hackneyed topics which Flaubert could have chosen for his novel. The question therefore arises whether, as Riffaterre claims, the adultery plot in *Madame Bovary* represents no more than the unfolding of a cliché.[20]

As early as 1840, Balzac had declared that 'adultery in literature has been done to death for a while, though it still wends its way in the world'; and, with characteristic self-reflexiveness, he had given one of his characters in *The Muse of the Department* the remark that 'the whole of your infamous literature rests on adultery'.[21] When, a decade and a half later, Baudelaire reviewed *Madame Bovary*, he imagined Flaubert choosing the subject for his novel in a mental dialogue which ends: 'What is the tritest theme of all, worn out by repetition, by being played over and over again like a tired barrel-organ? Adultery.' He went on to argue that the novel's distinction is the art which overcomes, indeed transcends, such unpromising subject-matter. For him, Flaubert 'deigned, with the chastity of an ancient teacher of rhetoric, to cast a mantle of glory over a bedroom-farce subject that would be repulsive and grotesque if it had not been touched by the opalescent light of poetry'.[22] However, having called attention to the novel's stylistic and technical brilliance, Baudelaire did not expand on this aspect of its achievement. Instead, he devoted most of his tribute to what he rightly saw as Flaubert's new and striking representation of the figure of the adulterous wife. This contemporary testimony strongly suggests that, contrary to Riffaterre's contention, Flaubert refrained from reproducing a stereotype in his handling of a much exploited topic. Indeed, in several decisive respects he transformed received conceptions of the situation of adultery itself.

First, Flaubert placed his heroine in a lower social class than had been conventional in any representations of the adulteress at this period or earlier. The portrayal of adultery in the libertine text is limited almost exclusively to the aristocracy and upper bourgeoisie. Mérimée follows suit in the two narratives discussed in Chapter 2; more surprisingly, perhaps, so does Balzac, both in *The Physiology of Marriage* and in his fiction. Feydeau's heroine Fanny is of a higher social class than her wealthy husband; and even Louise, in Champfleury's *Les Bourgeois de Molinchart*, is placed in the upper bracket of small-town society. The point is especially clear in Hippolyte Lucas's essay, because it distinguishes between adultery at different social levels. Lucas offers stock vignettes both of the aristocratic and of the bourgeois adulteress, but he gives only a few lines to the working class, where, he opines, because 'work maintains honour', adultery has less of a grasp.[23] Naturalist writers would convey a different view a generation later, although in their fiction adultery is only one among various forms of sexual promiscuity; the adulterous couple in Zola's *Thérèse Raquin* (1867) is lower middle-class. Even so, according to Huysmans, looking back at his novel *Against the Grain* (1884) early in the following century, adultery in fiction remained chiefly an upper-class affair:

> High life, it appears to me, has carried the day at present in the reader's good graces, for I notice that for the moment he hardly cares to regale himself on plebeian or middle-class amours, but still continues to savour the scruples and hesitations of the Marquise on her way to meet her seducer at a dainty little flat, whose aspect changes according to the varying fashion in furniture.[24]

Flaubert, in contrast, not only places his heroine in the lower reaches of the middle class, but emphasizes her rustic origins, for instance when he remarks that she is 'like most people of country stock, who always retain in their souls something of the calloused hardness of their fathers' hands' (I.ix.52, TM; 68).[25] This emphasis is without precedent in the fictional representation of the adulteress, and even in later novels of adultery it is rarely followed. Flaubert also broke with convention by placing both of Emma's lovers in the bourgeois class. This refusal of stereotype must have been too much for the writer of the entry on the novel in Larousse's *Dictionary*, who banally assumed that Rodolphe is the Viscount with whom she waltzes at the ball.[26]

Second, and relatedly, Flaubert again broke with convention in his choice and treatment of a rural, small-town setting. For Hippolyte Lucas, Paris is the native land of adultery: 'It is there that it is at its ease, that it parades itself, and that it raises its head, humbly lowered in the provinces.'[27] The stereotype is sustained at length by Balzac, and also in both of the novels by Champfleury and Feydeau. The heroines of *A Woman of Thirty* and *The Muse of the Department* keep their chastity while they remain in the country;

Louise, in _Les Bourgeois de Molinchart_, first succumbs to her lover only as he takes her from the provinces to Paris; and, in Feydeau's novel, Fanny is essentially a Parisienne. Two facts about _Madame Bovary_ highlight how different Flaubert's novel is in this respect. First, Flaubert abandoned his original design of a visit for Emma to Paris. Instead, the place in the novel's action which this visit would have occupied is filled by the operation on Hippolyte's foot;[28] and Rouen is not only the most exotic place Emma visits, but Flaubert transferred to that city an episode conventionally located in the capital, the adulterous jaunt in a cab.[29] The second and more important difference is that in _Madame Bovary_ Flaubert pays a quite new kind of attention to provincial life. Yonville, where most of the action takes place, resembles neither the setting of a country estate in the provincial scenes of _A Woman of Thirty_ or _The Muse of the Department_, nor the small town of Champfleury's novel. Indeed it is a humbler place even than Molinchart; yet, in describing it, Flaubert discards the conventions of genre picture and comedy alike. Again, no novel of adultery written later, let alone earlier, focuses on such humdrum surroundings. All but one of the examples discussed later in this book present adultery in a metropolitan setting. The exception is Fontane's _Effi Briest_, where the affair takes place in a provincial town and comes to light several years afterwards in Berlin. Flaubert's way of describing provincial life was a startling innovation in its range and detail, though Balzac had prepared the ground for it in part. But this aspect of the novel's originality is attested so fully in criticism and scholarship that it needs no further discussion here.[30]

The third main difference between _Madame Bovary_ and previous fiction dealing with adultery is centred in the situation of adultery itself. Although Hippolyte Lucas portrayed female adultery as a moral slide leading, in stages glossed by Michael Riffaterre, from '_femme sensible_ (one lover) to _femme galante_ (more than one)' and then to '_femme entretenue_ (more than one lover, with financial backing)',[31] it is unusual for the heroine in novels of adultery to have more than one illicit partner, far less to end in prostitution. There is only one such example among all the novels of adultery discussed in this book; and the character in question, Fortunata in Pérez Galdós's _Fortunata and Jacinta_ (1887), takes other lovers out of indigence, not lust. In Balzac's fiction there are figures such as Madame de Beauséant in _A Forsaken Lady_, or Valérie Marneffe in _Cousin Bette_ (1847), who have more than one affair. But this is not the case in *A Woman of Thirty* or *The Muse of the Department*, his works which most closely anticipate the novel of female adultery. In the latter novel, Dinah enters only one liaison, with Lousteau – whom she lives with but leaves to return to her husband. In the former, Julie d'Aiglemont only begins an affair after the death of her partner in a platonic liaison; a pattern echoed in part by Julie Chaverny, who, in Mérimée's *The Double Mistake*, falls for Darcy after first having been attracted by Châteaufort. The same pattern reappears in *Madame Bovary*, where Emma's attraction to Léon prepares the way for Rodolphe; but Flaubert completes it with a full-blown affair when both have gained more experience.

On the evidence of Lucas's essay and Larousse's *Dictionary*, Riffaterre suggests that the adulterous woman of nineteenth-century French ideology typically ends in prostitution or death. He further claims that, although Flaubert's heroine dies by her own hand, the entry in Larousse for *Madame Bovary* 'cannot resist playing out the alternative unactualized by the novel'; and he subsequently argues that the same alternative of prostitution is shadowed in the novel itself: 'we see Emma on her last day run from one male neighbour to the other in her village, seeking help, money, and either Emma or the man (for the sake of covering all possible options) recoiling from the venal option'.[32] But neither of these summaries is entirely accurate. The episode from the novel is complex and will be considered below. The *Dictionary* entry, however, actually contradicts its own suggestion that Emma should have ended as a prostitute. It offers two views of the novel, the second more favourable than the first, in order that the reader will have enough information on which to base a judgement. The statement that Emma 'should have dragged out the rest of her days on some common street corner of ill fame' occurs in the earlier part of the entry, where it is argued that the novel lacks a moral lesson. Later, when the opposite view is put forward, the stock notion that Emma ought to end on the streets is retracted. Instead, the writer declares that she could not do so 'without an enormous inconsistency', and that, 'given this woman, only two endings were possible: the convent or death'.[33] This suggests a different slant from the one Riffaterre presupposes. It is a salutary reminder that ideology is rarely all of a piece.

The way in which Flaubert motivates his heroine's death supplies the fourth and last illustration to be given here of his originality in treating the theme of adultery. In Hippolyte Lucas's scenario, the adulteress ends in prostitution or suicide because, forced by inevitable discovery to leave her family and the place where she has lived, she has no means of support.[34] In *Madame Bovary*, on the contrary, not only does Emma's adultery remain undiscovered until after her death, but she poisons herself in panic and despair when she can no longer stave off total financial collapse. In other words, Flaubert has Emma die less as a result of adultery than of debt. The shopkeeper who causes her ruin, Lheureux, sets out to entangle her before she enters into either of her affairs; and, although she greatly increases her liabilities by her extravagance in both, she and Charles are already living beyond their means when Lheureux first loses patience, after the operation on Hippolyte.

Among the adultery texts discussed so far, money is an issue of explicit concern in only two, both by Balzac: in *Gobseck*, the Restaud property is saved from ruin at the hands of the Comtesse's lover; and in *La Grenadière* the mother dies with little to leave her children. So restrained an interest in capital is surprising, given that one of the reasons most often cited for the wickedness of adultery was that it was thought to threaten the transmission of property by placing legitimacy in question. The likely explanation for this paradox lies in two ideological twists. First, in the two novellas by Mérimée, and in the work of Balzac, it is among the aristocracy and the upper bourgeoisie that discreet adultery is tolerated. Here, some of the freer manners of the Old Regime still obtain; still more important, money and status insulate against, and, overtly in Balzac, outweigh morality. Thus, in *The Muse of the Department*, Lousteau remarks that a woman can overcome public opinion by becoming Madame de Staël or by possessing a yearly income of 200,000 francs (203; 757); and La Baudraye shrugs off his wife's adultery, secure in his hold not only of estate and title but of a family and heirs – even though not sired by himself. Second, despite the example of Balzac, money was still often regarded as too low a subject for extended treatment in literature. In the Romantic confession it is almost beneath notice, so that in *Adolphe*, for example, the changes in Ellénore's fortunes are not of interest in themselves but are mere devices necessary to the development of the emotional plot. Flaubert himself reflects a similar view, even though he took great pains over the details of Emma's financial embarrassment, for he complained to Louis Bouilhet at the time when he was describing them: 'I am enmeshed in explanations of promissory notes, interest charges, etc., which I don't understand much'.[35] But the importance he attached to the economic pressures on Emma is clear in his use of the *Mémoires de Madame Ludovica*, a third-party account of the married life of Louise Pradier, with whom he had an affair in the 1840s. What he took from this manuscript was not the account of Louise's adulteries, beside which, as Claudine Gothot-Mersch puts it, Emma is a mere apprentice.[36] Instead, in Stephen Heath's words, 'it is above all the financial imbroglio in which Louise entraps herself and her efforts to keep herself afloat and undiscovered, that gave Flaubert material'.[37] Indeed, the novel follows closely the details of that imbroglio and the inevitable collapse.

Emma's generosity to her lovers recalls Louise Pradier's, and it is in keeping with the image of profligacy presented by Hippolyte Lucas. The fact that Flaubert has her begin to exceed her means even before she takes a lover may imply a predisposition to excess. Again, however, he does not simply reproduce the pattern of female corruption propagated by Lucas and Larousse. Emma is represented as lacking fulfilment not only emotionally and sexually, but in her whole role as wife and mother. As a bourgeois wife, it is not her function to undertake paid work inside or outside the home; and she increasingly delegates even the duties of the household to others, especially the wet-nurse and maid. Flaubert has Emma relinquish the customs of thrifty self-help urged on her in vain by her outraged mother-in-law for a fashionable way of living which is, moreover, above her station as the wife of a humble officer of health. Richard Terdiman has commented suggestively on the complex of issues involved here in comparing *Madame Bovary* with Baudelaire's poem *Les fleurs du mal*. Both works, he observes,

> manifest a preoccupation with the means by which desire is engendered in society. In their own ways both Flaubert and Baudelaire clearly perceived the paradox that the very society that creates desire – by an increasingly dense circulation of images of social mobility and economic success, by an increasing identification of the erotic and the commercial – at the same time stringently restricts the means by which desire can be satisfied.[38]

But this engendering of desire was also a gendering. Flaubert places Emma at an historical juncture when, for the bourgeois wife, domestic duties were giving way to decorative; and at a social level which made the expense of playing such a role impossible to sustain. Bonnie G. Smith has pointed out that for middle-class women this was a period when, 'for the first time in history, the productive aspect of their lives virtually disappeared', but that it was not until after mid-century that organizations such as maternal societies, day-care centres and crèches developed to help fill the resulting vacuum.[39] The point is relevant to Flaubert's construction of Emma, even though the women studied by Smith are from a higher social class and from the industrialized north. Indeed, a *petite-bourgeoise* in a small rural town would have encountered very few legitimate channels of activity or sources of support.

In all these respects, Flaubert did very much more in *Madame Bovary* than draw out to novel-length the received idea of the adulterous wife. Not only is his version of that figure convincingly situated in a social and a material world, but for anyone to have portrayed life at so banal a social level, and in so prosaic a setting, dispassionately and without conventional humour, was quite unprecedented. Erich Auerbach best epitomizes this distinguishing quality of the novel in commenting on one of the scenes early in Emma's marriage. The passage is so perceptive as to require quotation at length:

The scene shows a man and wife at table, the most everyday situation imaginable. Before Flaubert, it would have been conceivable as literature only as part of a comic tale, an idyl, or a satire. Here it is a picture of discomfort, and not a momentary and passing one, but a chronic discomfort, which completely rules an entire life, Emma Bovary's. To be sure, various things come later, among them love episodes; but no one could see the scene at table as part of the exposition for a love episode, just as no one would call *Madame Bovary* a love story in general. The novel is the representation of an entire human existence which has no issue; and our passage is a part of it, which, however, contains the whole. Nothing particular happens in the scene, nothing particular has happened just before it. It is a random moment from the regularly recurring hours at which the husband and wife eat together. They are not quarreling, there is no sort of tangible conflict. Emma is in complete despair, but her despair is not occasioned by any definite catastrophe; there is nothing purely concrete which she has lost or for which she has wished. Certainly she has many wishes, but they are entirely vague – elegance, love, a varied life; there must always have been such unconcrete despair, but no one ever thought of taking it seriously in literary works before; such formless tragedy, if it may be called tragedy, which is set in motion by the general situation itself, was first made conceivable as literature by romanticism; probably Flaubert was the first to have represented it in people of slight intellectual culture and fairly low social station; certainly he is the first who directly captures the chronic character of this psychological situation.[40]

Auerbach's striking phrase 'unconcrete despair' may be glossed by Richard Terdiman's remarks on the role of desire in a culture based increasingly on conspicuous consumption, and by Bonnie Smith's account of the bourgeois lifestyle that went along with it. A further analogue is the eloquent account of a young woman of the period in anguished contemplation of marriage:

> I am not even able to live alone, being obliged to take from others, not only in order to live but also in order to be protected, since social convention does not allow me to have independence. And yet the world finds me guilty of being the only person that I am at liberty to be; not having useful or productive work to do, not having any calling except marriage, and not being able to look by myself for someone who will suit me, I am full of cares and anxieties.[41]

Emma Bovary has started from a position analogous to the one described here; but, lacking the ability to analyse it, she has entered marriage under similar conditions with the one suitor who has come forward, only to find herself still dependent, superfluous and unsatisfied. In such circumstances, despair is concrete enough.

Not least through the density of its social detail, Flaubert's novel provides the material for a feminist reading such as the one I have just outlined; yet, at the same time, its pervasive irony must perplex a response of that kind. Auerbach proposes that the attitude which Flaubert displays toward the reality of contemporary life could be called 'objective seriousness', and he remarks that such an attitude 'seeks to penetrate to the depths of the passions and entanglements of a human life, but without itself becoming moved, or at least without betraying that it is moved'.[42] The problem which must now be faced is that of Flaubert's famous impersonality. This is an issue consisting both in the nature of the story and in the way in which it is told.

Both questions, of course, have been discussed by writers and critics at great length. The best analysis, and probably the concisest, is provided by Stephen Heath. First, Heath points out that the reason so many of the novel's first readers found it scandalous, indeed the fundamental reason why author, publisher and printer were prosecuted, was that, despite Emma's suffering, it lacks a discernible moral design:

> The problem is that the punishment is not *clear*, not clearly related to any socially valid moral perspective. Adultery here is platitude, as flatly oppressive as all the rest. There is nothing to measure it against; or rather, everything else can just as well be measured by the adultery: nothing is any better, less mediocre. So what is the point of the novel, how is it to be read? The trial turned on this question, each side trying to *settle* a reading: glorification of adultery for the prosecution, condemnation of adultery for the defence; but *Madame Bovary* does not fit any such settlement, any such reading, which again was the question for the trial.[43]

Second, Heath argues that this indeterminacy results in part from a refusal by the author to give priority to any of the voices in his narrative: 'discourses are presented in circulation and in play with one another, but no particular discursive position is taken, no one discourse assumed; the writing remains impersonal, uncommitted, other than to the work of art, the perfection of the sentences Flaubert turns'. He goes on to show that even such a commitment to be uncommitted is itself 'subject to self-ironic deflation'.[44]

The novel does, nevertheless, offer some points of purchase against an eternal regress. First, despite frequent shifts in point of view, and despite a more than conventionally impersonal narrator, the character whose perspective Flaubert reflects most often is Emma. The contrast is clear when his novel is compared with those of Champfleury and Feydeau. *Fanny*, as a personal narrative, is confined to the lover's perspective; and, although most of *Les Bourgeois de Molinchart* is told impersonally, it not only has little room for the woman's point of view, but ends with the personal narrative of the lover's letter. As I have suggested above, such a narrative strategy and emphasis links these texts to the Romantic confession. Flaubert echoes that tradition at the beginning of his novel by implying that the story is to be told by a personal narrator who was one of Charles's classmates; readers familiar with the conventions of confessional narrative might even be forgiven if they were to speculate that the narrator would be Emma's seducer. But the echo is little more than a trace, quietly parodic. What is more significant is the opening word, 'We'. Flaubert does not quite begin and end his novel with Charles, as is often asserted. Instead, its frame and setting is the bourgeois order in which schooling is by rote and in which, as its last words disclose, Homais, supreme epitome of that order, can be awarded the Legion of Honour.[45] The fact that Flaubert would later accept the same honour only rubs in an all-encompassing banality.

The second point of purchase is, then, the novel's unremitting offensive against the bourgeoisie. For all the indeterminacy of its discourse, no reader could for a moment doubt that *Madame Bovary* expresses a profound contempt for the social world it portrays. It was, as Baudelaire recognized, in order to vent that contempt that Flaubert chose the provincial setting, the petty characters in petty positions, the trite theme of adultery; and that, in composing his novel, he went on to deny his readers any of the conventional satisfactions they might have expected. But he also went further, to convey a corrosive disillusionment and scepticism about almost all aspects of life except those concerning his art. This critique is so full and so searching that Tony Tanner hails *Madame Bovary* as 'the most important and far-reaching novel of adultery in Western literature'.[46] But, if it does go so far, the question arises as to why Flaubert chose Emma for its focus. According to Stephen Heath,

> Simply, he takes and defines his realism, the reality of the social world, from woman, from Emma, grasps *her* as the key point for the interrogation of that world, the demonstration of its oppressive mediocrity. His separation from Emma is then that she is contained within this mediocrity, lacks access to art which for him is the sole possibility of liberation from it all. The position of the artist writing against, outside, in the margins, is brought together with the position of the woman as different, socially marginal, and simultaneously distanced, since *she* becomes *his* figure for a writing that is *his* art.[47]

This is a brilliant observation, but in two respects it gives the novel's game away. It revealingly conflates 'woman' with 'Emma'; and it suggests that Flaubert's relation to that figure is parasitic: in other words, that the writer makes his character both vehicle and, in part, target for his own alienation and despair. This is probably what Michael Riffaterre means when he declares: 'The novel is not about adultery, but rather about boredom.'[48] It is not by accident, for instance, that boredom is the focus of the only extended passage presenting Léon's state of mind, as he waits interminably in Rouen Cathedral for Emma to arrive. The passage on which Auerbach comments is only a brief example of others of the same kind. There is even a sense in which the attitude Auerbach terms 'objective seriousness' might be seen as response and counterpart to boredom, at the level of style.

However, despite Flaubert's ambitions to write 'a book about nothing',[49] he had to write about something, and he chose an adulterous woman. The equation in Heath's analysis between 'woman' and 'Emma' is supported by Naomi Schor's suggestion that, just as 'Homais' was meant to evoke *homme*, so 'Emma' evokes *femme*.[50] It is a sign that although, as Heath points out, no particular discourse dominates *Madame Bovary*, the novel was still determined in part by the ideological field within which women at this period were defined. Flaubert's version of the adulterous woman may be much less crude than those of Lucas and Larousse, but it is informed by cognate assumptions and stereotypes. Thus, it could be argued, *Madame Bovary* offers materials for a masculinist, even a misogynist reading, as well as for a feminist one. Two examples are Flaubert's way of describing Emma's physical appearance, and his emphasis on her corruption. A paragraph during the height of her affair with Rodolphe illustrates both:

Never had Madame Bovary been so beautiful as at this time; she had that indefinable beauty which comes from joy, from enthusiasm, from success, and which is simply the harmony of temperament with circumstances. Her cravings, her sorrows, her experience of pleasure and her still-fresh illusions had, as manure, rain, wind and sun do for flowers, developed her gradually, and she was blossoming at last in the fullness of her nature. Her eyelids seemed perfectly fashioned for those long ardent looks in which the pupils lose themselves, while deep breathing dilated her fine nostrils and lifted the plump corners of her lips, shadowed in the light with a faint black down. One would have said that an artist skilled in corruption had arranged on her nape the coiling of her hair: it twined in a heavy mass, negligently, and in keeping with the chance accidents of adultery, which every day took it down. Her voice was now taking on more mellow inflections, her figure too; something subtle that ran straight through you spread out even from the folds of her gown and from the curve of her foot. Charles, as in the first days of his marriage, found her delicious and quite irresistible. (II.xii.157, TM; 199–200)

This set-piece invites a response which is implicitly and at times explicitly male. Well might not only Charles but any reader alive to female sexual allure find Emma 'quite irresistible'. The appeal is direct when the passage attributes to the reader a feeling, clearly sensual, 'that ran straight through you'; and even more in the whole impression it creates of a woman ripe for sexual love – especially as it is erotic pleasure which has completed her ripening. Flaubert's choice of the word 'nature' suggests that it is for this that Emma is made; a suggestion amplified by art when he goes on to invoke conventions of female portraiture. Although an extended example, this way of describing Emma is by no means exceptional. Maria Vargas Llosa illustrates it in one way by pointing to the images of Emma's shoes and feet which occur in the novel, and to their importance in 'the erotic life of male characters', as he styles it; Tony Tanner in another way by discussing what he calls Flaubert's 'morselization' of Emma.[51] Only once, and very briefly, is any comparable kind of attention given to the physical appearance of a man. This occurs in Emma's response to Léon before their sexual liaison begins:

Never had any man appeared to her so beautiful. An exquisite candour arose from his bearing. He lowered his long, fine, curling eyelashes. The soft skin of his cheek was turning pink – she thought – with desire for her, and Emma felt an invincible urge to press her lips upon it. (III.i.192, TM; 242)

Here, however, responses are attributed not to the reader but to Emma from the start. The fact is emphasized by the expression 'appeared to her' and, especially, by the interpolation 'she thought'. Unlike the language describing Emma, these phrases leave open the question whether the responses of the observer, here Emma herself, are valid: it is not clear whether Léon really is beautiful, and whether he also desires her. The passage even suggests that it is her own desire that Emma reads into Léon's blush, for, timidly, he is already beginning to hold back. Indeed, to denote her wish for physical contact as 'an invincible urge' is to hint at sexual impulses which are excessive.

Such a hint does no more than pick up, from the description of Emma just discussed and elsewhere, a flavour of what the narrator calls 'corruption'. The flavour strengthens as the sexual liaison with Léon unfolds. One chapter ends with a question ambiguously located, as so often in this novel, between narrator and character: 'Where then had she learned this corruption, almost intangible by dint of being profound and dissembled?' (III.v.226, TM; 284). In the following chapter the narrator describes Emma's corset as slithering from around her hips like a snake, and he continues:

> Yet there was on that brow covered by cold drops, on those murmuring lips, in those distracted eyes, in the clasping of those arms, something extreme, vague and mournful, which seemed to Léon to be sliding between them, imperceptibly, as if to separate them. (III.vi.230, TM; 288)

This vignette is especially interesting, as it hints not only at excessive and unsatisfied sexual desire, but at an all-embracing unfulfilment, dissatisfaction and anxiety.

The same ambivalence marks the episode in which Emma tries frantically to raise money to stave off the sale of her home. This episode is more complex than Michael Riffaterre allows when he suggests that, true to conventional formulas for the adulteress, it stages prostitution as the alternative ending to death. It is built on a progressive and symmetrical series of scenes in which Emma visits three different men. The first shows her indignantly refusing the lawyer Guillaumin when he begs her for sex in exchange for money; the second leaves ambiguous whether the proposition she puts to the tax-collector Binet is sexual as well as financial; but the third, when she rushes to Rodolphe, brands her with 'prostitution', the word on which the chapter categorically ends. Each step in the series is carefully graded. After the visit to Guillaumin, the narrator implies that Emma's anger is in part artificial by remarking that 'the disappointment of failure strengthened the indignation of her outraged modesty' (III.vii.248, TM; 310); and he insinuates a page later that 'now perhaps she was repenting her refusal to yield to that man'. The word 'perhaps' relays an indeterminacy maintained by narrative technique in the scene with Binet. By presenting it from the viewpoint of two respectable women who watch from an attic, Flaubert limits the evidence available to the reader to what they see and how they interpret it. On the one hand, they have no doubt that she offers herself to him; on the other, they are eager to believe the worst; the text refrains from resolving the question either way. In a further symmetry, the three scenes are punctuated by interludes with lower-class women. Emma goes to Guillaumin after advice from her maid Félicité; she returns for a more agitated discussion with Félicité before she rushes to Binet in order to avoid her returning husband; and she flees in turn from Binet to the wet-nurse Mère Rollet, whom she sends to her home to find if Léon has arrived.

Flaubert's presentation is finely poised between embracing and complicating the stereotype of the adulteress. Through its complex structure, the episode shows Emma sliding from outraged refusal to involuntary acceptance of prostitution, as all other resources fail her, and as her panic, anguish and confusion mount. However, it is revealing that the text should construct as prostitution Emma's appeal for money from the lover who had left her three years before. Such an appeal is scarcely on the same level as the one she rejects from Guillaumin. The comment in the Larousse entry on the novel identifies the real issue by crudely drawing attention to the superior power of the male: 'does one pay a woman whom one has already possessed for nothing?' But this emphasis on the rejected woman's weakness can be understood in two ways. While the episode invites an orthodox reading, in which she sinks further into corruption, it does not entirely resist an alternative in which the accent falls on her dependency and subjection. The same vein of ambiguity runs through the whole novel.

In his theory of the aesthetics of reception, Hans Robert Jauss discusses the contrasting fortunes of *Madame Bovary* and *Fanny*, first among contemporary and then among later readers. Feydeau's novel is now hardly known except as a footnote to Flaubert's. Yet in its own day, as Jauss observes, *Fanny* achieved 'a success the likes of which Paris had not experienced since Chateaubriand's *Atala*';[52] while *Madame Bovary*, thanks in part to the trial of author, publisher and printer for obscenity, found as much notoriety as esteem. Jauss suggests that the two writers 'put the worn-out theme of jealousy in a new light by reversing the expected relationship between the three classic roles': for, while *Fanny* centres on the lover's jealousy rather than the husband's, *Madame Bovary* ends by giving some dignity to 'the laughable figure of the cuckolded Charles Bovary'.[53] He goes on to argue, however, that what more than anything accounts for the reversal in each novel's valuation is a fundamental difference in narrative form: Feydeau wrapped his provocative variation on a stock fictional theme in the familiar package of the Romantic confession, appealing to the taste of the day at the cost of the interest of posterity; while Flaubert shocked and perplexed contemporaries, but has continued to fascinate later readers, not by any special variation of theme but through the radical formal innovation of narrative impersonality.

Jauss's explanation of why the two novels should have enjoyed such opposite fortunes is in several ways persuasive. However, his analysis of how they vary a commonplace plot is limited, and his distinction between content and form is schematic and misleading. To deal first with *Fanny*, from the viewpoint of the Romantic confession there was nothing remarkable in Feydeau's attribution of jealousy to the lover; indeed, this followed directly from the convention. What is genuinely unusual, within that convention, is that the lover's mistress is married, and that he does not take for granted that her relationship with her husband is only nominal. In these respects *Fanny* differs from *Adolphe*, and, more significantly, from *Confession of a Child of the Century*, in which the hero also shows violent jealousy. The novel does not reduce the deceived husband to the banal belittlement of a cuckold; instead, it suggests that the lover has every reason to fear his rivalry. But the fact that in *Fanny* it is the lover rather than the husband who suffers jealousy amounts to more than the facile reversal of a conventional formula suggested by Jauss. In putting such a view, Jauss follows Feydeau's contemporary Émile Montégut in his review of *Fanny*.[54] Accusing the novel of immorality, Montégut argues that its entire *donnée* is factitious and implausible. His attack is forceful, but it depends on disclaiming the main feature which gives *Fanny* its interest: the lover's jealousy for a husband. This takes on its full significance in light not only of Freud's theory of the Oedipus complex, but of the tradition of the Romantic confession, in which a husband's rivalry with the lover was quite new.

The role Feydeau gives to the relation between husband and wife highlights the importance of marriage in the novel of female adultery. Nevertheless, that importance becomes pivotal for the first time in *Madame Bovary*. Jauss rightly points out that Flaubert played with social and literary convention by inviting a qualified sympathy for his cuckold. However, the novelist took a much more important and influential step when he centred his narrative on the adulterous wife and consigned her lovers to the margins. This was considerably to outstrip Feydeau, for in *Fanny* the mistress, though a wife, remains secondary to the conventional lover-narrator. The distance Flaubert travelled may be appreciated further by looking back to *Adolphe* and also to Balzac's *Muse of the Department*, along with an essay on Constant's novel by Gustave Planche which was reprinted as a supplement to the editions of 1839 and 1843.[55]

In *Adolphe*, as in other confessional narratives, marriage is given little importance, and the woman's position is largely taken for granted. Planche shows even less consideration than the novel does for Ellénore's vulnerability as an unmarried mother who has left an irregular relationship for a man who has tired of her. The issue in his essay is how to end a liaison which has failed because each partner entered it for motives which it could not answer. In *The Muse of the Department*, Balzac to some extent redresses the balance. Dinah can avoid the fate of Ellénore partly because she has studied Constant's novel and Planche's article, but chiefly because she has a marriage to go back to. When she realizes that it is useless for her to continue her affair with Lousteau, it is she who takes the initiative and leaves him. However, for Dinah to return from an inadequate lover to an inadequate husband does not solve the problem of her marriage. It is this which is recognized increasingly as the novel of female adultery develops.

The new departure represented by *Madame Bovary* stands out clearly against these earlier paradigms. First, Flaubert locked his adulterous wife into a marriage which permitted neither escape nor even the unsatisfactory but, for Balzac, acceptable expedient represented by Dinah's return to her husband. Second, he rejected not only the single viewpoint of confessional narrative, but Balzac's combination of a stable, authoritative narrative voice with the viewpoints of various characters. Third, like Balzac, but unlike Constant, Champfleury and Feydeau, Flaubert gave a serious role to the adulteress's offspring. This is an important enlargement of focus, because his presentation of the mother/child relationship goes well beyond Balzac's. Little space is given to the portrayal of that relationship in *A Woman of Thirty*, and none at all in *The Muse of the Department*. The role played by the children of both novels is limited – largely in the one case, and entirely in the other – to instruments of the plot: as agents of punishment, or of dynastic ambition followed by marital reunion. In contrast, Flaubert displays not only what the child signifies for the mother, but in what ways she relates to her child in consequence; though the emphasis falls on Emma as an inadequate mother rather than on the position of the child herself. This is a development which later novels of female adultery, notably *Anna Karenina*, would take much further.

The fundamental shift achieved by *Madame Bovary* is, then, towards the adulterous woman herself. This, as Baudelaire saw, is where the novel most decisively broke new ground. However, it is essential to recognize that, in addressing the woman's experience much more fully, Flaubert did not relinquish a masculinist outlook. First, the novel maintains, often in highly sophisticated forms, various assumptions about women current at the period. Indeed, *Madame Bovary* may have owed its later success not only to its formal innovations, but to a contribution which far outwent that of *Fanny* to a developing discourse on the female. It was partly on such a basis that Flaubert's defence counsel at his trial was able to represent the novel as a moral work. Even Montégut, whose review of *Fanny* marks a change in the climate of French critical opinion, and who probably helped ensure that *Fanny* did not enjoy its success for long, did not find Flaubert's novel immoral in comparison with Feydeau's.[56]

Second, and paradoxically, later nineteenth-century discourse on woman was not only, or even primarily, moral, least of all in France. Flaubert himself provides an example. As Stephen Heath points out, the novelist was fascinated by adultery from his youth. Almost ten years before beginning *Madame Bovary*,

in the autobiographical *Novembre*, he records how the very word 'adultery' conjured up a whole poetry of desire: 'a word which seemed supremely beautiful among human words . . . An exquisite sweetness hangs vaguely over it. A singular magic fills it with perfume.'[57]

This fascination helps explain why Flaubert presents Emma not only from her own point of view but from that of a male admirer, for whom part of her beauty is the seductiveness of corruption. What is even more ironic, however, is that the cynical element in this vision was informed by the novelist's own alienation. Baudelaire again recognized this exactly, in his image of a world which had already seen, before the Revolution of 1848, 'the final outbursts of a spirit still willing to be stimulated by the display of imaginative powers', and of a writer, in this case still unpublished, 'confronted with a completely worn-out public or, worse even, a stupefied and greedy audience, whose only hatred is for fiction, and only love for material possession'.[58]

For male writers in Continental Europe, female adultery became one of the pre-eminent fictional subjects through which to interrogate a whole society. Writing from the standpoint defined so indignantly by Baudelaire, Flaubert used the theme as his vehicle for a corrosively sceptical critique not only of mid-nineteenth-century French provincial culture, but of a whole range of human behaviours and institutions, including the forms in which they are perceived and understood, even those of language itself. In this latter respect no novelist has pushed the theme so far.

5

Alternatives: George Sand and Others

The foregoing chapters have shown the emergence in France of the novel of female adultery up to the point when, after 1857, it became established in its classic form with Flaubert's *Madame Bovary*. Part of my aim has been to define what is specific to works of this kind, and to distinguish them from other works in which adultery is not the leading issue. The differences are fundamentally ideological. Self-evidently, the dominant ideas of the period about marriage are crucial to this kind of fiction, especially through their consequences for the role of the wife. What defines the novel of female adultery, however, is not simply the fact that its action hinges on the wife's betrayal of wedlock, but, above all, that it displays a specific set of attitudes towards such conduct and indeed towards women in general. The purpose of the present chapter is to demonstrate this essential difference by discussing a number of other narratives which raised questions concerning marriage and adultery during the period in which the novel of female adultery developed.

The writer whose treatment of these questions had most impact was George Sand. That impact was important in itself, but there are also several further reasons why it is vital to consider Sand's fiction about marriage and adultery. First, her writing spans almost the whole period during which the novel of female adultery developed and flourished in France: the first novel she published as her own work appeared in 1832, and she wrote prolifically until her death in 1876. Second, although she was notorious for portraying illicit love, including adultery, in her fiction, she produced only one narrative which might be classed as a novel of female adultery. This work, *Le Dernier amour* (*Last Love*), first appeared late in her career, in 1866, as a serial; but, as the discussion below will make clear, it is revealingly untypical of the tradition. Third, and by extension, in her fiction and her non-fiction alike, Sand represented marriage and adultery in very different ways from those characteristic of the novel of female adultery. Given that the form is a project peculiar to male writers, the nature of those differences, in the work of the leading woman writer of her period, is highly significant.

In 1836 Sand published an open letter to the critic Désiré Nisard who, in an article by no means without enthusiasm for her novels, had alleged that they constituted an attack upon marriage and, in particular, upon husbands. It was important for Sand to rebut this interpretation, which appeared at a time when her husband had appealed against the legal separation decreed at her instance earlier in the same year.[1] She wished not just to explain her actual views, but to prevent Nisard's article from influencing the outcome of the appeal. The letter appeared in the number of the *Revue de Paris* which followed the one containing the misleading article, and it was later collected in *Lettres d'un voyageur*. It is a key statement of Sand's thinking about marriage and adultery, produced at a critical point in her personal life, and when she was in a position to take stock of her first eight novels. In reply to Nisard's claim that 'the purpose of all [her] books is to discredit marriage' (292; 936),[2] she defends them one by one. She points out that marriage is not even mentioned in *Lélia* (1833), and she suggests that the focus of this most notorious of her novels is spiritual rather than sensual. With cordial irony she continues:

> Nor when I was writing it did *Indiana* seem to me to be a defence of adultery. I believe that in this novel (where, if I remember rightly, no one commits adultery) the *lover* (*that king of my books* as you wittily call him) cuts a poor figure compared to the husband. *Le Secrétaire Intime* [1834] is (if I'm not entirely mistaken as to my intentions) about the joys of conjugal bliss. *André* [1835] is neither *against* marriage nor *for* adultery. *Simon* [1836] ends with a marriage just like a fairy-tale by Perrault or Madame d'Aulnoy; and as for *Valentine* [1832] whose conclusion, I admit, is neither original nor skilful, the expected calamity intervenes to stop the adulterous wife from enjoying in a second marriage a happiness for which she has failed to wait. (292–3; 936–7)

She goes on to insist that *Leone Leoni* (1834), written as a counterpart to *Manon Lescaut*, portrays as critically as Prévost's novel 'desperate love for an unworthy object and the subjection imposed by the strength of a corrupt being on another blinded by its own weakness' (293; 937). Only in the case of *Jacques* (also 1834) does she concede that there is a case to answer. Her response is to point out that, while her critic presents the novel as hostile to domestic order, other people have drawn quite opposite conclusions, and to submit that she may not sufficiently have realized her intentions as an author. She goes on to agree with Nisard that the aim of her work is indeed 'the downfall of husbands, or at least their unpopularity' (294; 939). But she qualifies this crucially by citing her answer to members of the Saint-Simonian movement, who had asked her what she would put in place of husbands: 'I replied in all innocence that it would be *marriage*, just as I believe that religion should be substituted for those priests who have given it such a bad name' (295; 939).[3] In other words, Sand's protest is directed not against marriage but against the abuse of marriage as a result of the husband's superior power. She asks Nisard why he had not taken the opportunity 'to chide the dissolute, violent behaviour of men which so often authorizes or provokes the criminal acts of women' (297; 941), and she trenchantly declares: 'Every kind of marriage will be intolerable so long as custom persists in showing unlimited indulgence to the errors of one sex while the austere and salutary rigour of past ages is retained solely to judge those of the other' (297; 942).

Nisard's misreading of Sand is instructive, not least because it has much in common with other contemporary reactions to her work. On the one hand, it was difficult for many readers and critics to accept that a critique of the practice of marriage was not also an attack on the institution. The distinction was especially hard to recognize in the shadow cast by the author's gender, the gossip about her own marriage and her actual and alleged love affairs, and, perhaps most of all, her challenge to masculinist assumptions. On the other hand, it was that very challenge which alarmed so many of her contemporaries. The main reason, for instance, that *Lélia* caused such a scandal, and was read by Nisard and others as hostile to marriage, was Sand's presentation of a woman in the Byronic role, male by definition, of alienation, dissidence and despair.[4] What was fundamental to Sand's representation of love, marriage and adultery was her keen awareness of the inequality between men and women sanctioned by custom and vested in law. That awareness led her to set adultery in a wider context than is characteristic of the novel of female adultery. The assumptions behind her work not only have little in common with those behind the developing form, but in several ways put it in question.

Although adultery is one of the themes of *Indiana* and *Valentine* (both 1832), as well as of *Jacques*, it is not the principal theme in any of the three. Each is concerned much more with relationships of equality between men and women, and also with general questions of social power. The first chapter of *Indiana* opens just such an expanded outlook. It presents a scenario composed of pretty young wife, irascible older husband and handsome young man which might at first seem to promise only too plainly a story of adultery. But the narrator soon emphasizes that the husband has no cause for jealousy, and directs attention instead to his arbitrary power. Indiana's unhappiness stems not only from an ill-matched marriage but from her husband's wilfulness and violence. This is shown when he vents his irritation on his friend's hunting dog, and is reminded by his wife, begging him for mercy, that he had killed her own spaniel. The chapter ends by suggesting that the husband's abuse of his power is not confined to private life. Warned by his steward of wood-thieves, Colonel Delmare goes out armed and ready to kill any trespasser as the law entitles him.

In this way *Indiana* begins by transforming an apparently adulterous scenario to one of husbandly oppression, and then by enlarging the perspective from domestic to social and political. The rest of the novel follows suit. Not content with wrong-footing the reader in her first chapter, Sand repeats the move much more intricately through the character she introduces next. Indiana's would-be lover, Raymon de Ramière, illustrates even more than her husband how men may abuse their power over women. Raymon has already seduced and impregnated Indiana's maid, Noun, who commits suicide in fear of her mistress's response and in despair at her lover's attempt to abandon her. Despite pretending passionate love, he goes on to fail Indiana comprehensively. When she puts herself wholly in his power, compromising her own reputation to protect his, he backs off and gets his doting mother to rescue him. Then, once Indiana has had to go with her husband, whose business has collapsed, to the island in the Indian Ocean where he hopes to retrieve his fortunes, Raymon compounds the betrayal. She responds to his letter promising renewed love by leaving her husband and braving the return journey alone, only to be ejected, sick and destitute, from the home that used to be hers by the rich wife he has already taken.

Earlier in the story the narrator drily remarks of Indiana: 'It was not the first time that Raymon saw a woman take love seriously, although, fortunately for society, such cases are rare; but he knew that promises of love are not binding on a man's honour, again fortunately for society' (XII.101; 136).[5] This is not only to expose and underline the double standard of sexual morality for men and women, but to direct attention from adultery to infidelity. Love, the narrator observes, 'is a contract as much as marriage is' (IV.39; 52), and the novel invites condemnation of Raymon for breaking that contract with Noun as well as with Indiana. Sand shows how the unhappy wife is injured even more by her would-be lover than by her husband. Having defied the latter by telling him: 'morally you're not my master' (XXI.177; 226), Indiana makes the mistake of returning to Raymon to offer just such a relationship: 'Take me, I am your property, you are my master' (XXVIII.232; 301). The novel does not use the language of property lightly, for it connects female subjection with slavery. Indiana, brought up in the colonies 'by an eccentric, violent father', has developed sympathy for the slaves around her and a capacity for 'mental resistance' (VI.51; 68–9). This makes it all the more ironic that, on her return to Raymon, she should present herself with the words: 'it's your slave, whom you have recalled from exile' (XXVIII.231, TM; 300). Having learned her error the hard way, she is saved by her companion of the novel's opening scene. She and her partner return to the colony where, although freed from her husband by his death, they do not, pointedly, marry.[6] The novel ends in an idyll where, at one with each other and their servants, they devote most of their income to buying people out of slavery.

As Naomi Schor has demonstrated, the theme of slavery is one of the means by which Sand extended her portrayal of love and marriage in *Indiana*.[7] Although Sand did not develop the colonial motif very far, it illustrates the care she took in associating the behaviour of her characters with particular social and political positions. The novel also indicates that the power structures which inform relations between men and women are replicated in various ways in society at large. For example, Raymon is able to discard Noun all the more easily because 'for him a working-girl was not a woman' (IV.38; 52); Colonel Delmare's tetchy but vulnerable authoritarianism is linked to his support of the former Empire; and Raymon's self-interest and opportunism connect with his role as an aristocrat bent on improving his standing by political manoeuvres and ultimately by marriage. Indeed, the crisis of the novel's action, which coincides with the Revolution of 1830, looks set to establish Raymon as a characteristic figure of the new regime. Indiana's eventual partner, Sir Ralph Brown, is less representative. As an Englishman from the colonies, his political position in France is detached, so that, though an aristocrat, he can champion republican and humanitarian ideals without incongruity. Just as Sand traces Raymon's arrogant self-interest not only to his social position but to an overindulgent mother, so she suggests that Sir Ralph escaped being spoiled by his social privileges through an unhappy childhood in which he was rejected by his mother and was slighted by the rest of his family.[8] This psychological sidelight on the action is one of the further ways in which the novel expands the fictional agenda concerning issues of love and marriage.

Like *Indiana*, Sand's next novel, *Valentine*, is also named after its heroine. The two contrast in several ways, however, and especially in their representation of a woman tempted by adultery. While Indiana offers herself twice to the man she loves, and is met by his cowardice and desertion, Valentine struggles against adultery but eventually has to succumb. Yet, as in the earlier novel, what is at issue is not adultery itself but the social and political structures which condition marriage and love. The highly artificial plot which Sand devised for *Valentine* casts those structures in relief.

The heroine is of aristocratic birth and is heir to a wealthy estate. When the novel begins, she is engaged to a man of her own rank whom she scarcely knows but whom she believes she may come to love. Her grandmother is a hedonistic survivor from the Old Regime; her mother, who supports the marriage out of ambition, had been the lover of a man who also seduced her elder daughter, Louise, and she had kept her own affair secret by applauding her husband for killing the seducer in a duel. Valentine's lover, Bénédict, is an orphan of peasant extraction who is talented and well educated, but who lacks occupation and standing. The two fall in love when he helps her to meet her half-sister, who had been rejected by the family 15 years earlier when her seduction had resulted in her bearing an illegitimate child. Valentine's fiancé, the Comte de Lansac, sees her rarely, but she is given no alternative except to marry him, although she comes to realize that she cannot care for him and that she is in love with Bénédict. Although

Valentine fails to prevent her marriage, it is never consummated. Lansac spends nearly all his time away from her, and it transpires that he married her in order to liquidate massive debts. For this reason he is prepared to connive at a liaison on her part, so long as it is discreet; he himself keeps a mistress in St Petersburg, where he goes as a diplomat. Valentine's mother also absents herself after the marriage, and she repudiates her daughter and goes abroad when Valentine writes to her for help. The action is further complicated by unrequited love for Bénédict on the part both of Valentine's sister, Louise, and of Athénaïs, the daughter of the farming family in which he had been brought up, and whom he had been intended to marry. While Louise has to stifle her jealousy, Athénaïs marries a neighbouring farmer in pique.

The schematic nature of the novel's design is clearest at its climax, when Bénédict and Valentine have become lovers, and the news arrives that Lansac has been killed in a duel. While Bénédict believes they have been providentially set free, Valentine cannot help feeling that she deserves not reward but punishment. In his response, Bénédict summarizes the difficulties she has faced:

> 'But, Valentine, think of all that you had to excuse you. Think of your miserable and false position. Remember the husband who drove you to your ruin deliberately, the mother who refused to open her arms to you in time of danger, the old woman who could think of nothing better to say to you on her deathbed than these pious words: "My dear, take a lover of your own rank".'
>
> 'Ah! it's true,' said Valentine, reflecting bitterly on the past; 'they all treated virtue with incredible levity. I alone, whom they accused, understood the importance of my duties, and I wanted to make the marriage a sacred and mutual obligation. But they laughed at my simplicity; one talked of money, another of dignity, a third of the proprieties. Ambition or pleasure, that was all the morality of their actions, all the meaning of their precepts. They invited me to fall, and urged me to know only the outward practice of virtue. If, instead of being a peasant's son, you had been a duke and peer, my poor Bénédict, they would have borne me in triumph!' (XXXVIII.328–9; 354–5)[9]

Not for nothing does the narrator observe of Valentine that 'fate seemed to take pleasure in forcing her into exceptional situations and surrounding her with perils which were beyond her strength'

(XXVII.228; 246). After long resisting inordinate temptations, she only yields to Bénédict's desire and her own after he has barely survived a suicide attempt, she has nearly died after contracting cerebral fever in reaction, and he has fainted in her bedroom after risking his life to get there. But 'fate' in fiction is a metaphor for the writer's design. The novel's events, which are often implausible, are important less in themselves than for the questions they highlight.

The most obvious of these questions is the conflict between love and the obstacles against it created by class barriers and by the use of marriage to transmit property. Not only may Valentine not marry Bénédict, but her marriage to Lansac is nominal, and she is treated by him less even as a chattel than as possessor of the signature which will settle his debts. However, the minimal nature of his expectations does not prevent Sand from drawing attention to other ways in which marriage is abused. He plans at first 'to hold his wife in complete subjection' (XVIII.144; 155), and this is his right, although her willingness to part with her property makes coercion unnecessary. Bénédict passionately denounces the husband's associated power over his wife's body: '"O outrageous violation of the most sacred rights!" he exclaimed inwardly; "shocking tyranny of man over woman! Marriage, society, all existing institutions, I hate you!"' (XXII.183; 198). Neither Bénédict nor the narrator hesitates to call by its proper name, rape, the forcible exercise of that power (XXII.184; 198). It is an adroit move on Sand's part, comparable with her adoption of a male pseudonym, to place this protest in the mouth of a man. Equally adroit is her use of an explicit accusation rather than a narrative event to which readers would probably have objected.[10] But there is also a further implication, as Bénédict's protest cannot be altogether disinterested. What is at issue is not only female subjection in marriage, but the impact both on him and on Valentine of thwarted sexual desire.

Two scenes between Valentine and Bénédict show the effects of sexual repression. The first occurs on Valentine's wedding night, when Bénédict goes to her bedroom determined to keep her chaste by killing either Lansac or Valentine herself. Here Sand underlines Bénédict's sexual jealousy by switching to his distorted point of view when he wildly suspects that Valentine is about to let her husband in: he moves forward with the intention 'to blow out that shameless, lying woman's brains' (XXII.189; 203). Then, after Valentine, still unaware of his presence, has taken opium, Bénédict enjoys the liberty not only of gazing at her sleeping form, but of undoing her hair, filling his mouth with it, and even biting 'the round, white shoulder which she uncovered before him' (XXIII.196; 211). He is on the point of yielding to what the narrator calls 'the violence of his agonizing desires', or, in other words, of raping her, when her nurse mistakes his cries for Valentine's and comes in (XXIII.197; 211). It is after the nurse has gone that he decides to kill neither Valentine nor her husband but himself. This is the most violent outcome of his need to repress his desire, but Sand uses the letter in which he explains his intention as a further way of exposing male sexual possessiveness. Bénédict begins the letter with a phrase which stresses how completely Valentine has been in his power: 'I am [. . .] more your master than your husband will ever be' (XXIII.199, TM; 214).

The second scene takes place following Bénédict's recovery and a long interlude during which the lovers meet chastely in Valentine's pavilion. Nancy K. Miller has shown that the pavilion in Sand's novel, as well as in other novels by Frenchwomen, is a sanctuary which preserves female space and independence.[11] Lansac violates both with his unexpected return, and precipitates a crisis in which Valentine avoids Bénédict by retiring to the chateau to await advice from her mother. Bénédict's anxiety leads him to gain entrance to the dangerous space of her bedroom, where their passion is finally consummated. Here again the narrative insists on the violence of his repressed desire. Bénédict not only faints from frustrated passion, but he so frightens Valentine after he has come round that he causes her to scald herself with the tea with which she has revived him. The kiss he gives her reddened foot through its transparent stocking has been discussed as an instance of fetishism by Naomi Schor.[12] Whatever its psychoanalytical significance, however, what the novel emphasizes is the wounding of Valentine, as in the bite Bénédict gives her sleeping body earlier. When the two at last make love, the narrator describes her as 'conquered by pity, by love, above all by fear' (XXXVI.306, TM; 331). Suppressed desire then takes its toll of her in a different way from its effect on him: 'Valentine, naturally calm and reserved, had become passionate to the point of delirium as the result of a pitiless combination of misfortunes and allurements which had developed within her new powers of resisting and of loving. The longer and more determined her resistance, the more violent her fall' (XXXVI.308, TM; 333). Sand also portrays Valentine as racked by remorse, but her portrayal of the heroine as sexualized by suppressed longing, rather than naturally sensual, is one of the qualities which distinguish *Valentine* from the novel of female adultery.

Although Nancy K. Miller has called *Valentine* a novel of adultery,[13] it might better be termed a novel of abused marriage and tortured love. The primary focus is not on adultery, but on the human and social consequences of a system which stacks the odds heavily against fulfilled love in a legitimate relationship. Sand creates a situation which renders the adultery of Valentine and Bénédict virtually inevitable, and then produces a swift and manifestly novelistic retribution. No sooner are the two free to marry than Bénédict is killed by the husband of Athénaïs in the mistaken belief that he is her lover, and Valentine dies soon after in fever and madness. This way of resolving the action further illustrates the injustice of the social and legal codes governing marriage, for Bénédict's murderer can escape without punishment from the law. Though it is melodramatic, as Sand recognizes wryly in her letter to Nisard (292–3; 936–7), its effect is to expose the costs of a system which is not only destructive but militates against the ideal of 'true conjugal fidelity' (296; 941).

As Sand also acknowledged in her response to Nisard, *Jacques*, published in 1834, two years after *Indiana* and *Valentine*, is more vulnerable to the charge of approving adultery. The novel's basic action is simple: Jacques marries Fernande, who is much younger than himself; she falls in love with Octave, whose interests as well as his age are nearer hers, and after an honourable resistance becomes his lover; and Jacques enables the two to marry by discreetly committing suicide. However, the novel is reticent about the affair between Fernande and Octave, and adultery in itself is not its main concern. Once more, Sand's governing interest is in marriage. *Jacques* shows the dynamics and the pathology of a marriage entered with the best of apparent intentions but which fails to survive for long.

The novel is told entirely through letters between the principal characters. This is a narrative method perfectly suited to conveying misunderstanding; also, because of the very different perspectives it makes possible, it helps explain the misreading of the novel by Nisard and others. The chief correspondences are on the one hand between Jacques and the foundling Sylvia, and on the other between Fernande and at first her convent friend Clémence but later Octave. The characters write to each other not only about what happens, what has happened in the past, and their various relationships, but, more significantly, about the nature of love, marriage and fidelity. In the course of the action, the relationship which develops between Fernande and Octave, who begins as Sylvia's lover, becomes a counterpart to the relationship between Jacques and Sylvia. This interplay between two sets of partners is not the only feature of the novel to recall Goethe's *Elective Affinities*, a work which plainly fascinated Sand.[14]

It is pivotal to the effect of *Jacques* that the most important correspondent is a man, and that his behaviour is not altogether consistent with his views concerning matrimony. Early in the novel there are two parallel discussions about marriage: between Fernande and Clémence, and between Sylvia and Jacques. However, the opening five letters, which immediately precede the first from Jacques, are all from the three women, each of whom has a different age, position and outlook. Fernande, on the threshold of marriage to Jacques, is 17; Clémence, already widowed, is a little older; and Sylvia, who is 25, is single, sexually experienced, and opposed to marriage. While Clémence advises Fernande almost as a mother, it is not until Letter XVIII, after Fernande and Jacques are married, that it is made clear that Sylvia's relation to Jacques is not that of a former lover, as the reader might at first imagine. In that letter he tells her he believes she is his father's illegitimate daughter, and therefore his own half-sister. He will not reveal who her mother is because, it later transpires, this is Fernande's mother, Madame de Theursan. Sylvia and Fernande are consequently half-sisters, but, as Madame de Theursan had another lover at the same time as Jacques's father, she cannot tell whether or not Sylvia is also half-sister to Jacques. Several facts emerge from this tangle of licit and illicit sexual relationships and the uncertainties of parentage and kinship they have produced. First, Jacques's father and the mother both of Fernande and Sylvia have been guilty of multiple adultery; second, what Jacques knows about this helps explain his own doubts about marriage and fidelity; third, Jacques is barred from any closer relation to Sylvia than that of a brother; fourth, as in *Indiana* and *Valentine*, it is a mother who receives almost all the blame. If, like *Indiana*, the novel begins by seeming to foreshadow adultery between two of its central characters, it then not only shifts attention from adultery to marriage, but displaces adultery to the past. Sylvia and Jacques, who have both had unhappy liaisons, have every reason to fear that sexual relationships will prove unstable, whether married or not. Jacques's first and perhaps largest inconsistency is therefore the decision to marry at all.

There are four major explanations for that decision. Jacques gives two of them in his first letter to Sylvia: that he loves Fernande, and can possess her only by marrying her; and that marrying her is also the only way of taking her out of the hands of a wicked mother and giving her an honourable and an independent life. As Kathryn J. Crecelius has suggested, a third but subconscious motive may be inferred from what Jacques suspects about Sylvia's parentage and knows about Fernande's: if he cannot marry Sylvia, because he thinks she is his half-sister, then her own half-sister, Fernande, is the closest possible surrogate.[15] The fourth motive only emerges later, shortly before the wedding, in his first letter to Fernande herself. This consists in a conception of marriage which he believes can overcome the deficiencies he has attributed to it in his earlier letter to Sylvia. The key to that conception is mutual trust and friendship. For Jacques, the trouble with marriage is that it seeks to enforce ties which should properly depend on individual responsibility and goodwill. Thus he tells Fernande that he disclaims the vows of fidelity and obedience: 'You cannot answer for your heart, even if I were the greatest and most perfect of men; you ought not to promise to obey me, because that would be degrading to us both' (XIV.73).[16] For his part he accepts the vow to protect his wife, but he adds a further pledge, essential in his own view, though not required by religion or law: that he will also respect her. The corollary is that, provided she keeps his respect, he will abide by her preference if she comes to love someone else. Jacques is as good as his word at the novel's crisis. In explaining his decision to Sylvia, he offers a striking redefinition of adultery:

No human being can control feelings of love, and none is guilty for having them and for losing them. What makes a woman vile is falsehood. It's this that constitutes adultery; it isn't the hour which she gives to her lover, but the night which she goes to spend afterwards in the arms of her husband. (LXXXI.339)

Because Fernande cannot overcome or conceal her love for Octave, or appease her own conscience about it, Jacques is able both to accept an illicit relationship on her part, and to clear the way for its legitimation by marriage.

Although Jacques and Fernande retain their mutual affection and respect, and although Jacques is true to his principles, at least two problems remain: first, their marriage fails; second, the unwanted partner's suicide seems an unduly drastic solution. The marriage fails because Fernande and Jacques are fundamentally ill-matched. It is clear from early on that they do not know each other very well, and that, crucially, they fail to confide in each other sufficiently. Indeed, their lack of mutual trust is demonstrated not only in their dialogues with each other and in their letters, but in the fact that both carry on important correspondences with others. It can best be explained by the inherent and radical inequalities between them. Jacques is twice the age of Fernande, and a rich man while she has no dowry; furthermore, a gulf of experience and knowledge divides them. Despite all his good intentions, Jacques's relation to Fernande is essentially patronizing. This he betrays involuntarily when he tells Sylvia that he proposes to devote to his wife all the advantages of power and independence which life has brought him:

> I want the object of my affection to profit from them – a poor, weak, oppressed being, who will owe me everything; I want to give her a happiness unknown here below; I want, in the name of the society I despise, to secure for her the benefits which society refuses to women. (VI.39)

Ironically, the relationship between Jacques and Fernande is so onesided that he cannot achieve these aims while remaining her husband. In this way the novel not only indicates that marriage may prove oppressive to erotic choice, but also asserts the woman's right to equality with the man. It suggests that equality as well as affinity between husband and wife are necessary conditions for successful marriage. Such a view was not held widely when Sand wrote *Jacques*, and it is not clear that these conditions can be met in the society which the novel portrays. While the relationship between Fernande and Octave may or may not prove happy, it is significant that Sylvia refuses to marry, although recommended to do so by Jacques.

Jacques's motives for committing suicide throw further light on Sand's thinking about love, marriage and adultery. In part, his act stems from a recognition that Fernande's union with Octave will not be tolerated without legal and social sanction. This is shown when Sylvia and Octave join Jacques and Fernande, and the two couples live together for a while. The suspicions which quickly arise grow into scandal when Octave pursues Fernande to Tours, and Jacques ludicrously finds himself having to fight duels to protect his wife's reputation. It is also worth recalling that, for most of the nineteenth century, divorce was not available in France, and that, as Sand knew only too well, a legal separation could not be obtained without difficulty. However, what determines Jacques's suicide is a factor which in the novel of female adultery plays a quite different role. In that tradition, from the beginnings with Balzac, and including the classic examples of *Madame Bovary, Anna Karenina* and *Effi Briest*, the adulterous woman is often punished through her offspring. Although both of the children die who are born to Fernande and Jacques, the emphasis in Sand's novel is opposite. Because it is a shared congenital defect that kills them, acknowledged by Jacques to Sylvia in Letter XCII, the fault is symbolically traced not to adultery but to a deficient marriage. When Fernande, having long ceased sexual relations with Jacques, becomes pregnant by Octave, the latter assures her: 'the children of love never die; God endows them with more promise and more vigour than those of marriage' (XCII.373). It is this phrase which catches Jacques's eye when he comes accidentally upon Octave's letter, and which he takes as his death warrant (XCIV.383–5).

Jacques cannot be said either to recommend or to discourage adultery. As with much of Sand's work, the novel's main effect is to examine what constitutes healthy marriage; though it also, less explicitly, explores the relationship between kinship and choice of sexual partner. At the same time, in *Jacques*, as in many of her novels, Sand makes the experience of a male character central; and this has the effect of undermining from within the unequal relation between husband and wife established by law and custom. She shows what in her view is wrong with bourgeois marriage, not only through Jacques's direct criticism of the failings in it which he can recognize, but through his inability to acknowledge and rectify others which escape him.

In *Le Dernier amour*, written and published over 30 years later, Sand reworked several of the themes she had treated in *Jacques*. The novel begins from an after-dinner discussion, apparently limited to men, concerning how a betrayed husband should punish an adulterous wife. Later it recalls the earlier work directly, through a self-reflexive passage in which the narrator takes issue both with *Jacques* and with one of Sand's more recent novels, *Valvèdre* (1861). However, *Le Dernier amour* is distinctive in that it is the only work in Sand's huge output of fiction in which the theme of female adultery is central. She was keenly aware of writing on the topic in the wake not merely of her own earlier fiction, but of *Madame Bovary* and other examples of a form which was now fully established. Not only did she dedicate the novel to Flaubert, with whom she had recently begun a famous correspondence, but she followed with interest the progress of *L'Affaire Clémenceau* (1866), another novel of female adultery which a further friend, Alexandre Dumas the younger, was writing at almost exactly the same time. Like Dumas's novel, *Le Dernier amour* differs from the novel of female adultery in its classic form in that the betrayed husband is not only the main character in the story but also its narrator.

Among the various problems of interpretation presented by *Le Dernier amour*, Sand's choice of narrator is the most obvious. In itself, personal narrative offers a range of interpretive possibilities. At one extreme, almost everything the narrator says may be open to question, including even what he or she reports to have happened; at the other, the text may encourage the reader both to accept the narrative as a true record of events and to endorse the judgements and values the narrator expresses. In *Le Dernier amour* the problem is further complicated by the fact that Sand committed the telling of the story to the betrayed husband. Given the superior power of the husband in nineteenth-century marriage, there could be no more interested role in a novel of female adultery.

Le Dernier amour contains no evidence that its central character, Sylvestre, is unreliable in the sense of having consciously distorted the record; a much more difficult question is how far the views he presents invite agreement. One item of evidence from outside the text is that Sylvestre is the eponymous philosopher and moralist of Sand's previous novel, *Monsieur Sylvestre* (1866). As Isabelle Hoog Naginski has shown, such a figure often occurs in Sand's work, and Sylvestre is certainly the mouthpiece in both novels for some of her thinking about religion and ethics.[17] However, Sylvestre plays the role of philosopher only after two disastrous marriages, and there is no need to assume that, whatever Sand's didactic intentions, he is beyond criticism as a fictional character. Indeed, in *Mauprat* (1837), as in several other works, Sand had already used a male narrator to subvert masculinist assumptions from within – rather as she had used the eponymous main character of *Jacques*. *Le Dernier amour* also distances the reader to some extent from Sylvestre by means of a kind of prologue in which he is introduced by an anonymous narrator who has no further function. But the novel's implications are best assessed by comparing Sylvestre's judgements as narrator with the circumstances the novel provides for him.

Sylvestre begins his story by telling how he embarked on a new life at the age of nearly 50. His first wife, who had almost ruined him by extravagance, has died; and he has settled his remaining money on his only child, a daughter who has fallen into disgrace, in an attempt to save her from further sexual temptation. After finding work in the Alps, Sylvestre is welcomed into the family of his employer, Jean Morgeron, for his practical and business skills. Jean encourages Sylvestre to marry his sister Félicité, whom he has supported despite her rejection by all around her after she had been seduced and abandoned at the age of 15. Félicité is in love with Sylvestre and is eager to marry him, but she has to deal with the jealousy of her cousin Tonino, eight or nine years younger than herself, who loves her and who has already exacted from her a promise never to marry. After Jean's death from the bite of a rabid dog, Tonino agrees to the marriage. Tonino then also takes a spouse, in part at least out of pique; not long afterwards, he begins an affair with Félicité. Sylvestre suspects nothing, but after a further year he is alerted by Sixte More, Félicité's jealous former suitor. The novel then confronts the question which Sylvestre's story is designed to illuminate: how should a betrayed husband punish his adulterous wife?

The parallel with *Jacques* is not as close as may appear initially. First, Jacques neither has any wish nor feels any need to punish Fernande. She cannot help falling for Octave, and she never treats either Jacques or her marriage lightly, whereas Félicité deceives Sylvestre both before and after she marries him. Second, Fernande and Octave have the prospect of a happy life together, provided that Jacques disappears; while the relationship between Félicité and Tonino can have no future, not only because Tonino is also married, but because he has tired of her. The fact that both lovers in *Le Dernier amour* are married is a further unusual feature in a novel of female adultery; but more unusual still is a third difference from *Jacques*. Whereas Fernande is a virgin when she marries Jacques, shortly after leaving her convent, Félicité is a fallen woman who has borne an illegitimate child. This motif of an adolescent female's seduction by an older man appears not only in *Valentine* but in other fiction by Sand, including *Rose et Blanche*, the novel she wrote with Jules Sandeau before she established herself as a writer.[18] It is also significant that Musset, in *Confession of a Child of the Century*, gives a similar experience to Brigitte, the character based on Sand. Whatever the biographical or other importance of the motif, Félicité's early seduction plays a critical role in *Le Dernier amour*.

The key question is the relationship between Félicité's seduction and her later adultery. According to received opinion in the period, a woman, however young, was usually more to blame for sexual activity than the man, and a woman who had succumbed once would be likely to succumb again. One possible interpretation is, then, that Félicité's seduction indicates a sensual predisposition on her part which she has already failed to restrain. Sylvestre voices such a view when he infers that she has allowed Tonino to conceive the hope of marrying her: what he calls 'her first transgression' suddenly seems to him 'an actual sullying, a precocious self-abandonment, a wholly animal enticement which modesty and pride had perhaps not even thought of overcoming' (131).[19] This is also in keeping with the Italian birth which Félicité shares in part with her cousin, as he reminds her in one of his letters. For Sand has Tonino link Italian blood with passion (201), and indeed Félicité speaks to Sylvestre in Italian when, near the end of the novel, she reproaches him for his lack of passionate feeling (292). But an alternative interpretation of the seduction is possible. Sylvestre has already remarked that seduction may sometimes be considered as a misfortune rather than as a transgression (58). The novel lends support for this view in that, through no fault of her own, Félicité had been effectively abandoned by her family and, at the age of 15, had been living alone, unprotected, and shunned by her neighbours when she met the man who was to seduce her (61).

If Sand's choice of narrator offers no way of resolving the questions raised by Félicité's sexual past, the novel leaves no doubt that its effect is permanent harm to the way in which she is seen both by others and by herself. Sylvestre declares that 'the violent emotions of her youth had left her the habit of dramatizing the least incident and of seeing a gaping abyss in all the ruts of life's prosaic path' (178). She herself says: 'It seems to me that I will always find hanging over my miserable head this contempt which must kill me' (169); and she accuses him of trying to convince people that he is not marrying a fallen woman for money (174). Indeed, so degraded is she in her own opinion that, after the marriage, she tells him how often she has been on the verge of saying: 'Love me and don't marry me! I will be your mistress and your slave; I do not feel myself worthy to be your wife' (179). Although in her marriage she is able for a while to forget her unhappiness, it is brought back only too easily, and she carries her past, in Sylvestre's words, like a brand on a convict's shoulder (220). She has, besides, a painful reminder in her inability to conceive again after the daughter born from her seduction, who died as a baby.

The novel leaves open a further possibility: that Félicité was not predisposed to unchastity, but sexualized by her carnal exploitation as an adolescent. When Sylvestre discovers her affair with Tonino, he intercepts a letter in which she tells her cousin: 'There were so many years when the fire was brooding under the ashes and I was thirsty for the pleasures you have given me!' (231). Here Félicité refers to the long period during which, following her premature sexual awakening, she had to repress her desires and consider herself unmarriageable. Though she adds that she 'did not know' these desires, her metaphors of suppressed appetite indicate otherwise. She goes on to suggest that Sylvestre has failed to satisfy her erotically; nevertheless, the affair with Tonino begins only after he has raped her (236). It is therefore possible that the rape re-enacts not only her seduction as an adolescent but its sexual consequences; for, after Sylvestre has put an end to the affair with Tonino, but has failed to resume sexual relations with his wife, Félicité has a brief adulterous episode with her former suitor. Unfortunately, Sand gives Félicité no chance to cast further light on her predicament.

Again, then, interpretation is vexed by Sand's choice of narrator. Although Félicité's perspective is represented in the narrative by letters and by her role in dialogue, it is always hedged about by Sylvestre's comments. The line he takes is austere. He not only deplores flirtation, and insists on absolute fidelity in marriage, but he deeply distrusts sensuality. When he tells how he first fell in love with Félicité, he remarks that at his age 'it is impossible not to distinguish in oneself the allurement of the senses from that of the heart' (95). He goes on to call the love he had experienced in his first marriage 'that fullness of instincts in which youth does not distinguish pleasure from happiness', and to reject it as impure (98). Sylvestre's moral code is so rigid that he is outraged when Tonino tells him he has long known of his cousin's seduction.

Tonino rejoins that the matter was public knowledge, and that Sylvestre's view that he should have kept silent on the subject, even to himself, is the response of 'an aristocrat and a philosopher' (163). But Sylvestre is inflexible. It is therefore not surprising that he should judge Félicité harshly when he reads the letters which have passed between Tonino and herself before her marriage, even though he concedes that they give no evidence that he has been wronged, and that she has sought to protect him from Tonino's jealousy. Pointing out that one of Félicité's letters clearly admits the possibility of yielding to Tonino's passion, he remarks: 'It is not in this way that a woman of courage and integrity makes herself respected' (204). Later, when there is no longer any doubt of their adultery, he blames Félicité more than Tonino. This is because she had been responsible for him since he was nine years old, and because, as he puts it, Tonino 'had obeyed the instinct of the male, the maddening curiosity of puberty, the first explosion of the senses which Félicité had suffered already to her cost and the danger of which she well knew' (252).

Despite the important differences between *Le Dernier amour* and *Jacques*, the magisterial tenor of Sylvestre's judgements points to an important parallel. Both Jacques and Sylvestre are 18 years older than the women they marry, and each plays a superior and even a patronizing role in his marriage. Both use the formal *vous* in addressing their wives, Jacques generally and Sylvestre invariably, while Fernande and Félicité use the intimate *tu* with their lovers. Sylvestre becomes Félicité's teacher, and she describes him more than once as a God not only to herself but to Tonino. Once the two have put themselves in the wrong, he has the fullest opportunity to play that role. But he does not forgive and withdraw, like Jacques; instead, he responds with what he calls 'the disdain of a just man' (251). Confronting neither of them with their crime, and explaining to neither the real reason for his actions, he sends Tonino away with the money he needs to establish himself and his family, and he treats Félicité gently when she breaks down in grief and remorse. Yet there are limits to Sylvestre's charity, if that is what it is. Citing the story of the woman taken in adultery, he observes that, although he can see Jesus telling those without sin to cast the first stone, he cannot see him taking the adulterous wife to the bed of the offended husband (275). In the discussion which begins the novel, he has styled his way of treating an adulterous wife as 'friendship' (28); friendly or not, it proves fatal. In the letter Félicité writes to Tonino before taking an overdose of laudanum, she asks: 'Can a woman forgive the most deadly of offences, indifference?', and she expresses the hope that, once she is dead, Sylvestre will think of her as purified by the punishment which he did not wish to give and which she has inflicted on herself (303).

In common with other novels of the period by Sand, *Le Dernier amour* was first published in the *Revue des Deux Mondes* as a serial. Soon after she began writing the novel, Sand told François Buloz, the editor: 'it is the portrayal of *adultery* which I am working on, the punishment of which has not yet been found, and which is as easy as saying hello. All the same it has taken me 25 years to think of it.'[20] This suggests that, at least while planning the novel, she meant to endorse Sylvestre's treatment of his unfaithful wife. The remark is in the same spirit as her comments on *Madame Bovary* ten years later in a letter to Flaubert:

> Although a section of the public made an outcry, the larger and saner part of it saw in the book a severe and striking judgment on a woman faithless and without conscience; a rebuke to vanity, ambition and folly. They pitied the woman, as art saw to it that they should, but the lesson was plain.[21]

But Sand was a far better writer of fiction than of literary criticism or moral doctrine, and the views she asserted at an abstract level are often belied by her imaginative representation of human behaviour. So, in *Le Dernier amour*, Sylvestre's didactic commentary is traversed and challenged by the twin strands of Félicité's story: her seduction and its ruinous impact on her life, and her strange, quasi-incestuous relationship with Tonino. As will already be clear, seduction and incest are recurrent themes in Sand's work; they constitute part of her distinctive contribution to the fiction of love and betrayal. What is special to *Le Dernier amour* is the novel's embedded account of a struggle between a male grown to maturity and the dishonoured cousin who has played the role of his mother, but who cannot finally prevent him from dominating her sexually and personally. Although Sylvestre claims that he treated Félicité according to Christian morality, the novel allows a less favourable view, both through its outcome and through the sexual politics implicit in its key relationships. It is even possible to suggest that *Le Dernier amour*, with its story of a man's emancipation from a woman, told by a male narrator to a group of men, is Sand's version, or parody, of the Romantic confession. This would not have been beyond a novelist who subversively rewrote *Manon Lescaut* in *Leone Leoni*, produced a female Byronic figure in *Lélia*, and who, in *Jacques*, glanced not only at Goethe's *Elective Affinities* but, through the novel's epistolary form and the resolution of its action, at Rousseau's *Julie, or the New Eloise* (1761).

Sand wrote *Le Dernier amour* during a period of moral reaction, when Proudhon, Michelet and others had produced influential misogynist works, and when even Louise Colet, Flaubert's former lover, had renounced the sexual libertarianism she had long maintained.[22] Sand was well aware of a corresponding change of policy in the *Revue des Deux Mondes*, for she records having told Buloz that she feared her novel might be 'too *frank* for the review which every day is becoming more prudish'.[23] Nevertheless, her correspondence with Dumas the younger shows that she had other ideas which she felt unable to express or, perhaps, to get published concerning the question of adultery. Commenting on *L'Affaire Clémenceau*, the parallel novel which Dumas had just finished, she suggested that the two should produce a 'pendant' in which the sexes would be reversed. She went on to sketch the betrayed wife's predicament:

> Here is a pure woman, charming, naive, with all the qualities and the appeal of a female Clémenceau. Her husband is physically in love with her, but he has to have mistresses; it is habitual with him and he degrades her by his behaviour. What can she do? She cannot kill him. She is gripped by disgust for him, his *returnings* to her turn her stomach. If she wants to deny herself to him, she does not have the right. – Ah, what will she do? She cannot take vengeance, she cannot even keep herself secure, since he can rape her and no one will stand in his way. She cannot run away; if she has children she cannot abandon them. Go to law? she will not win if the husband's adultery has not been committed in the home; she cannot kill herself, if she has a mother's heart.[24]

Sand adds that the subject 'is not new, but no one has ever treated it frankly'. She did not, unfortunately, feel equal to it herself. Dumas, whose novel was written to justify the hero's murder of his adulterous wife, offered scant sympathy for Sand's point of view. He suggested that a woman in the circumstances she outlined would inevitably take a lover, and he took his stand on the two articles of the Civil Code which prohibited inquiry into paternity and dissolution of marriage.[25] Such was the climate of opinion in which Sand wrote.

Sand was almost certainly correct in her statement that no one had treated adultery frankly from the viewpoint of the betrayed wife. Indeed, it is doubtful whether a novel based on such a plight would have found a publisher at the period. However, several other novelists offered alternatives to the dominant fictional construction of adultery during the period in which she worked. Two of these were women whom she knew: her former friend, Marie d'Agoult, and the pioneering socialist feminist, Flora Tristan.

Marie d'Agoult, who followed Sand in writing under a male pseudonym, Daniel Stern, published the short novel *Valentia* in 1847. This is notable in shifting the focus from female adultery to male sexual licence. The story is told by its high-born heroine, who is married for reasons of wealth and caste to a debauched aristocrat much older than herself. Worn down by his sexual demands, she goes on her doctor's advice to the Alps, where she begins a love affair with a man introduced to her as her husband's nephew. However, two obstacles prevent her fulfilment. First, in some ways like Sand's *Indiana*, she finds that her lover lacks her own commitment and courage. Second, and decisively, she discovers that her lover is her husband's illegitimate son. Unable to defeat the double taboo of adultery and incest, she commits suicide. As Leslie Rabine has pointed out, it is significant that the threatened incest is nominal, not rooted in consanguinity: 'In this story even the incest that the heroine must renounce is a false incest, determined by the social institutions and the paternal power of her husband, who always has God on his side.'[26] Rabine also calls attention to the scene in which, implicitly, Valentia's husband drugs her before taking her virginity on her bridal night.

In *Méphis* (1838), Flora Tristan presents an even more startling perspective on marriage and adultery. The keynote is, again, male exploitation of women, but Tristan takes this much further than Sand or Stern. Her main female character, Maréquita, is tricked into marrying Hazcal, who wishes to use his position as her husband to prostitute her. Hazcal's ruse is to convince her that she can save the life of the man she loves, Don Olivera, only by giving her virginity to an elderly duke. This leads to her abuse not merely by the duke, to whom she bears a child the duke takes as his own, but to rejection and attempted rape by Don Olivera, who rounds on her in humiliation. Not for nothing does Maréquita remark that woman 'is considered by man as solely intended for his pleasure and for reproduction';[27] though even these purposes scarcely exhaust those of Hazcal and Don Olivera.

Tristan pursues her critique of relations between men and women not only through Maréquita's story but also through that of her title character, Méphis. She reinforces the critique by parallels between the two stories and, even more, by contrasts determined by gender. For instance, in an episode partly analogous to that between Maréquita and the duke, Méphis impregnates a duchess who is in an arranged marriage with his employer, a much older man. While she dies in childbirth, Méphis escapes the consequences, the duke claiming the child as his. Another arranged marriage results from Méphis's betrayal by his beloved Clothilde and his foster-brother who has had him ostracized from polite society. The twist comes when Clothilde takes revenge on her husband by prostituting herself, especially when Méphis uses her role as a prostitute to exact his own sexual revenge. His experience in connection with arranged marriages does not prevent him from entering one himself. But, ironically, he finds that prostitution can work both ways, as his wife expects satisfaction from her handsome young husband in return for her wealth. As Sandra Dijkstra has observed, the marriages both of Méphis and Maréquita 'indicate the extent to which Tristan connected legitimate marriage with prostitution, and recognized the plight of the economically dependent person in any exchange'.[28] Yet the novel's originality consists much more in its repeated demonstration of the exploitative potential in any sexual relationship. It is because she recognizes that danger that Maréquita resolves to kill Méphis and herself once their adulterous passion is consummated; although, in the event, he is murdered by his social and political enemies and she dies of grief.

Méphis cannot be classed as a novel of adultery, let alone as a novel of female adultery. It is at least as much concerned with such further questions as social class, the power of institutionalized religion, and the role of art; and, even in the sphere of love and marriage, Tristan's emphases are very different from those which dominate the novel of female adultery. *Méphis* not only focuses more on male than on female adultery, but dramatizes a range of sexual abuses inside and outside marriage, most of them involving the victimization of women. It is not surprising that so radical an outlook was unwelcome, and *Méphis* has still never been reprinted. This neglect, along with that of *Valentia*, and to a lesser extent the work of George Sand, is a striking illustration of how powerfully the social and literary establishment has worked to exclude writing which has challenged dominant perspectives and values.

The connections between ideology and literary form are complex, but it is not a coincidence that each of these writers wrote within fictional conventions which were consigned to the margins when the realist tradition gained ascendancy. Leslie Rabine has pointed out the role of Romantic narrative conventions in *Valentia*, and still more, with its melodramatic plot, in *Méphis*; and Naomi Schor has called attention to the forgotten tradition of idealist fiction in which Sand was the leading figure.[29] Another work long slighted by bias in favour of realist conventions is Baudelaire's *La Fanfarlo* (1847).[30] This offers still another way of presenting adultery in fiction, and it could hardly be more different.

La Fanfarlo is remarkable for inverting most of the stereotypes of the novel of female adultery before the form had even become fully established. The action centres on a young man's failure to seduce an unhappily married woman, and his entrance into inglorious concubinage instead with a dancer. More surprisingly still, it begins from male rather than female adultery, and, thanks to the wife's intelligence and goodwill, it ends in her husband's reclamation. Madame de Cosmelly is a woman from the provinces who proves more than a match both for husband and would-be lover. When Samuel Cramer approaches her, she leads him on, but only in order to encourage him to court the dancer La Fanfarlo, her husband's mistress. Her plan succeeds so well that Samuel has almost forgotten the purpose of his new liaison by the time that, reunited with her husband, Madame de Cosmelly thanks him for his help and politely withdraws the amorous reward she had ventured.

Baudelaire's anti-novella, as Barbara Wright has called it,[31] looks back most obviously to Balzac, but also to Gautier, Mérimée and even perhaps to Constant;[32] yet at the same time, in its cult of art and sensation, its irony and iconoclasm, it anticipates Huysmans. Its irreverent wit sets it apart from the dominant tradition of realist fiction, especially from the novel of female adultery. But Baudelaire chose not to repeat the experiment. Instead he turned for his later main ventures into narrative to a still more subversive form, that of the poem in prose.[33] While *La Fanfarlo* does not present a radical view of love, marriage or prostitution, it questions some of the ruling fictional verities of its period through brilliant pastiche.

One of the narrative forms which gained fullest acceptance in nineteenth-century France, and which has long been established in the French literary canon, is described in this way by Leslie Rabine:

> The dominant masculine voice of traditional romantic narrative imposes a totalizing structure on romantic narrative and represses an independent feminine other. Reducing the heroine to a reflection of himself, the hero makes of her an 'intermediary,' as Simone de Beauvoir says, through whom he can realize his desire to return to a mythical union with himself. While by no means all nineteenth-century French novels are based on this structure, it is noteworthy that most of the prominent novelists wrote one such novel and that none of them wrote more than one.[34]

Rabine cites as examples Chateaubriand's *René*, Constant's *Adolphe*, Stendhal's *The Red and the Black* (1830), Sainte-Beuve's *Volupté* (1834), Balzac's *The Lily of the Valley* (1836), Dumas's *La Dame aux camélias* (1848), Nerval's *Sylvie* (1853), and Flaubert's deconstruction of the genre, *Sentimental Education* (1869). Although none of these texts is a novel of female adultery, all cast light on the form in various ways. In Chapter 2, I have shown how this type of fiction is anticipated by *René* and *Adolphe*, among other narratives. The present chapter, which addresses alternative constructions of the problems of marriage and adultery, ends by discussing two texts which complemented the novel of female adultery as it developed. Unlike the other works discussed in the chapter so far, these are firmly established in the French literary canon. The first is Balzac's *The Lily of the Valley*; the second is a novel of a similar kind, not mentioned by Rabine, Eugène Fromentin's *Dominique* (1863).

What distinguishes these two narratives from others of the same broad type is that they represent not only the temptation, or the threat, of female adultery, but its successful repression. Rabine traces a related theme to Prévost's *Manon Lescaut*:

> As bourgeois men reject their immediate passions, women even more than before are portrayed in literature as embodiments of those destructive passions that must be repressed, or buried.

Manon then is the first of a long series of romantic heroines who die, like Chateaubriand's Amélie in *René*, Constant's Ellénore in *Adolphe*, Dumas's *La Dame aux camélias*, Balzac's Mme. de Mortsauf in *The Lily in the Valley*.[35]

But Balzac's novel differs from the other examples cited here in that, like Fromentin's *Dominique*, it hinges on repression of a passion which is specifically adulterous. That repression is performed by the married woman involved with the hero as well as, centrally, by the hero himself. In this way the two texts parallel but never join the novel of female adultery.

The Lily of the Valley and *Dominique* are further examples of the Romantic confession, and, following the traditions of the genre, both are narrated by men. Balzac's narrator, Félix de Vandenesse, writes his past life to his married lover, Natalie de Manerville, at her request; more conventionally, Fromentin's narrator, Dominique de Bray, relates his story to an unnamed male figure who delivers it to the reader. Both novels present a sentimental education, but their emphases are quite dissimilar. The contrasts are rooted in the nature of the two focal relationships, and in the very different social and political orders in which the novels are set: the generation before and after the 1830 Revolution respectively.

Félix de Vandenesse gains his education from a surrogate mother, Madame de Mortsauf, the lily of the novel's title. He meets her in 1814 when he is a very young 21. She is 28 and she has been married since the age of 18 to a cantankerous former émigré, 17 years her senior. Félix has always been treated coldly by his family, thanks to his mother's example. Madame de Mortsauf gives him the mother-love he has never had. She also gives him not only a sentimental but a social and a political education, especially through the long letter she writes him when he leaves to pursue his career in Paris. Having taken her teaching to heart, and having established himself in the king's service, he declares: 'and so I owed everything to her: power and wealth, happiness and knowledge' (167, TM; 1108).[36]

However, Madame de Mortsauf is not only a mother to Félix. Not least, she is devoted to her children, both of whom are sickly thanks, implicitly, to their father's syphilis. But while, in *A Woman of Thirty*, discussed above in Chapter 3, Julie d'Aiglemont is punished for her adultery through her offspring, the husband's past sexual licence goes unpunished in *The Lily of the Valley*. Instead

Balzac reinforces the orthodox role of wife and mother by presenting Madame de Mortsauf's ailing children as perpetual reminders of her duty. What is even more remarkable is that she does not reject her husband, although their relationship is no longer sexual, but acts as a mother to him too. The motive for her dedication is the suffering he has experienced as a result of the Revolution – as so often in Balzac, the original sin from which the narrative issues. She tells Félix that, after the Revolution, it was the duty of women 'to heal the bruises of the time, to comfort those who had stood in the breach and come back wounded' (80; 1035). This not only highlights the mother's role as nurse and as fount of compassion, but condones male sexual promiscuity, at least in wartime, by equating syphilis with a war wound.[37]

A further explanation for Madame de Mortsauf's care for her family is the importance of succession to an aristocratic family threatened with extinction by the Revolution. The Mortsauf son is required to survive so that he may inherit the title; while Madame de Mortsauf, denying her own love for Félix, intends him for her daughter. In the analysis the novel suggests, these dynastic ambitions go hand in hand with the need to reinforce the social and political structures of the newly restored monarchy.

But Madame de Mortsauf's relation to Félix also goes beyond that of a surrogate mother. The lovers identify further because she too has suffered maternal oppression. If this makes them 'twins of the same womb', as Félix expresses it (74, TM; 1029), it also leaves Madame de Mortsauf in need of motherly love. She had married to live with her aunt, who, Félix says, 'was a second mother' for her (51; 1010); and she asks him to love her as her aunt had done (88; 1041). Therefore their love is not only potentially adulterous, but quasi-incestuous, both at the level of siblings and, because each figures as mother to the other, doubly at the level of parenthood. The expression 'fraternal marriage' which Balzac has Félix apply to his relationship with Madame de Mortsauf is bizarre but apt (96, TM; 1048). His novel certainly outdoes, with characteristic extravagance, the tradition established by Chateaubriand. But in several respects it goes further still.

It is, in particular, much more explicit about the sexual side of the relationship. While Félix and Madame de Mortsauf treat each other variously as mother, child and sibling, both are keenly aware of desiring the other sexually. However, although Félix leaves Madame de Mortsauf in no doubt about his feelings for her, it is not until she is dying that she confesses the strength of her desire for him. So direct an expression of a woman's sexual feelings was found scandalous when the novel was first published, especially before Balzac toned down Madame de Mortsauf's deathbed speech in deference to the dying wishes of his own former lover Laure de Berny.[38] Those who still found the confession shocking probably reacted not only to the expression of such feelings, but to the barely restrained regret that Félix had never taken the sexual initiative. For instance, in the letter he receives after her death Madame de Mortsauf exclaims: 'Oh! if in those moments when I was colder to you than ever, you had taken me in your arms, I should have died of happiness. Sometimes I have longed that you might be over bold – but prayer soon drove out that evil thought' (296; 1216). Though neither gives way to passion, the novel does not discourage the response that the cost of repression may exceed its value. In his Freudian interpretation, Peter Brooks goes so far as to suggest: 'The whole novel indeed reads as a deconstruction of virtue, virtue understood as renunciation in exaltation of the ego.'[39]

However, Félix realizes that, since Madame de Mortsauf's heart is, in her own phrase, 'drunk, so to speak, with motherhood' (80; 1034), she cannot give him undivided love:

> I was the object to which her thoughts, her unavowed sensations, had fastened themselves, as a swarm of bees clings to some branch of a tree in blossom; but I was not the essence – I was an accident in her life, I was not her life itself. A king unthroned, I walked on, wondering who should restore my kingdom to me. In my crazy jealousy I blamed myself for never having dared anything, for not having tightened the bonds of an affection which now seemed to me more subtle than sincere by the chains of absolute right created by possession. (188–9, TM; 1126)

This passage is conspicuous for the assumption that a man who has sex with a woman gains the right to own her, and for the related image of a dethroned king. It points to the system of patriarchy endorsed by the novel, in which the husband stands in the same relation to his wife as the king to his subjects, and in which the successful lover may overthrow him, or be in turn overthrown. Such imagery is especially resonant in the context of the Restoration. But the rule of men ensures that it is the woman who will be betrayed. The novel creates a double bind for Madame de

Mortsauf in that Félix cannot tolerate a rival in her love, whereas what distinguishes maternal love is that it is not necessarily limited to a single object. Given Balzac's tolerance for male sexual adventure, this renders it inevitable that Félix will be unfaithful.

Balzac further turns the ideological screw on women through his presentation of his hero's two mistresses. Framing Félix's narrative is his affair with Natalie de Manerville, for whom, long after the events, he writes it; enclosed within it is his affair with Lady Arabella Dudley, which seals Madame de Mortsauf's death. Balzac draws the contrasts starkly. The role of the mother in *The Lily of the Valley* is underpinned by Catholicism, especially by the values and imagery attached to the Virgin Mary.[40] If, then, Madame de Mortsauf is a type of the Virgin Mother, Lady Arabella is a kind of unrepentant Magdalene. The oppositions are familiar, and Balzac not only rehearses but extends them: body versus soul (213; 1146), earth versus heaven (239; 1168), Protestant versus Catholic (262; 1187), egoism versus self-sacrifice (261–2; 1186–7), and, of course, English versus French (260–3; 1186–7). Lady Arabella, it scarcely needs adding, neglects her children for her lovers. She seduces Félix out of jealousy, drops him from injured conceit, and ends by becoming his vengeful enemy. From the same point of view, Natalie de Manerville is little better. Although she occupies only the margins of *The Lily of the Valley*, the novel was written and published almost simultaneously with *The Marriage Contract* (1835), in which she betrays her doting husband. She treats Félix with no more mercy in the caustic letter which ends the novel, and in which she responds to the narrative she requested by dumping him.

The contrast between Madame de Mortsauf and Félix's two mistresses is especially interesting in light of the challenge Balzac had set himself in his Preface to the second edition of *Le Père Goriot*, the year before *The Lily of the Valley* was published. Responding to the charge that his portrayal of illicit love in his previous work had pandered to the seamier side of female taste, he undertook to present in a future novel 'a woman virtuous from preference'. Such a woman, he anticipated, must combine 'an imperious sensuality and a bad husband', or the motive for her virtue might be pleasure; and she should not be a mother, or her motive might be care for her children.[41] The novel he came to write completely belied the latter part of this prescription, because he clearly associated female love with maternal love, and because his idea of female virtue was closely bound up with his ideal of motherhood. Thus *The Lily of the*

Valley celebrates, in Madame de Mortsauf, an ideal of the mother, and criticizes, directly or by implication, women who betray that ideal: not only Lady Arabella Dudley and Natalie de Manerville, but the mother of Félix and of Madame de Mortsauf herself. Yet, at the same time, it not only implies more indulgence to sexual licence on the man's part than on that of his lovers, but has Madame de Mortsauf pay for her chastity with martyrdom.

The novel's treatment of the mother's sexual desire is still more interesting. Nancy K. Miller has suggested that, in having Madame de Mortsauf express such desire, 'Balzac attributes to his heroine the phallocratic discourse of an eighteenth-century roué'. This is in keeping with the enduring libertine element in his fiction, and it is that element which helps explain how the novel was able to interrogate, as Miller puts it, 'the ideology of representation that reposes upon the assumption that positive femininity (since Rousseau inseparable from the maternal function) and female sexual desire are incompatible in one and the same body'.[42] In this way Balzac has the cake of the novel of female adultery without, as it were, having to eat it. Indeed the novel's ending is thoroughly ambiguous. It celebrates Madame de Mortsauf as Virgin Mother, yet hesitates over the cost of her sexual renunciation; it allows Natalie's letter to be read not only as spiteful egotism but as sharp truth-telling; and, while administering the final lesson in the hero's sentimental education, it does not discourage the reader from identifying him as an ineffectual narcissist who fails all three of his lovers.

It is a measure of the distance between the period of the Empire and that of the July Monarchy that Fromentin's novel offers no such ambiguity. *Dominique* shares a similar narrative method with *The Lily of the Valley*, but it is much more emphatically a novel of adultery repressed. Written and set nearly 30 years apart, the two works are divided by a world of social, political and ideological differences. First, instead of dealing with the higher reaches of the nobility portrayed in *The Lily of the Valley*, *Dominique* turns to the provincial gentry. Second, while Balzac's aristocrats assert their position in the newly restored monarchy with some confidence, Fromentin's gentry beat a disillusioned or a prudent retreat. Third, whereas in *The Lily of the Valley* the hero's key relationships are with women, in *Dominique* they are predominantly with men.

Writing under the Empire, a generation on from his novel's action, Fromentin reflects a social order in which the monarchy is gone forever, sexual licence has been largely displaced to the *demi-monde*, middle and upper-class wives are for domesticity or social display, and bourgeois values reign.

The single most important difference between Fromentin's novel and Balzac's is that *Dominique* points to an unequivocal rejection of the illicit passion at its centre. The hero strikes the keynote himself at the end when he declares: 'I am atoning for a past that was undeniably harmful, and redeeming wrongs for which I still feel responsible' (XVIII.247; 311).[43] Such a judgement is built into the whole structure of the novel, which juxtaposes the lives of two other men with that of its narrator. Dominique has to accept that his love for the wife of another man can have no future, and takes a wife for himself to settle down on his provincial estate; while on the one side Olivier chooses the licence of a dandy but succumbs to emptiness and ennui; and on the other Augustin, Dominique's former tutor, struggles for and finds happiness in a public career anchored by marriage and a family. Indeed, the narrative is framed by an act on the part first of one and then of the other friend. Dominique is impelled to tell his story by Olivier's attempted suicide; and the unexpected arrival of Augustin – upright, successful and contented – marks its end. This shift between starting-point and finish plainly affirms the hero's ultimate choice to renounce passion and embrace husbandry.

Such a choice follows from the social and political changes I have indicated. It signifies a turning away not only from politics but from élite status. Dominique goes to Paris and becomes a minor celebrity on the strength of his political pamphlets and his poetry; realizing their mediocrity, he retires to the country, where he farms his land and serves as Mayor. It is significant that his estate is in the Vendée, long identified with counter-revolution and with royalism. Olivier, a kind of last gasp of aristocracy, expires through luxurious privilege. Scorning what he calls 'the commonplace and the boring', 'the two wretched little timid, stingy middle-class, custom-ridden demons' (XIV.205–6; 263), he wastes his life in search of what he cannot attain, unable to recognize that the social order in which he might have found himself is gone. Only Augustin succeeds, as a self-made man insulated from disillusion or disdain by the stigmas of poverty and illegitimacy. For all its nostalgia, the novel implies acceptance of the bourgeois values for which he stands. While

Balzac has Félix Vandenesse turn to the imagery of monarchy to define his position as a lover, Fromentin has Dominique adopt the language of finance. Separated from his beloved Madeleine, and trying to subdue his passion through activity, he describes himself metaphorically as 'accumulating capital, not spending it' (XVI.215; 274). Similarly, when he recalls appraising his personal situation, he tells how he drew up 'a straightforward balance-sheet of [his] knowledge', and completed it 'as methodically as the winding-up of a business' (XVI.219; 278). This is the discourse of the bourgeois system and ideology which were now established immovably.

It is that system which keeps Dominique and Madeleine apart. Almost of the same age, and not related, they would have made an eligible match had convention not favoured Madeleine's marriage to a wealthy older man before Dominique has even left school. This marriage is the only barrier between them, but it is unbreakable. When Dominique first gets to know of Madeleine's engagement, he remarks that her fiancé 'already symbolized the rule of reason, and soon he would be personifying the rule of right as well' (VII.100; 146). Neither he nor she ever questions this rule, though its basis is entirely secular and conventional. In contrast to *The Lily of the Valley*, religious belief plays no part at all in *Dominique*, either in the motivation of the characters or in any system of values which it implies or expresses. Instead, the novel suggests that the characters have internalized a secular code which is scarcely less rigid. This is vividly illustrated by the image Dominique presents of Madeleine as 'a statue kept upright by an iron rod, without which it would topple over' (XIII.187; 242).

The image of the statue is especially appropriate in that it highlights the decorative social role Madeleine is required to play. Dominique uses it more than once, and he later develops a fixation on her portrait which he happens upon in a gallery (XVI.222–3; 281–3). These representations are apt to a social order which keeps the bourgeois wife at a safe and an aesthetic distance. They also correspond to the effect of a narrative method which largely excludes Madeleine's perspective. She is given a fairly limited part even in dialogue, and, unlike Madame de Mortsauf, she is allowed no intimate letters and no confessions. Indeed, she becomes convinced of Dominique's love for her only some time after her marriage, and still further time goes by before she betrays the attraction she feels for him. Only at the point of parting forever, and on that condition, does she tell him that she loves him.

Although Madeleine's relationship with her husband is cool, and although she and Dominique share feelings of passion and affinity, the novel implies no criticism of marriage. The achievable ideal it suggests is the comfortable domesticity enjoyed by Augustin and accepted ultimately by Dominique. This ideal at least offers a means of preventing the loneliness and sterility which it strikingly features: the hero and his two male friends are orphans, Madeleine and her sister Julie have no mother, Olivier and Julie never marry, and Madeleine, in her loveless marriage, can have no children.

With its distinctive tone of nostalgic resignation, *Dominique* offers an account of adultery not so much repressed as sublimated. While the novel has much in common not only with *The Lily of the Valley* but with Sainte-Beuve's *Volupté*, of which Fromentin was especially fond, it reflects a later and a soberer generation. This is manifest in its conservative morality and in its idealization of a pastoral world which it associates with tradition and peace. *Dominique* was admired by Flaubert, who developed a similar story very differently in *Sentimental Education*; and by Sand, who suggested some revisions (not all of which Fromentin adopted), and to whom it was dedicated. Notwithstanding its hero's apparent ability to sublimate illicit passion, it is a deeply repressed text – not only in its representation of sexual relationships and female sexuality, but above all in its plangent acquiescence with bourgeois conventions of marriage and inheritance. Although it is not a novel of female adultery, it has much in common with the form, both in its use of realist narrative conventions and in the underlying assumptions it betrays.

The novel of female adultery would continue to flourish in France, where it had originated, in the work of Dumas and Maupassant among others. But, as the next three chapters will show, it was in other European countries that the form was to develop most fully.

6

What Is to Be Done? Chernyshevsky, Tolstoy, Chekhov

Paying tribute to George Sand on her death in 1876, Dostoyevsky recalled the impact of her work in Russia during the 1830s and 1840s when he was a young man. He reminded his readers that, at that time of rigid political censorship, fiction 'was all that was permitted; all the rest, including virtually every new idea, and those coming from France in particular, was strictly suppressed'. And he remarked on the irony that, whereas the works of writers such as Thiers and Rabaut were proscribed, new ideas were introduced through fiction 'perhaps by the standards of the day in an even more "dangerous" form, since there probably were not too many lovers of Rabaut, but there were thousands who loved George Sand'.[1]

Dostoyevsky rightly emphasized that Sand inspired progressive Russians not only through her feminism but her populism. Perhaps the most influential of her works, however, was *Jacques* – a novel concerned much more with problems of love and marriage than with more directly political questions. Richard Stites has called attention to no fewer than five Russian reworkings of Sand's story. The most important of these were Alexander Herzen's *Who Is to Blame?* (1847) and Nikolai Chernyshevsky's *What Is to Be Done?* (1863).[2] As Kathryn Feuer has indicated, Herzen took his title from that of the preface to *Jacques*,[3] although he also based his novel partly on Sand's *Horace* (1842). Chernyshevsky responded in turn to Herzen as well as to Sand, but his amendment to their title marks a critical change of direction. *What Is to Be Done?* raises questions not about fault but about the future. This future is one of hope and potential – in pointed contrast, as Joe Andrew has shown, to that assumed by Turgenev's *On the Eve* (1859), in which the heroine famously asks 'What is there to do in Russia?' and seeks her fulfilment abroad and through a man.[4] Rejecting Turgenev's liberal quietism, Chernyshevsky offers a blueprint for female emancipation as a key element in a general vision of human freedom and equality.

Although *What Is to Be Done?* is not a novel of adultery, it is significant to the fiction of adultery in several ways. First, it presents relations between men and women in a context of personal, social and political liberation; second, it calls in question the assumptions which construct female adultery as a leading social and moral issue; third, by doing so, it helped to provoke a powerful defence of traditional marital and other social values, notably from Tolstoy in *Anna Karenina*. Chernyshevsky adapted the plot he took from Sand and from Herzen as radically as he adapted their title. He centred his novel not on a male but on a female character, Vera Pavlovna; and he had Vera's first husband, Dmitri Lopukhov, effect a less drastic solution than Jacques to the problem of an unfulfilling marriage through a simulated rather than an actual suicide. This allows Vera to remarry, while Lopukhov emigrates under a different identity. He subsequently returns to marry again himself, and to live with his second wife in close and harmonious association with Vera and her second husband. Chernyshevsky offers to solve the problems caused by an unrewarding marriage, and by illicit sexual desire, through enlightened acknowledgement and negotiation on the part of each person involved. Adultery as an issue disappears because they take seriously each other's right to happiness and equality, because they are unconcerned with property, and because, ignoring the bigamous nature of the new marriages, they honour personal choice and commitment over legal bonds.

The changes introduced by Chernyshevsky in reworking *Jacques* go further still. In both novels, a young woman is rescued through marriage to an older and more experienced man from her mother's exploitation; but, despite his good intentions, the marriage fails to allow her enough scope to change and grow. However, where Sand demonizes Fernande's oppressive mother, Chernyshevsky defends Vera Pavlovna's because, in conditions of grinding poverty, her callous, rapacious tyranny has created the chance of a better life. At the same time, Chernyshevsky recognizes more explicitly than Sand that the marriage based on inequality leaves needs unsatisfied in the husband as well as in the wife. Understanding those needs enables Lopukhov to begin life again and find a new partner himself. Unlike Fernande's lover, Octave, the man Vera Pavlovna comes to love and to marry, Alexander Kirsanov, is her husband's close friend and his equal in age and abilities. Lopukhov never resents the intimacy which grows up between his wife and his friend, who behaves impeccably throughout. While Sand emphasizes heavily the unfruitfulness of the flawed marriage through the congenital and fatal illness of the children borne by Fernande to Jacques, Chernyshevsky merely leaves Vera Pavlovna and Lopukhov childless (indeed, it is not even clear whether the marriage is ever consummated), though in their second marriages each has a son.

If *Jacques* shows what is wrong with marriage in a bourgeois, patriarchal society, *What Is to Be Done?* proposes socialist solutions. Part of the solution consists in refusing to treat people as property. Vera Pavlovna, saved by Lopukhov from being sold into marriage by her mother, feels she owes him too much to turn away from him, even though her development takes her in a different direction. She must therefore be redeemed again, through his faked suicide, so that she can marry Kirsanov. The principle at stake is defined by the novel's hero, Rakhmetov, who remarks that jealousy 'shouldn't exist in a developed person', for it is 'the result of regarding a person as my own property, as an inanimate object' (III.xxx.305).[5] Instead each person has a right to freedom and self-determination. Lopukhov tells Vera Pavlovna 'there's no happiness without freedom' (III.xxvii.270); and Kirsanov, treating the patient who will become Lopukhov's second wife, puts it even more strongly: 'Freedom comes before everything, even life itself' (V.iii.391). But for Chernyshevsky personal fulfilment, though vital, is not in itself enough. Another part of the solution accordingly consists in socially useful work. Shortly after her marriage to Lopukhov, Vera Pavlovna starts a sewing co-operative which prospers and encourages others to follow her example; later, she embarks on training to become a doctor. In the same way, as Michael R. Katz and William G. Wagner have pointed out, while Jacques is advised unsuccessfully by Sylvia to begin a new life, perhaps in the New World, this is what Lopukhov actually does.[6]

Given that *What Is to Be Done?* looks forward to a utopian, post-revolutionary future, it may appear paradoxical that it should focus so closely on personal relationships. One reason is negative and practical: Chernyshevsky wrote the novel while awaiting trial on charges, largely trumped-up, of political subversion; and, even as it stands, it was only through accident and official obtuseness that it was published at all.[7] It was owing to his need to handle political themes discreetly that he gave his declared hero, Rakhmetov, an almost ostentatiously minimal role in the action. But there were also two positive motives for the particular focus he chose. First, he believed that love was crucial to the development of the person and her or his abilities. Second, he linked personal with social development. As Katz and Wagner have observed,

> In his view, the relationship of mutual dependence between the autocracy and privileged social groups precluded meaningful state action until a social revolution had restructured political power. Chernyshevsky believed, moreover, that if this revolution was to succeed, it would need to overturn the patriarchal relations that existed within the family as well as between social groups and between the state and society.[8]

What Is to Be Done? therefore offers to undo, from within, the patriarchal structures which thwarted progress, presenting a new model for the role of women in the family, in marriage and in employment. In keeping with this radical outlook, Chernyshevsky broke with realist fictional conventions. He introduced a narrator who addressed his readers directly, often to call stock assumptions and novelistic devices in question; he used coded language where he could not express himself explicitly; and, in Vera Pavlovna's four dreams, he outflanked the dominant fictional conventions of the period to give access both to the unconscious and to a utopian vision of the future.[9] It is in these respects, too, that the novel marks out a quite different path from that of the fiction of adultery.

Chernyshevsky's insistence on the importance of not treating people as property carries a special resonance in the wake of the emancipation of the serfs in 1861. As Evgeny Lampert has remarked, 'the question of the liberation of woman was [. . .] treated almost on a par with that of the liberation of the peasants'.[10] But this relationship was not one of cause and effect. Although Barbara Alpern Engel claims that, 'once the power of master over serf had been called into question, it was almost inevitable that progressive thinkers would be moved to examine other authority relations, including those between parents and children and men and women',[11] it is clear that Chernyshevsky saw these relations not only as complementary but as interlinked. Indeed, the emancipation of the serfs had a rapid and a material impact on the lives of many women from the aristocracy and gentry. According to Richard Stites,

> Many old 'gentry nests' that had sheltered large families with extended kinship groups, unmarried females, and retainers were no longer economically viable. For the women in such families, this meant a major change in life-style. Wives replaced their husbands as breadwinners. Daughters, no longer assured of support up to their wedding day, sought work both as relief for their hard-pressed parents and as the means to their own independence. Women who possessed no visions of marriage came to realize that the old dependent way of spinster life was quickly disappearing.[12]

This was the social reality for many of the gentry in the period leading up to Tolstoy's writing of *Anna Karenina*. Tolstoy, however, connected the position of women and the relationship between landowners and peasants very differently.

Unlike other European countries in the nineteenth century, Russia did not undergo a bourgeois revolution. It is therefore especially significant that *Anna Karenina* is the only classic instance of a novel of female adultery in Russian fiction of the period. Neither Turgenev nor Dostoyevsky, Tolstoy's great contemporaries, wrote a novel of female adultery, and the theme of adultery figures little in their work. It is not that other writers avoided the topic; rather that they gave it less than central importance. The work of Alexei Pisemsky, whose career as a writer coincided with the first half of Tolstoy's, is an interesting example. Pisemsky wrote a number of novels and plays which involve either male or female adultery, or both. However, when he took a verse from the prophet Jeremiah (7:9) as the epigraph to one of his later plays, *Baal* (1873), Pisemsky omitted the words 'and commit adultery'. Charles Moser, who points this out, remarks: 'Apparently for him adultery was hardly as heinous as the other sins listed.'[13] For Tolstoy, on the other hand, adultery was indeed a heinous sin, not least because it threatened what he took to be the keystone of Russian social life, the family.

At the beginning of *Anna Karenina* first Oblonsky, and then Anna, asks the question which Chernyshevsky had taken as the title to his novel: 'What is to be done?'[14] As might be expected, in Tolstoy's novel the question has a very different meaning. Oblonsky wants to solve the difficulties caused by his affair with his children's French governess, and his sister Anna comes to help him. She is instrumental in saving the marriage, though her way of answering the question, by glossing over Oblonsky's adultery, is evasive.[15] *Anna Karenina* suggests that what really needs to be done is to reaffirm marriage as the basis not only of family life but of social life in general. This suggestion, which might better be called an implicit injunction, came out of Tolstoy's response to a range of topical concerns in which he himself, directly or indirectly, had a personal stake. All these concerns were complex and to a large extent intractable. The most important were the problems arising from the emancipation of the serfs; Western influence, especially on economic development and on upper-class behaviour; and the growing movement for the education and emancipation of women.

The issue of female emancipation had begun to preoccupy Tolstoy from a much earlier date. Boris Eikhenbaum points out that the four comedies which he planned or sketched during 1856–7 had as their basic theme 'mockery of women's emancipation and of "the George Sand-style woman"'.[16] Several years later, following his own marriage in 1862, but more especially the publication in the following year of *What Is to Be Done?*, Tolstoy completed *The Infected Family* (1864), a play parodying Chernyshevsky's novel.[17] These crude attempts at dramatic satire, none of them published until after his death, are a far cry from his artistry in narrative fiction. The short novel *Family Happiness* (1859)[18] had already shown a more nuanced response. There is, admittedly, little subtlety in the plot, which shows how a marriage evoking that of Jacques and Fernande settles into mutual if resigned acceptance. The couple are of similar ages to their counterparts in Sand's novel, the husband is a paternal figure – indeed his wife's former guardian – and the wife soon finds life with him dull. But what gives Tolstoy's story most of its interest is less its reversal of Sand than his striking if not quite consistent success in projecting it through the voice of the wife. This imaginative and rhetorical device anticipates one of his strategies in *Anna Karenina*.

In the opening chapters of this study I have argued that the novel of female adultery arose in large part out of a fear among Frenchmen, first kindled chiefly by the Revolution, of women's emancipation in the home and in society. *Anna Karenina* was written out of a parallel reaction, though not from a bourgeois position. Tolstoy not only answered Sand's feminist challenge, its Russian rescension in Chernyshevsky, and, for example, J. S. Mill's *The Subjection of Women*, which appeared in two Russian translations as early as 1869. He also appropriated some of the contemporary French response. He had already read and, in 1861, probably visited Proudhon.[19] Just before beginning his new novel, he greeted Dumas's *L'Homme-femme* (1872) with great enthusiasm. According to Boris Eikhenbaum, it is very likely that Tolstoy knew Dumas's *L'Affaire Clémenceau* already; *L'Homme-femme* sought to justify discursively what the earlier work had presented in fiction: a husband's murder of his unfaithful wife.[20] However, if, as Richard Stites has put it, Tolstoy was 'the most influential of antifeminist writers', and 'also the bluntest and crudest, drawing as he did upon the church and upon the peasant ethos',[21] this was only part of his ideological position. In Eikhenbaum's words, his was 'the situation of a landowner-aristocrat in agreement neither with the official bureaucratic system, nor with the transformation of Russia into a bourgeois capitalistic country, nor with the ideas, theories, and behavior of the revolutionary democratic intelligentsia'.[22] In a bid to counter the threats he saw to Russian social and moral order, Tolstoy offered an idea of the family.

That idea is a patriarchal one, and it stems from the life of the landowner. It is illustrated in the novel by the story of Constantine Levin, which runs throughout in counterpoint to Anna's. Just before the turning point in his life, Levin reflects that, in the aftermath of emancipation, 'when everything has been turned upside down and is only just taking shape, the question of how to regulate things is the one important question in Russia' (III.xxvi.352).[23] What he has in mind is agricultural management, but a few chapters later, when he is discussing the same matter with his housekeeper, she draws what was to Tolstoy the vital connection: '"All I say is," replied Agatha Mihalovna, evidently not speaking at random but in strict sequence of ideas, "that you ought to get married. That's what it comes to"' (III.xxx.370). When, immediately afterwards, Levin's tubercular brother arrives, to confront him with imminent death, it is Levin who asks Chernyshevsky's question: 'Now what's to be done? What's to be done?' (III.xxxi.374). The answer Tolstoy offers is not the socialism of Chernyshevsky or, in the following chapter, of the latter's namesake, Nikolai Levin. It is marriage, which will assure the continuity both of Levin's family and of the agricultural community for which he is responsible. Levin marries soon after, and his spouse quickly assumes the role not only of wife but of landed housekeeper. More important still, she proves capable of dealing with death as well as with giving birth to his children. The first critical event related by Tolstoy in their married life is a visit to the dying Nikolai. Kitty insists on accompanying her husband, despite his objections to any contact on her part with his brother's mistress. She proves the perfect nurse; programmatically, Nikolai's death just precedes her announcement that she is pregnant.

The central part played in Tolstoy's thinking by an idea of marriage derived from the landowning aristocracy is clear from his adaptation, for the story of Anna and Vronsky, of a real-life liaison which came to a tragic end near his home. Just over a year before he started writing the novel, in C. J. G. Turner's summary, 'Anna Pirogova, the mistress of a neighbour, A. N. Bibikov, who was about to marry another woman, committed suicide by throwing herself under a train, having written him a note that he did not receive.'[24] The differences between the real and the fictional tragedy are as striking as the similarities. First, Tolstoy changed not only the social class of the woman who killed herself, as John Bayley has noted,[25] but her marital status. Second, and equally significant, he altered the social position of her lover, who was a member of the landowning gentry, born illegitimate; and he may have found in Anna Pirogova's rival, the German governess of Bibikov's children, a hint for Oblonsky's liaison.[26] The effect was to transform a tragic episode stemming from the irregular relationships of a member of the landed gentry into a plot of aristocratic adultery, filtered through a traditional conception of landed marriage and family. These are differences of substance, not nuance. As Eikhenbaum has proposed, citing a political analysis of the aristocracy exactly contemporary with the novel, Oblonsky, Vronsky and Levin 'seem to be representatives of the three parts of the nobility about which Meshchersky wrote: the serving, the court, and the landowning'.[27] Furthermore, it is an ideal model of the landowning class to which Tolstoy plainly gives priority as a source of values.

However, Eikhenbaum's link between Meshchersky's analysis and three of Tolstoy's characters needs to be extended in order to take two further factors into account: the role of Karenin, and changes in the roles both of Oblonsky and of Vronsky. Karenin, like Oblonsky at the start, is and remains a member of the serving nobility. Oblonsky, though, changes his position in two material ways. His sale of the forest which was part of Dolly's dowry, and

which so angers Levin, sacrifices his remaining ties with the
landowning tradition; worse still, from Tolstoy's point of view, his
success in obtaining a lucrative commercial post marks him out as
embracing the new capitalism. Vronsky, on the other hand,
abandons his military and court career in an attempt to claim a role
as a landowner, though the novel implies that his adoption of that
role is factitious. The differences between the three main families in
the novel are therefore not only marital but social and ideological.
The Karenins are both a family which breaks up as a result of the
wife's adultery, and one identified, through the husband's position,
with the bureaucracy; the Levins are represented both as an ideal
family and as an example of continuing landed traditions; while the
Oblonskys are both a family which does not break up, despite the
husband's adultery, and one split between the country, where
Dolly spends her time to save money, and, through her husband's
move into commerce, the new capitalism. These differences and
changes of position within the nobility provide the framework for
Tolstoy's fictive modelling of issues of marriage and family.

Anna Karenina is unique among novels of female adultery in
presenting, alongside its adultery plot, not only a normative marital
relationship, in Levin and Kitty, but, in the Oblonskys, the less
commonly emphasized situation of a family held together despite
the adultery of the husband. Not for nothing did Tolstoy remark, as
his wife recorded in her diary in 1877: 'For a work to be good one
must love the main, basic idea in it. So in *Anna Karenina* I love the
family idea.'[28] But the type of family idea he applied to the Karenins
and the Oblonskys, upper-class families based in Moscow and St
Petersburg respectively, is grounded, just as firmly as the Levin
marriage, on the traditions of the landed estate. The novel begins
with the crisis in the Oblonsky family. From the opening page,
when not only wife and husband are at odds, but children and
domestics, it is clear that the family is conceived not on the modern
Western model of a nucleus of parents and children, but as a
household, including the servants and often also other kin. In this
conception, ties of mutual though hierarchical obligation link not
only husband and wife but all their dependants. Dolly's discovery
of her husband's adultery produces chaos which extends both to
their children and to the servants, several of whom respond by
giving notice. Yet the two servants closest to their master and

mistress, Matvey and Matriona, do their best to help reconcile them. The Karenin family also has its trusted and long-serving valet, hall-porter, and nurse.

In this extended family the children, as future heirs, nevertheless remain crucial. It is therefore the preservation of the family which counts most. Thus, while Oblonsky is wrong to have affairs, Dolly is right not to leave him but to stand by her children. Presenting her at the start as tearful and seemingly broken, the novel has her grow in strength and integrity as it continues, while her husband slides morally downwards. Conversely, although the marriage between Anna and her husband is artificial, and although, vivacious and eager to live, she is physically repelled by him, for Tolstoy she has no right to desert her marriage and her son to seek happiness in another sexual relationship. The other female characters in *Anna Karenina* who are divorced or separated have no children. It follows that, as C. J. G. Turner has argued, the reason why 'Anna alone seems to be a social pariah in consequence of her separation [. . .] is probably to be sought in Tolstoi's peculiar stress on the family unit in which children were of the essence'.[29] Similarly, although Karenin agrees at one point to divorce, the fact that he continues married to Anna suggests that wedlock is not easily undone.

Although Tolstoy's design renders abundantly clear the novel's governing focus on marriage and the family, its ideological bearing is less obvious. This is largely because Tolstoy took great care to conceal it. At the time of writing *Anna Karenina* he had still to undergo the conversion which would lead him to produce works of such unmistakable moral purpose as *The Death of Ivan Ilyich* (1886) or *The Kreutzer Sonata* (1891). Instead, his position is represented by the often-quoted remark recorded by one of his correspondents about the scene between Levin and the priest in Part V, Chapter I:

> I myself, of course, am on the side of the priest and not at all on Levin's. But I re-worked this episode four times and it still seemed to me that it was noticeable on whose side I was. And I had noticed that every thing, every story made an impression only when one could not make out with whom the author's sympathies lay.[30]

The drafts for *Anna Karenina* show how painstakingly Tolstoy revised his work in an attempt to mask his own convictions.

Two shifts are especially important in his shaping of the novel.

First, Turner points out that in Tolstoy's initial draft the novel was to have been the husband's tragedy, not the wife's, and that the wife is clearly condemned; but that the redrafting soon began 'to elevate the character of Anna and lower that of her husband'.[31] This first main revision may suggest that, against his original intentions, Tolstoy could not help sympathizing with his adulterous heroine. Such a view appears to harmonize with his first recorded comment, over three years previously, on the story which was to become *Anna Karenina*: that 'his problem was to make this woman only pitiful and not guilty'.[32] It is more likely, however, that in revising his initial draft Tolstoy reverted to the approach he had outlined in his comment of 1870. On the evidence of the text and his revisions, he sought to achieve not only apparent authorial neutrality but an even more difficult aim. The case against female adultery would be all the stronger if readers could be brought to sympathize with the adulteress; if her transgression could be shown as arising out of circumstances which might seem to mitigate or even justify it; and if it still appears insupportable in its effects on others and on herself. The extenuating circumstances include an arid marriage to a cold husband, a passionate attraction to a remorselessly persistent lover, and peer-group connivance at extra-marital affairs. If this was Tolstoy's strategy, it has succeeded with many readers and critics from his own time up to the present. Anthony Thorlby provides a characteristic example when he argues that, while 'Anna is too radiant and too likeable a figure for us to disapprove of her', she has to be destroyed 'by some profounder necessity in the nature of things'.[33] Though such a response remains common, at least among Western critics, it forgets that the nature of things in the novel is Tolstoy's contrivance. This is epitomized by the celebrated epigraph he selected, 'Vengeance is mine, and I will repay.'

Tolstoy's second main change in constructing his novel was the introduction of Levin and Kitty, who did not appear until the third draft. Indeed, as late as the fifth draft Anna was to divorce and remarry, so that 'the titles *Two Marriages* and *Two Couples* that make a brief appearance most probably refer to her two marriages',[34] rather than to the parallel stories of the Karenins and Levins. Tolstoy's shift from two marriages for Anna to the respective marriages of Anna and Levin is a telling refinement. The attack on female adultery which was explicit in his early drafts gains strength not only when it is masked, and when mitigating factors are set up to fail, but when it is intertwined with the positive example of a marriage which is constructed as healthy. Such a design is much more effective, because less plainly tendentious, than condemning the adulterous wife and commending the betrayed husband.

A similar pattern is borne out by Tolstoy's detailed revisions. Turner notes that 'One theme that occurs in some drafts is Anna's "liberalism," which permits her to justify her position as a common-law wife; but, as such, she is no longer accepted by society and has to find friends among "nihilists" and (once) even a "communist".'35 In the final version Tolstoy altered this aspect of Anna's characterization. He transferred the theme of communism and free love to Levin's brother Nikolai, and he attributed to Anna and her lover a flirtation with Western ideas which was both more plausible, given their social position, and in his view more dangerous. When, for instance, Dolly visits Anna at Vronsky's estate in the country, she finds her sister-in-law surrounded by all the trappings of Western modernity, including tennis and contraception (VI.xvii.640–xxiv.673). This is, again, a much subtler way to stir doubts, especially because the episode is presented from the viewpoint of the admirable Dolly, who sympathizes with Anna but cannot help differing from her. Furthermore, as the example of Levin and the priest suggests, it was not only passages dealing with Anna that Tolstoy revised. Elisabeth Stenbock-Fermor points out that he omitted two scenes from Part III, centred on Levin's response to his dying brother, 'which made the author's intentions too obvious'. She also observes that Tolstoy chose but then rejected epigraphs for each of the novel's chapters.36

Konstantin Leontiev, a contemporary of Tolstoy who discussed his writing with him, remarked that, in comparison with *War and Peace*, *Anna Karenina* 'is a more subjective work, because of the closeness of the author to the epoch and the milieu, and because of the nature of the main character, Levin, but its subjectivity was *objectivized* to the highest degree of perfection'.37 This is a helpful guide to Tolstoy's success in tempering ideology and morality into art, even though it claims a neutrality which he did not realize and which is, indeed, impossible. The remark also suggests, though it does not identify, the main artistic device through which Tolstoy sought to 'objectivize' the novel's subjectivity. That device is control of point of view, as in the episode just cited in which Dolly visits Anna and Vronsky in the country. C. J. G. Turner emphasizes 'two examples of what is a frequent feature of Tolstoi's revisions: just as the viewpoint from which the ball is seen had been transferred from the narrator to Kitty, so what has originally been simply narrated is often put into the mouth of a character (sometimes a character introduced for this sole purpose)'.[38] These are sophisticated ways of inviting responses which overt use of the narrative voice might forestall. In the scene at the ball, for example, Kitty, faced by Anna's captivation of Vronsky, finds in her charm 'something terrible and cruel', and reflects: 'Yes, there is something strange, diabolical and enchanting about her' (I.xxiii.97). Such a response is entirely apt and convincing from the character, whereas the doubts it raises about Anna would have come much less discreetly from the narrator. Indeed, presented from Anna's perspective, the scene would have offered a different range of meanings still. The episode when, despite the publicity of her liaison with Vronsky, she visits the Opera is a classic illustration (V.xxxiii). To have presented from her own point of view the humiliation she suffers there would have encouraged a much more sympathetic response than is easily gained from the angle Tolstoy selected, which is Vronsky's. The scene's potential emotional impact is further diluted by his position as a distant spectator, and by his anger at Anna for attending against his advice.

It is largely by dramatizing the responses of individual characters that Tolstoy presents what were to him the human and moral questions at stake in adultery. He develops those questions to their fullest extent by exploiting the perspective of each main figure concerned: adulteress, lover, husband, and child. To begin with the lovers, the chapter showing Anna's and Vronsky's responses after they have made love for the first time is an especially powerful example. It is not possible to analyse the whole chapter here, but the following extract illustrates its emotional and rhetorical force:

She felt so sinful, so guilty, that nothing was left to her but to humble herself and beg forgiveness; but she had no one in the world now but him, and so to him she even addressed her prayer for forgiveness. Looking at him, she had a physical sense of her degradation and could not utter another word. He felt what a murderer must feel when he looks at the body he has robbed of life. The body he had robbed of life was their love, the first stage of their love. There was something frightful and revolting in the recollection of what had been paid for by this terrible price of shame. Shame at her spiritual nakedness crushed her and infected him. But in spite of the murderer's horror before the body of his victim, that body must be hacked to pieces and hidden, and the murderer must make use of what he has obtained by his crime.

And, as with fury and passion the murderer throws himself upon the body and drags it and hacks at it, so he covered her face and shoulders with kisses. She held his hand and did not stir. 'Yes, these kisses – these are what have been bought by my shame! Yes, and this hand, which will always be mine, is the hand of my accomplice!' (II.xi.165–6)

The chapter's importance is marked by Tolstoy's comment in a letter: 'this is one of the passages on which the whole novel stands. If it is false, then everything is false.'[39] Part of its impact is to present the first act of adultery as devastating to Anna and Vronsky alike. This emphasis, which is unique in novels of adultery, turns on special ways of constructing each of the two lovers.

It has often been noted that Anna's response to her adultery differs sharply from that portrayed on the part of other adulterous women in the novel to theirs. Princess Betsy, for example, carries on affairs which escape not only social disapproval but any guilt or remorse of her own. Three ways of explaining the paradox may be suggested. First, from a moralist's standpoint it is the passionate, committed affair, like Anna's with Vronsky, which most threatens social order; second, and relatedly, a passionate affair is much more likely to end in such a way as to provide an inescapable moral example; third, the moral law is most plausibly, and most effectively, enforced against a character if she is presented as having internalized it. The last of these possible explanations is the one for which there is most evidence in the novel's texture. Tolstoy builds the moral law, so to speak, into his characterization; so that it is by her own responses to her adultery that Anna is destroyed. For instance, although he nowhere presents Anna as a person of special religious convictions, throughout the chapter presenting her response to her first act of adultery he constructs that response in specifically religious terms. In the passage quoted she feels 'sinful' and ashamed of 'her spiritual nakedness'; and she addresses to Vronsky the 'prayer for forgiveness' – 'Oh God, forgive me!' – which she can offer neither to God nor to anyone else. Later in the same chapter, she cannot 'profane' her 'sense of shame, rapture and horror' by trying to put into words 'all that was in her soul'.

A second example of how Tolstoy attributes to Anna a sense of what he took to be the moral law occurs further on in the action, when she is agonizing over her position. Here, in soliloquy, she puts a case on her own behalf which, in his well-known comments on the novel, D. H. Lawrence would restate 50 years later: 'the time came when I realized I couldn't deceive myself any longer, that I was alive, that I was not to blame, that God had made me so that I need to love and live' (III.xvi.314). Lawrence argued that Tolstoy should have allowed Anna to leave her husband and live with Vronsky free and unashamed.[40] In the novel, she takes such a step only to fail in it. Yet the failure is predetermined, for, even at the point when Anna first considers leaving Karenin for Vronsky, Tolstoy has her realize that, 'however much she might struggle, she could not be stronger than herself' (III.xvi.316). He has, indeed, designed her self to founder in such an attempt.

The chapter presenting Anna's and Vronsky's responses to their first act of adultery also predetermines what will become of them through its most striking, not to say shocking, feature – its use of the metaphor of murder. The metaphor is first introduced from Vronsky's viewpoint in order to convey his sense of the irrevocable step he has taken in entering upon sexual relations with the woman he loves. It is the narrator, however, who goes on to generalize from it and to equate Vronsky's frantic kisses with the murderer's repeated blows on the dead body; yet the passage ends with Anna implicitly taking it over in her reference to Vronsky as her 'accomplice'. In transferring the metaphor from Vronsky through the narrator to Anna, Tolstoy not only attributes to each character, especially to Vronsky, a horrified and disturbing reaction to illicit intercourse. Through relentless repetition and expansion, he also has the metaphor exceed its initial sense to suggest that adultery, even the sexual act as such, is itself murderous. Since the metaphor is introduced from one character's point of view, and ends in the other's, the narrator's role in developing it is partially masked, while none of the powerful associations and forebodings it carries is forfeited. Indeed, the rhetoric of the passage is scarcely less full of meaning and portent than the whole later episode in which Vronsky causes the death of his racehorse (II.xxiv–xxv).

The presentation of Vronsky has its own importance. First, it suggests that Tolstoy was far from condoning the role of the adulterous lover, even though it is a woman's adultery which he emphasizes. This is a view which no novels of adultery prior to *Anna Karenina*, and few subsequently, so much as intimate; and it is reflected in Tolstoy's developing presentation of Oblonsky during the novel, as well as of Vronsky himself. Second, Tolstoy switches decisively from an external view of Vronsky as a stereotypical seducer, 'with a proud, glad smile lurking under his moustache' (II.iii.144), to the moral confusion and panic of the chapter just discussed. At its height, Vronsky's anguish leads to his suicide attempt following Anna and Karenin's temporary reconciliation; and, after Anna's death, to his virtual suicide in going to war. In this way Tolstoy not only highlights the responsibility of the lover in seducing a married woman, but has the seduction produce consequences which are disastrous for himself as well. Third, Tolstoy also exploits Vronsky's point of view in order to assert what was to him the insubstantiality of happiness as a motive for adultery. After Vronsky and Anna have escaped to Italy, she is at first 'unpardonably happy', but the narrator remarks:

> Vronsky, meanwhile, notwithstanding the complete fulfilment of what he had so long desired, was not entirely happy. He soon began to feel that the realization of his desires brought him no more than a grain of sand out of the mountain of bliss he had expected. It showed him the eternal error men make in imagining that happiness consists in the realization of their desires. (V.viii.490–1)

As so often in the novel, the character's thoughts are presented from his own point of view, but through the narrative voice. Yet the notion that people are wrong in assuming that happiness consists in the realization of desire does not come naturally from a figure who is scarcely portrayed as reflective about moral or philosophical questions. Tolstoy has, as it were, smuggled into his interior view of Vronsky a conviction which is fundamental to the novel's whole purpose: that the pursuit of personal happiness is not only wrong but self-defeating. He later shows Levin grasping a complementary idea from the peasant Fiodor – 'it is wrong to live for one's belly; we must live for truth, for God' (VIII.xii.830) – but from him it comes much more convincingly.

If *Anna Karenina* is highly unusual among novels of adultery in giving moral and psychological weight to the figure of the lover, it is without parallel in the extent and quality of attention it pays to the betrayed husband. As has been noted above, Karenin became a much less sympathetic figure in Tolstoy's successive drafts than in his original conception. Nevertheless, the finished novel presents a character who has his own perspective and interest, and who undergoes deep and ultimately destructive personal change. He is seen at first from the outside, with protruding ears and cracking fingers, next from the inside, in his denial of emotion and imagination. Then, through a stunning reversal, Karenin becomes capable of love and forgiveness in response to Anna's words of contrition in her delirium from puerperal fever, only to find himself shunned and disdained after she recovers and leaves him. This is the point Tolstoy chose for his most intimate and moving portrayal of the feelings of the betrayed husband:

> He felt that he could not endure the general shock of contempt and exasperation which he had distinctly read on the face of the man from the shop and of Korney, and of everyone, without exception, whom he had met during the last two days. He felt that he could not divert people's hate from himself, because that hate was not caused by something fundamentally wrong in himself (in that case he could have tried to do better), but because he was disgracefully and odiously unhappy. He knew that people would be merciless for the very reason that his heart was lacerated. He felt that his fellow-men would destroy him, as dogs kill some poor cur maimed and howling with pain. He knew that his only salvation lay in hiding his wounds, and he had instinctively tried to do this for two days, but now he no longer had the strength to keep up the unequal struggle. (V.xxi.534)

Karenin's inability to bear his position, all the more pitiable for his self-pity, lays him open to the hypocrisy and fake spirituality of Countess Lydia Ivanovna. By rendering him vulnerable to scorn and rejection, his moral and emotional breakthrough in forgiving Anna leads him back to a different kind of hollowness, reflected in his cold and oppressive relationship to his son. As with the figure of the adulteress, the characterization of the betrayed husband in the finished novel is far more subtle and effective than in the heavy-handed early conception revealed by Tolstoy's drafts.

It is the Karenins' son, Seriozha, who provides the remaining key vantage point for Tolstoy's presentation of adultery. Shortly before the race in which Vronsky is to kill his horse by his clumsy riding, Vronsky visits Anna and comes up against 'the most painful side of his relations with her – her son with his (as he fancied) questioning, hostile eyes'. Although Seriozha is not at home when Vronsky arrives, the narrator expands on the boy's point of view towards his mother and her lover:

> The child did in fact feel that he could not understand this relation; and he tried but could not make out what feeling he ought to have for this man. With a child's sensitiveness to feeling in others, he saw distinctly that his father, his governess, and his nurse all not only disliked Vronsky but regarded him with aversion, though they never said anything about him, while his mother looked on him as her greatest friend.
>
> 'What does it mean? Who is he? How ought I to love him? If I don't know, it's my fault: it means I am a silly boy, or a bad boy,' thought the child. (II.xxii.203)

This wonderfully perceptive account of a young child's confusion, unhappiness and guilt about a situation he cannot understand is completely without precedent among novels of adultery. Tolstoy was the first writer in this tradition to take the adulterous mother's child seriously as a figure in his own right; and, once more, what helps makes the passage so telling is its presentation from the character's viewpoint. The passage prepares the way for the two poignant episodes which dramatize the impact on Seriozha of his mother's subsequent desertion: the scene in which she visits him clandestinely on his birthday (V.xxix), and the even more painful scene in which he is visited by his uncle Stiva Oblonsky (VII.xix).

The four interior views discussed above demonstrate that, while *Anna Karenina* is informed by an intense and even uncompromising moral vision, it is also distinguished by an acute attention to the particulars of human behaviour, and by a scrupulous respect for individuals which extends sympathetic understanding to all the main characters. Thus *Anna Karenina* is the only novel of female adultery which pays serious and sustained attention not only to the role of the wife, but to that of the lover; to the response not only of the betrayed husband, but of the child.

However, it has to be recognized that the novel's magnificent strengths are not separable from its agenda. In rebutting D. H. Lawrence's critique of *Anna Karenina*, Raymond Williams declares:

> The social convention invoked against Anna is indeed shallow and hypocritical, but take a society in which there is no difficulty in divorce, in which an Anna would not be pointed at and

avoided, and the human difficulty in substance remains. The child of the body is there, in any society. Frustration and hatred are there, under any laws, if the relationships are wrong.[41]

Williams argues that Lawrence's fundamental mistake is to separate the personal from the social and to glorify it. In response, he contends that the problems caused by marital breakdown are universal: 'the human difficulty', 'in any society', 'under any laws'. This is a powerful and in many ways a convincing argument, but human difficulties take various forms and find various outcomes in different societies. What in large measure determine those forms and outcomes are history and ideology. It is therefore necessary, while responding to the novel's images of human life, to recognize that they are not only fictional but culturally determined. When Williams goes on to remark that 'the significance of Anna, at the highest point of her growth, is that she must live her feelings right through',[42] he accepts the novel's invitation to understand her as if she were real, and in doing so he risks endorsing the ideological assumptions Tolstoy built into her.

For the novel's qualities are indivisible from Tolstoy's commitment to the twin idea of the landed marriage and family. He emphasizes that idea in recoil from the threats he saw in commercialism, modernizing Western influence, and the emancipation of women. When, with almost overwhelming power and conviction, he explores the perspective of deserted child or betrayed husband, and shows the mutual destruction of adulterous partners, it is to serve an ideal of marriage. This recognition must go along with tribute to his outstanding achievement as a novelist in *Anna Karenina*, since that achievement is so humanly and artistically persuasive that its ideological implications easily escape notice. The fact is that, in keeping with the tradition, the novel's fundamental concern is still the adultery of a woman. Crucially, Tolstoy types Anna as a bad mother through the impact of her adultery on the children she has both by her husband and by her lover.[43] While perhaps the most moving and original part of the novel deals with the experience of her son, the presentation of Seriozha, in its acuteness, works to further not just Anna's suffering, but the appeal for her condemnation which the novel tenders.

Just as Tolstoy, in *Anna Karenina*, responded to an ideological challenge represented in part by Chernyshevsky's *What Is to Be Done?*, so, in various short stories, Chekhov responded in turn to Tolstoy. The extent of the older writer's influence over the younger is still a matter of debate, although it was attested by Chekhov himself and although a number of his earlier stories recall the moral parables to which Tolstoy turned after *Anna Karenina*.[44] However, there are several instructive differences between Chekhov's and Tolstoy's fictional treatments of adultery.

First, although adultery is a frequent motif in Chekhov's stories, it is the principal issue only in a few. In this respect his approach, restrained and non-judgemental, recalls that of Pisemsky.[45] Second, while Tolstoy's design in *Anna Karenina* is confined almost wholly to the aristocracy, the social range of Chekhov's stories – whether featuring adultery or not – is much broader. As Boris Eikhenbaum has observed, 'it would seem that there is no profession, no class, no corner of Russian life into which Chekhov has not peered'.[46] Third, through the form of the short story, with its built-in bias towards the episodic or even the fragmentary, Chekhov presents a wide variety of points of view. Though some of his stories, such as 'The Butterfly' (1892) or 'His Wife' (1895), centre on the married woman's transgression, others, including 'Lights' (1888), 'Terror' (1892), and 'The Two Volodyas' (1893), highlight her exploitation and betrayal by men.[47] At the same time, and especially as his career as a writer progressed, Chekhov increasingly situated both male and female adultery in an array of social contexts which reorient or even redefine what is at issue. Two early examples, both dating from 1886, are 'Misfortune' and 'Agafya'.[48]

'Misfortune', often cited as a story influenced by *Anna Karenina*, is more striking for its divergence from Tolstoyan models. In particular, it is inconclusive, unmoralistic and, on occasion, ironical or even comic. Strictly speaking, the story is not an adultery text at all, because the ending leaves unresolved what Mrs Lubyantsev does when she walks out into the night. Instead its concern is with the mixture of invincible impulse, self-deception and other human inadequacies which lay the ground for adultery, whether or not, after the closing ellipsis marks, the central character actually goes on to betray her husband. What connects 'Misfortune' to the fiction of adultery is that it centres in a woman the experiences of frustration with marriage and temptation to sexual infidelity. What distinguishes the story from previous works in the tradition is that, as its title suggests, it represents such experiences not as part of a moral or an ideological agenda but as human problems. This key departure is clearest in Chekhov's handling of point of view.

In the same way as the main character is by definition always a woman in the novel of female adultery, and the author a man, so the two viewpoints presented in 'Misfortune' are those of the male narrator and of the tempted wife. The narrator is marked as male by generalizations such as 'a woman's egoistical feeling of superiority over the man who is in love with her' (33), 'the sort of discomfiture decent women feel at suddenly being discovered naked' (34), or 'the phrase which all ordinary women use on an occasion like his' (42). If, and most clearly in the third example, these carry a humorous intonation, the narrator also ventures one conventionally moral remark: 'The pettiness and egoism of youth seemed never to have revealed themselves in her as strongly as on that evening' (41). But the story's dominant emphasis emerges in a quite different kind of observation. Halfway through, the narrator comments: 'Only when in trouble do people realize how difficult it is to master their own feelings and thoughts. Mrs. Lubyantsev said afterwards that her mind was "in a state of confusion which was as difficult to sort out as to count the number of flying sparrows quickly"' (38–9). Part of what is extraordinary here is the shift to an unspecified time subsequent to the events related in the story – events which are themselves left unresolved by the ellipsis marks with which it ends. But the effect of this shift is to bring home the truth of the generalization, which in itself seems so banal, on misfortune; and with it the stress and perplexity of Mrs Lubyantsev's predicament. Although the story shows her insincerity and self-deception very clearly, it also underlines the power of the desire against which she struggles and the frailty of the resources on which she can draw: 'She understood now how strong and implacable the enemy was. To fight him she had to possess strength and determination, but her birth, her upbringing, and her life had given her nothing to fall back on' (43). The point is pressed home when she appeals to her husband for help and, half-comically, he fails her, replying to her faltering confidence, 'I – I think I am in love', with the inapposite query 'Who with?', yawning and telling her she is imagining things, and then, 'frightened all the same', expressing his views on family life and on infidelity (44). Chekhov caps this fruitless exchange with a further ironic generalization: 'There are a great many opinions in the world, and a good half of them are held by people who have never been in trouble!'[49] Such a remark, wry and without self-righteousness, taking the pressure of the individual case independently of any moral formula, strikes a quite new note in nineteenth-century representations of female adultery.

Chekhov does not consistently sustain this approach of attentive equity throughout 'Misfortune'. Beverly Hahn, while recognizing that his portrayal of Mrs Lubyantsev's thoughts and feelings is 'detailed and sympathetic', also detects an externality which for her represents 'the difficulty of a male writer whose own prose presence, in this story, is quite strong'.[50] She goes on to argue that two later stories, 'Lights' and 'The Party' (1888), present 'women who are subtly emancipated from direct commentary'. In 'Agafya', however, first published a few months before 'Misfortune', Chekhov had already tried a method which achieves the same effect. Again, the key to the story's distinctiveness is the standpoint from which it is told.

'Agafya' is in several ways highly unusual as an adultery text. Its action consists of a single undramatic episode; its social setting is neither the aristocracy nor the bourgeoisie, but the peasantry; it is told by a leisured gentleman distanced by social class from the adulterous couple and the cheated husband; and, perhaps most surprising of all, during most of the story the focus is not on the erring wife but on her indolent lover. 'Agafya' unfolds through a series of carefully layered phases. It begins with the narrator, enjoying his ease for a day or two in the company of the layabout Savka. Next, it shows Savka himself, engaging in his relaxed self-acceptance despite his irresponsibility. Finally it presents Agafya, torn between Savka's attractions and the demands of her lawful husband. The focus shifts in further stages to the irresistible desire which brings Agafya, with a laugh of 'reckless determination, weakness, and pain' (29), to stay all night with her lover, then to her wretched, zigzag walk back to the husband who she knows will beat her, and lastly to her spirit once she tosses her head and steps out, having 'evidently plucked up her courage and made up her mind' (31, TM).[51]

Beverly Hahn has suggested that, although 'Agafya' shows the 'callous lightheartedness' of the lover and the 'threatening austerity' of the husband as 'two kinds of masculine tyranny between which Agafya is trapped', the story nevertheless achieves 'no real sense of protest'.[52] This, however, is to underrate several important factors.

First, despite Savka's demeaning attitude, it is the strength of Agafya's desire for him which drives her to affront her husband. As Barbara Heldt has pointed out, 'words meaning decisiveness or decision are paradoxically applied to the character who is the least free of the three in the story: married, a woman, and a peasant.'[53] Second, as Heldt also indicates, the husband is associated not just with social obligation and law but with the ordered routine of the railway for which he works. Third, that routine casts light on why Agafya, married to 'a fine young fellow, only about a year before' (24), might find Savka's carefree irresponsibility so attractive. Fourth, the narrator's social position both helps to explain his detachment from Agafya's plight and points to two contradictions betrayed by his own fascination with Savka. Not only does Savka's freedom appeal in comparable ways to the narrator and to Agafya, but the narrator's leisure, though authorized by his class, is not easy to distinguish from that of his peasant friend. In other words, the meaning of each character's behaviour is strongly inflected by social position and gender – factors which privilege the narrator to enjoy Savka's company without discredit. Chekhov's presentation of this episode of adultery shows an unobtrusive but complex attention to social context which he would develop much more fully in the work of his maturity.

Chekhov's best-known story of adultery – indeed, as Ronald Hingley has said, 'probably the best-known' of all his stories[54] – is 'A Lady with a Dog' (1899). What has given the story much of its appeal is the irony by which a casual holiday affair between a rather cynical older man and a naive young woman unexpectedly flourishes into passionate, committed love. But what distinguishes 'A Lady with a Dog' as an adultery text is that, unusually, both the lovers are married, and that, almost without precedent, the point of view from which the story is told is the man's. Gurov embarks on the affair with a demeaning, exploitative attitude towards women which recalls Savka's in 'Agafya'; yet he discovers in himself a previously unsuspected capacity for love. The story shows the seeds of this transformation after the couple have made love for the first time. Faced by what seems to him Anna's stereotyped shame, as she pours out her distress, Gurov responds on two different levels. The first is conscious and superficial: 'Gurov was bored with all this. He was irritated by the naïve air, the unexpected, uncalled-for remorse' (IX,131). The second consists in the actions and tone of voice which he appears to adopt instinctively:

'I don't understand,' said he softly. 'What is it you want?' [. . .]
'There there, that's enough,' he muttered.

He looked into her staring, frightened eyes, kissed her, spoke softly and gently. She gradually relaxed and cheered up again. Both laughed. (IX,131)

The scene could hardly contrast more decisively with its famous forerunner in *Anna Karenina*, discussed above. Lightly but firmly bypassing Tolstoy's example, Chekhov emphasizes how both characters grow beyond roles dictated by social convention. While Anna, before her outburst, is 'like the Woman Taken in Adultery in an old-fashioned picture', so Gurov, despite himself, sheds the seducer's casual misogyny to show care and tenderness.

'A Lady with a Dog' also implies a connection between the jaded unfulfilment of both characters' lives and the social order they inhabit. Gurov is in an arranged marriage, contracted in his second college year, with a wife who 'seemed half as old again as himself' (IX,127); he has a position in a bank though he has trained as an opera singer. Anna has been transplanted two years earlier, at the age of 20, from St Petersburg to the provinces by her marriage to an official whom she cannot help despising. Though neither situation is particularly remarkable, both gain significance from an interior view of Gurov near the end of the story. The passage begins with Gurov explaining to his young daughter how sleet is possible even though the thermometer is above zero: 'it's only the ground which is warm, you see – the temperature in the upper strata of the atmosphere is quite different' (IX,139). This remark stands in discreet metaphorical relation to his ensuing reflections on the difference between his public and his most fully personal life:

He was living two lives. One of them was open to view by – and known to – the people concerned. It was full of stereotyped truths and stereotyped untruths, it was identical with the life of his friends and acquaintances. The other life proceeded in secret. Through some strange and possibly arbitrary chain of coincidences everything vital, interesting and crucial to him, everything which called his sincerity and integrity into play, everything which made up the core of his life . . . all that took place in complete secrecy, whereas everything false about him, the façade behind which he hid to conceal the truth – his work at the bank, say, his arguments at the club, that 'inferior species' stuff, attending anniversary celebrations with his wife – all that was in the open. He judged others by himself, disbelieving the evidence of his eyes, and attributing to everyone a real, fascinating life lived under the cloak of secrecy as in the darkness of the night. Each individual existence is based on mystery, which is perhaps why civilized man makes such a neurotic fuss about having his privacy respected. (IX,139)

The idea of a double life both parallels and helps explain the two separate levels on which Gurov responds to Anna before he, and their relationship, develop. But the passage also goes much further, suggesting that the division between public and private lives is not only radical but general. By changing tense in the final sentence to the present, Chekhov switches unobtrusively from conveying Gurov's point of view to a narratorial statement about civilized life as such. Given his insistence that his work referred specifically and exclusively to Russia, and could not otherwise be understood,[55] it is not too much to suggest that the generalization reflects on a social world which he perceived as fatally out of joint.

Like 'Misfortune', 'Agafya', and many other stories by Chekhov, 'A Lady with a Dog' ends with no conventional resolution. Able to meet only rarely and in secret, the lovers hope for 'a wonderful new life' but recognize 'that the most complicated and difficult part was only just beginning' (IX,141). In this respect the story is true to the precept Chekhov had expressed to his friend and publisher Alexei Suvorin in 1888: 'You are right in demanding that an artist should take an intelligent attitude to his work, but you confuse two things: *solving a problem* and *stating a problem correctly*. It is only the second that is obligatory for the artist'.[56] Although Chekhov never wavered from this, in the work of his maturity he gave detailed attention to the social factors by which the problems he addressed were determined. Several of these factors, which are left largely implicit in 'A Lady with a Dog', are highlighted by two longer narratives, published earlier in the decade, before Chekhov began to give more time to his dramatic work: 'An Anonymous Story' (1893) and 'Three Years' (1895).

Both these narratives work by juxtaposition and displacement. The narrator of 'An Anonymous Story' is an undercover agent who takes a post as a valet in order to gain information about his employer's politician father. Though he discovers almost nothing, he finds himself learning instead about his employer's private life, especially his treatment of his mistress. Zinaida Krasnovsky leaves her husband to live with Orlov, whose increasing neglect and ill-treatment finally drive her out in the company of the scandalized narrator; she ends by poisoning herself after giving birth to a daughter whom the narrator adopts. 'An Anonymous Story' not only shifts from conventionally political questions to the politics of personal relationships. It also implies that there is a connection between these: as a well-connected civil servant who lives for his own pleasures, Orlov reflects the power of a corrupt establishment. Not for nothing does the narrator find himself deflected from his undercover work into helping Orlov's abused victim.

Similarly, in 'Three Years', male adultery becomes part of the story's foreground even though it is never its subject. The main narrative is divided between Alexis Laptev's marriage with Julia Belavin and his obligation to take over the rich and harshly exploitative business which produces his wealth. Laptev has a mistress whom he abandons after his marriage and who takes up with Yartsev, one of his best friends; and also a married sister, Nina, who dies in the course of the story, and whose husband has been living openly in the same town with his mistress and the children he has by her. The story is full of ironic reversals. Laptev comes to recognize that he is no longer in love with his wife, while she, having married him for lack of other prospects and to escape her overbearing father, has grown to love him. Again, having dropped his mistress, a married woman scraping a living after long separation from her husband, Laptev comes to realize how much better suited she was to him than his wife, and to regret the liaison with Yartsev to which she has been driven by economic as well as emotional needs. Later, after his sister's death, her husband deserts his mistress who, almost destitute, goes to Laptev for help; and the story ends by showing Yartsev playing suitor to Julia. Juxtaposed with this array of unhappy and fluctuating relationships, in which men hold almost all the power, is Chekhov's account of Laptev's induction into his father's business, which prospers through tyrannical oppression of its workers. Characteristically understated, the story implies a complex causal relationship between personal misery, lives out of joint, and social and economic inequality.

The same linkage is implied by two later stories, 'A Case History' (1898) and 'A Marriageable Girl' (1903). In the first of these, Korolyov, a young house-surgeon, is sent in place of his superior to attend to the young heiress of a recently deceased factory-owner.

Korolyov soon finds that the problem is nervous, not physical, and his first thought is: 'time she got married' (IX,71). However, after staying the night, during which the poverty and brutality of life in the mills come home to him, the view he expresses to her is quite different: 'You, as mill-owner and rich heiress are dissatisfied, you don't believe you have the right to such things' (IX,77). Though Korolyov finds it impossible to give Liza the prescription directly, he believes her best hope is to renounce 'her five mills and her million roubles'. He ends by sketching for her a future in which 'this problem of right and wrong will have been solved', but without suggesting how.

'A Case History' recalls *What Is to Be Done?* both in its utopian closing vision and in its central situation. Specifically, Liza's illness parallels that of Katerina Polozov in the penultimate chapter of Chernyshevsky's novel; but, though Chekhov's story offers no clear way forward, it eschews that part of Chernyshevsky's remedy which involves marriage. 'A Marriageable Girl', Chekhov's last story, points in the same direction. Again the central character is a dissatisfied young woman, but Nadya has a friend, Sasha, to advise her: 'you're living on others, you're ruining the lives of people you don't even know' (IX,212). At Sasha's prompting, Nadya breaks her engagement and leaves her provincial home to find herself through education in St Petersburg. The story ends with her returning for the holiday to reaffirm her faith in a new life and, after news arrives of Sasha's death, to leave again, as the closing words express it, 'for ever, presumably' (IX,223).

Chekhov was always at great pains to stress that he subscribed to no particular politics or ideology. If, therefore, it may seem strained to compare his work with that of so politically committed a writer as Chernyshevsky, what must be remembered is his sense of responsibility to the conditions of life around him, and the climate of censorship and repression in which he wrote. Two examples may, in conclusion, serve to illustrate his engagement in contemporary issues. First, it has been argued that 'A Lady with a Dog' 'was very likely a polemic response to a story, "Mimochka Taking the Waters," by L. I. Veselitskaia, which appeared in *The Herald of Europe* in 1891 and had met with Tolstoi's approval'; predictably, Tolstoy took a dim view of Chekhov's contribution.[57] Second, there is the testimony of Chekhov's contemporary readers. In her discussion of the correspondence he received, much of it from women, Carolina De Maegd-Soëp has observed: 'The tormented questions "What is to be done?" and "Where is the way out?," so recurrent in Chekhov's stories and plays, are echoed in many letters.'[58] These were inherently risky questions to raise at a time when, for instance, Chernyshevsky's novel was still banned. Thus, though rejecting programmatic Soviet interpretations, Ronald Hingley has pointed out Chekhov's fear that 'An Anonymous Story' and 'A Marriageable Girl' would be censored, and has shown that Nadya in the latter story was widely understood by contemporaries 'as a revolutionary by implication'.[59]

Of course, neither 'A Case History' nor 'A Marriageable Girl' is an adultery text; but that is part of their significance. In keeping with the attention he paid in many stories to the social context of marriage and adultery, Chekhov quite literally changed the subject.

7

Protestant Fiction of Adultery: Blicher, Jacobsen, Fontane

Whether or not they are, strictly speaking, novels of adultery, nearly all of the texts I have discussed so far were produced by writers from Catholic France or Orthodox Russia. Balzac wrote as a monarchist and a Catholic, though in ways which were often highly idiosyncratic; and his contemporaries and his successors show the influence of Catholicism even when, like Zola, they rebelled against it. Tolstoy, though no orthodox believer, tried in *Anna Karenina* to reaffirm what he took to be the essentials of popular Orthodox faith; while, in contrast, Chernyshevsky and Chekhov wrote from secular, non-traditional, positions. It is in novels from Spain and Portugal, which will be addressed in the next and final chapter, that the role of religion is strongest. This chapter deals with works by three of the few writers from Protestant cultures to have produced narratives of female adultery: the Danes Steen Steensen Blicher and Jens Peter Jacobsen, and the Prussian Theodor Fontane.

Blicher's short story 'Tardy Awakening' (1828) is the earliest nineteenth-century narrative I have come across to centre on female adultery. It differs from the tradition which would develop later in the century not only in that it is a short story rather than a novel, but in that it is a personal and not an impersonal narrative. Part of the distinction of 'Tardy Awakening' consists in the story's brilliant narrative technique. The narrator is a pastor, identified only by his first name, Wilhelm. He tells his story to explain the sudden suicide of Doctor L——, his friend of many years' standing. In relating it he not only reveals how the long-sustained and long-concealed liaison between Elise, the wife of L——, and a mutual friend, a captain in the army, had come to light. He also describes why he himself had had reason to suspect the liaison, and how he did his best to cover it up even when the evidence confirmed it all too plainly.

It is entirely possible to read 'Tardy Awakening' in the terms of its narrator's summary: 'how a sensual and unscrupulous woman's crime brought ruin to two families, and to many others a sorrow that gave deep pain for a long time and will never wholly be forgotten' (145).[1] Elise betrays her faithful and devoted husband over a period of about 20 years, bearing children not only to him but to her lover whose own marriage is childless; the lover's guilty conscience reveals the affair to his wife, as well as to the narrator and his friend, in his delirium during an illness from which he dies. The narrator relates two incidents which caused him to suspect Elise long before the discovery of the affair. First, soon after his arrival in the town, Elise accepted his offer of a dance which she had already promised to L——; and she twice squeezed his hand. He then entered a close friendship with L——, who told him later that he was already engaged to Elise, secretly because of opposition from her parents. Second, the narrator had involuntarily witnessed the meeting from which the affair later turns out to have begun. During a masquerade he had withdrawn because of a headache to rest in a dark room. The captain and Elise, both masked, had entered and, at the latter's instigation, they had made love. What the narrator heard them say establishes that the captain believed he was with his wife, while it is uncertain whether Elise had believed or had pretended to believe that she was with her husband. When a sudden light revealed themselves to each other, the captain had responded in horror, Elise in apparent distress, and they had left separately. Both L—— and the captain had been costumed, ironically, as Don Juan; whereas Elise, the narrator affirms, had changed her costume from one like that of the captain's wife by the time she returned to the ball. After the ball both the narrator and his wife had noticed a great change in the captain's behaviour; but, though the narrator had known its cause, he had sought to reassure her and to defend Elise. When, 20 years later, the affair is revealed, the captain's delirium uncovers letters from Elise which strongly suggest that the initiative throughout had been hers. He, his wife Charlotte tells him in her anguish, is 'the one who has been seduced' (136).

The narrator offers evidence which, for him, justifies his belief that, if 'vampires' existed, Elise would be one (125). He emphasizes what he terms her 'cold fire' (127) and, later, the 'hellish calm' of her self-control (131). At the same time, however, his own comments and behaviour are open to question. For example, there is a strange disparity between the aspersions he casts on Elise, as in the phrases just quoted, and his attempts not only to defend her against suspicion but to cloak the affair even when it is all but completely exposed. The narrator tries to persuade his wife, the captain's wife and L—— himself that their suspicions may prove unfounded, even though he has every reason to believe otherwise. Although it is possible to explain his words as well-intentioned efforts at reassurance, they conflict so clearly with what he knows and suspects that they may instead be interpreted as attempts to protect not only Elise from exposure but himself from certain knowledge of her transgression. For the story also offers evidence that the narrator is attracted to Elise. It is difficult to reconcile his claim at the beginning that, when he danced with her, he was not especially impressed by her looks, and that neither his heart nor his senses 'felt the slightest excitement', with the fact that he 'perhaps kissed her hand rather warmly' and returned the pressure of hers (124). Still more suggestive is his remark later on, before the affair begins, that he, L——, the captain and their respective wives might be better suited by switching partners:

> If similarity of character were the foundation of matrimonial bliss, we six people should have been quite differently matched; there should have been a complete change-about. My even temper and natural gravity, which was strengthened by the dignity of my office, should have been united with Mrs. L——. Her frank, merry, brisk, and bold husband would have found his congenial match in Mrs. H——. And my gentle, meek, and mild wife should have been chosen for the captain's companion on the way of life. (129)

It is not only through the names of the captain and his wife Charlotte that Blicher's story evokes Goethe's *Elective Affinities*.

'Tardy Awakening' offers a standard attack on female adultery while providing materials for its subversion. The narrator's double view of the adulteress, whom he portrays as calm but secretly passionate, and whom he both condemns and defends, may be read as reflecting the familiar male image of woman as both virgin and whore. But the brief examples of Elise's voice in the narrative enable a quite different response. In her letter to the captain in which she tells him she is pregnant by him, and that she is glad she will be giving him the child his own marriage lacks, it is love above all that she expresses: 'My conscience reproaches me with the sin against my husband, but love knows only one sin – unfaithfulness toward the beloved; it has only one duty – to do everything for the dear object of affection, to give it both body and soul and if necessary sacrifice both.' In the next letter quoted she declares: 'I have a new heart, a new soul', and: 'It is not sensuality that draws me to you; no, my love for you is pure' (139). These letters are, of course, as open to interpretation as the narrator's testimony; but they offer a point of view quite different from his condemnation of her adultery as a male and as a pastor. Through his choice of narrative method, Blicher threw into relief much of what is at issue psychologically and ideologically in a tradition which was still to develop, almost all the examples of which are both male-authored and narrated impersonally.

Blicher shows a strong predilection in his stories not only for the device of the personal narrator, but for the theme of oppressive parental control of female choices in marriage. A daughter's parents oppose her marriage both in 'Tardy Awakening' and in such stories as 'The Hosier and his Daughter' (1829), 'Marie' (1836), 'Three Holiday Eves' (1841) and 'Brass-Jens' (1842); and, in 'The Journal of a Parish Clerk' (1824), 'The Robber's Den' (1827) and 'An Only Child' (1842), the daughter and her lover elope in order to escape an arranged or a forced marriage. 'The Journal of a Parish Clerk' is of special interest as the first of three fictional treatments in Denmark of the story of Marie Grubbe, who was twice divorced on grounds of adultery. Although that story is historical, each of the three constructs it differently. Blicher's version is not a narrative of adultery, as the woman who stands for Marie Grubbe, and whom he calls Sophie, elopes with her low-born lover while she is still engaged to the king's illegitimate son. Instead, the story centres on the humble, pious narrator's unreturned love for Sophie, the vicissitudes he undergoes, and his dismay at seeing her again, many years later, corrupted by the life of degradation she has led. Hans Christian Andersen's version, 'The Family of Hen-Grethe' (1870), conforms much more closely to the historical record.[2] Here the emphasis is on recovering the past through the few links which remain, not least the title character, Marie Grubbe's granddaughter, who ends her life keeping the hen-house where the Grubbe manor-house stood. Andersen's version, written with an audience of children in mind, elides both divorce and adultery completely. Not so Jens Peter Jacobsen's *Marie Grubbe* (1876), the third and best known rendering of the story.

There are significant differences between the fictional treatments given to adultery by Jacobsen and Theodor Fontane and those given by their predecessors and contemporaries. While these differences may be attributed to various disparities of culture and history, many of them specific to Denmark or Germany, one which stands out is the influence of Protestant doctrine and tradition concerning marriage. As Roderick Phillips has shown, the Protestant Reformers of continental Europe rejected the Catholic principles that marriage was a sacrament and was indissoluble. On that basis, 'all of the Protestant states of continental Europe and Scandinavia had legalized divorce by the end of the sixteenth century'.[3] What Phillips calls 'the first coherent divorce legislation' in Denmark and Norway were the Articles of Marriage of 1582. These were modified over the next two centuries by the introduction and extension of royal dispensation.[4] In Prussia the legal code of 1794 laid down provisions for divorce which were amended, after unification, by the Personal Status Act of 1875, applying to all of Germany.[5] As has been pointed out in Chapter 1, divorce did not exist in France for most of the nineteenth century, between 1816 and 1884; and, as *Anna Karenina* underlines, divorce in Russia, though possible for the well-off, was not easy. Ute Frevert has shown that, like France, though to a lesser extent, Prussia saw a conservative backlash against the legal reforms set in motion by the Enlightenment, so that 'both the Catholic and Protestant clergy increasingly refused to marry divorcees', and 'from the 1840s onwards the Prussian Ministry of Justice was drawing up plans to make divorce far more difficult'.[6] Roderick Phillips, referring to the same plans, cites a divorce rate in Prussia of about 3,000 a year at this period.[7] Nevertheless, despite opposition to divorce, it continued on the statute books both in Denmark and in Germany. Its acceptance and availability, past and present, in the countries of Jacobsen and Fontane constitute a key influence on the representation of adultery in their work.

By choosing a pastor to narrate 'Tardy Awakening', Blicher had raised questions about the dangers of hypocrisy inherent in a puritan, Protestant code. Jacobsen's novel draws on another part of the Protestant inheritance in its attitude to marriage and divorce. *Marie Grubbe* is in several respects highly unusual as a novel of female adultery. First, this is the sole such novel I have encountered which is not only set in the distant past but based closely on historical events. Second, female adultery in *Marie Grubbe* is firmly and clearly embedded within a narrative framework in which men are portrayed as routinely exploiting, oppressing and betraying women. Third, the society represented, that of later seventeenth-century Denmark, is unique among those portrayed in novels of female adultery in that, at least at the social level of the main characters, divorce and remarriage are both permitted and obtainable. Fourth, the novel shows the power of female as well as of male sexual desire, but, while it presents this power as mysterious, it does not suggest that it is in any way shameful. Fifth, even though Marie's desire results in her social degradation, the novel carries no conventional moral judgement but affirms her determination to live her life in her own way.

Marie Grubbe does not correspond to the classical form of the historical novel as defined by Georg Lukács. In particular, as Lukács pointed out, the central action has no connection with historical events, and 'as a *typical* destiny Marie Grubbe's story has its place in Jacobsen's own time, the second half of the nineteenth century'.[8] Jacobsen cast a woman as his main character, and, though he set some of the novel's early scenes during the Swedish siege of Copenhagen, he focused the action on personal rather than on historical events. But nothing emphasizes the novel's contemporaneity more clearly than its role in the Scandinavian Modern Breakthrough, proclaimed and inaugurated by Georg Brandes in a famous introductory lecture of 1871.[9] Like other contributors to the movement, among them Ibsen and Strindberg as well as Brandes himself, Jacobsen questioned traditional thinking on a range of topics including religious belief, the position of women, and sexual morality. Marie Grubbe parallels Ibsen's Nora Helmer (in *A Doll's House*, 1879) and Rebecca West (in *Rosmersholm*, 1886), along with Strindberg's eponymous Miss Julie (1888), all of whom figured in the often heated debates which took place across Scandinavia at this period about marriage and sexual morality.[10] Jacobsen's choice of historical material gave him a warrant to depict a degree of female sexual independence which, especially by the standards of his own time, was extraordinary, and to exemplify, through his heroine's life, a code of fatalistic individualism.

Marie Grubbe is married at the age of 17 to Ulrik Frederik, an illegitimate son of the king whose own previous marriage, unacceptable to his father, has been dissolved by royal decree. Ulrik leaves Marie to go to war in Spain, rapes her on the first night of his return, takes up with a mistress, and, when Marie responds by spurning him, has sex with common women and installs his mistress in the marital home. After Marie leaves him and they are divorced, she goes abroad with Sti Högh, the spendthrift, philandering husband of her elder sister, but the affair does not last for long. On her return, almost destitute, she is married by her father to a mercenary official with whom she lives uneventfully but in petty, stifling tedium for 16 years until she falls in love with his coachman Sören. Marie initiates and carries on an all but open affair with Sören, to which her husband raises little objection, until, chiefly at her father's instigation, she is divorced again. She marries her lover, and the two scrape a living for a while as the most lowly of fairground entertainers, until, thanks to a legacy her father cannot withhold from her, they are able to buy a ferry inn which enables them to support themselves through arduous labour till they die.

Two of the novel's emphases stand out from this brief summary: the power of men in a patriarchal society, and Marie's initiative in attempting to counteract it. She has much to struggle against. Erik, her father, is instrumental in arranging her first two marriages and both her divorces. Though he pleads injured morality in petitioning for her second divorce, he is himself notorious for sexual licence; indeed, following the death of his wife, while Marie is still young, he lives with and has a child by his housekeeper. The narrator of *Marie Grubbe* ventures few moral judgements, but he remarks with good reason that Erik 'was the last person who had any right to cast at her the stone of righteous retribution' (XVI.234).[11] Similarly, Ulrik Frederik, Marie's first husband, and Sti Högh, her first lover, are both infamous for debauchery; yet, while Marie's standing suffers from her divorce, Ulrik is able to further his ambition by remarrying to advantage. Although Ulrik also suffers from patriarchal power, through the enforced dissolution of his marriage to Sofie Urne, this pales into insignificance beside Sofie's fate, pregnant at the wedding yet not only promptly denied her husband but consigned to a convent. An exchange of letters between Marie and her elder sister shows that neither has any power to restrain the sexual licence or extravagance of her spouse. Yet, whether through indifference, powerlessness, or even some form of female or sisterly solidarity, there is no hint of complaint from Marie's sister once Marie goes off with her brother-in-law after her divorce.

The novel indicates that much of the power held by men over women is economic. Seeking to improve his own position at any cost to his daughter's, it is for material motives that Erik Grubbe arranges Marie's marriages and divorces. Ulrik Frederik accepts the dissolution of both his marriages for political and economic profit, and Sti Högh spends all his wife's money as well as his own. When Marie leaves her first husband, she is deprived of money both by him and by her father, though each in turn allows her a home; not surprisingly, she experiences 'a sense of powers and possibilities without limit' (XIV.185) when, after her first divorce, she has money of her own for the first time in her life.

What distinguishes Marie, in a world harsh even for upper-class women, is the strength of her passions and her determination to live them through. She is capable of violent, impulsive action, as when she tries to stab Ulrik Frederik the night after he has raped her, and when on two separate occasions she attacks his mistress. Yet the novel represents no special plea for female independence, for it suggests that its heroine courts domination by masterful men. It begins strikingly by juxtaposing Marie's adolescent sensuousness with her father's sordid brutality. After describing her gathering and scattering roses in her luxuriant garden, the first chapter presents her father being nagged coarsely by his concubine housekeeper, and then drinking and riotously quarrelling with the pastor till both fall asleep. But this initial contrast is complicated by Marie's daydream about the ill-treatment of two women from legend, one of them Patient Griselda, by violent, cruel men. The reverie not only prefigures her own maltreatment, but intimates a masochistic attraction on her own part to male power and female martyrdom. Each time she is strongly drawn to a man, his display of strength or violence is decisive: 'a strange peace' comes over her when Ulrik Christian forces a kiss (V.60); she first yields to Sti Högh only after he shows his 'latent savagery' in fighting with two men who have insulted her (XIV.193); she is first taken by the 'beautiful, gigantic form' of Sören when he is manhandling horses out of a burning stable (XVI.211); and her love for Sören is sealed by his attempt to kill the servant-girl she thinks is her rival. Following the failure both of her first marriage and her first affair, the narrator outlines the motives which drive Marie in her relationships with men:

She had left Ulrik Frederik urged on partly by accidental events but chiefly because she had kept certain dreams of her early girlhood of the man a woman should pay homage to, one who should be to her like a god upon earth from whose hands she could accept, lovingly and humbly, good and evil according to his pleasure. And now, in a moment of blindness, she had taken Sti for that god, him who was not even a man. (XV.203)

The dreams mentioned in this passage are highlighted several times in the narrative, and they seem at first to link the young Marie with Flaubert's heroine in *Madame Bovary*, a novel Jacobsen must certainly have known. But her yearnings are more substantial than Emma's, and, unlike Emma's, they prove capable of satisfaction. Though Marie is given to sitting at windows, suffering 'the pain of longing' (II.23), the novel soon suggests that what she needs is a man. She finds her first object of desire in the war-hero Ulrik Christian, whose kiss makes her feel, and yet accept, 'a dull sense of bondage, of being no longer free' (V.60). After Ulrik Christian sickens and succumbs to penitence and death, she enters a religious phase, again reminiscent of *Madame Bovary*, until she agrees to marry Ulrik Frederik. He, and then Sti Högh, fail her in turn; so too does a young man who falls in love with her in Nuremberg and who dies in an accident. Finally, when she is well into her forties, she finds in the peasant Sören, much younger than herself, a man she can love. Jacobsen presents Marie as enthralled by the coachman's physical strength. Yet what is most significant about his construction of her desire is that he represents it both as inviting domination and as essentially feminine:

She thought of his coarse habits and his ignorance, his peasant speech and poor clothes, his toil-hardened body and his vulgar greediness. Was she to bend beneath all this, to accept good and evil from this black hand? In this self-abasement there was a strange, voluptuous pleasure which was in part gross sensuality but in part akin to whatever is counted noblest and best in woman's nature. For such was the manner in which the clay had been mixed out of which she was fashioned.... (XVI.217)

Jacobsen hedges his generalization about women by displacing it with the words 'akin to' and by attributing it to accepted opinion. Nevertheless, the judgement represented by the phrase 'whatever is counted noblest and best in woman's nature' is all the more notable for his usual narratorial reserve. The suggestion is that 'natural' femininity consists in a woman devoting – even subjugating – herself to the man she loves. Thus Marie bears terrible poverty, hardship and labour for a man much below her class who later turns to beating her, but who has demonstrated his love not only as her husband but by attempting suicide and murder for her sake.

As Niels Lyhne Jensen has remarked, 'Jacobsen unquestionably held progressive views on women's rights, but his insistence in the novel that Marie's disposition for humiliation and subjection to a man is an element of what is most valuable in woman's nature reflects a decidedly masculine view of the female psyche'.[12] Nevertheless, although *Marie Grubbe* generalizes female desire as masochistic, in other respects it presents a more challenging perspective. On two occasions Jacobsen has Marie deliver what amounts to a personal testimony. First, when Sti Högh mistakes her for a disillusioned pleasure-seeker like himself, she passionately explains that she despairs not because life disappoints her but because she feels excluded from it: 'this life – this earth – seems to me so splendid and wonderful I should be proud and happy beyond words just to have some part in it. Whether for joy or grief matters not, but that I might sorrow or rejoice in honest truth, not in play like mummeries or shrovetide sports' (XI.149–50). Marie achieves this sense of full participation in life only through marriage, in exacting conditions, to a husband she loves. Jacobsen underlines the point in the novel's closing scene by expanding on the account given by the Dano-Norwegian historian, dramatist and essayist Ludvig Holberg of his acquaintance with her near the end of her life. She responds to Holberg's incredulity about her choice of partner and her bypassing of conventional morality with the simple affirmation: 'I believe every human being lives his own life and dies his own death; that is what I believe' (XVIII.250). She goes on to ask the writer whether a sinner who dies repenting on his deathbed 'is more pleasing to God than another who has likewise sinned and offended against Him but then for many years of her life has striven to do her duty, has borne every burden without a murmur, but never in prayer or open repentance has wept over her former life' (XVIII.251). Though Holberg has no answer, the response the novel invites is in keeping with Jacobsen's own declared interest in 'the struggle of one or more human beings for existence, that is their struggle against the existing order of things for their right to exist in their own way'.[13] Marie's independence is all the more impressive in comparison with the behaviour of the two main female characters in Jacobsen's later novel, *Niels Lyhne* (1880).[14] One sacrifices her freedom for a conventional marriage, while the other refuses to elope with the hero, but has a clandestine affair with him till she rejects him in moral panic after her husband dies in an accident.

It is through Jacobsen's emphasis on freedom that *Marie Grubbe* differs most radically from previous novels of female adultery. The implications of that emphasis are to some extent mixed. If, on the one hand, the person shown struggling for freedom is a woman, on the other hand the form in which she finds it is in devotion, though chosen by herself, to a man. However, despite Jacobsen's dubious notions about female desire, he also demonstrates, through Marie's life, the oppression and lack of opportunity suffered by women. *Marie Grubbe* highlights male, not female, sexual transgression. Indeed, in a revealing deviation from historical record, Marie does not begin her first affair until after she is divorced;[15] and, in her second loveless marriage, she turns adulteress only to become a better wife. Jacobsen emphasizes Marie's role as a married woman through the word *Fru* in his title. Yet the novel is driven by an ideology not of marriage or of family – it is significant that Jacobsen's heroine never has children – but of individualism. What is most unusual about *Marie Grubbe* as a novel of female adultery is, finally, that its heroine survives – even though she compounds her transgression by breaking taboos both of social class and of age.

Jacobsen's work, including *Marie Grubbe*, was greatly admired by Rilke and other modernist writers. Yet, if the individualism celebrated by his novel links with that of the alienated artist in the late nineteenth and earlier twentieth centuries, it has its roots in an essentially Protestant tradition. That tradition, strong in Denmark, to which the Reformation had spread quickly, explains in part the marked differences between *Marie Grubbe* as a novel of female adultery and examples from predominantly Catholic or Orthodox cultures. Its influence is equally important in the work of Theodor Fontane.

Fontane published his first novel at the relatively advanced age of 58. He was already well known as a writer of ballads, travel books, theatre reviews and general journalism; indeed, for some time after his death he was better remembered for his travel writing and his ballads than for his fiction. As a novelist, his governing concern was the representation of social behaviour and values among the old Prussian aristocracy and the new metropolitan bourgeoisie which burgeoned in the aftermath of German unification. This concern was intrinsically historical. It is reflected not only in his several historical novels, including the first novel he published, *Before the Storm* (1878), and a work he projected but was unable to begin before he died, *Die Likedeeler* (*The Sharers*),[16] but also in his fiction of contemporary life and of the recent past. Among his fiction addressing his own times are no fewer than three novels of adultery. Like Jacobsen's *Marie Grubbe*, the first two of these display striking differences from the patterns, chiefly derived from *Madame Bovary* and *Anna Karenina*, which are most often held to characterize nineteenth-century adultery fiction. In the first, *L'Adultera* (1882), the adulterous wife not only achieves a divorce but a successful and happy remarriage; more surprisingly still, the second, *Beyond Recall* (1891), is a novel of male rather than of female adultery. The third of Fontane's novels of adultery, *Effi Briest* (1895), appears to follow more closely the precedents set by Flaubert and by Tolstoy. Yet it would be wrong to suggest that *L'Adultera* and *Beyond Recall* constitute failed attempts on Fontane's part on his way to realizing some kind of normative model for a novel of adultery in *Effi Briest*. Each of the two earlier novels has its own special qualities, not least of which is a capacity to put social and fictional conventions in question. Furthermore, if comparison is extended beyond the customary trio of *Madame Bovary*, *Anna Karenina* and *Effi Briest*,[17] so that it also includes Fontane's two other novels centred on adultery, his own contribution to the theme emerges much more clearly.

First published only four years after *Anna Karenina*, *L'Adultera* invites comparison with Tolstoy's novel through several detailed parallels. The most specific of these are that, like Tolstoy's, Fontane's adulterous couple also escape to Italy where their child is born; that the child is female; and that her name, Aninette, recalls that of Anna's daughter, Ani. Similarly, Fontane follows Tolstoy in having his heroine sensitized to faults in her husband and in her marriage by her response to a man she loves. Just as Anna, returning from Moscow, recognizes Karenin's protruding ears and feels a quite new awareness of dissatisfaction (I.xxx.119), so Melanie, in Fontane's novel, feels ashamed of her husband for the first time when he indulges in the risqué humour she has always accepted from him unthinkingly in the presence of the man with whom she has fallen in love (IX.55; 63).[18]

Another parallel is the role played by paintings in the two novels, though this is quite different in each. In *Anna Karenina* the portrait of Anna highlights the charm and attractiveness of the adulteress, impressing everyone, including Levin on the one – guilty – occasion when he meets her, 'not only by its likeness but also by its peculiar beauty' (V.xiii.503; VII.x.728–9). Fontane, however, uses the painting he features in *L'Adultera*, and from which he took his title, as a way of complicating responses to Melanie's transgression. The painting is a copy of a Tintoretto depicting the woman taken in adultery.[19] Introduced at the start of the novel by Melanie's husband as, in his words, 'a sort of memento mori' (II.10; 15), it offers, through Melanie's comments, an image of the adulteress which is fully in keeping with the tolerance of the Bible story:

> She's been crying. Of course she has. You know why? Because they've told her over and over again how wicked she is. And now she believes it, or at least she wants to believe it. But her heart rebels and just won't accept it . . . I must confess, I really find her very touching. There's so much innocence in her guilt. And it's as if it had all been predestined. (II.9, TM; 13)

This comment prefigures not only Melanie's adultery, but the response Fontane invites towards it. For *L'Adultera* is distinguished not only by its happy ending but by its adumbration of a quite different set of values from that which applies in *Anna Karenina*. After Melanie's divorce, return from Italy, and remarriage, she speaks of the hurt she has caused her husband as 'a wrong which is not diminished just because, in my heart, I don't quite feel it to have been a wrong' (XIX.104; 115). The paradox echoes her previous comment on the painting, and it is explained not so much by her assertion that she has 'never lied or pretended' (XX.111; 121), as by her belief that her first marriage was in itself a lie which was better put straight. On the point of leaving to elope with her lover, she declares to her husband: 'I must start a new life and find in *him* what was missing from my old life, and that is truth' (XVI.92; 102). This is to suggest a morality like that discussed by Michael Black in his book *The Literature of Fidelity*, in which fidelity means truth to the self rather than to others or to social, religious or institutional codes.[20] It is in this sense that Melanie replies to her servant: 'one can be true by being untrue. Truer than by remaining faithful' (XV.86; 96).

It is startling to find in a work by a novelist noted for his tact and discretion so explicit a statement of an individual's right to fulfilment of her emotional needs. What makes this position all the more notable is the fact that the individual in question is an adulterous wife in a society for which, according to Ute Frevert, 'pre- and extra-marital sex was an absolute taboo that few dared to question', including even members of the women's movement.[21] It is true that it is the character who challenges the taboo, not the narrator. Indeed, *L'Adultera* is the first of Fontane's novels in which the form of presentation is mainly dialogue. Yet the novel bears out its heroine's stand through its emphases and its ending, despite not only a period of almost complete ostracism but alienation from the children of her first marriage.

First, the new couple justify themselves in the eyes of society by their love and commitment to each other, especially after a business failure destroys their affluent way of living. Fontane finesses an outcome which seems all too rosy for conviction by means of a narratorial comment which is characteristically ironic and sceptical: 'The state of mind that first condemned and then pardoned was basically the same: at first people had reveled in the thrills of indignation; now they were able to speak with scarcely less satisfaction of "the inseparables" and to sentimentalize their "true love"' (XXII.126, TM; 137). In the process Melanie changes from bourgeois wife, subject and object of conspicuous consumption, to working mother. Second, both Melanie and the narrator are clear about her priorities with her children. When she leaves her husband, she refuses his invitation to look at them for the last time. Later she explains why: 'I had to make a choice. [. . .] If you run away from your marriage for no other reason than because you love another man, then you give up your right to play the tender mother' (XX.111; 122). As Henry Garland has remarked, this clarity of mind and purpose recalls Nora's in Ibsen's *A Doll's House*, which had scandalized audiences in Germany only two years before, though Ibsen's heroine leaves her husband for quite different motives.[22] It survives, though not without difficulty, a meeting with her children in which her older daughter rejects and quits her in hatred (XX.115; 125). In the novel's final chapter Melanie's ex-husband sees and praises her new baby out in the park with her nurse, and sends her as a Christmas present a miniature of the Tintoretto. To cite Garland again, 'the diminished format is a sign that her "offence" is no longer a matter of resentment'.[23]

It is significant that *L'Adultera* is the only one of Fontane's three novels of adultery to end happily, and also the only one of the three to deal with the bourgeoisie rather than with the old aristocracy. Melanie's husband, Ezekiel van der Straaten, is a successful if, according to Berlin society, an underbred member of the new bourgeoisie who, well aware of prejudice against Jewish origins, takes care to emphasize his Protestantism. He has married Melanie ten years before the action begins, when he was 42 and she was 17. Melanie, who comes from an aristocratic Swiss-French family, had accepted him when her father died suddenly, leaving her with nothing but debts. Her lover and second husband, Ebenezer Rubehn, is another businessman of Jewish descent, younger and more cultivated than his predecessor. Van der Straaten not only foreshadows his wife's adultery by acquiring and commenting pointedly on the Tintoretto, but partly enables it by taking Rubehn into his home as a business favour. His indulgence in familiar Berlinisms and in humorous, sometimes mildly salacious, innuendo often produces a comedy of social embarrassment, but Fontane makes him neither a conventional cuckold nor a figure of fun. Though at times overbearing in his attempts to demand a social regard proportional to his business position, he is generous both with his wealth and in his tolerance and forgiveness to Melanie. These attitudes contrast sharply with those of his brother-in-law Major Gryczinski, married to Melanie's younger sister.

Gryczinski's attitudes, which are much more characteristic of the establishment, prefigure the rigidity of code and behaviour depicted in *Effi Briest*. They give a flavour of a social world in which the first topic of conversation at the van der Straatens' dinner party is the prospect of a war to follow the Prussian victories of 1864, 1866, and 1870 (V.21–4; 26–9); in which members of the police and of the army respectively find it embarrassing to be a Catholic (V.29; 35) or to have Catholic relatives (XIX.106–7; 117); and in which to use the word 'trousers' or to allude to fallen women in polite company is considered indecorous (V.27; 33, IX.54; 61). A staff officer and a 'careerist' (IV.17; 22) – a word which, as Henry Garland points out, 'in Fontane's usage is contemptuous'[24] – Gryczinski cannot bring himself to offer his arm to the Police Commissioner with whom he dines regularly 'as to an equal'

(IV.20; 25), and forbids his wife to see Melanie on her return from Italy. Melanie's sister, who takes nearly all her opinions from her husband, is delighted at seeing so much as a shadow of Frederick the Great's statue as her carriage passes by it (VI.31; 37), and is prepared even to contemplate war for the sake of his promotion (XIX.107; 117). Even she, nevertheless, questions his priorities: 'Gryczinski never stops saying that what matters in life is controlling one's feelings . . . I am not so sure he's right' (XX.113; 123). *L'Adultera* registers the same doubts, less tentatively. They reappear in a poignant key in *Effi Briest*.

What stands behind the presentation of female adultery in *Marie Grubbe* and *L'Adultera* are distinctively Protestant positions on the integrity of the individual conscience and on marriage. Just as Jacobsen's heroine insists at the end of her life that she had a right to live in her own way, so Fontane's maintains that she cannot live at peace with herself while unhappily married and returning the love of another man. Paradoxically, as Roderick Phillips has suggested, it was because the Protestant reformers valued marriage as an institution for the legitimate expression of 'God's gift of sexuality' that they were prepared to accept divorce.[25] The Reformers did not, however, allow remarriage for those convicted of matrimonial fault. Thus *Marie Grubbe* and *L'Adultera* reflect secular developments which emphasize not fault but the kinds of incompatibility which resulted when, for instance, an adolescent female entered an arranged marriage, especially to a man older than herself. However, along with *Marie Grubbe* – and unlike Ibsen's *A Doll's House* – none of Fontane's novels of adultery questions marriage as such. It is as a wife that Marie Grubbe at last finds fulfilment; and Melanie van der Straaten breaks a failed marriage to make a good one. Fontane's second novel of adultery, *Beyond Recall*, is, so far as I know, unique in the nineteenth-century canon in that it centres on the adultery of a husband. But it is entirely in keeping with other fiction of adultery in the seriousness it attaches to marriage.

Beyond Recall is set 30 years before it was published, on the eve of the Austro-Prussian war with Denmark over Schleswig-Holstein in 1864. At two strategic points, early and late in the novel respectively, newspaper reports are cited which refer to the change of government and rearmament in Prussia which heralded the war

(III.20–1; 23–4, XXXI.280; 236).[26] Although Fontane keeps the political context unobtrusive, it is also a period of crisis in Denmark: 'they were days when not only a ministry but even the monarchy itself seemed threatened' (XVII.142, TM; 123). The novel begins in September 1859, when the marriage of Helmut and Christine von Holk, having lasted for 16 years, has reached a turning point. Christine is anxious about the children and wishes to send them away to complete their education; while Holk, in his mid-forties, is at the stage of what would now be called a mid-life crisis. By Christmas the two are separated, thanks to Holk's fleeting affair with a lady-in-waiting; and less than two years after, following a brief and unsuccessful reconciliation, Christine has committed suicide. The Holks live near the Danish border, and Holk, though a Schleswig aristocrat like his wife, spends part of his time as a gentleman-in-waiting at the court of Princess Maria Eleanor, aunt to the Danish king. While Holk's main links are with Denmark, Christine strongly inclines to Germany where she has been educated by a strict Protestant sect, the Herrnhuter. In this way the Holk marriage is divided, like Schleswig-Holstein itself, between the claims of both Denmark and Prussia.

Like *L'Adultera* and Fontane's mature work in general, *Beyond Recall* unfolds largely through conversations between or about the main characters. An early discussion in which Holk takes the side of Denmark and Christine of Prussia foreshadows the conflicts between states and partners alike. While Holk scoffs at the idea of Prussia as a nation, Christine speaks up for Prussian moral rigour against what she sees as Danish licence. She believes that Prussia is bound to outstrip Denmark because it is inspired by 'an idea, a faith' (IV.27; 28); and, speaking as a Schleswig-Holsteiner, she declares: 'German, not Prussian, that is what we must become' (IV.29; 30). The contest of values presented by the novel is therefore simultaneously personal and national.

Though *Beyond Recall* was written from the vantage point of a Germany united under Prussian hegemony, it offers nothing so crude as historical allegory. Rather, its portrayals of a failing marriage, of the husband's unfaithfulness, and of life both in a noble Schleswig family and in the Danish court are woven into a fabric of national traditions and of historical process. Since it is while he is attending the Danish court that Holk betrays his wife, it is not for nothing that a series of conversations brings to light a whole history of sexual immorality in the Danish royal family. Not only is the present king, Frederick VII, who is also Duke of Schleswig, notorious for living all but openly with his mistress, but he is shown to be following long-established precedents. There are also allusions to the sixteenth-century Christian II, and his mistress of humble origins, Dyveke (XVI.136–7; 119); to Struensee, executed as lover of the wife of the eighteenth-century Christian VII (XVI.139; 121, XVII.143; 124); and to the seventeenth-century Christian IV and his tiff with his mistress (XXII.196–7; 167–8). The last of these anecdotes is especially revealing for the discussion it provokes. The pastor who relates it notes that the king's mistress 'was his wife without being his wife, unfortunately a rather frequent occurrence in our history' (XXII.197; 167). Holk, teased by the flirtatious Ebba von Rosenberg, responds by calling the story trivial, only to find himself further embarrassed by her rebuttal. Denmark aside, she remarks that Germany cannot compete for royal love affairs with England or France, and she mockingly adds: 'last of all, there comes Prussia with a complete blank in this sphere' (XXII.200; 170). Ebba has already drawn attention to the dangers she poses by mentioning that her name means 'Eve' (XIII.112; 99) and that she was born in Paris on the day the Revolution broke out in 1830 (XIII.114; 100). She ends by giving her attack a personal application: 'Loose living only harms morals but the pretence of being virtuous harms the whole man' (XXII.200; 170).

What is at issue in discussions like these is not only Holk's division between his wife's austere morality and Ebba's witty sexual allure, but a debate about cultural values and a reading of Danish history. Another conversation gives a view of an earlier, heroic Denmark in which a woman played the role not of seducer and mistress but of religious champion and wife. It arises from a painting at the royal castle depicting a sixteenth-century sea victory by Denmark over Sweden. The pastor explains that the woman who later married Herluf Trolle, the victorious admiral, was the pillar of the new Lutheran faith, and that without her Denmark might 'have remained wrapped in Popish darkness' (XX.180; 154). What gives the anecdote further force is the history of Frederiksborg castle itself, built by an earlier Danish king to replace the old castle, razed to the ground, which he had obtained from Herluf Trolle. For the turning point of the novel comes when part of the castle is destroyed by fire just after Holk has succumbed to temptation with Ebba. The burning of Frederiksborg, which actually happened in December 1859, illustrates the rich web of

historical and political implication which Fontane wove into his
novel of adultery. It both suggests the danger of passion, or licence,
not only for the main characters but for the Danish court as a
whole, and points a sharp contrast to the story of Herluf Trolle and
his wife Brigitte – who, ironically, has the same first name as
another of Holk's temptresses, his landlady's beautiful daughter.

Beyond Recall is, then, an historical novel as well as a novel of
adultery, and more truly so than *Marie Grubbe* in that the personal
is linked with the historical throughout. At one point, for example,
Holk asks himself:

what, in fact, could be considered entirely beyond question?
Nothing, absolutely nothing, and every conversation with the
Princess or with Ebba only served to confirm him in that opinion.
Everything was provisional, everything a mere majority decision
of the moment: morals, dogma, taste, everything was uncertain
and it was only for Christine that every question had been settled
once and for all. (XIX.162; 139)

Here, Holk's sense of his wife's inflexibility is expressed in the
language of parliamentary government, the personal merging with
the political.

In its dramatization of tension and misunderstandings between
husband and wife, *Beyond Recall* offers a painfully convincing
account of marital breakdown. The narrator observes that 'Holk,
though a kind and excellent husband, was none the less a man of
rather ordinary gifts and in any case markedly inferior to his wife'
(II.7; 12); and Holk himself reflects ruefully that 'Christine was a
woman with less geniality than was desirable and more principles
than were necessary' (XXIV.215; 183). While Fontane indicates that
neither husband nor wife is blameless, the novel is presented
mainly from Holk's point of view and it attributes most of the
responsibility for their separation to him. Alan Bance has claimed
that *Beyond Recall* 'contains some of the very few overtly moralizing
sentiments in Fontane's works', and he suggests that one reason for
this may be that the writer's previous novel, *Irrungen, Wirrungen*
(1888), which turns on a pre-marital affair between a seamstress
and an aristocratic officer, had been widely criticized for its
supposed immorality.[27] For Bance, the moral to the tale is to be
found, if anywhere, in what Holk reads from the expression of the
usually free-thinking Princess when he goes to tell her that he

intends to leave his wife and marry Ebba: 'The only lesson that could now be read in her haggard face seemed to be that boldness and excess had little to offer as a rule of life; that keeping a promise and obeying the law were the only things really to be recommended and, above all, that a genuine, not a reluctant, marriage, was the only safe haven' (XXVIII.249–50; 211). However, Fontane rarely encourages any absolute judgement, and this is no exception. In two ways the context is important. First, what Holk reads in the Princess's face is merely inference, while she is still shocked and exhausted after the fire, and anxious to avoid further distress. Second, the assessment of Holk which the novel puts forward is conditioned by a political parallel between him and his native Schleswig-Holstein.

It is, again, Alan Bance who has suggested that 'the union of Holk and Christine resembles the troubled "marriage" of Denmark and Schleswig-Holstein on the eve of the German-Danish war'.[28] The analogy is tempting, but it leaves out the third and crucial item of Prussia, and it neglects the fact that the action turns on the divided loyalties of Holk himself. Ebba von Rosenberg pinpoints the divisions in Holk long before he yields to her at the novel's climax. She tells the Princess:

He pretends to be a Schleswig-Holsteiner and yet he serves as gentleman-in-waiting to an obviously Danish princess; he's a living work of reference on genealogies [. . .] and yet he sets himself up as an enlightened liberal. [. . .] As far as his morals are concerned, he is what one might describe as almost virtuous and yet he has a yearning to be a man of the world. (XVIII.155; 133–4)

When, having fallen to Ebba, Holk believes he is leaving his wife to marry her, he fatuously imagines a Danish friend rejoicing that, 'with the help of a beautiful Swede, a Schleswig-Holstein heart had been won over to Denmark' (XXX.263; 222).

Beyond Recall denies its hero what *L'Adultera* had permitted to its heroine. However, the cases are far from similar. Though Holk may seem to echo Melanie in declaring at his moment of decision: 'it's my right to have what I want' (XXIX.251; 212), he has fundamentally misunderstood both himself and Ebba, and she rejects him. The novel has already highlighted the dangers for Holk through such scenes as those in which a wax angel falling from a Christmas tree punctuates the discussion about Christian IV and his mistress

(XXII.200; 170), and in which he and Ebba literally skate on thin ice (XXV.221–3; 187–9). Similarly, the narrator conveys Holk's moral failure by pointing out that, 'if he had been able to step outside himself and listen to his own arguments, he would have realized that he was studiously avoiding two words: God and heaven' (XXVIII.244; 206), and then, categorically, that 'he finally lost all sense of judgement and reason' (XXVIII.245; 207). Nevertheless, the sharp sense of marital discord created in the novel comes at least as much from Christine as from Holk. The marriage is not helped by the use Christine makes of her companion, an unmarried friend from her schooldays. Worse, her religion is harsh and unyielding – even her brother finds her 'so obstinate and unapproachable' (V.33; 33) – and she repeatedly fails to restrain her impulse to criticize and correct faults in others, especially her husband. Richard A. Koc pertinently compares Christine to Geert von Instetten in *Effi Briest*.[29] Both betrayed spouses show a rigidity of principle and a zeal for education which their partners find oppressive; and neither conveys affection easily. Christine agrees to a reconciliation with Holk because, as her brother puts it, 'what she might be incapable of doing for love, she will find herself impelled to do out of her conception of duty' (XXXI.282, TM; 238). But duty proves insufficient to quell her resentment of her husband's infidelity. As Alan Bance has observed, 'her suicide bears witness to the unendurable strength of her feelings, and, paradoxically enough, it is the first occasion on which she bends her inflexible Christian principles'.[30]

Beyond Recall is further distinctive in declining to condemn the adulteress. Not only is Ebba witty and highly perceptive, but she shows a moral realism which contrasts favourably both with Holk's muddled attitudes and with Christine's austerity. Ebba states her position when she remarks: 'of course I know that people ought to be virtuous but they are not, and if you accept this, on the whole things are better than when morality is a mere façade' (XXII.200; 170). However, although this freedom from hypocrisy is refreshing, it does not alter the human impact of infidelity. Before Christine dies, Holk comments: 'The light of our life is joy, and once the light goes out, then night must fall, and if that night means death, it is still for the best' (XXXIII.292, TM; 245). This note of fatalistic Nordic acceptance accords with Fontane's composed, unsentimental portrayal of what is no more. The novel is a humane, manysided account of a marital breakdown and a declining social and political order both of which are indeed irretrievable.

L'Adultera was Fontane's first novel of contemporary life, coming after the historical narratives *Before the Storm, Grete Minde* (1880), *Ellernklipp* (1881) and *Schach von Wuthenow* (1882).[31] Although he moved to the recent past for *Beyond Recall*, all his novels after *Schach von Wuthenow* offer what Alan Bance has called 'essentially a historical view of contemporary life'.[32] This remark is true above all of *Effi Briest*. The novel not only reflects Fontane's disquiet about social and political developments in the Germany of his time, but portrays a society obsessed by history.

Most of the history invoked in *Effi Briest* concerns the military successes through which Prussia had achieved pre-eminence. Effi herself refers to the battle of Fehrbellin in 1675, in which one of her ancestors led an attack (VIII.65; 64),[33] and which began 'the process of sweeping the Danes right out of Brandenburg-Prussian territory';[34] and also to the massacre carried out by the Danes at Stockholm in 1520 (XIII.105; 109). Joachim Nettelbeck's role in the defence of Kolberg against the French in 1806–7 persuades Effi's husband, Geert von Instetten, and another patriot to bid for the hero's unappealing portrait (XIX.142; 152); the successful bidder had distinguished himself in the first Schleswig campaign of 1848 (XVIII.140; 150), under the same general whom Effi's father had served as adjutant (VII.57; 55). But it is the Franco-Prussian war, of more recent memory, which commands most attention. Major von Crampas, who becomes Effi's lover, reminds her husband that they were comrades at Vionville (XV.118; 124–5);[35] and Effi and Instetten visit the panorama of St Privat (VI.46; 43), which commemorates another Prussian victory. Volker Berghahn has pointed out the building, up till the eve of the First World War, of 'innumerable monuments that commemorated the victory of 1870 and other historical events', adding that 'the intent of patriotic edification and indoctrination was highlighted at both the pompous opening ceremony and at annual festivities like Sedan Day'.[36] Indeed the Sedan Day celebrations feature early in the novel (IV.33–4; 28–9), and Fontane shows the cult of militarism infiltrating even the domestic and the familial. When Effi gives birth on the anniversary of the victory over the Austrians at Königgrätz in 1866, the doctor regrets that she has not produced a son; and there are objections from some families when the christening takes place on the birthday of Napoleon (XIV.110–11; 115–16). At Effi's parental home the garden contains a monument to Waterloo (XV.113; 119), while there are even pictures showing scenes from the wars of 1864 and 1866 in her bedroom (XXIV.199; 218).

Fontane believed that the task of the modern novel was 'the description of a life, a society, a group of people, as the undistorted reflection of the life we lead'.[37] The military traditions represented so extensively in *Effi Briest* are part of the phenomenon in German life at this time which has subsequently been called 'social militarism'.[38] David Blackbourn has cited as an example of deference to authority during the Wilhelmine period 'the particular respect accorded to the army', which 'found vivid expression in the way a middle-aged and respected citizen would step off the pavement in order not to impede a young lieutenant';[39] and Giles MacDonogh has highlighted the 'aggressive nationalism' which overtook Prussian conservatism in the 1880s.[40] Although Fontane offers his historical and military allusions without narratorial comment, and although he took pride in his Prussian heritage, it is clear that he was greatly disturbed by these developments. Eda Sagarra quotes him saying in 1887: 'The military world in particular is getting beyond itself. It is the spoiled child of the family, just because the military are the best riders and dancers, and the parents let them do anything they want.'[41] In 1894, the year in which he completed *Effi Briest*, he wrote to his publisher: 'How fortunate we are that we still have a non-Prussian Germany. Oberammergau, Munich, Weimar – those are the places that make one happy. Faced with standing-at-attention, fingers-to-the-trouser-seam, Leist and Wehlan, I get sick. And I am a dyed-in-the-wool Prussian.'[42] This was also the year in which the government proposed an anti-subversion bill, to which he strongly objected. Joachim Remak indicates that the bill, which was ultimately defeated in the Reichstag,

would have provided for prison terms of up to two years for offenses as vaguely defined as "enticing various classes of the population to commit acts of violence against one another," or "publicly attacking, in a manner insulting or designed to endanger the public peace, religion, monarchy, marriage, family, or property." The bill so bothered Fontane that he took the unusual step of adding his name to a public protest against it and agreed to solicit the signatures of some socially prominent friends of his as well.[43]

Though set at an earlier date than its publication, by inference in the years 1878 to 1891, the novel gives various examples of social and political unrest, including the assassination attempt on the Kaiser in 1878 (IX.67; 67), and local incidents of arson (XII.95; 98, XVII.127; 135).

What renders this carefully inscribed setting of militarism, nationalism and political repression significant, in Fontane's third novel of adultery, is its entanglement with a rigidly stratified social structure and a culture of conformity and emotional-sexual repression. The seed from which Fontane develops the action of *Effi Briest* is Frau Briest's refusal of Instetten's proposal of marriage, 18 years before the novel begins. Having married an older and better established man instead, Frau Briest is in a position to offer her 17-year-old daughter to her former suitor, who now more than compensates for his previous youth and inadequate prospects. Through Effi's dress, talk and play the novel's opening scene emphasizes that she is still virtually a child; and there is a repugnant hint of paedophilia about the mother's inspiration that Effi might better go to Instetten without changing her clothes, 'still flushed from the excitement of her game' (II.24; 17). Alfred G. Meyer has shown from the memoirs of Lily Braun, born to a military family in 1865, the twin codes of seductiveness and of chastity impressed on girls of good family:

Braun tells us that she was seven or eight when older relatives introduced her to this role of women: to be pretty, to be seductive, to dominate others through sexuality, and to learn that these love games are intriguing and enjoyable. Rule number two commanded chastity, unapproachability, and untouchability. Women were to be seen but not to be touched, and to be seen only under controlled conditions. [. . .] Violation of this code was a serious, often unpardonable offense against respectability.[44]

A trivial but telling example of such violation in *Effi Briest* is the censure passed by Frau Briest on Fräulein Hulda for clinking her glass too hard against Lieutenant Nienkerken's at Effi's wedding (V.44; 40). Meyer goes on to infer that 'the code of behavior obviously was designed to train men and women, and especially the latter, for frigidity, for only a negative attitude toward sex, arising from fear, from disgust, or from disdain of the opposite gender'.[45] This attitude is also reflected at Effi's wedding, for an elderly male guest says to his friend, 'still a bachelor, and doubtless for that reason at the moment involved in his fourth liaison': 'What really prevents anyone from succeeding in life? It's always fervour' (V.40, TM; 36).

Fontane presents in Effi and Instetten two people not only brought up in but fully accepting such contradictory rules of behaviour. Thus, after Effi has borne her child, still at the age of 17, she is delighted when Instetten says, 'There's something seductive about you,' and she answers: 'Did you know that that's what I've always wanted to be? We have to be seductive or else we're nothing at all' (XV.116; 123). Instetten is amazed when she goes on to attribute this article of wisdom to her childhood pastor, but it is paralleled by his own liking for other people, including Crampas, to admire his wife (XVIII.136–7; 145–6). While Crampas indeed finds Effi attractive, he also pays her the consideration which Instetten neglects. Fontane even appears to suggest that, like Melanie's husband in *L'Adultera*, Instetten invites betrayal through his inattention to Effi and his permissiveness in her relation to a man he knows to be a philanderer.

Emotional and sexual repression loom as large in *Effi Briest* as military and nationalistic tradition. Again, the novel builds up its picture by accumulating details small in themselves. In the opening scene, Frau Briest reproves Effi for impulsiveness when she runs to embrace her (I.16; 9); and 15 months later, when Effi, now a married woman herself, dashes over and kisses her hand, she says, 'Effi, you're so impetuous' (XXIII.177, TM; 192). Two examples of prudishness are of truly Victorian hypersensitivity: Effi's nursemaid Roswitha removes from a list of library books a title including the word 'trousers' (XXIII.182; 198), and the more genteel maidservant Joanna finds that 'the emphasis on wife and mother' in a rhyme welcoming Effi home 'somehow contained a suggestion that might give offence' (XXVI.208; 228). Actual sexual misdemeanour is much more dangerous. Before Effi is married, her father has to dismiss his overseer for carrying on with the gardener's wife (IV.30; 25); while, shortly after her arrival in Kessin, a neighbour 'is obliged to dismiss her maid on the spot because of an unfortunate incident' (XI.86; 87). Effi herself, despite or even because of her affair with Crampas, tries to police Roswitha's behaviour with the coachman; and the nursemaid tells how she was pursued with a red-hot iron by her father, a blacksmith, when he found she was pregnant, how her illegitimate child was quickly taken away from her, and how she was sent away as a wet-nurse (XXI.163–5; 176–8). As Roswitha has discovered, the only safe mode of behaviour in such circumstances is conformity. This is displayed to perfection by the concert-singer Fräulein Trippelli, who will not go on the stage for fear of damaging her reputation, who sings 'with a virtuosity only equalled by her lack of emotion' (XI.90; 92), and whose views on morality are all the stricter because 'she personally had the great advantage of not believing in anything at all' (XII.92; 95).

The novel presents its heroine as a child of this society in only too full and literal a sense. Strikingly, it never occurs to Effi that her Cousin Dagobert, an eligible young officer who is strongly attracted to her, might be a more appropriate partner than a man old enough to be her father. She is so thoroughly socialized that, for her, 'anyone is Mr Right', so long as he has 'a title and a situation in society and look[s] presentable' (III.26; 20). She later explains in all seriousness to her husband that she married him only 'out of ambition' (X.81; 82), and there is no sign that the marriage is anything but a success, according to the principles of their culture, at the point when the evidence of Effi's adultery comes to light. Michael Minden quotes Roy Pascal's view that 'if the letters had not been discovered [Effi] would have become something not very different from Botho's wife in *Irrungen, Wirrungen*, elegant, ambitious, superficial', and adds: 'I do not feel that from any easily discernible point of view one could say that this would have been a human catastrophe'.[46] Perhaps 'catastrophe' would be too strong a word for such an outcome; but the issue at stake is what Minden has already formulated as 'the growth of an individual towards the specific possibilities of adulthood offered by a certain stratum of society at a certain historical moment'.[47] For the novel suggests that those possibilities are cripplingly meagre not only for Effi but to some extent for Instetten too. The point is clear, at least in relation to Effi, when Minden, having put the case for what he terms 'the world of tact', declares:

The apparent mistake made by the society in which she lives, that is, marrying her too young, is no mistake at all, but, as with the over-zealous education by Instetten, inseparable from the process through which women must go if they are to assume the only place available to them in this world of tact. Effi's development *must* be arrested at the stage of childish spontaneity – and this childishness must be linked with sexuality, as it is both symbolically and literally in the affair with Crampas – for only this combination, childishness plus an erotic dimension, can fit a woman to her social role.[48]

But it is unnecessary to assume that the novel encourages complicity with a form of 'arrested development' which is the emotional equivalent of foot-binding or clitoridectomy. After Effi has been taken in again by her parents after several years of almost total ostracism, Fontane describes her wearing the same dress as on the day of her engagement (XXXIV.252; 278); and his choice of her maiden name for the novel's title not only echoes the inscription she chooses for her tombstone but suggests that at the end she is still in important respects the child she was at the beginning.

The question then arises as to how far adultery is central to *Effi Briest* – and even the question how far it is proper to term *Effi Briest* a novel of female adultery. Referring to this novel and to *L'Adultera* during a discussion of *Beyond Recall*, Frances M. Subiotto has remarked: 'Ebba, like the Crampases and Rubehns of his other novels, is nothing more than a catalyst in the break-up of the marriage. She merely confirms the flaws that already exist in the relationship.'[49] Fontane's famous discretion in all three novels over the act of adultery – a discretion so exquisite that the fact is plain only after the event – may indicate not just deference to a world of tact, but an implicit denial that in these circumstances it is the fact of most significance. The same point is suggested by the leading differences between *Effi Briest* and the events on which Fontane based it.[50] Of these there are four. First, in the real-life tragedy the husband was only five years older than his wife, who was 19 when he married her; second, the wife and her lover had no fleeting affair, but continued to meet after she returned with her husband to Berlin, and planned to elope and marry; third, the incriminating letters were discovered not by accident, long after the affair had ended, but as a result of suspicions provoked in the husband; fourth, the wife did not decline and die after her husband killed her lover in a duel and divorced her, but lived on till the ripe age of 99. The key changes made by Fontane to his source material construct the adulterous wife as little more than a child, present her adultery as inconsequential in itself, and define her as the principal victim. They also raise questions about a code which requires, even though the affair ended over six years before, not only that a husband challenge and if possible kill his wife's former lover, but that he instigate her exile both from the marital and the parental home and from any meaningful social role.

Female adultery is not, then, the subject of *Effi Briest*, but the index to an emotional and moral vacuum within the social order displayed. Effi commits adultery not, like Anna Karenina, because she is a mature woman longing for sexual fulfilment, but because she is a lonely, confused adolescent; not because she is in love, let alone passionately in love, but because she is neglected and bored. Instetten does not kill Crampas because he hates him, or because he has any belief in the code of honour by which he acts, any more than he banishes Effi from himself and her daughter because he does not love her, but because he cannot face the consequences for his social and official position of failing to heed the unwritten law. What makes it worse is that Instetten acts in full awareness that the code is both draconian and arbitrary. He agrees when his friend Wüllersdorf calls the cult of honour 'idolatry' and yet concludes: 'But we must submit to it, as long as the idol stands' (XXVII.216; 237). Again, it is not because they do not love her that Effi's parents reject her until she is dying, but because they defer to a taboo which is as much social as moral and which demands, whatever the circumstances, her sacrifice. The price of these repressions is the *Angst* – a word for which there is no match in English – which stalks the inner lives of nearly all the characters in *Effi Briest*. This is shown even in so marginal a figure as Effi's Cousin Dagobert when he states his wish for a war: '"people like us would like a chance to get rid of this horrible empty space," and he ran his hand across his chest' (XXIII.179; 194). Erika Swales has defined *Angst* as 'the psychological precipitate of a society whose members are denied a sense of personal authenticity in their experience, without being able to silence their disquiet by acquiescence in the public sphere', and has shown how delicately, but also how pervasively, the novel represents inward despair and unease through a tissue of mythological and otherwordly allusion.[51]

In his comparison of *Effi Briest* with *Madame Bovary* and *Anna Karenina*, J. P. Stern claims that Flaubert's main preoccupation is psychological, Tolstoy's moral, and Fontane's social. Arguing that this distinction marks the pre-eminence of *Anna Karenina*, Stern pays special attention to the relationships between each adulterous mother and her offspring. For him, the limitation of *Effi Briest* as compared with *Anna Karenina* is that, 'wherever the embodiment of the novel's moral scheme may lie, it is not where we might expect it, in the child-mother relationship'.[52] As this remark makes clear, not only is the distinction between psychological, moral and social too sweeping, but Stern entirely overlooks ideology. Loralee MacPike supplies a necessary corrective in an essay on childbearing in nineteenth-century fiction as an epitome of attitudes to female sexuality.

According to MacPike, in the nineteenth-century novel 'good women bear sons, bad women daughters who cannot carry on the family line, thus ensuring that negative qualities in the parents (particularly the mother) will not be part of the moral "genealogical continuity"'.[53] Among other examples, MacPike discusses Balzac's *A Woman of Thirty*, in which, she points out, the drowning of the adulterine son negates 'any possibility of paternal succession through illegitimacy'.[54] She does not consider *Madame Bovary*, though it conforms to her paradigm in that the adulterous mother's child is female; it might also be added that, despite Flaubert's innovation in paying serious attention to the role of the child, its effect is chiefly to indicate that Emma is a bad mother. *Anna Karenina*, which she does discuss, is more complex, for Anna has a son by her husband before her affair, and a daughter by her lover. This, again, is consistent with the paradigm, since Anna bears a male child while she is a 'good' wife, a female child while she is a 'bad' one. It is also psychologically convincing, as Tolstoy takes care to ensure; for, while Anna channels into her relation with her son the need for loving which is not met by her marriage, her daughter represents for her the danger not only of dying in childbirth but of losing Vronsky through impairment of her looks. Anna is presented as a bad mother when Dolly visits her in the country; and, in the scenes presenting the feelings of her son, the focus is poignantly on his sense of confusion and betrayal. Once more in accordance with MacPike's paradigm, this son is available at the end as a line for legitimate inheritance; whereas, because of her gender, though she survives and is adopted by Karenin, the adulterine child is not.

MacPike discusses no novels by Fontane, and it is revealing that none of his novels of adultery bears out her generalization. In *L'Adultera*, Melanie has two daughters by her husband and one by the lover who later marries her. She is prepared to abandon the children of her first marriage in order to seek fulfilment in her second; and the novel implies no criticism of her decision. *Beyond*

Recall, as a novel of male adultery, could hardly be expected to fit the paradigm, but what is remarkable here is that, although the Holks have two adolescent children, the narrative pays them little attention. Instead, as in all of Fontane's novels of adultery, the focus is on the marriage. Where Fontane gives more prominence to the figure of the child is in *Effi Briest*. Here, however, although in one sense Effi is punished for her adultery through her daughter, since she is deprived almost completely of contact with her, the novel implies that responsibility for this cruelty lies with her husband, to some extent with her parents, and with the social codes which they allow to govern their behaviour. Effi denounces her husband when, after asking and being allowed to meet her daughter, she finds that she has been brought up to treat her with cool reserve. The scene pointedly contrasts with a similar scene in *L'Adultera*, in that the child's rejection of her mother in the earlier novel is motivated by her jealousy of the lover, but in the later by a pseudo-moral rigour on the part of the father which is unthinking and heartless.

But the key to the question consists in the fact that Effi Briest has been married while herself still all but a child. When J. P. Stern remarks that, 'of the three women, Anna is the only wholly adult character',[55] he begs several questions at once. What is at issue is, in Michael Minden's phrase, quoted above, 'the specific possibilities of adulthood offered by a certain stratum of society at a certain historical moment'. Leaving aside the question how far Anna might be said to achieve adulthood, it is crucial to Flaubert's novel that Emma Bovary's social class, education and circumstances offer her little chance to develop; while much of the point of Fontane's is that Effi's adultery results from a development which is deliberately arrested. The very different outcome of *L'Adultera* suggests that *Effi Briest* is in part a critique of the military and civil service aristocracy whose power Fontane increasingly feared. What enables Melanie van der Straaten to achieve more freedom and self-realization than either Effi Briest or Christine von Holk is the greater enlightenment and tolerance attributed by Fontane to the commercial bourgeoisie. The condition of Melanie's development is not only her own resolution, but what is made possible by two men of Jewish extraction: one her lover, the other her husband. Taken together, Fontane's three novels of adultery may even suggest that the Protestant values of self-determination and fulfilment in marriage are still alive in an aspiring bourgeoisie, but lost to a decadent aristocracy.

8

Church and State: Eça de Queirós, Alas, Galdós

In most accounts of nineteenth-century fiction, the novel of adultery is seen as a standard narrative form showing little essential deviation from one example, one national setting, to another. The cases of Jacobsen and Fontane demonstrate that individual novelists, working in different cultures and out of different traditions, varied the theme considerably. Although both followed precedent as male writers who produced impersonal narratives centred on female adultery, both also challenged it. As the previous chapter has shown, both *Marie Grubbe* and *L'Adultera* vindicate the heroine; while Fontane went further still by basing *Beyond Recall* on male adultery, and by foregrounding, in *Effi Briest*, a culture of rigid conformism and emotional repression.

There are equally important differences between novels of female adultery from the Iberian peninsula and their much better-known predecessors. Again, however, these are commonly elided in mainstream literary history. The stock comparison is between *Cousin Bazilio* (1878), the second novel published by the Portuguese Eça de Queirós, and *Madame Bovary*. J. P. Stern declares, for instance: 'Once again we have the exposure of an oppressive, sultry *milieu*, done unsparingly, with deadly accuracy and a cold eye for every sham detail; once again an unsuspecting husband, a worthless lover, a heroine, Luiza, who has little beyond her "romantic" imagination to fall back on.'[1] Similarly, in a brief discussion of the novel of adultery, F. W. J. Hemmings remarks that *Cousin Bazilio*

> could fairly be described as an adaptation of *Madame Bovary* to a Lisbon setting. Superficially, at least, the resemblance is flagrant: Eça's heroine is linked to her husband by nothing stronger than a community of material interests; her only refuge from the deadly tedium of conjugal life is to indulge her taste for romantic

novelettes, and she falls an easy prey to the first unscrupulous philanderer who presents himself.[2]

However, 'superficial' rather than 'flagrant' is the right word for the similarities between Eça's novel and Flaubert's. As Alexander Coleman has remarked of Eça's various borrowings from other literatures, 'The borrowed elements are there, for sure, and cannot be denied. But they *do* undergo a sort of sea change and become quickly acclimated and assimilated into the peculiar structure of Portuguese society and Eça's theory about that society.'[3] Although Luiza is portrayed as dreamy, sensual, and a devotee of romantic fiction, the main concerns of *Cousin Bazilio* lie elsewhere. This becomes clear when the two novels are compared more closely.

They differ in their construction of female adultery, in the social context and setting they exhibit, and therefore also in their wider implications. In fact, Luiza Carvalho's adultery has little in common with Emma Bovary's. The action of Flaubert's novel lasts several years, that of Eça's several months. Emma gets married, grows to hate and despise her husband, moves house, bears a child, falls ill, has two affairs and poisons herself in despair when her extravagance and her exploitation by Lheureux produce bankruptcy. Luiza, on the other hand, begins in contentment with her marriage, which is childless, and she is seduced and abandoned during the absence of Jorge, her husband, by the cousin to whom she had been engaged seven years previously. Jorge's return from his travels as a mining engineer renews Luiza's affection for him, and he forgives her even when, during the illness from which she dies, he discovers her infidelity. But the most significant difference in the action of *Cousin Bazilio* consists in the role played by the jealous, resentful servant, Juliana. Luiza's affair seems to end like Emma's with Rodolphe when she scares her lover off by asking him to elope with her. What precipitates this appeal, however – and at a point when she has already begun to regret the liaison – is Juliana's attempt at blackmail; an attempt which succeeds all too well after Jorge's return, driving Luiza to her fatal breakdown. Luiza has none of Emma Bovary's passionate frustration or recklessness. Instead she is passive and vulnerable: to Jorge's advances, before the action begins, when he wanted a wife; to Bazilio's seduction; and to exploitation by Juliana, whom she tries to propitiate not only by money and gifts but by taking on nearly all of her work. When Luiza finally rebels against her servant, it is because Jorge has forced the issue by demanding her dismissal; and, even then, Eça has Luiza depend on male help in resorting to Sebastian, her husband's friend, who silently adores her. Indeed, in contrast to Flaubert's heroine, Eça's is never shown as initiating action.

In 1871, during the period in which he probably wrote a first draft of *Cousin Bazilio*,[4] Eça published a wide-ranging critique of Portuguese society. One of his targets was contemporary literature, especially fiction. He declared:

The novel is the apotheosis of adultery. It studies nothing, it explains nothing; it doesn't draw characters nor outline temperaments, it doesn't analyze passions. It has no psychology, no action. Pale Julia, married to burly António, hurls the conjugal manacles at her husband's face and faints lyrically into the arms of Arthur, who is disheveled and gaunt. In order to move the sensitive reader more deeply and in exculpation of the unfaithful wife, António works, which is a bourgeois ignominy, while Arthur is a loafer, a Romantic glory. Honest women have been weeping the tears of their own sensibility on account of such whorehouse dramas as this since 1850.[5]

Cousin Bazilio was clearly designed to explode such sub-Romantic claptrap for good. However, if Eça followed Flaubert not only in writing a novel of adultery but in rejecting sentimental formulas about love and marriage, he focused his attack much more directly. *Cousin Bazilio* is unique among novels of female adultery in that, although the heroine, by definition, is the centre of narrative interest, Eça's title highlights not Luiza but her seducer. In a way, this is consistent with Luiza's passivity; but, given the limited part Bazilio takes in the action, the distinction given by the title can only be ironic. Eça's presentation of Bazilio is part of his offensive against Portuguese corruption and decadence. Rich on his return from Brazil, Bazilio indulges physical desire, fashionable taste and self-interest. All these features are displayed by the novel's ending: a sardonic vignette in which, having heard of Luiza's death and regretted her briefly, Bazilio falls in with the cynicism of his companion, an aristocrat selling off his last piece of land, and blames himself only for having returned to Lisbon without another mistress to fall back on. Such behaviour is wholly in keeping with the hypocrisy, corruption and sexual licence which the novel attributes to Lisbon society. One scene, which has almost no bearing on the adultery plot, shows a bachelor dinner-party attended among others by a newspaper editor, perpetrator of 'so many platitudes and lies' (X.206; XI.760), and by a lackey, famous mainly for his handwriting, who divides most of his time 'not dedicated to the service of the State [. . .] between pastry-shops and brothels' (X.213, TM; XI.767).[6] The host is Councillor Accacio, a long-standing friend of Jorge's family, who boasts civic and social distinction but sleeps with his housekeeper on the quiet. Accacio declares: 'I am a liberal. I believe in God. But I recognize that religion is a restraint' (X.209, TM; XI.762), and his bedroom reveals religious paintings on the wall and pornographic poems in the bedside cabinet. The chapter which opens with this scene closes by showing Luiza repelling the obscene advances of the businessman to whom, in her need to buy off Juliana, she had tried to prostitute herself.

Unlike Flaubert, Eça did not set out to attack the bourgeoisie as such. *Cousin Bazilio* encourages no special interest in Jorge's work as an engineer, but neither does it satirize him for it, any more than it invites scorn for the conventional values of his friend Sebastian. Eça introduces no petty representatives of bourgeois life such as Homais, Léon or Charles Bovary as objects of satire, but ridicules instead the attitudes of the upper and aspiring middle class. The narrator scathingly comments that the wealthy would-be purchaser of Luiza's favours prefers the women of France because, 'like the bourgeois of his circle, he valued twelve million Frenchwomen by the six prostitutes of the café-chantant, who had cost him dear and bored him hugely' (X.229, TM; XI.779). Another minor character is said to write from 'a deep-rooted passion for art – because he was employed on a good salary in the Customs Office, and had an income of 500,000 *reis* from his investments' (II.32, TM; II.575); and still another, on finally obtaining promotion, switches from 'terrible revolutionary' to 'friend of Order' (XIII.282, TM; XIV.824). Part of Bazilio's shallowness is his jumped-up scorn for what he takes to be bourgeois. Once he is tired of the affair which he had initiated, he contemptibly judges it 'supremely bourgeois, a little *vulgar*', and he applies the first of these damning epithets to Luiza's well-justified terror of blackmail (VII.160, TM, 161; VIII.716).

A further important contrast between Eça's novel and Flaubert's consists in location. While *Madame Bovary* is set, pointedly, in the provinces, *Cousin Bazilio* is set in a capital city, Lisbon. Eça presents a much more densely populated world than Flaubert, one in which gossiping neighbours and chance passers-by play a prominent role.

It is also a world in which adultery and fornication are common. Unlike Emma Bovary, adulteress in isolation, Luiza is surrounded by examples of sexual transgression. This is part of Eça's attack on Portuguese decadence, and it draws on influences he had absorbed from the contemporary Naturalist movement. Bazilio finds his affair with his cousin all the more exciting because 'it was quite complete! It had adultery, it had incest' (VII.162, TM; VIII.717); and the narrator states that Jorge loves Luiza more 'since he supposed her unfaithful, but with another love, carnal and perverse' (XIII.273, TM; XIV.817). It is therefore within a double frame of reference that Luiza is to be understood: the social context of the city, the cultural context of Naturalism. Eça goes beyond Flaubert in giving his heroine not only a weakness for sentimental fiction, but sensitivity to music; and he constructs her not only as sensual but passive. He describes her, for instance, as gazing at herself in front of a mirror, 'enjoying the feeling of being so white, stroking the softness of her skin, with the languid yawns of a happy tiredness' (III.53, TM; III.592); and, during a lull in Juliana's blackmail, he comments: 'She gave herself up to an inertia that felt almost voluptuous in its abandonment, passing days without taking interest in anything' (VIII.179, TM; IX.734).

The passivity which Eça gives to his heroine echoes strictures he published in 1872 on 'the general type that is the unmarried young lady from Lisbon'. At a time when, according to Alexander Coleman, he 'had probably completed the first draft of what was to become *Cousin Bazilio*', he wrote: 'A Portuguese girl has no initiative, no determination, no will. She has to be ordered and governed. If not, she remains on the median of life, arms lowered, irresolute, and in a state of suspension.'[7] What is odd about this satirical attack is that, by recognizing how completely Portuguese women are excluded from taking part in public life, it provides an implicit explanation for the debility it attributes to them. It is according to such assumptions that Eça presents Luiza's agreement to marry Jorge: 'without loving him, she felt beside him a kind of weakness, a dependency, and a languor, a wish to sleep leaning on his shoulder, and to remain so for many years, in comfort, without fearing anything' (I.15, TM; I.562). She later responds with the same passive lethargy to Bazilio's seduction: 'Luiza listened to him without moving, her head lowered, her eyes to the ground. That ardent, powerful voice, from which she took in his words of love, dominated and conquered her; Bazilio's hands suffused her own with a feverish warmth; and, overcome with lassitude, she felt as if she were falling asleep' (IV.83–4, TM; IV.620).

As in Flaubert's portrayal of Emma, there are elements both of misogynism and of masculine eroticism in Eça's presentation of Luiza. Although Eça satirizes Bazilio as a paltry, cynical Don Juan, in several passages he follows Flaubert in encouraging complicity with the seducer's gaze. For example, just before Bazilio first enters, the narrator anticipates his way of appraising her sexually: 'Her low-cut chemise showed her white shoulders, round and smooth, her pale, soft neck, azured with tiny little veins; while her arms, slightly plump, pink at the elbows, revealed underneath, when she raised them in fastening her tresses, fine blonde threads curling to form a nest' (III.44, TM; III.585). Eça's Brazilian contemporary, Machado de Assis, had passages such as this in mind when he denounced the novel as crude, contrived and salacious.[8] Extending Machado's analysis, it would be easy to criticize *Cousin Bazilio* as a moralistic sham in which male fears and desires about women produce an adulteress as both sexual object and scapegoat. For example, Alexander Coleman has suggested that Eça responded to the misogynism as well as to the socialism of Proudhon.[9] However, as Coleman further indicates, Eça was also influenced by the work of Comte, Taine and other exponents of social and historical science, as well as by the related Naturalist movement. Although never a doctrinaire adherent of Naturalism, he was clearly guided by Naturalist principles in his portrayal of Luiza as a creature of her environment who lacks any real scope to challenge it.

But the key point – and one which partly offsets the charge of misogynism – is that these assumptions inform Eça's presentation of all the characters. *Cousin Bazilio* draws dispassionate attention to the physical and sexual drives not only of the adulteress but of her seducer and even her husband. The double standard wobbles when Luiza discovers that Jorge is tempted to betray her from a letter which his friend Sebastian allows her to read by accident, and in which he boasts of his admirers. She responds by expressing the same wish to kill her spouse, if he proves unfaithful, which before her affair he had strongly endorsed himself (VII.174, II.35–6; VIII.728, II.577–8). The parallel is all the more striking because, although Eça had been reading Dumas's *L'Affaire Clémenceau*, which attempts to justify a husband's murder of his adulterous wife,[10] he has Jorge forgive Luiza when he finds she has cuckolded him. Indeed, the novel sets male and female sexual need on the same moral level, whether it is that of Councillor Accacio with his concubine, or of his unrequited adorer Dona Felicidade; that of Luiza's friend Leopoldina, with her various lovers; or that of the cook Joanna and her carpenter from across the street. Even Juliana, the servant who blackmails Luiza, is not actuated by religious or moral principle. Eça presents her as reacting not only against her exploitation as a servant, labouring in miserable conditions for subsistence wages, but out of the sexual frustration to which her unbecoming looks and low social status have condemned her.

Machado was right to point out the contradiction in *Cousin Bazilio* between the ostensible moral message and its sometimes salacious delivery. Nevertheless, it is necessary to qualify his critique. First, Juliana is much more than an arbitrary means of punishment for Luiza's adultery; second, Luiza's passivity may be understood not as that of a 'puppet'[11] but as that of a victim; third, the novel's chief aim, though not realized consistently, is satire on behaviour and values at the hub of Portuguese culture, Lisbon. All these themes coalesce in Eça's presentation of women.

In what happens to Luiza, Juliana and Dona Felicidade, the novel offers a subtext of female dependence and oppression. Jorge, who had kept a part-time mistress while a student, decided to marry when his mother suddenly died; he took the initiative in choosing Luiza, who was not at first attracted to him. Bazilio, Luiza's first love, left her to seek his fortune in Brazil when his father's business failed; when he returns, he coolly informs her that he has deliberately chosen to visit while Jorge is away. On the occasion when Luiza visits the Promenade with Bazilio and Dona Felicidade, she is tracked by a man who stares at her with 'large, languid and silvery eyes' (IV.68, TM, 70, 72, 74; IV.607, 608, 610, 612); and later, on her way to the sordid room her lover has rented, she is unable to shake off the persistent Councillor Accacio until Bazilio has already left (VII.141–7; VII.698–703). Luiza's lack of choice is also reflected in her dearth of friends. Her husband severely disapproves of her seeing Leopoldina, her closest friend since childhood, while her only other female visitor is the religiose Dona Felicidade, friend of her late mother. Jorge, on the other hand, is surrounded by male friends and relatives, including the faithful Sebastian; and three of them achieve ill-deserved preferment or honour by the end: Accacio, the doctor Juliao, and the aspiring dramatist Ernestinho. This stands in ironic contrast to the fate of the three main female characters: Dona Felicidade twists her foot in a fall, and, 'becoming a ruin' from the failure of her love for Accacio (XIII.275; XIV.819), she retires to a hospital; Juliana dies from a burst blood vessel when Sebastian, accompanied by a brawny policeman, puts a stop to her extortions; and Luiza expires from cerebral fever caused by blackmail and fear of exposure. Alexander Coleman, developing Machado's critique, has argued that the two deaths with which the novel ends are 'capricious events, imposed [. . .] upon the fabric of the novel by Eça'.[12] But this is to discount Luiza's vulnerability, the impact of her ordeal from blackmail, and Juliana's own suffering from perpetual neglect and ill-treatment. The fact that Luiza dies after the threat of blackmail has been removed, and after Jorge has forgiven her, shows that her death is the result of her protracted ordeal; while Juliana capitulates to the vested interests which have kept her in subjection. Yet the crucial point is Eça's striking reversal of expectations in that, despite Jorge's foreboding words in the opening chapter, and a culture which justified crimes of 'honour', the husband does not kill his adulterous wife.

Analysis of the novel on the lines laid down by Machado also fails to take account of what Mikhail Bakhtin would have termed its dialogical character.[13] *Cousin Bazilio* is composed of a medley of voices, none of which is given any obvious priority; indeed, Eça's most significant debt to Flaubert is his suppression of narratorial comment. Much of the text is in the form of free indirect speech, in which the narrator renders the thoughts of various characters in their own idiom and from their own perspective. Eça's extensive use of this method, and the paucity of narratorial comment, work against interpretive closure and leave the novel open to a diversity of readings. This fact is related in turn to the notorious question of Eça's literary borrowings. Machado based his attack on Eça in part on allegations of plagiarism, but the novel is much more deliberately and indeed mischievously allusive than he appreciated. Not only does its action span, self-reflexively, the production by one of its characters of a play which questions whether a husband should forgive his unfaithful wife, but another character even compares the dramatist to Dumas as writer of *L'Affaire Clémenceau*. Eça also builds in references to other literary prototypes: Dumas's *The Lady of the Camélias*, and Octave Feuillet's more recent and more scandalous novel, *Monsieur de Camors* (1867), along with Proudhon, Claude Bernard and others; and he goes so far as to have one of his characters produce a further intertextual link, to Balzac's *Eugénie Grandet*.[14] Though he coined the bitter formula, 'Portugal is a country translated from the French into slang,'[15] Eça also showed, through his creative exploitation of allusions and borrowings, how to transcend it.

The passivity and powerlessness of Eça's heroine make *Cousin Bazilio* a very different novel of female adultery from *Madame Bovary*. But it would be a mistake to infer from this that the novel represents any special plea for female rights; instead, the one respect in which it speaks unequivocally is in satirizing the Portuguese establishment. In converting the theme of adultery into a vehicle for social criticism, Eça was carrying further an attack he had already initiated. Alexander Coleman goes so far as to claim that *Cousin Bazilio* and Eça's first independently published novel, *The Sin of Father Amaro*, 'are essentially the same works'.[16] The two were probably begun at the same period; and, although *Cousin Bazilio* originally appeared after the first two versions of *The Sin of Father Amaro*, published in 1875 and 1876 respectively, it predates the definitive version published in 1880. Eça's second novel carries to a provincial city, Leiria, the attack on Portuguese society trained in his first on the capital. Its main target, however, is the Church. *The Sin of Father Amaro* is not a novel of adultery, female or otherwise. Ironically, it escapes this category not because the seducer is a priest, but because the death of his lover takes place before she can be married to a convenient husband. The novel is particularly interesting for its portrayal of the power of the Church, especially in the provinces; and for the comparison it offers with another Iberian novel, Leopoldo Alas's *La Regenta* (1884–5), which deals both with clerical power and with adultery, and which will be discussed next.

Despite almost identical titles, there is little essential similarity between *The Sin of Father Amaro* and Zola's *The Abbé Mouret's Sin*, published in the same year as the first version of Eça's novel.[17] Although both works centre on a young priest's fornication, their themes are quite different. While Zola takes as his subject the priest's denial of natural growth and fecundity, and his morbid enslavement to mystical doctrine, Eça scathingly attacks the corruption of the Roman Catholic Church in Portugal and, by extension, of the whole Portuguese social order.

Eça directs his offensive through the affair carried on by his central character, Father Amaro Vieira, with Amelia Joanneira, the unmarried daughter of his landlady. He presents from the start a social and a religious system based on an unhealthy symbiosis between clerics and women. Amaro both becomes a priest and obtains preferment in Leiria by way of female patronage, exercised in the latter instance through a government minister not averse to clerical support in return. Like most of his colleagues, he then profits by feeding the warped religious scruples of his wealthier female votaries, especially through confession. He soon discovers that his landlady, one of a group of religiose women only too devoted to the clergy, is the mistress of Canon Dias, his former 'master of moral' at the seminary; and this prompts him not only to recognize the truth of the remark, 'They all play the same game!', but to join in (V.59).[18] It is not surprising that Amelia, 'brought up amongst priests' (IV.49), should be drawn to the personable Amaro; still less so that he should follow both nature and example by seducing her. As the rationalist Dr Gouvea points out,

> As a man he has passions and organs which make him want a woman; and as her confessor he has the importance of a God in her eyes. It is evident that he must utilize this importance in order to satisfy these passions; and he has to cover these natural satisfactions with the appearance and under the pretext of a divine service. (XII.161)

Like *Cousin Bazilio*, but to more powerful effect, *The Sin of Father Amaro* joins Naturalist analysis with social satire. The clerical seducer not only gets off scot free. He also ends up complacently in a better position, despite offences which include the exploitation of others in carrying on the affair, including a congenitally disabled adolescent girl and her ailing, devout father; the dropping of hints to blame the pregnancy on others; the attempt to marry his lover to her former fiancé, with the full intention of carrying on the affair after her marriage; and finally the entrusting of the baby to a known child-murderer in whose hands, within a day, he dies. Amelia, on the other hand, breaks off her engagement with the eligible João Eduardo, and has to bear Amaro's child in secret. She spends the final months of her pregnancy in a gloomy country retreat watched over by a vindictive, ageing spinster whose religion is neurotically fanatic, and, her baby snatched away immediately after birth, she dies in convulsions exacerbated by her loss.

The novel's satirical attack is fiercest in the final chapter, set in

Lisbon a few years after the main action. Amaro's panic-stricken flight from Leiria has not hampered his further preferment, and he now seeks a position closer to the capital, where, sleek in his prosperity, he bumps into Canon Dias, who has supported him through all his iniquity, and his patron, the Conde of Ribamar. It is 1871, and, amidst bourgeois outrage at news of the Paris Commune, both the priests and the Conde speak up for religion and conservatism against the forces of change. The Conde not only forecasts what will happen in France with ludicrous inaccuracy, but paints a picture of Portuguese stability and prosperity blatantly belied by the scene before him. The novel ends by juxtaposing 'the representative of the state, the two representatives of religion' (XXV.352), with the monument to Luis de Camões, a writer who did full justice to the glories of Portugal's past. Alexander Coleman points out that this mordant contrast appears only in the final version of the novel, published in 1880, 'the same year in which Portugal underwent a veritable paroxysm of civic pride and messianic hopes for a new day – the tricentenary year marking the death of Camões himself'.[19] This political and historical perspective distinguishes Eça's novel from Zola's especially sharply. While, as Elliott M. Grant observes, with pardonable exaggeration, *The Abbé Mouret's Sin* could have been set 'at almost any time and at almost any place',[20] Eça depicts a decadent generation failing at a specific historical moment to respond either to change in the world around it or to the message of its past.

As in *Cousin Bazilio*, Eça's Naturalist assumptions about human behaviour both enable and limit his satire. For instance, the novel emphasizes the unnaturalness of a vow of chastity because it takes for granted that sexual desire is instinctive and unavoidable. It is this which explains the fact that Amaro does not emerge as the brute which his actions seem to suggest, but rather as a man of ordinary drives and appetites who takes the path of least resistance for lack both of vocation and of positive example. Similarly, the narrator appears to endorse Abbot Ferrão's view that Amelia is 'all woman and full of sexual desires' (XXII.302); indeed, the Abbot's ideological antagonist Dr Gouvea has just told her his own version of the same belief: 'You have been true to nature, who ordered you to conceive, not to marry' (XXII.300). In one of those borrowings which Eça made his own, *The Sin of Father Amaro* recalls *Madame Bovary* when, while Amelia is dying, and despite her increasingly desperate condition, Ferrão and Gouvea keep on arguing the convictions of Church and rationalism respectively. But it is a mark of Eça's distinction as a novelist, and of the difference between his kind of emphasis and Flaubert's, that this is no slanging-match between two such almost equally contemptible representatives of competing stale orthodoxies as Homais and Bournisien. Instead Gouvea, whose views are not far from those implied by the novel itself, shows an unappealing and even a doctrinaire insistence on his own opinions, along with little care for his patient; indeed, as the prostitute-turned-midwife points out, and for all his medical science, his treatment of bleeding a woman who has just given birth is almost criminally stupid (XXIII.332). On the other hand, Ferrão, though as keen to stand up for the dignity of the Church as Gouvea is for secularism, is a genuinely good man whose religion is sincere, in many ways practical, and above all humane and tolerant. Not surprisingly, Ferrão stays confined to his country parish, though the only fault held against him is his love of hunting.

In his argument with Ferrão, Gouvea maintains that the Church no longer has any significant power:

> Formerly the Church was the nation; today it is just a small minority tolerated and protected by the state. It used to dominate in the law-courts, in the councils of the crown, in the disputes of the peasantry, on the seas; it made wars and dictated peace; today a deputy of the government has more power than all the clergy in the kingdom. (XXIII.329)

However, although Eça's clergy cannot help cherishing 'grand ambitions for the return to the world of Catholic tyranny' (VI.80), the novel suggests that in many ways they exercise hardly less power, especially in the provinces and particularly among women. Eça depicts them as self-interested, gluttonous, and lecherous, cynically supporting each other through the most flagrant wrongdoing; and sustained by their cosy, collaborative relationship with the aristocracy and upper bourgeoisie. *Cousin Bazilio* and *The Sin of Father Amaro* exploit and vary respectively the form of the novel of female adultery, delivering a scabrous indictment of contemporary Portugal.

Introducing his translation of *La Regenta*, John Rutherford remarks that on its publication in the mid-1880s Leopoldo Alas's novel 'was attacked as an obscene irreligious monstrosity and a plagiarism of Flaubert's *Madame Bovary*'.[21] Although these charges echo those launched a few years previously at Eça, *La Regenta* is very much more than a Spanish blend of *Cousin Bazilio* with *The Sin of Father Amaro*. Like Eça, Alas turned the theme of female adultery into a vehicle for social and political criticism. *La Regenta* recalls *Cousin Bazilio* in presenting the adultery of a childless married woman with an accomplished seducer, and in alluding self-reflexively to Spanish honour drama; it recalls *The Sin of Father Amaro* in portraying a priest's adulterous passion, along with conflict and scandal over clerical power and influence. Despite these and other parallels, however, several qualities distinguish Alas's novel not only from the two by Eça but from all other examples of the form discussed in this book. *La Regenta* is the only canonical novel of female adultery to show the heroine's early life in detail, and to connect that life with her transgression; it is unique in locating the heroine's adultery at the centre of a power struggle between two men, one of them a leading cleric; and it is outstanding both for its painstaking attention to the minutiae of social life in a provincial city, and for a narrative stance which, though often witheringly sceptical, does not withhold compassion.

Although *La Regenta* depicts a clerical establishment soiled by abuse of power, by corruption, faction and backbiting, it differs from *The Sin of Father Amaro* in that it is neither an anti-clerical work nor, in essence, satirical. A key example is Alas's presentation of one of his leading characters, Don Fermín De Pas, canon theologian of the cathedral. It is significant that, as John Rutherford has remarked, and with a single exception, only two of the characters are allotted extended interior monologues: the heroine, Ana Ozores, and Don Fermín.[22] This narrative privilege gives much greater emphasis to the character and situation of De Pas than of any other male figure in the novel, including Ana's husband and her seducer; and it invites a measure of sympathy as well as substantial criticism. On the one hand, De Pas typifies arrogant clerical power. He is ruthless, domineering and self-seeking. The opening scene introduces him surveying the city of Vetusta like a magnate from his cathedral tower; and he has no qualms about exploiting others, including the bishop whom he dominates and his own devotees whom he milks for favours and donations. For the sake of his own prestige and that of the church, he is even prepared to justify the continued existence of a convent in an insanitary location, despite the illness and death there of a daughter from one of the families which idolize him. On the other hand, De Pas also presents a remarkable image of the hollowness of clerical ambition and of the church's increasing impotence. What gives this image its force is that it is embedded in a detailed social context and history.

The position of De Pas is doubly contradictory. First, he owes his rise from the peasantry to his widowed and ambitious mother. Disempowered by gender as well as by class, Doña Paula has been able to advance only through the agency of men of standing. Wishing to escape the poverty of her home, and recognizing the opportunities offered by the church, Doña Paula has kept house for a succession of priests – blackmailing one after he made an advance to her, controlling another who later become bishop, and best placed of all as housekeeper to her son. Thus, though De Pas has learned his ambition from his mother, who has put him through the seminary and gained him preferment through the bishop, he is more radically her surrogate. The second contradiction is that, while the church represents a means of progress for the aspiring poor, as an institution it is not only in decline but fundamentally reactionary. Alas shows the pressure of these contradictions on De Pas. Canon theologian by ability as well as patronage, and at the earliest age for admission to the office, he finds himself blocked from further promotion by neglect outside Vetusta and enmity within. At the same time, and unlike his mother in both respects, material acquisitions do not satisfy him and he chafes against the vow of celibacy which denies him emotional and sexual fulfilment. Lacking the piety and spirituality of his bishop, De Pas finds a way of meeting his needs for power and love when an ageing colleague suggests that he take over as confessor to Ana Ozores, styled by her aunts as 'the First Lady of Vetusta, [. ...] the Judge's Wife' (V.121).

The nature of De Pas's relationship with Ana and its ultimate outcome epitomize several of the chief differences between Alas's novel and Eça's. First, unlike Father Amaro, De Pas never seeks to seduce Ana; indeed, for a long time he deceives himself about the physical, sexual element in his attraction to her. Second, although he abuses his role as confessor, if nothing so flagrantly as Amaro, he fails to keep Ana's faith – both in him and in her religion – once she realizes that he is in love with her. Third, and perhaps most interesting, the novel displays his agonizing frustration as a strong, handsome man in his prime neutered by clerical vows. No other novel of female adultery presents a rival to the heroine's lover, least of all one whose position obstructs a physical relationship and whom she herself sees as her moral and religious guardian. The triangle formed by Ana, her lover, and her confessor – a triangle which excludes the husband – offers a telling analysis of the roles played by church, class and gender in Restoration Spain. De Pas is a patriarch; as John Rutherford points out, the Spanish word rendered by the unavoidably colourless phrase 'canon theologian' is *el magistral*, 'the man who is the master'.[23] Yet the man is a master thanks to the channelling of a poor woman's ambitions, and his attempt to realize his mastery founders on the contradictions of his relationship with the judge's wife.

Alas begins his novel from De Pas's vantage point on the cathedral tower; he ends its first volume by relating how, through his mother, the canon theologian had reached such a height from an impoverished beginning. In the same way Ana's story is developed from an early life the social and personal details of which are highly significant. Whereas Percy Lubbock famously called Anna Karenina 'a wonderful woman whose early history has never been fully explained',[24] Alas presents Ana as a woman whose treatment before marriage largely governs her destiny after it. Although few novels of female adultery pay much attention to the early lives of their heroines, most construct them as effectually or actually motherless from adolescence or childhood. *Madame Bovary* as well as *Anna Karenina* are examples; so too are Jacobsen's *Marie Grubbe*, Eça's *Cousin Bazilio* and Galdós's *Fortunata and Jacinta*; and, while Fontane's *Effi Briest* is a rare exception, both *L'Adultera* and *Beyond Recall* conform to type. The same pattern appears not only in such prototypes as Musset's *Confession of a Child of the Century* and Balzac's *A Woman of Thirty* and *The Muse of the Department*, but in cognate examples such as Fromentin's *Dominique*, in which heroine and hero are orphans, and in Balzac's *The Lily of the Valley*, where both are slighted by their mothers. Indeed, even antitypes such as various novels by Sand follow suit: the heroine either lacks a mother, as in *Indiana*, or, more often, as in *Valentine*, *Jacques* and *Le Dernier amour*, is estranged from or persecuted by her.

What is striking about *La Regenta* is that, especially through a long retrospect early in the narrative, Alas demonstrates the impact of his heroine's motherlessness. Deprived of her mother at birth, Ana yearns for the love and care she has never enjoyed: 'Her young head had never been pressed to a soft warm breast, and the girl had searched everywhere for something similar' (III.66). One substitute

Ana tries is religion. Thus she is described as having 'wept over St Augustine's *Confessions*, as over a mother's breast' (IV.92). Much of De Pas's appeal for her stems from the same source: 'she was content to be by his side, still thinking of him as her strong, well-fashioned shield'; 'the judge's wife smiled at him as she would often have smiled at her mother, had she known her' (XIII.309, 310). Ana can even respond in the same way to Don Víctor Quintanar, her ineffectual husband, as when, during one of her breakdowns, she thinks of him as 'her father, her mother, her brother – the gentle strength of the familiar caress, the spiritual protection of domestic love' (XIX.422). But it is Don Alvaro Mesía, her eventual seducer, who most fully, though briefly, gives her the sense of meaning and purpose denied her by motherlessness: 'she was determined to remove all blame from her Mesía, from her lord and master, from the man to whom she had given her body and her soul for the rest of her life [. . .]. Whenever the idea of losing Don Alvaro seized her she shuddered in horror, as she had shuddered in former times whenever she had been afraid of losing Jesus' (XXIX.650–1).

While Ana's motherlessness helps account both for her leanings to mysticism and for her attraction to powerful men who appear to offer support, the novel has her experiences as a girl compound her vulnerability. Her father, inept though well-meaning, is absent for much of her childhood; his family traduce her mother, who had been a dressmaker, out of prejudice against her Italian extraction and her class; and she is brought up mainly by a spiteful governess and by two maiden aunts who malign not only her mother and father but Ana herself, thanks to an innocent escapade as a child which they falsify grossly as sexual laxity inherited from her mother. Worse still, Ana has almost no choice in her future life:

> She wanted to liberate herself, but how? She could not work for her living – the Ozores sisters would sooner kill her than allow that to happen – and so there was no decorous way out, other than marriage or the convent.
>
> But Ana's devotion had already been judged and condemned by the proper authorities. Her aunts, who knew something of her transient mysticism, had made cruel fun of it. Besides, the girl's false piety was complicated by the greatest and most ridiculous defect which a young lady could have in Vetusta: literature. This was the only serious vice which the aunts had discovered in the girl, and it had already been rooted out. (V.111–12)

So, while Ana reads widely and much more seriously than Emma Bovary or Luiza, she can rarely speak her mind with her aunts; and, derisively labelled as a bluestocking and a George Sand, she is denied the chance to find and express herself through writing. Soon the only, minimal, choice she can exercise is escaping the coarse millionaire her aunts design for her at the cost of accepting the amiable but inadequate Quintanar, already nearing an early retirement and over 20 years older than herself.

Perhaps no other novelist has presented the fate of a fictional adulteress as so completely and remorselessly determined. Writing a generation on from *Madame Bovary*, Alas is much more explicit than Flaubert in emphasizing the very limited choices available to a woman of Ana's class. He is scathing at the expense of upper-class marriage: Ana's aunts are 'society procuresses', and she feels as if she is being fattened up 'like a cow for market', to be 'put up to public auction' (V.110, 103, 110). Once married, Ana's role is further restricted still. As Adrian Shubert indicates with reference to Spain, a woman's position in nineteenth-century Iberia was in some respects even more oppressive than in other European countries:

Upon marriage she automatically lost most of her legal rights and became an appendage of her husband. [. . .] The Civil Code told wives that they should obey their husbands and punished disobedience with jail terms of five to fifteen days. This legal subordination remained in effect until 1931. Wives had to live where their husbands did and could not leave without permission. [. . .] Any sexual infidelity committed by a wife was defined as adultery. A husband's affairs had to cause 'public scandal' before they constituted a legal offence. Women were also punished more severely for crimes of passion, receiving life imprisonment compared to the six months to six years of exile for their husbands. Real divorce, with the right to remarry, was unavailable until March 1932.[25]

Since Ana's affair is short-lived, and since it occurs late in the action, the novel directs most of its scrutiny to her experience in the unsuitable marriage she has been forced to contract. In Vetusta, a good wife is defined as one who 'attended to her property and her household chores with care and diligence' (VIII.176). But Ana, without any children, has her work done for her by her servants, and her household tasks do not occupy her mind 'for so long as half an hour' (XXV.567). Her relationship to her husband, an avid hunter and, ironically, an enthusiast for Spanish honour drama, offers her no more. In one bizarre but pathetic scene she comes home at Christmas to find him in bed in his nightclothes, declaiming and brandishing a sword:

> her heart sank to her feet when she considered that this man sitting in his bed at two o'clock in the morning, wearing a cap and a flannel jacket, and flailing the air, was her husband; the only person in this world with a right to her caresses and her love – with a right to give her the delights which she believed motherhood to contain and for which she was aching, thanks to the stable in Bethlehem and other such reminders. (XXIII.537)

Alas goes on to imply, delicately, that Ana has gone to Don Víctor partly for sexual love; but he suggests with equal delicacy elsewhere that, even if her husband were similarly inclined, he is impotent.

A further respect in which Alas develops Flaubert's presentation of the adulterous wife is through the theme of mental breakdown. Part of this development consists, again, in clarifying and drawing out what is implicit or merely latent in *Madame Bovary*. Alas derives Ana's nervous illness not only from the emptiness of her life and the defeat of her attempts to fill it. In part, her psychological fragility results from the insecurities of her childhood: she initially breaks down a few days after her father's burial, and relapses when she is adopted by her aunts. In addition, and more fundamentally, the novel suggests that what Ana's doctor and husband call her nerves is 'in reality the very essence of her being, where she was most herself: in short what she was' (XVI.369). This is not the same as saying that Ana is subject to nerves because she is female. It is true that, as Noël Valis has remarked, 'The medical profession throughout nineteenth-century Europe and America repeatedly conflated signs of weakness, hysteria and sickness in general (mental and physical) with what was considered the essential female persona.'[26] But Ana is constructed not as a generalized figure of the female, but as a woman subjected to specific experiences which have produced psychological instability and disturbance. Her character is, on the other hand, representative insofar as oppression and absence of personal choice were common, though usually in less extreme forms, among young women of her class. If, as Jo Labanyi proposes, Alas 'seems to be suggesting, in keeping with patriarchal discourse, that women have an intrinsic disposition to neurotic forms of hypnotic possession',[27] he has shown very fully that such a disposition in Ana stems from her history and circumstances. However, while Alas presents Ana's mental suffering as serious and important in itself, it is in two further ways that this theme extends his version of the novel of female adultery.

First, it is a striking paradox that the woman who, in all Vetusta, is most admired and coveted has so slender and uncertain a sense of her own personality. Although Ana is the cynosure for everyone in the city, most notably when she walks as a penitent in the Good Friday procession, there is an absence at her centre. What helps explain this absence is that her social role is to represent the status of powerful men. That role is encoded in the name by which she is known: *la Regenta*, the judge's wife. The arbitrariness of the title is compounded by the fact not only that Ana's marriage is empty, but that it denotes a position she no longer occupies, since her husband is retired; absurdly, her successor is called 'the *other* judge's wife' (II.55). Ana's value as a signifier of status stems from her beauty, her aristocratic rank and her exemplary reputation: 'to say the judge's wife was to say the perfect wife' (III.78). The novel's action therefore begins with her change of confessor to the most powerful cleric in the city, De Pas; and it culminates in her seduction by his secular rival, Mesía, president of the Gentlemen's Club and leader of the Dynastic Liberal Party. Alas has very little happen until he has introduced, in turn and at length, not only Ana in relation to her background and history, but also, each in his own domain, the two rivals for her love: De Pas in the cathedral chapter, Mesía in the Gentlemen's Club. The significance of Ana's change of confessor is lost on no one in Vetusta. Similarly, because Mesía designs Ana's seduction for prestige as well as pleasure, he intends it to become equally public: 'This was why he wanted his triumph to take place at the Vegallanas' place: so that everyone should see' (VII.153). Ana, already a symbol of one man's status, becomes a pawn in a conflict between the two others and the order each represents. As Alison Sinclair has pointed out, Alas underlines the ludicrous collapse of categories that results when De Pas thinks of Ana, the judge's wife, as his own wife (XXIX.662);[28] an absurdity surpassed only by Quintanar when he urges Mesía to seduce Ana to prevent her from falling further into De Pas's clutches (XXVI.597).

Ana's suffering foregrounds the emptiness of her role not only as bourgeois wife, but as symbol of male power and vehicle for male aspiration. Furthermore, however, Alas develops in Ana the radical doubt which Flaubert stops short of attributing to Emma but which suffuses the whole of *Madame Bovary*. Thus, during the breakdown which follows her ordeal as object of everyone's gaze in the Good Friday procession, Ana is tortured by 'scorn for logic, doubt about the laws of thought and language, and finally the disappearance of her awareness of her own unity: she believed that her moral faculties were falling apart, that inside her there was nobody who was *she, Ana*, essentially, really' (XXVII.606). This torment reaches its height after Mesía, challenged by her husband to a duel, has killed him and cravenly fled: 'someone was arguing inside her, inventing sophisms to which there were no answers and which did not relieve the pain of remorse but which did make her doubt everything, doubt whether there were such things as justice, crime, piety, God, logic, soul . . . Ana. "No, there is nothing, said the torment in her brain"' (XXX.705).

The crucial difference between such a denial of meaning in *La Regenta* and in *Madame Bovary* respectively is that in Flaubert's novel it defines the author's position rather than the heroine's. Alas shows fully and clearly that Ana's vertiginous doubts are socially produced; they spin out of her conflict-ridden position as a woman whose role is to symbolize the meaning of others. It would be naive to suggest, however, that Alas's presentation of his heroine is broadly objective or disinterested, for another respect in which it goes beyond Flaubert's is that she also functions as a channel for expression of a critical, even contemptuous, attitude towards provincial Spanish society. Among all the characters, it is only Ana who recognizes the cliché-ridden vacuity of Vetustan life:

That afternoon Ana hated the Vetustans even more than usual. Those traditional customs which they observed without any awareness of what they were doing, without any faith or enthusiasm, and to which they returned with a regularity as mechanical as a madman's rhythmical repetition of phrases and gestures; that atmosphere of gloom about which there was no grandeur, and which did not have to do with the uncertain fate of the dead but rather with the certain boredom of the living – it all weighed upon her heart. (XVI.354)

Although, later the same day, Mesía comes to challenge what seems to Ana 'the great sin of human stupidity' by riding into the square 'with a touch of colour, grace and strength' (XVI.363), within a few pages even he has become 'part of the dull prose all about her' (XVI.375–6).

Ana's disgusted and despairing sense of meaningless rote and denial of purpose is confirmed in the grotesque farce produced by the novel's social and political analysis and by several of its leading scenes. Alas satirizes the *turno pacífico*, the cosy arrangement by which conservatives and liberals in Restoration Spain handled power between them,[29] by portraying the leader of the Dynastic Liberal party in Vetusta as hand in glove with his opposite number: 'Like a man playing himself at chess and taking as much interest in the white pieces as in the black, Don Alvaro looked after the commercial concerns of conservatives as much as those of liberals' (VIII.157). He also presents corruption and backbiting among the clergy, posturing, self-seeking and crass stupidity at the Club; and he brings all this to a climax in the rasping comedy of the scenes surrounding the deaths of Don Santos Barinaga, a drunkard who, not without justice, blames De Pas for his ruin, and of Don Pompeyo Guimarán, Vetusta's only atheist. The canon theologian's enemies triumph when Barinaga dies cursing him, not least by turning the funeral into a hostile demonstration – only for the tables to be turned when Guimarán, the dead man's sole friend, repudiates his atheism on his own deathbed and insists that he receive extreme unction from none other than De Pas. In the same way, just as Mesía is humiliated when he fails and his rival succeeds in freeing a swingboat in which a friend of Ana is suspended, so De Pas suffers shame and chagrin when, during a thunderstorm, he drags Quintanar along in an attempt to surprise Ana with Mesía. The sole evidence of illicit love found by the two is a garter which, though originally Ana's, accuses each of them instead – Quintanar because he has seen Petra the maidservant wearing it during a fruitless attempt at seduction, De Pas because Petra has lost it while having sex with him earlier the same day.

While *La Regenta* provides an astonishingly full and perceptive analysis of Spanish provincial society, along with keen, sympathetic insight into the position of a distressed and exploited wife, no other novel of female adultery contains such scenes of ludicrous and at times excruciating farce. There are two further and related ways in which the novel renews this fictional type. First, in one sense *La Regenta* looks back to an earlier, eighteenth-century form: the novel of seduction. Much of its action centres on the rivalry between

Ana's two lovers, and in no other example of adultery fiction does the heroine hold out so long: only in the penultimate chapter is it revealed that Ana has yielded. Secondly, however, and in sharp contrast with the narrative of seduction, in *La Regenta* the seducer is himself an object of criticism and satire. For all his social prestige and his ultimate success with Ana, within the text Mesía is increasingly mocked and undermined. It is not just that on occasion the narrator sardonically refers to him as 'the Don Juan of Vetusta', or that he discloses his prudent recourse to flannel underwear and to measures for sustaining his waning sexual vigour. Much more withering is his demonstration of the seducer's moral and intellectual bankruptcy. *La Regenta* is a novel of female adultery in which the seducer's behaviour, not the heroine's, comes out of fashionable fiction: 'Don Alvaro was only imitating the heroes of these elegant books – and imitating them badly' (VII.156). But, as an example of a seducer, Mesía is most interesting in embracing a cut-down model of nineteenth-century materialism. Having 'asked a friend for books which would prove materialism in a few words' (IX.199), Don Alvaro is equipped with an ideology which appears to justify his way of life and, more to the point, assists his main occupation: 'Mesía's materialism was easy to understand. Once a woman was convinced of the non-existence of metaphysics, things took a much smoother course for Don Alvaro' (IX.200). But Alas does not stop at exposing the seducer's philosophy as a self-interested sham. He also reveals its complacent and demeaning inadequacy:

> Mesía did not need any encouragement to think obscene thoughts about priests and women. He did not believe in virtue. The version of materialism which was his religion led him to believe that nobody was capable of resisting natural impulses, that all priests were therefore hypocrites, and that ill-contained lust gushed out of them however and whenever it could. (XIII.290)

In this way Mesía and De Pas are not only rivals for influence in Vetusta and for Ana's love. Each also represents one of the two ideologies dominant in late nineteenth-century Spain. If, then, the novel shows self-seeking and corruption in the church, it also lays bare the superficial rationalism of the anti-clerical elements typified by Mesía. What gives this opposition further significance in a novel of female adultery is that *La Regenta* highlights the latent or manifest misogynism of both.

However, the view of women implied by *La Regenta* is itself not entirely dispassionate. For example, Alas offers a rare generalization during a scene in which, with obscene erotic relish, De Pas visits a convent school. As one of the girls recites propaganda she has not been educated to understand, the narrator describes her and comments: 'What was speaking there was the blind obedience of woman: the symbol of sentimental fanaticism, the initiation of the eternal feminine into eternal idolatry' (XXI.482). Although the scene demonstrates how girls are conditioned for the convent, it also suggests a predisposition to naive acquiescence which it presents as typical of women. It is almost as if the the narrator is indicting not only the church for its policy of female moral enslavement, but women themselves for compliance. Lower down in the social scale, however, Alas attributes only too much aggression to De Pas's mother and to Ana's maid, Petra; and, crucially, it is Petra whom he has bring about the novel's catastrophe by betraying Mesía to Ana's husband and to De Pas. 'The sensual blonde', as the narrator styles her, has sexual episodes with all three of the men who are rivals for her mistress. Unlike Eça with Juliana, Alas presents this betrayal not as revenge for slights and oppression, but as driven by 'vanity' and 'what was perhaps her favourite passion apart from lust – vindictiveness' (XXIX.654). The success of Petra's scheming mocks the assurance of canon theologian and professional seducer alike; but her promiscuity and her vengeful manipulativeness hint at misgivings in the novel over active female sexuality as well as over lower-class resentment. Anxiety about women and sex is also reflected in the portrayal of Obdulia and Visitación, familiars of Mesía who are constructed as sensual and intriguing.

Nevertheless, two points must be set against this. First, the novel presents sex in general as degrading. This applies to male as well as to female characters, including minor figures such as the country priest whom De Pas disciplines for fornication; the shy antiquarian Don Saturnino Bermúdez, who ventures out at night in disguise to haunt the doors of brothels; or the Marquis who repairs to the country for sex as others do for hunting, but whose home is a warren for seduction, exploited among others by his son. Second, the reason why Ana and De Pas are the central figures is that, unlike almost all the others, both have higher aspirations – though each is driven to profane them by a particular personal history and a compound of hostile forces. It is important to recognize this distinction when interpreting the final scene. Here, sexual disgust reaches a climax when Ana, having fainted in the cathedral after her rejection by the infuriated De Pas, is kissed while unconscious by the homosexual acolyte Celedonio. The closing words – 'she thought that she had felt on her lips the cold and slimy belly of a toad' (XXX.715) – present an image of nausea and terror hardly outdone by novels of female adultery which, more conventionally, end with the heroine's death. John Rutherford has claimed that the repellent kiss is Ana's 'final degradation and punishment: a specifically sexual retribution for her sexual transgression'.[30] But such a judgement is belied by Alas's presentation of Ana as vulnerable, oppressed and tormented; and it forgets the corrosive narrative irony which allows her cowardly seducer to escape scot free, and her husband, who generously fires wide in the duel, to die from a bullet in the bladder he has neglected to empty. The slimy kiss is less Ana's punishment than an expression of the debased world about her, to which she is forced to succumb.

Unusually among novelists of adultery, Alas points to an alternative for the heroine in her aspirations as a writer; equally unusually, he does not disparage her ambition, but shows how crushingly it is denied. Nevertheless, it was specifically a novel of female adultery which he elected to write as the vehicle for his critique of Spanish provincial society; and, as Stephanie Sieburth has observed, although his narrator 'decries the Vetustan norms which prevent a healthy sexual life, he does not support Ana in her rebellion against these norms'.[31] The connection drawn by *La Regenta* between social corruption and a woman's sexual downfall is therefore of critical importance.

Robert M. Jackson has put an interesting case for regarding *La Regenta* as an allegory of contemporary Spanish political life. He suggests that nearly all the characters, not only De Pas and Mesía, are social or political types; he points to an historical explanation for the minimal role played in the novel by the working class; and he contends that Ana is 'the incarnation of both the virtues and the vices of Spain'.[32] However, these parallels can only apply to the novel at a certain level of abstraction. For example, the complexity of its social detail will not allow De Pas or Mesía in themselves to personify, respectively, 'a selfish Church' and 'an oligarchic state';[33] conversely, there is no historical equivalent for Ana's rejection and soiling at the end. Although the allegorical parallels are resonant and suggestive, they amount to no more than an outline.

At a more general level still, Noël Valis has argued that *La*

Regenta 'depicts through the decline and fall of an individual the profound pervasiveness of evil and decay in Spanish Restoration society'; and Jo Labanyi that 'Ana's adultery stands as a metaphor for an adulterated society.'[34] What has to be set against this kind of view is the fact that Ana's fall is brought about by factors almost entirely beyond her control, and that she herself is decidedly critical of the social life around her. Her ruin is determined by social institutions – the Church, the political order, marriage, the family – which are themselves corrupt. The novel cannot be said to align its heroine with a society which impels her to enter an empty marriage and from which she is, at the end, excluded. No other novel of female adultery presents so full an account as *La Regenta* of what drives its heroine into sexual transgression; no other offers so intensive a critique of the society of which she is part.

Nevertheless, it is also crucial to the novel's implications that its heroine's fall is sexual. On the one hand, *La Regenta* suggests that sex is shameful and that few can escape its degradation. De Pas has furtive intimacies with his maid Teresina as well as his episode with Petra, and he is shocked and dismayed to recognize the nature of his desires for the judge's wife; while she, unlike all the women and nearly all the men of her circle, stays chaste till she can struggle no longer. On the other hand, Ana does finally succumb; for all its other qualities, *La Regenta* is unequivocally a novel of female adultery. The novel's social criticism is complicated and even in part compromised to the extent that it relies on a sense of sex as intrinsically nasty. That sense ensures in turn that Alas, like most other novelists of adultery, could not avoid creating a heroine who is scapegoat as well as martyr.

The distinction is clarified sharply by a novel published shortly after *La Regenta*, Emilia Pardo Bazán's *The House of Ulloa* (1886).[35] As I have pointed out in Chapter 1, Pardo Bazán never wrote a novel of adultery, female or otherwise. Instead, though she does not avoid the portrayal of sexual relationships in her fiction, she highlights the unequal and oppressed condition of Spanish women. In *The House of Ulloa* she shows how a woman is abused through a totally unsuitable arranged marriage. The abuse takes several forms. First, there is the choosing of the bride, Nucha, who is averse to marriage but who has no real power to refuse an eligible suitor. Her selection by Don Pedro, so-called marquis of Ulloa, against his physical attraction to her nubile elder sister, Rita, further illustrates not only the pressures on daughters to marry but the demands of money and of masculine honour. Ironically, however, Nucha loses her financial expectations to Rita, and it is the elder sister's vivacity, the source of her appeal to Don Pedro, which raises the doubts about her reputation which decide him against her. Second, having taken his bride back to his country estate, Don Pedro resumes his liaison with the maidservant who has already borne him a son, and bullies Nucha for what he assumes is her inability to produce one. After a protracted labour which results in the birth of a daughter and which weakens her permanently, Nucha is unfit for further pregnancies. Don Pedro suspects her of a liaison with the young priest Julián, who agrees to help her escape; and she dies several months after he has violently accused her and had Julián sent away.

Judith Drinkwater has demonstrated that Pardo Bazán's earlier novel, *A Wedding Journey* (1881), undermines the conventions of romantic fiction.[36] In a similar way, *The House of Ulloa* may be read as an implicit response to other fiction of the period which focuses on romantic or sexual relationships between women and priests. Pardo Bazán's novel could scarcely contrast more strongly with *The Sin of Father Amaro*, *The Abbé Mouret's Sin* and *La Regenta*. Not only is its central female figure a woman whose cruel treatment in an arranged marriage culminates in her death after a false accusation of adultery, but its central male figure is a priest who is stigmatized as feminine on account of his innocence and vulnerability. Pardo Bazán shows the force of Spanish machismo both in its victimization of women, and in the oppressive gender roles it enforces on men.[37]

Benito Pérez Galdós was a colleague both of Alas and of Pardo Bazán, and, for a time, the latter's lover. Although he developed feminist sympathies – which did not, however, go far enough for Pardo Bazán[38] – his main aim in his fiction was to represent the history and society of his period. Between 1873 and 1912 he produced two massive series, the *National Episodes* and the *Contemporary Novels*, which offer nothing less than a fictional history of nineteenth-century Spain. As Robert M. Jackson has pointed out, Galdós anticipated Alas in building political and historical parallels into a novel of contemporary life.[39] But his use of these parallels was more explicit and more systematic. Peter A. Bly groups eight of Galdós's novels, all published in the 1880s, under the heading 'Fiction as Allegory of History'.[40] The first of these, *La desheredada* (*The Disinherited*), dates from 1881; two of the group are also novels of adultery. *La de Bringas* was first published in 1884, the same year as the first volume of *La Regenta*, and *Fortunata and Jacinta: Two Stories of Married Women* appeared a few years later in 1887. In both novels Galdós goes much further than Alas towards challenging the conventions of the novel of female adultery. It is not a coincidence that he also allows much less of a role to the church than either Alas or Eça. Although he does not neglect the role of religious belief and of religious institutions, his is a much more secular world. His fundamental concerns lie with the bourgeois family and the bourgeois state.

La de Bringas follows the example of nearly all novels of female adultery by taking its title from the name of the adulterous woman. Indeed, the use of the possessive term relating the heroine to her husband goes even further than, for instance, *Madame Bovary* by underlining her subordination in marriage. In most other respects, however, the novel refuses to conform to type. First, it might better be termed a novel of prostitution than of adultery. Rosalía Bringas betrays her husband not because she is in love but because she is in debt. Ironically, the man to whom, on a single occasion, she gives herself fails to help her; she is saved by her relative Refugio whom she despises as a fallen woman; and she ends by supporting her husband and children through sexual liaisons. Second, although Rosalía spends more than she has on dress, it is not as a result of vanity that she falls into debt. As Peter Bly has suggested, her love of fine outfits stems partly from sexual frustration;[41] indeed, when her husband Francisco surprises her with a roomful of rich material, the narrator remarks that she is 'caught *in flagrante*' (XIII.62: XV.78).[42] But Rosalía's obsession with clothing also points to a need for independence. Though Francisco Bringas is in some ways benign, he is also sufficiently authoritarian and tight-fisted to keep the family's money to himself and to monitor all its expenditure. Rosalía contracts most of her debt by lending money to a friend during her husband's temporary loss of his sight; and, though she is naive, one of her motives is an enterprising wish to earn interest. Thus Lou Charnon-Deutsch has rightly emphasized that Rosalía's behaviour can be interpreted as an attempt to gain 'some measure of self-determination'.[43]

The third respect in which *La de Bringas* diverges from more conventional novels of female adultery is through its handling of Galdós's key innovation: the incorporation of historical analogies.

Although Galdós relates the novel's action very closely to the Revolution of 1868, the parallels are far from straightforward in their implications. Peter Bly has shown that Rosalía evokes Isabel II, especially in her love of dress and her sexual licence; but that at the same time she is 'also a figure in revolt' against her husband.[44] This invites the inference drawn by Maurice Hemingway: 'If the comparison to the Queen's fall is unmistakably critical, the comparison to the Revolution which deposed the Queen is not.'[45] It is further significant that the coup coincides not with Rosalía's adultery but with the crisis of her debt. Yet what is still more telling is the fact that the Revolution is presented almost as a farce. Not only does it cause minimal damage – despite the fears of Rosalía's husband, an ardent monarchist, the revolutionaries cannot even bag the Palace pigeons. It also turns out that many of the same faces stay in power, including the lover to whom Rosalía has uselessly yielded, and, even more strikingly, the narrator. For *La de Bringas* also departs from a formal convention which is invariable in nearly all novels of female adultery: that of impersonal narrative. The personal narrator takes little part in the action, but at the end he is an important official in the new regime, and it is implied that he has himself enjoyed Rosalía's favours.

La de Bringas paints a satirical picture of a world of graft and corruption which even a revolution changes little. If, as I have suggested, it might be called a novel of prostitution rather than of adultery, it is not only Rosalía who sells herself; and what the narrator calls 'Rosalía's consciousness of her role as a corner-stone of the household in these tragic circumstances' (XLVII.237; L.204) is not in any simple way ironic. The undermining of the narrator's authority, and the sustained dry comedy of the whole, are highly unusual in the fiction of female adultery; though in some respects the comic tone recalls Balzac and Mérimée.

Fortunata and Jacinta: Two Stories of Married Women, published three years later, develops and extends much of Galdós's achievement in *La de Bringas*. The novel's action and construction clearly identify it as a novel of adultery. Although it is a work of unusual length and diversity, its nucleus is the liaison between Fortunata and Juanito Santa Cruz, husband to Jacinta, the other wife of the subtitle. The first of the novel's four volumes shows the initial meeting of the two lovers, and closes by foreshadowing the adulterous affair which will begin at the end of its second; the third volume ends with their reunion, following a period in which both return to their spouses; and, after a further break-up, the action closes with Fortunata's death. However, even this brief summary points to a crucial distinction between Galdós's novel and other leading works of the tradition. Galdós not only anticipated Fontane by portraying the adultery of a husband, as in *Beyond Recall*, and double adultery, as in *Effi Briest*. He also, and much more remarkably, presented the lover of the adulterous wife as her seducer and exploiter – both before and after her marriage.

This fact casts into relief a further respect in which *Fortunata and Jacinta* breaks with the novel of female adultery in its classic form. Unlike heroines from the aristocracy, such as Ana Ozores, Anna Karenina, Marie Grubbe, or Effi Briest, or from the bourgeoisie, such as Emma Bovary, Melanie van der Straaten, or Bazilio's cousin Luiza, Fortunata is an adulteress from the margins. Orphaned before her adolescence, she is poor, unemployed and illiterate when Juanito first meets her. Her only hope of a decent life – and, as Galdós makes clear, her only effective choice – lies in marriage to a respectable working man. This prospect is crushed at every step by Santa Cruz. After the first stage of their affair, before either is married, he leaves her pregnant, thrown out by her aunt and dependent on a drunkard pedlar. Having lost her child in poverty, Fortunata lives as a mistress in Barcelona and Paris, while Juanito marries and quickly gets bored with Jacinta; but, after returning to Madrid, and with no interest and little aptitude for life as a courtesan, she falls into part-time prostitution. Her sole chance of redemption occurs when Maximiliano Rubín, a trainee pharmacist who suffers from congenital mental and physical disabilities, falls in love with her and offers her marriage. At the insistence of Maxi's family, she undergoes six months of so-called purification in a convent; but she spends her wedding night nursing her sick husband, and within two days she has succumbed again to Santa Cruz – who, in his relentless pursuit, has not only bribed her maid but rented the flat next door. The second stage of the affair ends like the first, with Juanito deserting her; and, having already left her husband, Fortunata once more accepts protection from a lover, Don Evaristo Feijóo. Partly out of concern for her welfare, and partly because his age overtakes him, Feijóo arranges Fortunata's reunion with Maxi. But the marriage breaks down again when Juanito takes up with her for a third time, only to fail her once more not only by leaving her but by having an affair with one of her friends. While still convalescing from the birth of the second child she has by him, Fortunata dies after attacking his new mistress in revenge.

Fortunata's children, both by Santa Cruz, point to a third respect in which the novel parts company with other nineteenth-century fiction of adultery. In *Madame Bovary*, Emma's daughter Berthe indicates her inadequacy as a mother; in *Anna Karenina*, Anna's children figure both as evidence of her crime and, in different ways, as parts of her punishment. Fontane's more liberal position allows Melanie van der Straaten, in *L'Adultera*, not only to leave her children but to have a child by her lover and marry him after her divorce; while in *Effi Briest* the function of the heroine's daughter is to show Instetten's cruelty in dividing her from her mother rather than to convey criticism or retribution. The role of the adulteress's child in *Fortunata and Jacinta* contrasts with all these alternatives.[46] The two married women of the novel's subtitle differ not only in their social position, but in that only one of them, Fortunata, is able to have children by Santa Cruz. Jacinta, desperate for a son, tries to adopt a boy who is offered to her as the child Fortunata had borne to Juanito, not knowing he had died in infancy. Juanito callously shatters her credulity. Later, after he has returned to Jacinta for a second time, Fortunata cherishes the idea that her own ability to bear a child by him confirms that she herself is more properly his wife than his spouse by law. This idea vindicates her not only in her own eyes but in Jacinta's when, before she dies, she wills her second son, to whom she has just given birth, to her wealthy counterpart. The child is joyfully adopted as the Santa Cruz heir; but at the price of Fortunata's death.

The role played by the adulteress's children in *Fortunata and Jacinta* is critical in a number of ways. First, Juanito's inability to have children with his wife emphasizes the barrenness of the marriage,[47] arranged by his mother in an attempt to tie him down and welcomed by Jacinta's with all due gratitude for the splendid settlement of her third – of seven – slenderly dowered daughters. Second, the failure of the marriage to produce an heir emphasizes an obligation laid almost exclusively on the wife in patriarchal society. It is because of that obligation, quite apart from her own longings for motherhood, that Jacinta tries desperately to find a surrogate child, even – indeed preferably – fathered by her husband with another woman. Third, the fact that the child's mother is from the proletariat raises difficult questions about the relation of the upper to the lower class. From one point of view, that relation is clearly exploitative. Not only does Juanito seduce Fortunata and wreck her life, but she ends by providing the child needed by his wife and the heir required by his family. Although Fortunata names her son after the three men whom she believes to have been most important to her life, Jacinta has no sooner adopted him than she begins to fantasize that he is indeed her own and, spiritually, the son of her admirer Isla-Moreno, who has died without ever having declared his love. From another point of view, however, the adoption illustrates that mingling of the classes which the narrator claims to be one of Spain's distinctions. Early in the novel, for instance, he remarks: 'Imperceptibly, and aided by bureaucracy, poverty, and education, all classes have gradually mixed; the members of one migrate to another, making a strong network that holds together and toughens the national fabric' (I.vi.i.81).[48]

I will return below to the questions raised by this statement, including its pertinence to the Santa Cruz adoption. However, whether it is valid or not, it highlights several further distinguishing qualities of *Fortunata and Jacinta* as a novel of adultery. First, Galdós builds round his adultery plot an entire social history of the middle class in Madrid during the nineteenth century. Itself the eleventh of his series of 28 *Contemporary Novels*, *Fortunata and Jacinta* begins with a long, detailed exposition of the commercial and social development of the Santa Cruz family as an epitome of the rise of the Madrilenian middle class. No other novel of adultery presents so spacious a view of its society. While Tolstoy, in *Anna Karenina*, maintains control of his great panorama of Russian aristocratic life through the overriding themes of marriage and adultery, Galdós builds into *Fortunata and Jacinta* many details, incidents and characters whose bearing on those themes is slight or even entirely absent. A case in point is Fortunata's brother-in-law, Juan Pablo Rubín. Although Juan Pablo involves himself not at all in his brother's problems, either before or after Maxi's marriage, Galdós devotes many pages, including all six sections in the first chapter of Volume III, to his life in Madrid café society, his debts, and his half-baked opinions. The effect of this and other apparent digressions, such as the space given to Guillermina, founder of an orphanage, or even to Maxi's moneylending aunt Doña Lupe, is to set the adultery plot in a context of social and historical process in which, as is only plausible, much happens that does not concern it directly.

Second, however, there is a further and a related implication in the narrator's comment, quoted above, on how the mixing of the social classes strengthens the national fabric. The remark introduces an array of metaphors which figure the nation as an immense organic unit, as when, a few lines later, Madrid society is imaged as 'an extensive and labyrinthine tree [. . .] whose branches crisscross, shooting up and down, disappearing into pockets of thick shrubbery' (I.vi.i.82); or when, much later, the death of Moreno-Isla is portrayed as a tearing away from 'the great tree of humanity', from which, 'at the same moment, leaves and more useless leaves were falling; but the next morning would reveal countless fresh new buds' (IV.ii.vi.689). According to such a metaphor, which is founded in the organicist assumptions of much nineteenth-century thinking,[49] everything is interrelated, however distantly.

Third, a well-known and a striking example of the novel's patterns of relatedness consists in repeated parallels between private and political events.[50] Indeed, it is in this respect, rather than through the theme of adultery, that *Fortunata and Jacinta* recalls *La de Bringas* most directly. The echoes initially sound in a minor key, as when the narrator aligns 'the evolution in education' with 'the evolution in politics' (I.i.iv.23), or when he tells how Jacinta's mother, who is herself to die on the same date as the prime minister's assassination (I.iv.ii.53), associates the births of her many children 'with famous dates in Isabel II's reign', including the besieging of Madrid by the Carlists, and an assassination attempt on the queen (I.ii.vi.30). Of more direct interest, however, are the novel's parallels between Juanito in shifting between his wife and Fortunata, and Spain in seesawing between monarchy and republic. The analogy is brilliantly introduced in a sequence during which Juanito's friend Villalonga, mindful that Jacinta not overhear the news that he has just seen Fortunata, transformed on her return from Paris and Barcelona, intersperses this with an eyewitness account of the scenes of General Pavía's coup (I.xi.i–ii). Later in the action it is extended in chapters entitled 'The Victorious Restoration' (III.ii) and 'The Revolution Fails' (III.iii), which mark not only the return of the Bourbon Alfonso XII in January 1875, and the consequent eclipse of the republic, but Juanito's desertion of Fortunata for Jacinta. The narrator points up the parallel with a remark from Juanito's father:

> What Don Baldomero had observed about Spain was also true of his son: he suffered alternate fevers of total liberty and absolute peace. Two months after one of the gravest periods of 'distraction'

in his life, he began to covet his wife as if she belonged to somebody else. [. . .] This paralleled another notion of Don Baldomero's; namely, 'When the country yields and supports authority, it's not because it truly loves law and order, but because it has to convalesce, strengthen its blood so that it can later satisfy its appetite for squabbles more enjoyably.' (III.ii.ii.461)

Shortly afterwards the narrator employs the same analogy with more than a hint of mockery: 'He simply had to switch regimes every so often; when the republic was in power, the monarchy was so tempting!' (III.iii.i.475). On the same page he even puts it into Juanito's mouth: 'Down with the republic!'

Several questions are raised by Galdós's analogy between monarchy and Juanito's marriage on the one hand, and republicanism and his liaison with a lower-class woman on the other. First, though the parallel might seem to suggest that marriage and monarchy are the norm, and that republicanism is as wrong as infidelity, both the private and the political contexts undermine so simple a view. While the marriage is rightful by law, it is also virtually empty; and, though the narrator's attitude is tolerant, he depicts a social order which is shallow, complacent and corrupt. Not for nothing does Peter Bly ask whether Galdós might be suggesting 'that the Restoration of the Bourbons was not the wisest move for Spain, that it did not take into account the real needs of the country'.[51] It is in the aftermath of the Restoration that, in his campaign to secure Fortunata, Don Evaristo Feijóo is able to find lucrative jobs for both her brothers-in-law: the gluttonous priest Nicolás Rubín, and the idle, self-deluding Juan Pablo. Indeed, the code of 'appearances' which Feijóo tries to instil in Fortunata, as a way to combine happiness with security, represents a similar though pragmatic complicity with a hollow system.[52] Second, and from the opposite point of view, Fortunata's resistance to deception and collusion might be taken to indicate a more positive scale of values. Her return to Maxi is also compared to the return of the Bourbons, not only by a further chapter title, 'Another Restoration', but by Maxi himself and by the narrator (III.v; III.v.ii.536, 538). This time, however, it is the restoration which fails; and it fails because Fortunata cannot deny either the love which ties her to Juanito or her repulsion from Maxi.

A third question arising from Galdós's analogies between private and political life is, then, the significance of Fortunata as a woman of the people. It is Juanito who, talking with Fortunata, introduces the notion that the people represent 'the essence of humanity, raw material', to which 'civilization' must return when it 'allows great feelings and basic ideas to be lost' (II.vii.vi.405). As the narrator signals by remarking that Santa Cruz is talking 'somewhat pedantically', this is an attempt to rationalize his exploitation of a lower-class woman. Later, however, the narrator's own judgement comes into question when he puts the same view himself: 'in our society it is the common people, the *pueblo*, who conserve basic ideas and feelings in their raw fullness, just as a quarry contains marble, the material for forms. The *pueblo* possesses truth in great blocks, and civilization, when it uses up the smaller pieces it lives on, goes back to the *pueblo* for more' (III.vii.iii.606). There is in fact little difference between the views of the narrator and those of the bourgeois characters. As John H. Sinnigen argues, 'the narrator has presented a comprehensive bourgeois consciousness; even his criticisms of the status quo have been only vague commentaries which in no way threaten the interests of the ruling class'.[53] Yet the novel, as distinct from the narrator, shows the different moral code by which Fortunata lives. According to that code, the fact that Juanito is her first lover, and that she bears his children, makes her properly his wife. So, when she says on meeting Jacinta for the first time that she has been married for five years (III.vi.v.571), she is referring not to her marriage to Maxi but to her relationship with Juanito, at that time not yet Jacinta's husband. Thus the novel opposes conventional bourgeois marriage, used by Juanito to exploit both Fortunata and Jacinta, with a code of natural love and fidelity.

In taking his adulteress from the people, in showing her abuse by an upper-class philanderer, and in attributing to her values which he presents as natural, Galdós challenged the received form of the novel of female adultery. From his position as a bourgeois intellectual, he portrayed what he saw as Fortunata's limitations as well as her strengths: ignorance and naivety, as well as passion both in love and revenge. He underlined both through the character of her friend Mauricia, the passionate, violent woman who encourages Fortunata in the rightness of her love, and twice acts as a catalyst for her return to Juanito; and he contrasted Mauricia, by no means all to her discredit, with Jacinta's friend Guillermina, whose immense practical activity in charitable work lacks any particular sympathy or compassion.

While *Fortunata and Jacinta* stands apart from the classic novel of
female adultery in the ways I have discussed, its most radical
difference consists in its narrative discourse. First, whereas all
canonical examples of the tradition are, without exception, told in
an impersonal narrative voice, Galdós deploys a dramatized,
personal narrator who frequently cites his sources of information
and refers to his acquaintance with many of the characters.
Although, unlike his counterpart in *La de Bringas*, this narrator
plays no part in the action, the fact that his viewpoint is personal
means that it is limited and even, at various points, questionable.
Fortunata and Jacinta therefore does not lay claim to the impartiality
of presentation and objectivity of judgement implied, for example,
by *Anna Karenina* through Tolstoy's narrative method. Instead, the
bourgeois point of view reflected by the narrator is not necessarily
authoritative. The reader is not discouraged from qualifying or
even disputing the opinion that Spain presents 'a happy confusion
of social classes, or, rather, their harmony and reconciliation'
(I.vi.i.81); or that the common people provide a quarry of ideas and
feelings for 'civilization' to draw upon. Similarly, moral stereotypes
are also put in question, especially through the narrator's use of the
convention of referring to individuals by stock phrases. This
provides a classic example of the dialogical discourse which,
according to Mikhail Bakhtin, characterizes the novel as a literary
form – and all the more because, as Stephen Gilman has shown,
Fortunata and Jacinta is unusually exuberant in colloquial idioms.[54]

The narrator applies the widest variety of labels to Fortunata.
Though he refers to her most often by her first name, occasionally
he calls ironic attention to her bourgeois marital status with the
expressions 'Señora Rubín' (III.iii.ii.480), 'Rubín's wife' (III.vi.i.547)
and even 'the Rubín woman' (IV.vi.vi.769). Elsewhere his most
frequent variation is 'the sinner', but when she attacks Juanito's
new mistress he goes so far as to call her 'the beast' (IV.vi.vi.770)
and even 'the she-devil' (IV.vi.viii.778). However, these derogatory
phrases are opposed by several others. Shortly before the assault
the narrator calls her 'the unfortunate girl' (IV.vi.ii.752), and shortly
after it 'the unhappy young woman' (IV.vi.xi.791). Contrasting still
further with conventional moral responses is his use, several times
in the same episode, of the phrase '*la Pitusa*' (IV.vi.iv.760; v.766,
vii.772), a familiar, affectionate expression normally applied to
children, and already established as the nickname of the child who
had been represented to Jacinta as Fortunata's first son. But the play

of terms signifying Fortunata reaches its height in her deathbed dialogue with Guillermina, the most conventionally virtuous woman in the novel. Tireless and dedicated in her charity work, Guillermina is frequently referred to as 'the founder' and 'the saint' – though also, with cordial irony, as 'the ecclesiastical rat'. Yet the opposition of 'saint' to 'sinner' breaks down at the novel's climax. Fortunata declares as she dies, 'I'm an angel' (IV.vi.xiv.808), claiming the epithet she has previously applied to Jacinta. Guillermina, on the other hand, comes to resemble a saint increasingly less; for, in her preoccupation with obtaining the baby in healthy condition for her friend, she fails to respond to the generosity and suffering of the so-called sinner. While Fortunata is stigmatized as a common woman and an adulteress, Jacinta is respected for her superior status and – even by her husband – for her chastity; and Guillermina is honoured for both these attributes and also for her zeal in one of the few activities permitted to unmarried middle or upper-class women. Nevertheless, the novel not only deconstructs the accepted ethical labels, but suggests that they derive less from any absolute moral code than from bourgeois social convention. In this way, as Catherine Jagoe has shown, *Fortunata and Jacinta* subverts the patriarchal stereotype of the Angel in the House, common in conduct books of the period.[55]

In keeping with the dialogical character of the text, and with his Cervantine inheritance, Galdós also parodies the stereotypes of adultery fiction. He introduces the theme through José Ido del Sagrario, a mentally unstable former schoolteacher and novelist reduced to canvassing for book subscriptions. Ido is the first of three husbands in the novel who are maddened by the conviction that their wives are cuckolding them. Galdós has him refer to Santa Cruz as 'Sr. Don Juan' with good reason (I.viii.iv.120); the name follows the philanderer through the novel, usually in the form of the diminutive 'Juanito'. Ido is as wrong as Fortunata's doctor Quevedo will be later in believing his wife unfaithful; but Juanito gets cruel fun from kindling one of his paroxysms of enraged honour. The two self-imagined cuckolds invite comparison with Maxi, who loses his mental balance through actual betrayal as a husband. But it is Ido who first mentions the supposed Santa Cruz heir Pitusín; and in this way Galdós further parodies stock fictional conventions. Though Jacinta at first tries to persuade herself that 'It's only in bad novels that unexpected children turn up, when they're needed to thicken the plot' (I.viii.v.126), her suspicion is only too correct. Not only is it ironic that Ido is a writer of adultery fiction – both his wife and Santa Cruz suggest that this is the source of his mania (I.ix.vii.156; I.viii.iv.123) – but the narrator adopts a phrase from Juanito by referring to Ido's account of the spurious son as 'the "Pitusian novel"' (I.xi.i.213). These are only a few examples of the novel's playful self-reflexiveness, but they are especially important as part of its continual interrogation of ideological and fictional clichés.

Fortunata and Jacinta is a wonderful achievement by any standard, not least because it questions so many of the conventions of adultery fiction. In addition, for instance, to the examples I have given of its challenges to the tradition, it is remarkable that it does not invite a voyeuristic view of its heroine, unlike *Madame Bovary* or *Cousin Bazilio*; and that, in contrast to both these novels, along with *Anna Karenina*, it portrays mental instability and hysteria not in a woman but in another man, Fortunata's husband. But there is a limit to the ideological open-endedness of any novel of female adultery – especially one which presents a lower-class adulteress from a middle-class point of view. Although John H. Sinnigen argues that Fortunata 'turns out to be the most powerful agent of this novel', his own analysis closes by conceding that 'she is unable to break definitively with the bonds which tie her to her "betters", and consequently she ends up making a sacrifice for a "healthier" continuation of bourgeois society'.[56] That sacrifice depends on her death, a device of closure which is almost universal in the tradition.

The fundamental question, as in all the works discussed in this study, is what is at issue in a male writer's employment of an adultery plot centred on a woman. In *Fortunata and Jacinta* the problem is compounded by Galdós's choice for his heroine of a woman of the people; and it is further complicated, as in *La Regenta*, by historical allegory. Peter Bly differs from most other critics in claiming that Spain is represented in the novel not only by Juanito Santa Cruz, in his swings between rebellion and order, but also by Fortunata, betrayed by the fraud and hypocrisy of the Restoration. He also suggests that in Fortunata 'Galdós puts forward the possibility of a redemptive love capable of withstanding the forces of history'.[57] But these allegorical links have implications with respect not only to social class, as Sinnigen has shown, but to gender. Catherine Davies observes that in *La Regenta* and *Fortunata and Jacinta* 'woman is equated with the malleable, potentially dangerous and irrational forces of the "madre patria"/"pueblo" shaped by man'.[58] It is also highly significant that Fortunata is constructed in terms of two further stereotypes of femininity: an ideal of absolute emotional fidelity, and a capacity for redemption. This is the clearest evidence that her role is subject to a double ideological determination combining class and gender.

In 1885, two years before the publication of *Fortunata and Jacinta*, Galdós wrote in a newspaper article:

> Everything has changed. The extinction of the race of tyrants has brought with it the end of the race of liberators. I use the word tyrant in its old sense, because tyranny still exists, but now we are the tyrants, we who in days gone by were the victims and martyrs, the middle class, the bourgeoisie, who fought against the clergy and the aristocracy [. . .] those who before were disinherited now occupy the position of privilege.[59]

This remark casts light both on Galdós's choice of a woman of the people for the heroine of his novel, and for that element of her role which underlines bourgeois exploitation. It also suggests a parallel with the continuing subordination of women. There is no doubt that Galdós's sympathies went well beyond his position not only as a member of the bourgeoisie but as a male. For this reason feminist as well as Marxist critics have found much to value in his work. Catherine Jagoe, writing on *Fortunata and Jacinta*, goes so far as to declare: 'Beneath the overtly middle-class and patriarchal value system of the narrative lies a protofeminist statement'; and Lisa P. Condé has demonstrated at length how Galdós's work shows the development of a 'feminist consciousness' into the 1890s and beyond, especially in his writing for the theatre.[60]

But the fact remains that in the case of this novel, which many critics consider his best, Galdós, like other male writers of his period, chose the theme of female adultery as a medium for social and political comment. The theme kept its importance and influence in the masculine literary establishment of Continental Europe until the end of the century, although, as I have tried to show, it underwent many changes of shape and emphasis within the various national traditions in which it flourished. Nevertheless, if Galdós did not overthrow the novel of female adultery in *Fortunata and Jacinta*, he provided an outstanding demonstration of what could still be achieved within it.

Notes

PREFACE

1. Baltimore and London: Johns Hopkins University Press, 1979. Page numbers for references to this book in the Preface are given in parentheses in the text.
2. The other main studies in English of the novel of adultery are Judith Armstrong, *The Novel of Adultery* (London: Macmillan, 1976); Naomi Segal, *The Adulteress's Child: Authorship and Desire in the Nineteenth-Century Novel* (Cambridge: Polity Press, 1992); and Alison Sinclair, *The Deceived Husband: A Kleinian Approach to the Literature of Infidelity* (Oxford: Clarendon Press, 1993).

1 FEMALE ADULTERY, IDEOLOGY AND NINETEENTH-CENTURY FICTION

1. *What Is Art? and Essays on Art by Tolstoy*, trans. by Aylmer Maude (London: Oxford University Press, 1930), p. 154. The title essay, from which the quotation is taken, first appeared in 1898.
2. See Keith Thomas, 'The Double Standard', *Journal of the History of Ideas*, 20 (1959), 195–216; and Roderick Phillips, *Putting asunder: A history of divorce in Western society* (Cambridge and New York: Cambridge University Press, 1988), pp. 344–54.
3. *The Sin of Father Amaro* is discussed in Chapter 8, pp. 195–8. In *The Deceived Husband*, pp. 47–8, Alison Sinclair cites a twentieth-century Norwegian novel, Johan Falkberget's *The Fourth Night Watch* (1923), which centres on adultery committed by a priest.
4. *Comparative Studies in Kinship* (London: Routledge and Kegan Paul, 1969), p. 24.
5. *Adultery: An Analysis of Love and Betrayal* (New York: Basic Books, 1988; repr. Oxford: Oxford University Press, 1990), p. 37.
6. *Adultery*, pp. 43 and 37. The prosecution took place in Georgia in 1984.
7. *The Adulteress's Child*, p. 58; *The Deceived Husband*, pp. 18 and 217–26. Segal's ten examples are Prévost, *Manon Lescaut*; Chateaubriand, *René*; Constant, *Adolphe*; Gautier, *Mademoiselle de Maupin*; Musset, *Confession of a Child of the Century*; Mérimée, *Carmen*; Nerval, *Sylvie*; Fromentin, *Dominique*; Gide, *Strait is the Gate*; and Bernanos, *The Diary of a Country Priest*. Only the last two of these feature adultery.
8. *Putting asunder*, p. 345.
9. *A Long Time Burning: The History of Literary Censorship in England* (London: Routledge and Kegan Paul, 1969), pp. 267–9 and 259.
10. *A Long Time Burning*, p. 239.

11. *Mudie's Circulating Library and the Victorian Novel* (Bloomington and Indianapolis: Indiana University Press; Newton Abbot, Devon: David and Charles, 1970), p. 27.
12. *A Long Time Burning*, pp. 248–9 and 253–4.
13. *Myths of Sexuality: Representations of Women in Victorian Britain* (Oxford and New York: Basil Blackwell, 1988), p. 48.
14. *Myths of Sexuality*, p. 73.
15. *The New Review*, 2 (1890), 6–9 (p. 9).
16. Harlow, Essex: Longman, 1988, p. 623.
17. *Fallen Women in the Nineteenth-Century Novel* (London: Macmillan; New York: St Martin's Press, 1994), pp. 8 and 74. See further Jeanne Fahnestock, 'Bigamy: The Rise and Fall of a Convention', *Nineteenth-Century Fiction*, 36 (1981), 47–71.
18. *The Novel of Adultery*, p. 29.
19. *The Deceived Husband*, p. 200.
20. 'Emilia Pardo Bazán: *Un viaje de novios* and Romantic Fiction', in *Feminist Readings on Spanish and Latin-American Literature*, ed. by L. P. Condé and S. M. Hart (Lewiston, NY, Queenston, Ont., and Lampeter, Wales: Edwin Mellen Press, 1991), pp. 63–76 (p. 71).
21. *French Feminism in the Nineteenth Century* (Albany: State University of New York Press, 1984), p. 21.
22. *French Feminism in the Nineteenth Century*, p. xi.
23. *Women and the Public Sphere in the Age of the French Revolution* (Ithaca, NY, and London: Cornell University Press, 1988), p. 27.
24. *Women and the Public Sphere*, p. 168.
25. *Women and the Public Sphere*, pp. 165–6 and p. 158.
26. Claire Goldberg Moses and Leslie Wahl Rabine, *Feminism, Socialism, and French Romanticism* (Bloomington and Indianapolis: Indiana University Press, 1993), p. 37.
27. 'Of maenads, mothers, and feminized males: Victorian Readings of the French Revolution', in *Rewriting the Victorians: Theory, history, and the politics of gender*, ed. by Linda M. Shires (New York and London: Routledge, 1992), pp. 147–65 (p. 150).
28. *Victorian Women: A Documentary Account of Women's Lives in Nineteenth-Century England, France and the United States*, ed. by Erna Olafson Hellerstein, Leslie Parker Hume, and Karen M. Offen (Stanford, CA: Stanford University Press, 1981), pp. 118 and 120.
29. *French Feminism in the Nineteenth Century*, p. 22.
30. The most notorious example of such censorship is the successful prosecution of Charles Baudelaire in 1857 for a number of poems in *Les Fleurs du mal*. This was the same year as Flaubert's acquittal on charges of obscenity arising from *Madame Bovary*.
31. *French Feminism in the Nineteenth Century*, p. 33.
32. A reconstruction of this text, which only survives in part, was first published by Maurice Bardèche as *La Physiologie du mariage préoriginale* (Paris: Droz, 1940). See the textual notes in *Balzac: La Comédie humaine*, 12 vols, ed. by Pierre-Georges Castex and others (Paris: Gallimard, 1976–81), XI, 1754–60.
33. *La Comédie humaine*, XI, 1769.

34. Herbert J. Hunt gives details of Balzac's classifications for the *Human Comedy* in *Balzac's Comédie Humaine* (London: Athlone Press, 1959), pp. 125–34 and 457–61.
35. As Arlette Michel suggests in her introduction to the text in *La Comédie humaine*, XI, 866.
36. Trans. by Francis Macnamara (London: Casanova Society, 1925); *La Comédie humaine*, XI, 865–1205. Short extracts are available in Honoré de Balzac, *Conjugal Life: Pinpricks of Married Life and The Physiology of Marriage* (London: Neville Spearman, 1957), pp. 181–230; but most of this work is made up of a translation of Balzac's later compilation *Petites misères de la vie conjugale* (1846).
37. *Flora Tristan: Feminism in the Age of George Sand* (London: Pluto Press, 1992), p. 9.
38. *A Social History of France, 1780–1880* (London and New York: Routledge, 1992), p. 110.
39. See Antony Copley, *Sexual Moralities in France, 1780–1980: New Ideas on the Family, Divorce and Homosexuality* (London and New York: Routledge, 1989), pp. 20–24. There is an outline of the history of divorce legislation until 1884 in *La Comédie humaine*, XI, 1776.
40. *Sexual Moralities in France*, pp. 86–7.
41. *Policing Prostitution in Nineteenth-Century Paris* (Princeton, NJ, and Guildford: Princeton University Press, 1985), pp. xviii–xix.
42. *Restoration and Reaction, 1815–1848*, trans. by Elborg Forster, Cambridge History of Modern France, I (Cambridge and New York: Cambridge University Press; Paris: Editions de la Maison de l'Homme, 1983), p. 381.
43. *Restoration and Reaction*, pp. 391 and 387.
44. *A Social History of France, 1780–1880*, p. 124.
45. 'Men's Reading, Women's Writing: Gender and the Rise of the Novel', in *The Politics of Tradition: Placing Women in French Literature*, *Yale French Studies*, 75 (1988), 40–55.
46. The anecdote is in Meditation XXIV, 236–49 (*La Comédie humaine*, XI, 1132–44). See further the textual notes in this edition (1905–11).
47. See *La Comédie humaine*, XI, 865.
48. *A Social History of France, 1780–1880*, p. 125.
49. *La Comédie humaine*, XI, 1920.
50. *La Comédie humaine*, XI, 1845–6.
51. Claudine Gothot-Mersch discusses the relationship between the *Physiology* and *Madame Bovary* in *La Genèse de 'Madame Bovary'* (Paris: Corti, 1966), pp. 50–4.

2 TOWARDS THE NOVEL OF FEMALE ADULTERY: CHATEAUBRIAND, CONSTANT, MUSSET, MÉRIMÉE

1. *The Adulteress's Child*, p. 58.
2. 'Our Lady of the Flowers', in *Violetta and her Sisters: The Lady of the Camellias, Responses to the Myth*, ed. by Nicholas John (London and Boston: Faber and Faber, 1994), pp. 161–7 (p. 163).

3. *Atala and René*, trans. by Rayner Heppenstall (London and New York: Oxford University Press, 1963); *Chateaubriand: Oeuvres romanesques et voyages*, ed. by Maurice Regard, 2 vols (Paris: Gallimard, 1969), I, 15–146.
4. 'Triste Amérique: Atala and the Postrevolutionary Construction of Woman', in *Rebel Daughters: Women and the French Revolution*, ed. by Sara E. Melzer and Leslie W. Rabine (New York and Oxford: Oxford University Press, 1992), pp. 138–56 (p. 149).
5. 'The Engulfed Beloved: Representations of Dead and Dying Women in the Art and Literature of the Revolutionary Era', in *Rebel Daughters*, pp. 198–227 (p. 222).
6. 'Being René, Buying Atala: Alienated Subjects and Decorative Objects in Postrevolutionary France', in *Rebel Daughters*, pp. 157–77 (p. 164).
7. 'Being René, Buying Atala', pp. 170–1.
8. *The Male Malady: Fictions of Impotence in the French Romantic Novel* (New Brunswick, NJ: Rutgers University Press, 1993), p. 17.
9. Constant's manuscript contains a passage, suppressed at the request of Lady Charlotte Campbell, which also attributes sexual experience to Ellénore before her liaison with the Count. See *Benjamin Constant: Oeuvres*, ed. by Alfred Roulin (Paris: Gallimard, 1957), p. 1413.
10. *Adolphe*, trans. by Leonard Tancock (Harmondsworth: Penguin, 1964); *Benjamin Constant: Oeuvres*, pp. 5–83.
11. 'George Sand and Alfred de Musset: Absolution Through Art in *La Confession d'un enfant du siècle*', in *The World of George Sand*, ed. by Natalie Datlof, Jeanne Fuchs, and David A. Powell (New York and London: Greenwood Press, 1991), pp. 207–16 (p. 211).
12. *La Confession d'un enfant du siècle*, trans. by G. F. Monkshood (pseudonym of W. J. Clarke) as *A Modern Man's Confession* (London: Greening, 1908); *Alfred de Musset: Oeuvres complètes en prose*, ed. by Maurice Allem and Paul-Courant (Paris: Gallimard, 1960), pp. 65–288.
13. *The Adulteress's Child*, pp. 20–1.
14. *The Deceived Husband*, p. 6.
15. *The Male Malady*, pp. 97 and 112.
16. See Jeanne Fuchs, 'George Sand and Alfred de Musset', for a reading of the novel which emphasizes the theme of religious conversion.
17. *The Adulteress's Child*, p. 228.
18. 'Men's Reading, Women's Writing: Gender and the Rise of the Novel', 44.
19. For a discussion of writing by Crébillon, Duclos, Laclos and others, see Peter Brooks, *The Novel of Worldliness: Crébillon, Marivaux, Laclos, Stendhal* (Princeton, NJ: Princeton University Press, 1969). Crébillon's *Les égarements du coeur et de l'esprit* has been translated into English by Barbara Bray (London: Oxford University Press, 1963).
20. *Manon Lescaut*, trans. by Leonard Tancock, 2nd edn (Harmondsworth: Penguin, 1991), p. 5; ed. by Frédéric Deloffre and Raymond Picard (Paris: Bordas, 1990), p. 6.
21. Francine du Plessix Gray gives an account both of the taking of lovers and of the Parisian salon in *Rage and Fire: A Life of Louise Colet* (London: Hamish Hamilton; New York: Simon and Schuster, 1994).

22. See *Mérimée: Théâtre de Clara Gazul, Romans et nouvelles*, ed. by Jean Mallion and Pierre Salomon (Paris: Gallimard, 1978), pp. 1545–6; and A. W. Raitt, *Prosper Mérimée* (London: Eyre & Spottiswoode, 1970), pp. 210–11.

23. I have not been able to consult a copy of any of the few English translations of *Arsène Guillot*. All references are therefore to the text in *Mérimée: Théâtre de Clara Gazul, Romans et nouvelles*, pp. 891–935, and translations are my own.

24. According to David Coward, Dumas probably borrowed the idea of the camellias from George Sand's novel *Isidora* (1846), for he adopted the same unusual spelling. See *La Dame aux Camélias*, trans. by David Coward (Oxford and New York: Oxford University Press, 1986), p. 207. Dumas, however, would certainly have known Mérimée's story.

25. *Théâtre de Clara Gazul*, p. 1544.

26. *Prosper Mérimée*, p. 102.

27. *A Slight Misunderstanding*, trans. by Douglas Parmée (London: John Calder, 1959); *La Double Méprise*, in *Théâtre de Clara Gazul*, pp. 605–68.

28. In his *Mérimée*, André Billy points out that the reference to Saint-Cloud, and Chaverny's ambition to become a gentleman of the bedchamber, identify a Restoration setting (Paris: Flammarion, 1959, p. 77). *Arsène Guillot* is located in the Restoration by its reference to Madame la Dauphine, the aunt of Charles X, who was noted for her rigid devotion (*Théâtre de Clara Gazul*, p. 1548).

29. *Théâtre de Clara Gazul*, p. 1408 (my translation).

30. *Théâtre de Clara Gazul*, pp. 1406–8 and 1416–18.

31. Mallion and Salomon point out Mérimée's unkind use of Mélanie's first name for the courtesan brought into Julie's box at the Opera (*Théâtre de Clara Gazul*, p. 1421); a pun on her surname may also be suspected in the story's title.

3 THE FORMATION OF THE NOVEL OF FEMALE ADULTERY: BALZAC

1. Herbert J. Hunt, *Honoré de Balzac: A Biography* (London: Athlone Press, 1957), pp. 2–5 and 89, 21–3, and 51–2 and 56 respectively. Further details are given in *La Comédie humaine*, ed. by Pierre-Georges Castex: e.g. on Balzac's resentment of his brother in II, 1031, and on Madame de Castries in V, 752–62. Graham Robb brings together many of the connections between Balzac's life and his fiction in *Balzac: A Biography* (London: Picador, 1994), e.g. pp. 3–33, passim, on his attitudes to his mother and brother, and pp. 213–21 on Madame de Castries.

2. *Gobseck*, first published as *Les Dangers de l'inconduite*, acquired its definitive title only in 1842. See *La Comédie humaine*, II, 945–59.

3. *History of the Thirteen*, trans. by Herbert J. Hunt (Harmondsworth: Penguin, 1974); *La Comédie humaine*, V, 737–1112.

4. *The Male Malady*, pp. 177–8, citing Naomi Schor, *Breaking the Chain: Women, Theory and French Realist Fiction* (New York: Columbia

University Press, 1985), p. 30.

5.　*A Social History of France, 1780–1880*, p. 126.

6.　'Textuality and the Riddle of Bisexuality', in *What Does a Woman Want? Reading and Sexual Difference* (Baltimore and London: Johns Hopkins University Press, 1993), pp. 41–67.

7.　'Textuality and the Riddle of Bisexuality', p. 65.

8.　*Balzac's Comédie Humaine*, p. 26. The two volumes were the first collection of *Scènes de la vie privée*.

9.　*Gobseck*, in *La Comédie Humaine*, ed. by George Saintsbury, 40 vols (London: Dent; New York: Macmillan, 1895–8), XL, *A Woman of Thirty*, trans. by Ellen Marriage (1897), 307–75; and *La Comédie humaine*, II, 945–1013.

10.　As far as I know, there is no version in English of *Le Conseil*. References are therefore to the text in *La Comédie humaine*, II, 1365–73, and translations are mine.

11.　See *The Message*, in the Saintsbury ed., XL, *A Woman of Thirty*, 291–306 (p. 299); and in *La Comédie humaine*, II, 387–407 (pp. 401 and 1375). Kathryn Norberg gives further details about the texts to which Balzac refers, and also their author, in '"Love and Patriotism": Gender and Politics in the Life and Work of Louvet de Couvrai', in *Rebel Daughters: Women and the French Revolution*, pp. 38–53.

12.　*La Comédie humaine*, II, 393.

13.　*Another Study of Woman* in the Saintsbury ed., XVII, *La Grande Bretèche and other stories*, trans. by Clara Bell (1896); *Autre étude de femme* in *La Comédie humaine*, III, 657–729. For the textual details, see the latter, 657–71 and 1485–1519. There is a more accessible English version of *La Grande Bretèche* in Honoré de Balzac, *Selected Short Stories*, trans. by Sylvia Raphael (Harmondsworth: Penguin, 1977).

14.　Both stories are in the Saintsbury ed., XL, *A Woman of Thirty*, 263–90 and 213–262; and in *La Comédie humaine*, II, 411–43 and 447–503.

15.　E.g. Arlette Michel attributes feminism to Balzac in discussing, of all texts, *The Physiology of Marriage* (*La Comédie humaine*, XII, 885–91). Though Balzac invites sympathy for various female characters, his position is scarcely feminist.

16.　The very complex textual history of *La Femme de trente ans* is summarized by Bernard Gagnebin and René Guise in *La Comédie humaine*, II, 1584–90.

17.　*La Comédie humaine*, II, 1018–27.

18.　*Balzac: Fiction and Melodrama* (London: Edward Arnold; New York: Holmes and Meier, 1978), pp. 132–3.

19.　*Balzac: Fiction and Melodrama*, p. 134.

20.　*The Adulteress's Child: Authorship and Desire in the Nineteenth-Century Novel*. Segal does not, however, discuss any texts by Balzac.

21.　*La Comédie humaine*, II, 1033 (my translation).

22.　See the remarks quoted by Prendergast, pp. 130–1 and 136.

23.　*Balzac: Fiction and Melodrama*, p. 135.

24.　Again, the textual history is complex. Full details are given by Anne-Marie Meininger in *La Comédie humaine*, IV, 1351–87.

25.　Jean Pommier compares the two novels, and *The Double Mistake*, in

'*La Muse du département* et le thème de la femme mal mariée chez Balzac, Mérimée et Flaubert', *L'Année balzacienne*, 1961, 191–221. See also Claudine Gothot-Mersch, *La Genèse de 'Madame Bovary'*, pp. 54–60.

26. *The Muse of the Department* in *La Comédie Humaine*, ed. by George Saintsbury, XXVIII, *Parisians in the Country*, trans. by James Waring (1898), 118. See further *La Comédie humaine*, IV, 1409.

27. *Les Français peints par eux-mêmes: encyclopédie morale du dix-neuvième siècle*, 8 vols (Paris: Curmer, 1840–2), VI, 1–8. The full text is given in *La Comédie humaine*, IV, 1378–87.

28. Jean Pommier discusses this episode and its links with the carriage scenes of Mérimée's *The Double Mistake* and Flaubert's *Madame Bovary* in '*La Muse du département* et le thème de la femme mal mariée', 208–14.

29. Camille Maupin appears often in *The Human Comedy*, especially in *Beatrice* (1839–45). To compound the irony, she is herself based in part on George Sand. See further Janis Glasgow, 'George Sand's Multiple Appearances in Balzac's *La Muse du département*', in *The World of George Sand*, pp. 217–25.

4   FROM OLD PARADIGMS TO NEW: CHAMPFLEURY, FEYDEAU, FLAUBERT

1. See 'Flaubert's Presuppositions', *Diacritics*, 11 (1981), 2–11, repr. in *Flaubert and Postmodernism*, ed. by Naomi Schor and Henry F. Majewski (Lincoln and London: University of Nebraska Press, 1984), pp. 177–91; and 'Relevance of Theory/Theory of Relevance', *Yale Journal of Criticism*, 1 (1988), 163–76.

2. 'La Femme adultère', in *Les Français peints par eux-mêmes*, III, 265–72 (p. 272). Translations are mine.

3. This is further borne out by the two illustrations to the text and by the epigraph, 'Go in peace and sin no more', spoken by Jesus to the woman taken in adultery (John: 8.11).

4. Paris: Larousse et Boyer. The work was first published serially, the seventeenth and final volume (a supplement) in 1886. Translations are mine.

5. Part 5, Chapter 8.

6. VIII (1872).

7. VIII (1872). Flaubert, who claimed that he undertook *Madame Bovary* 'in hatred of realism', would hardly have accepted such a designation. See *Correspondance*, 3 vols, ed. by Jean Bruneau (Paris: Gallimard, 1973–), II, 643 (30 October 1856).

8. Examples are *Contes domestiques*, *Contes de printemps*, *Contes d'été*, *Les Oies de Nöel*, and *Contes d'Automne*, all published in the three years before the first appearance of *Les Bourgeois de Molinchart*.

9. 'Champfleury, Flaubert and the Novel of Adultery', *Nineteenth-Century French Studies*, 20 (1991–2), 145–57.

10. Paris: Librairie nouvelle, 1855. This is the second edition, and the first

to be published in one volume. The novel has not been translated into English; translations are therefore mine.

11. 'Champfleury, Flaubert and the Novel of Adultery', 156–7.
12. Sainte-Beuve's review (14 June 1858) is collected in *Causeries du lundi*, 4th edn, 16 vols (Paris: Garnier, n.d.), XIV, 163–78. Sainte-Beuve was attacked for commenting favourably on a book which many found scandalous, and he defended himself in an open letter published on 20 February 1860 in which he declined the invitation to review Feydeau's later novel *Catherine d'Overmeire* ('La Morale et l'Art', *Causeries du lundi*, XV, 345–55).
13. Freud first published his theory in *The Interpretation of Dreams* in 1900. See especially *Introductory Lectures on Psycho-Analysis*, in *The Standard Edition of the Complete Psychological Works*, trans. by James Strachey, 24 vols (London: Hogarth Press, 1953), XV–XVI, 329–38.
14. The edition cited of *Fanny* is the fourth (Paris: Amyot, 1858); translations are mine.
15. Anon (London: George Vickers, 1860).
16. See Claire Goldberg Moses, *French Feminism in the Nineteenth Century*, pp. 152–61; Charles Bernheimer, *Figures of Ill Repute: Representing Prostitution in Nineteenth-Century France* (Cambridge, MA, and London: Harvard University Press, 1989), pp. 202–12; and Stephen Heath, *Gustave Flaubert: Madame Bovary* (Cambridge and New York: Cambridge University Press, 1992), pp. 81 and 87–8.
17. *Causeries du lundi*, XIV, 164 and 167–75; *Fanny*, pp. xi–xiii. The Preface was first printed in the second edition of the novel.
18. 'Flaubert's Presuppositions', pp. 181–9 (p. 182).
19. 'Relevance of Theory/Theory of Relevance', 173.
20. 'The whole of Gustave Flaubert's masterpiece, at any rate its plot, Emma Bovary's fall, crime and punishment, and the setting and props that help stage that exemplary drama are all derived from time-sequenced actualisations of a semanalysis of the word adulteress' ('Relevance of Theory/Theory of Relevance', 171).
21. Quoted by Stephen Heath in *Gustave Flaubert: Madame Bovary*, p. 80. The remark from *The Muse of the Department* is on p. 108 (*La Comédie humaine*, IV, 680).
22. *Madame Bovary*, Norton Critical Edition, ed. by Paul de Man (New York: Norton, 1965), pp. 339 and 342; *Baudelaire: Oeuvres complètes*, ed. by Claude Pichois, 2 vols (Paris: Gallimard, 1975–6), II, 80 and 84.
23. 'La Femme adultère', 270–1 (p. 271).
24. 'Preface, Written Twenty Years After the Novel', in *Against the Grain* [trans. by John Howard, pseud.] (New York: Three Sirens Press, 1931; repr. Dover, 1969), p. xxxv; *Oeuvres Complètes de J.-K. Huysmans*, ed. by Charles Grolleau, 18 vols (Paris: Crès, 1928–34), VII, *À Rebours*, p. x.
25. *Madame Bovary: Provincial Lives*, trans. by Geoffrey Wall (Harmondsworth: Penguin, 1992); *Madame Bovary: Moeurs de Province*, ed. by Claudine Gothot-Mersch (Paris: Garnier, 1971).
26. *Grand Dictionnaire universel*, II (1867), 1167–8, under '*Bovary*'.
27. 'La Femme adultère', 269.
28. See Flaubert's first scenario for the novel, discussed by Claudine

Gothot-Mersch in *La Genèse de 'Madame Bovary'*, pp. 89–119 (repr. on pp. 292–4; trans. by Paul de Man in the Norton Critical Edition, pp. 259–61). Gothot-Mersch is inaccurate in stating that the trip to the theatre in Rouen replaces the visit to Paris (p. 102), as in the first scenario there is a gap between the Paris visit and Léon's return.

29.   For the motif of sex in a cab, see note 28 to Chapter 3 (p. 231, above) and Riffaterre, 'Flaubert's Presuppositions', pp. 186–7. Jean-Paul Sartre relates the cab episode in *Madame Bovary* to the occasion when Flaubert and Louise Colet first made love. See *L'Idiot de la famille*, 3 vols (Paris: Gallimard, 1971–2; rev. edn, 1988), II, 1285–93.

30.   See, for instance, Alison Fairlie's discussion in *Flaubert: Madame Bovary*, Studies in French Literature, 8 (London: Arnold, 1962), pp. 28–32.

31.   'La Femme adultère', 267; 'Flaubert's Presuppositions', p. 184.

32.   'Flaubert's Presuppositions', pp. 185; 'Relevance of Theory/Theory of Relevance', 172.

33.   *Grand Dictionnaire universel*, II (1867), under '*Bovary*'; my translation.

34.   'La Femme adultère', 267.

35.   *Correspondance*, II, 585 (27 June 1855); my translation.

36.   *La Genèse de 'Madame Bovary'*, p. 46. Gothot-Mersch discusses Flaubert's use of the *Mémoires* on pp. 43–50.

37.   *Gustave Flaubert: Madame Bovary*, p. 34.

38.   'Bonapartism', in *A New History of French Literature*, ed. by Denis Hollier (Cambridge, MA, and London: Harvard University Press, 1989), pp. 717–22 (p. 720).

39.   *Ladies of the Leisure Class: The Bourgeoises of Northern France in the Nineteenth Century* (Princeton, NJ, and Guildford: Princeton University Press, 1981), pp. 48–9, p. 45 and passim.

40.   Norton Critical Edition, p. 389; first published in English in *Mimesis: The Representation of Reality in Western Literature*, trans. by Willard Trask (Princeton, NJ: Princeton University Press, 1953), pp. 425–33. The passage discussed is the last paragraph on p. 51 of the 1992 Penguin edition and on p. 67 in the Gothot-Mersch edition (I.ix).

41.   'A Parisian bourgeoise contemplates marriage: Stéphanie Jullien', in *Victorian Women*, ed. by Erna Olafson Hellerstein, Leslie Parker Hume, and Karen M. Offen, pp. 144–9 (p. 147).

42.   Norton Critical Edition, p. 391.

43.   *Gustave Flaubert: Madame Bovary*, p. 82.

44.   *Gustave Flaubert: Madame Bovary*, p. 102.

45.   It is worth noting that Flaubert's first scenario for the novel does not mention Homais, though it does indicate that Emma's first lover 'has a room in the house of the pharmacist across the street' (Norton Critical Edition, p. 260).

46.   *Adultery in the Novel*, p. 235.

47.   *Gustave Flaubert: Madame Bovary*, p. 87.

48.   'Relevance of Theory/Theory of Relevance', 175.

49.   *Correspondance*, II, 31 (16 January 1852); English translation in the Norton Critical Edition, p. 309.

50.   'For a Restricted Thematics: Writing, Speech, and Difference in *Madame Bovary*', trans. by Harriet Stone, in *Breaking the Chain: Women,*

Theory, and French Realist Fiction, p. 12. Rosemary Lloyd points out that Flaubert wrote in one of his scenarios for the novel: 'Homais comes from Homo = man' (*Madame Bovary*, Unwin Critical Library, London: Unwin Hyman, 1990, p. 30).

51.   *The Perpetual Orgy* (London and Boston: Faber, 1987; first published in Spanish, 1975), pp. 28–30 (p. 29); *Adultery in the Novel*, pp. 349–56.

52.   *Toward an Aesthetic of Reception*, trans. by Timothy Bahti (Brighton, Sussex: Harvester, 1982), p. 27.

53.   Ibid.

54.   'Le roman intime de la littérature réaliste', *Revue des Deux Mondes*, 18 (1858), 196–213, cited by Jauss on p. 198.

55.   'Essai sur Adolphe', in Benjamin Constant, *Adolphe* (Paris: Charpentier, 1839), pp. 371–87. The essay has been discussed in its relation both to Constant's novel and to Balzac's by Bernard Guyon in '*Adolphe, Béatrix et La Muse du département*', *L'Année balzacienne*, 1963, 149–75.

56.   'Le roman intime de la littérature réaliste', 198–9. Montégut indicates a new moral emphasis when he remarks, for instance: 'Good taste is only the moral sense applied to literary matters' (p. 213).

57.   *Gustave Flaubert: Madame Bovary*, p. 82.

58.   Norton Critical Edition, p. 338.

5   ALTERNATIVES: GEORGE SAND AND OTHERS

1.   For an account of the separation, see Curtis Cate, *George Sand: A Biography* (Boston: Houghton Mifflin; London: Hamish Hamilton, 1975), pp. 371–86 and 397–9; Sand's response to Nisard is discussed on p. 392.

2.   *Lettres d'un Voyageur*, trans. by Sacha Rabinovitch and Patricia Thomson (Harmondsworth: Penguin, 1987); *George Sand: Oeuvres autobiographiques*, ed. by Georges Lubin, 2 vols (Paris: Gallimard, 1970–1), II. The fact that the Larousse entry on *Indiana* (IX, 1873) calls it 'this first appeal against marriage' shows that the misreading illustrated by Nisard's article became entrenched.

3.   Sand had written to the Saint-Simonian Marie Talon to this effect in November 1834. See *Correspondance de George Sand*, ed. by Georges Lubin, 24 vols (Paris: Garnier, 1964–90), II, 739–42 (10 November 1834).

4.   See Margaret Waller, *The Male Malady*, Chapter 6, 'Towards a Feminist Mal du Siècle: Sand's *Lélia*'.

5.   *Indiana*, trans. by Sylvia Raphael (Oxford and New York: Oxford University Press, 1994); ed. by Pierre Salomon (Paris: Garnier, 1962).

6.   Indeed, Sand does not even make it clear whether they become lovers. See Naomi Schor, *George Sand and Idealism* (New York and Chichester, West Sussex: Columbia University Press, 1993), p. 106.

7.   *George Sand and Idealism*, p. 53. See also Schor's Introduction to *Indiana*, p. xxi.

8.   The absence or the harmful influence of the mother often features in Sand's work. Sand's own mother left her to be brought up by her

grandmother at the age of seven when she went to live in Paris.

9. *Valentine*, trans. by George Burnham Ives (Philadelphia: G. Barrie, 1902; repr. Chicago: Academy Press, 1978); Perrotin ed. of 1843, repr. Paris: Éditions d'Aujourd'hui, 1976.

10. Leslie Rabine cites such an event in Daniel Stern's *Valentia*, where, she suggests, an event which cannot be acknowledged in orthodox discourse is refracted through Gothic narrative conventions. See 'Feminist Writers in French Romanticism', *Studies in Romanticism*, 16 (1977), 491–507 (pp. 499–500). *Valentia* is discussed above in Chapter 5, p. 117.

11. See 'Writing from the Pavilion: George Sand and the Novel of Female Pastoral', in *Subject to Change: Reading Feminist Writing* (New York: Columbia University Press, 1988), pp. 204–28.

12. 'Female Fetishism: The Case of George Sand', *Poetics Today*, 6 (1985), 301–10; repr. in *The Female Body in Western Culture: Contemporary Approaches*, ed. by Susan Suleiman (Cambridge, MA: Harvard University Press, 1986), pp. 363–72.

13. *Subject to Change*, p. 207.

14. Kathryn J. Crecelius compares the two novels in her discussion of *Jacques* in *Family Romances: George Sand's Early Novels* (Bloomington and Indianapolis: Indiana University Press, 1987), pp. 127–40.

15. See *Family Romances*, pp. 135–7.

16. Perrotin ed. of 1842, repr. Paris: Éditions d'Aujourd'hui, 1976. References are given by letter as well as by page number. The only English translation, by Anna Blackwell, 2 vols (New York: J. S. Redfield, 1847), is very rare; translations are therefore mine.

17. *George Sand: Writing for Her Life* (New Brunswick, NJ, and London: Rutgers University Press, 1991), pp. 186–9.

18. *Rose et Blanche* is the novel written and published jointly by Sand and Sandeau in 1831 and published under the pseudonym 'J. Sand'. Kathryn J. Crecelius discusses it and several other novels by Sand which feature rape or seduction in *Family Romances*, pp. 40–56.

19. *Le Dernier amour*, introd. by Mireille Bossis (Paris: Éditions des femmes, 1991). This text is a reprint of the first edition (Paris: Michel Lévy, 1867). The novel has not been translated into English; translations are therefore mine.

20. *Correspondance*, XIX, 739 (24 February 1866). Translations from Sand's correspondence are mine except where noted otherwise.

21. *Flaubert–Sand: The Correspondence*, trans. by Francis Steegmuller and Barbara Bray (London: HarperCollins, 1993), pp. 385–6 (12 January 1876).

22. See Chapter 4, p. 75, and p. 234, note 56; and Francine du Plessix Gray, *Rage and Fire: A Life of Louise Colet*, pp. 340–2. Proudhon had attacked Sand in *On Justice in the Revolution and in the Church*; Michelet was a friend, but Sand thought that *L'Amour* was a mistake (*Correspondance*, XV, 197; 3 December 1858).

23. *Correspondance*, XX, 19 (9 June 1866).

24. *Correspondance*, XX, 46–7 (5 July 1866).

25. *Correspondance*, XX, 47. Dumas wrote a play, *La Princesse Georges*, in

response to Sand, but the ending, in which the wife forgives her husband, puzzled her. See Eve Sourian, 'The Important, Little-Known Friendship of George Sand and Alexandre Dumas fils', in *The World of George Sand*, pp. 243–53.

26. 'Feminist Writers in French Romanticism', 501. My discussion of *Valentia* is indebted to Rabine's.

27. *Méphis*, 2 vols (Paris: Ladvocat, 1838), II, 56. Quoted by Sandra Dijkstra in *Flora Tristan: Feminism in the Age of George Sand*. My discussion is indebted to Dijkstra's chapter on the novel.

28. *Flora Tristan: Feminism in the Age of George Sand*, p. 100.

29. 'Feminist Writers in French Romanticism'; *George Sand and Idealism*, especially Chapter 1, 'Idealism in the Novel: Recanonizing Sand'.

30. *The Prose Poems and La Fanfarlo*, trans. by Rosemary Lloyd (Oxford and New York: Oxford University Press, 1991).

31. Barbara Wright and David H. T. Scott, *La Fanfarlo and Le Spleen de Paris*, Critical Guides to French Texts, 30 (London: Grant & Cutler, 1984), p. 23.

32. Baudelaire indicates one of his debts to Balzac in a footnote to the story (27; *Oeuvres complètes*, I, 578); Claude Pichois discusses these and other echoes, allusions and parodies at length in *Oeuvres complètes*. Francis Scarfe proposes a link to Constant and *Adolphe* in the introduction to his translation in *Baudelaire: The Poems in Prose with La Fanfarlo* (London: Anvil Press, 1989), pp. 17–19.

33. See Richard Terdiman, *Discourse/Counter-Discourse: The Theory and Practice of Symbolic Resistance in Nineteenth-Century France* (Ithaca, NY, and London: Cornell University Press, 1985).

34. *Reading the Romantic Heroine: Text, History, Ideology* (Ann Arbor: University of Michigan Press, 1985), p. 7. Rabine's reference is to *Le Deuxième Sexe*, 2 vols (Paris: Gallimard, 1949), I, *Les Faits et les Mythes*, 234; *The Second Sex*, trans. and ed. by H. M. Parshley (London: Jonathan Cape, 1953; repr. Harmondsworth: Penguin, 1972), p. 173.

35. *Reading the Romantic Heroine*, p. 69.

36. *The Lily of the Valley*, trans. by James Waring, in *La Comédie Humaine*, ed. by George Saintsbury, XXI (1897); *Le Lys dans la vallée*, *La Comédie humaine*, IX (1978).

37. A striking parallel to this example of the double standard of sexual morality is that, as Jill Harsin points out, 'in the peculiar politics of venereal disease, women were always the guilty transmitters, men (and the wives and children of these men) their hapless victims' (*Policing Prostitution in Nineteenth-Century Paris*, p. 258).

38. See *La Comédie humaine*, IX, 1650–1 and 1747–8.

39. 'Virtue-tripping: Notes on *Le Lys dans la vallée*', in *Intoxication and Literature*, *Yale French Studies*, 50 (1974), 150–62 (p. 158).

40. Jean-Hervé Donnard goes so far as to call the novel 'a Catholic work'. See *La Comédie humaine*, 905–13 (p. 913).

41. *La Comédie humaine*, III, 41.

42. '"Tristes Triangles": *Le Lys dans la vallée* and Its Intertext', in *Pre-Text, Text, Context: Essays on Nineteenth-Century French Literature*, ed. by Robert L. Mitchell (Columbus: Ohio State University Press, 1980), pp.

67–77 (pp. 70 and 75).

43. *Dominique*, trans. by Sir Edward Marsh (London: Soho Book Company, 1986; first published London: Cresset Press, 1948); ed. by S. de Sacy (Paris: Gallimard, 1966; repr. 1974).

6   WHAT IS TO BE DONE? CHERNYSHEVSKY, TOLSTOY, CHEKHOV

1. *A Writer's Diary*, trans. by Kenneth Lantz, 2 vols (Evanston, IL: Northwestern University Press, 1993–4; London: Quartet, 1994–5), I, 507–8. Louis Adolf Thiers (1797–1877) was a statesman and historian; Jean-Paul Rabaut, known as Rabaut-Saint-Etienne (1743–93), a political writer and activist in the early years of the French Revolution.
2. *The Women's Liberation Movement in Russia: Feminism, Nihilism, and Bolshevism 1860–1930* (Princeton, NJ: Princeton University Press, 1978), p. 20. The other three novels are: Alexander Druzhinin, *Polinka Saks* (1847), Mikhail Avdeev, *Underwater Stone* (1860), and Innokenti Fedorov-Omulevsky, *Step by Step* (1870); Stites inadvertently cites Vasily Sleptsov as the author of the last-named text, and I am grateful to him for his help in clarifying this. Dawn D. Eidelman discusses *Who Is to Blame?*, *Polinka Saks* and *Underwater Stone* (the title of which she renders as *The Reef*) in *George Sand and the Nineteenth-Century Russian Love-Triangle Novels* (London and Toronto: Associated University Presses, 1994).
3. Introduction to reprint of *What Is to Be Done?*, trans. by N. Dole and S. S. Skidelsky (Ann Arbor, MI: Ardis, 1986; first published New York: T. Y. Crowell, 1886), p. xiii.
4. *Women in Russian Literature, 1780–1863* (London: Macmillan, 1988), Chapter 7; *On the Eve*, trans. by Gilbert Gardiner (Harmondsworth: Penguin, 1950), XXXV.229.
5. *What Is to Be Done?*, trans. by Michael R. Katz (Ithaca, NY, and London: Cornell University Press, 1989). All references are to this edition.
6. Introduction to *What Is to Be Done?*, p. 24.
7. The story of the novel's publication and subsequent suppression until after the 1905 Revolution is told by E. Lampert in *Sons against Fathers: Studies in Russian Radicalism and Revolution* (Oxford: Clarendon Press, 1965), pp. 128 and 364–5 (note 51). Chernyshevsky spent most of the rest of his life in prison or in exile.
8. Introduction to *What Is to Be Done?*, p. 14.
9. For a discussion of Chernyshevsky's formal innovations, see Gary Saul Morson, *The Boundaries of Genre: Dostoevsky's Diary of a Writer and the Traditions of Literary Utopia* (Austin: University of Texas Press, 1981), pp. 99–104.
10. *Sons against Fathers*, p. 108.
11. *Mothers and Daughters: Women of the Intelligentsia in Nineteenth-century Russia* (Cambridge: Cambridge University Press, 1983), p. 51.
12. *The Women's Liberation Movement in Russia*, p. 56.

13. *Pisemsky: A Provincial Realist* (Cambridge, MA: Harvard University Press, 1969), p. 162.
14. See the examples in *Anna Karenin*, trans. by Rosemary Edmonds (Harmondsworth: Penguin, 1954; rev. edn, 1978), I, i.15, x.52, xi.55, xix.82. The Russian text has further examples, which Edmonds renders differently: 'Oh dear, what am I to do?' (I.ii.16), 'What else can you do?' (I.ii.18), 'What can I do?' (I.iv.24), 'And what can one do?' (I.xi.55), 'What could I do?' (I.xv.68), and 'What am I to do?' (I.xix.84). I am grateful to Elaine Hobby for pointing these out to me, and for other advice on questions of translation from the Russian.
15. See Mary Evans, *Reflecting on Anna Karenina* (London and New York: Routledge, 1989), pp. 26–30.
16. *Tolstoi in the Sixties*, trans. by Duffield White (Ann Arbor, MI: Ardis, 1982), p. 130.
17. Ibid. See also Eikhenbaum's discussion in *Tolstoi in the Seventies*, trans. by Albert Kaspin (Ann Arbor, MI: Ardis, 1982), p. 95.
18. Trans. by Rosemary Edwards as 'Happy Ever After' in *The Cossacks, Happy Ever After, The Death of Ivan Ilyich* (Harmondsworth: Penguin, 1960).
19. *Tolstoi in the Sixties*, pp. 176–89.
20. *Tolstoi in the Seventies*, pp. 100–5. Eikhenbaum points out (pp. 104–5) that *L'Homme-femme* is discussed in one of the early drafts of the dinner at the Oblonskys (*Anna Karenina*, IV.ix–x).
21. 'Women and the Russian Intelligentsia: Three Perspectives', in *Women in Russia*, ed. by Dorothy Atkinson, Alexander Dallin and Gail Warshofsky Lapidus (Stanford, CA: Stanford University Press, 1977; Brighton, Sussex: Harvester, 1978), p. 45.
22. *Tolstoi in the Seventies*, p. 86.
23. As C. J. G. Turner remarks in *A Karenina Companion* (Waterloo, Ont.: Wilfrid Laurier University Press, 1993), p. 153, 'This sentence has been made famous through being quoted by Lenin in his assessment of Tolstoi's perception of Russian social history.'
24. *A Karenina Companion*, p. 4.
25. Introduction to *Anna Karenina*, trans. by Louise and Aylmer Maude (Oxford, 1918: repr. Oxford University Press, Oxford and New York, 1980), p. ix.
26. *Tolstoy's Letters*, trans. and ed. by R. F. Christian, 2 vols (London: Athlone Press, 1978), I, 256; Henri Troyat, *Tolstoy*, trans. by Nancy Amphoux (New York: Doubleday, 1967; London: W. H. Allen, 1968; repr. Harmondsworth: Penguin, 1970), p. 477.
27. *Tolstoi in the Seventies*, p. 76.
28. *A Karenina Companion*, p. 49.
29. 'Divorce and *Anna Karenina*', *Forum for Modern Language Studies*, 23 (1987), 97–116 (p. 112).
30. *A Karenina Companion*, p. 50.
31. *A Karenina Companion*, p. 15.
32. *A Karenina Companion*, p. 47.
33. *Leo Tolstoy: Anna Karenina* (Cambridge: Cambridge University Press, 1987), pp. 21 and 22.

34. *A Karenina Companion*, p. 18.
35. *A Karenina Companion*, p. 30. Turner also notes that in one of the drafts the 'St. Petersburg view' which Countess Vronsky is discussing with Anna as Vronsky meets them at the station is 'that there cannot be anything honourable in nihilists' (p. 134; *Anna Karenin*, I.xviii.75). Tolstoy does not identify this view in his final version, but Anna's disagreement with it constitutes her first speech in the novel.
36. *The Architecture of Anna Karenina: A History of its Writing, Structure, and Message* (Lisse, Neth.: Peter de Ridder Press, 1975), pp. 33 and 23.
37. Quoted by Boris Eikhenbaum in *Tolstoi in the Seventies*, p. 134.
38. *A Karenina Companion*, p. 20.
39. *A Karenina Companion*, p. 40. The letter was to Mikhail Katkov and dates from mid-February 1875 (*Tolstoy's Letters*, I, 274).
40. *Study of Thomas Hardy and Other Essays*, ed. by Bruce Steele (London: Grafton, 1986), pp. 25–6.
41. *Modern Tragedy* (London: Chatto and Windus, 1966; repr. Stanford, CA: Stanford University Press, 1987), p. 129.
42. Ibid.
43. The significance of Anna's children, and of children in the novel of female adultery in general, is further discussed in Chapter 7, pp. 184–6.
44. Chekhov's response to Tolstoy is discussed by Thomas Winner in *Chekhov and his prose* (New York: Holt, Rinehart and Winston, 1966), especially Chapter 4; and by Donald Rayfield in 'Chekhov and the Literary Tradition', in *A Chekhov Companion*, ed. by Toby W. Clyman (Westport, CT, and London: Greenwood Press, 1985), pp. 35–51 (pp. 41–3).
45. See p. 133 above and Boris Eikhenbaum, 'Chekhov at Large', in *Chekhov: A Collection of Critical Essays*, ed. by Robert Louis Jackson (Englewood Cliffs, NJ: Prentice-Hall, 1967), pp. 21–31 (pp. 21–2). Eikhenbaum goes so far as to say of Pisemsky and Leskov: 'In what is most basic and essential, Chekhov's literary origins come from them' (p. 22).
46. 'Chekhov at Large', p. 23.
47. All five stories are included in *The Oxford Chekhov*, trans. by Ronald Hingley, 9 vols (Oxford and New York: Oxford University Press, 1965–80), vols VI, VIII, IV, VI and VII respectively. Except where otherwise stated, all references are by volume and page number to this edition.
48. *The Oxford Chekhov* includes no stories first published before 1888. References to 'Misfortune' and 'Agafya' are therefore to the texts which are currently most accessible, in *Lady with Lapdog and Other Stories*, trans. by David Magarshack (Harmondsworth: Penguin, 1964).
49. This sentence, which is mistranslated by Magarshack, is quoted from Constance Garnett's translation, 'A Misfortune', in *The Tales of Tchehov*, 13 vols (London: Chatto and Windus; New York: Macmillan, 1917–23), IV, *The Party and Other Stories*, p. 291.
50. *Chekhov: A study of the major stories and plays* (Cambridge and New York: Cambridge University Press, 1977), pp. 222–3.

51. This more accurate rendering is again quoted from Garnett's translation (*The Tales of Tchehov*, VI, *The Witch and Other Stories*, p. 134).
52. *Chekhov: A study of the major stories and plays*, pp. 217–18.
53. *Terrible Perfection: Women and Russian Literature* (Bloomington and Indianapolis: Indiana University Press, 1987; repr. Midland Books, 1992), p. 51.
54. *The Oxford Chekhov*, IX, 1.
55. See, for instance, his remarks quoted in *The Oxford Chekhov*, IX, xvi.
56. *Letters on the Short Story, the Drama and Other Literary Topics*, ed. by Louis S. Friedland (New York: Minton, Balch, 1924; repr. Dover, 1966), p. 60.
57. See Victor Terras, 'Chekhov at Home: Russian Criticism', in *A Chekhov Companion*, pp. 167–83 (pp. 173 and 180–1), citing an article by the Russian scholar A. M. Turkov. Tolstoy's comments on 'A Lady with a Dog' are in *Tolstoy's Diaries*, trans. and ed. by R. F. Christian, 2 vols (London: Athlone Press, 1985), II, 475.
58. *Chekhov and Women: Women in the Life and Work of Chekhov* (Columbus, Ohio: Slavica, 1987), p. 57.
59. *The Oxford Chekhov*, VI, 287–8; IX, 10–11; IX, 10. The fact that both stories were unusually long in gestation and show many textual variants suggests Chekhov's nervousness about them.

7   PROTESTANT FICTION OF ADULTERY: BLICHER, JACOBSEN, FONTANE

1. *Twelve Stories by Steen Steensen Blicher*, trans. by Hanna Astrup Larsen (Princeton, NJ: Princeton University Press, 1945).
2. *The Complete Fairy Tales and Stories*, trans. by Erik Christian Haugaard (New York: Doubleday, 1974), pp. 954–66.
3. *Putting asunder: A history of divorce in Western society* (Cambridge and New York: Cambridge University Press, 1988), p. 40.
4. *Putting asunder*, pp. 51–2 and 200.
5. *Putting asunder*, pp. 201 and 430–1.
6. *Women in German History: From Bourgeois Emancipation to Sexual Liberation*, trans. by Stuart McKinnon-Evans in association with Terry Bond and Barbara Norden (Oxford and Hamburg: Berg; New York: St Martin's Press, 1989), pp. 11–19 and 64.
7. *Putting asunder*, p. 429.
8. *The Historical Novel*, trans. by Hannah and Stanley Mitchell (London: Merlin Press, 1962), p. 200.
9. Brandes published his lectures in 1872–90; they are translated as *Main Currents in Nineteenth-Century Literature*, 6 vols (London: Heinemann, 1901–5); the term 'Modern Breakthrough' comes from *Det moderne Gjennembruds Mænd* (*The Men of the Modern Breakthrough*, 1883).
10. See Elias Bredsdorff, 'Moralists *versus* Immoralists: The Great Battle in Scandinavian Literature in the 1880's', *Scandinavica*, 8 (1969), 91–111. I am grateful to Michael Robinson for this reference and for advice about the whole chapter, especially the Scandinavian section.

11. *Marie Grubbe: A Lady of the Seventeenth Century,* trans. by Hanna Astrup Larsen of *Fru Marie Grubbe,* 2nd edn, rev. by Robert Raphael, The Library of Scandinavian Literature, 30 (Boston: G. K. Hall, 1975).
12. *Jens Peter Jacobsen* (Boston: G. K. Hall, 1980), p. 68.
13. Quoted from a letter by Jacobsen in Larsen's Introduction to her translation of *Marie Grubbe* (New York: American-Scandinavian Foundation; London: Oxford University Press, 1917) p. xi.
14. Trans. by Tiina Nunnally (Seattle: Fjord Press, 1990).
15. Larsen notes that the historical Ulrik Frederik divorced Marie Grubbe 'for her alleged relations with Sti Högh', and quotes a contemporary witness to the same effect *(Marie Grubbe,* pp. 257 and 259). Jacobsen makes no reference to this ground for divorce in his novel, and has the affair begin subsequently.
16. *Before the Storm,* trans. by R. J. Hollingdale (Oxford and New York: Oxford University Press, 1985); for details of *Die Likedeeler,* see Henry Garland, *The Berlin Novels of Theodor Fontane* (Oxford: Clarendon Press, 1980), p. 239.
17. Representative comparisons of the three novels are by J. P. Stern in *Re-Interpretations: Seven Studies in Nineteenth-Century German Literature* (London: Thames and Hudson, 1964; repr. Cambridge and New York: Cambridge University Press, 1981), pp. 316–39; and by Stanley Radcliffe, in *Fontane: Effi Briest,* Critical Guides to German Texts, 6 (London and Wolfeboro, NH: Grant & Cutler, 1986), pp. 74–7.
18. *Two Novellas: The Woman Taken in Adultery and The Poggenpuhl Family,* trans. by Gabriele Annan (Chicago and London: University of Chicago Press, 1979; repr. Harmondsworth: Penguin, 1995); *Theodor Fontane: Werke und Schriften,* 54 vols, ed. by Walter Keitel and Helmuth Nürnberger, VII, *L'Adultera* (Carl Hanser: Munich, 1971; repr. in Fontane Bibliothek, Frankfurt-am-Main, Berlin, Vienna: Ullstein, 1991). I am grateful to Keith Overton for advice about translation from the German. Where I have modified the translation, this is indicated by the abbreviation 'TM'.
19. The painting, which is not now thought to be by Tintoretto, is in the Accademia at Venice where Fontane saw it. See Rodolfo Pallucchini and Paola Rossi, *Tintoretto: Le opere sacre e profane,* 2 vols (Milan: Gruppo Editoriale Electa, 1982), I, 255 (notes), and II, 683 (illustration).
20. London: Chatto and Windus, 1975.
21. *Women in German History,* p. 135.
22. *The Berlin Novels of Theodor Fontane,* p. 60. *A Doll's House* was first staged in Germany in 1880.
23. *The Berlin Novels of Theodor Fontane,* p. 65.
24. *The Berlin Novels of Theodor Fontane,* p. 49.
25. *Putting asunder,* pp. 41–5 (p. 43).
26. *Beyond Recall,* trans. by Douglas Parmeé (London and New York: Oxford University Press, 1964); *Werke und Schriften,* XV, *Unwiederbringlich* (1971), repr. in Fontane Bibliothek (1991).
27. *Theodor Fontane: The Major Novels* (Cambridge and New York: Cambridge University Press, 1982), pp. 105–6 (p. 105); *Irrungen, Wirrungen,* trans. by Derek Bowman as *Entanglements: An Everyday*

Berlin Story (Bampton, Oxfordshire: Three Rivers Books, 1986).

28. *Theodor Fontane: The Major Novels*, p. 109.
29. *The German Gesellschaftsroman at the Turn of the Century: A Comparison of the Works of Theodor Fontane and Eduard von Keyserling* (Berne and Frankfurt-am-Main: Peter Lang, 1982), pp. 22–4.
30. *Theodor Fontane: The Major Novels*, p. 125.
31. As A. R. Robinson points out, most of *Schach von Wuthenow* had been written before Fontane began *L'Adultera*, although it was published later. See *Theodor Fontane: An Introduction to the Man and his Work* (Cardiff: University of Wales Press, 1976), p. 80.
32. *Theodor Fontane: The Major Novels*, p. 19.
33. *Effi Briest*, trans. by Douglas Parmée (Harmondsworth: Penguin, 1967); *Werke und Schriften*, XVII (1974), repr. in Fontane Bibliothek (1979). The superior translation by Hugh Rorrison and Helen Chambers (London: Angel Books, 1995) became available too late for me to use it.
34. Giles MacDonogh, *Prussia: The Perversion of an Idea* (London and Auckland: Sinclair-Stevenson, 1994), p. 27.
35. The allusion to the Prussian victory at Vionville is not represented in Parmée's translation. See the note in *Werke und Schriften*, XVII, 366.
36. *Imperial Germany, 1871–1914: Economy, Society, Culture, and Politics* (Providence, RI, and Oxford: Berghahn Books, 1994), p. 134.
37. Quoted by Roy Pascal in *The German Novel: Studies* (Manchester: Manchester University Press, 1956), p. 178; review of Paul Lindau, *Der Zug nach dem Westen*, in *Sämtliche Werke: Aufsätze, Kritike, Erinnerungen*, ed. by Walter Keitel, 5 vols (Munich: Carl Hanser, 1969), I, 568.
38. See David Blackbourn, 'The German bourgeoisie: an introduction', in *The German Bourgeoisie: Essays on the social history of the German middle class from the late eighteenth to the early twentieth century* ed. by David Blackbourn and Richard J. Evans (London and New York: Routledge, 1991), p. 42, note 93.
39. 'The German bourgeoisie: an introduction', p. 24.
40. *Prussia: The Perversion of an Idea*, p. 291.
41. *A social history of Germany, 1648–1914* (London: Methuen, 1977), pp. 248–9.
42. Joachim Remak, *The Gentle Critic: Theodor Fontane and German Politics, 1848–1898* (Syracuse, NY: Syracuse University Press, 1964), p. 63. Remak notes that Leist and Wehlan were 'German colonial officials accused of mistreating African natives' (p. 93, note 21); it is relevant to recall that Instetten briefly has colonial ambitions in *Effi Briest* (XXXV.260; 288).
43. *The Gentle Critic*, p. 44.
44. 'The Radicalization of Lily Braun', in *German Women in the Nineteenth Century: A Social History*, ed. by John C. Fout (New York and London: Holmes and Meier, 1984), p. 221.
45. 'The Radicalization of Lily Braun', p. 222.
46. '"Effi Briest" and "Die Historische Stunde des Takts"', *Modern Language Review*, 76 (1981), 869–79 (p. 874, note 3), quoting Pascal, *The*

German Novel, p. 201.
47. '"Effi Briest" and "Die Historische Stunde des Takts"', 872.
48. '"Effi Briest" and "Die Historische Stunde des Takts"', 879. Writing in 1912, Havelock Ellis observed: 'though extra-conjugal intercourse is in Germany almost a crime, sexual offences against children are far more prevalent than in France, while family life is at least as stable in France as in Germany, and more intimate'. See *The Task of Social Hygiene* (London: Constable, repr. 1927), p. 269.
49. 'The Function of Letters in Fontane's "Unwiederbringlich"', *Modern Language Review*, 65 (1970), 306–18 (p. 314).
50. The details are summarized by Stanley Radcliffe in *Fontane: Effi Briest*, pp. 9–10.
51. 'Private Mythologies and Public Unease: On Fontane's "Effi Briest"', *Modern Language Review*, 75 (1980), 114–23 (p. 122).
52. *Re-Interpretations*, p. 337.
53. 'The Fallen Woman's Sexuality: Childbirth and Censure', in *Sexuality and Victorian Literature*, ed. by Don Richard Cox, Tennessee Studies in Literature, 27 (Knoxville: University of Tennessee Press, 1984), pp. 54–71 (p. 57). The phrase 'genealogical continuity' is from Tony Tanner, *Adultery in the Novel*, p. 4.
54. 'The Fallen Woman's Sexuality', p. 60. MacPike is, however, mistaken in asserting that the offspring of Julie d'Aiglemont's first passionate affair is a girl; it is a boy, Charles. The boy's drowning is caused by Hélène, Julie's daughter by her husband. See above, pp. 56 and 59–60.
55. *Re-Interpretations*, p. 324.

8 CHURCH AND STATE: EÇA DE QUEIRÓS, ALAS, GALDÓS

1. *Re-Interpretations*, p. 322.
2. 'Realism in Spain and Portugal', in *The Age of Realism*, ed. by F. W. J. Hemmings (Harmondsworth: Penguin, 1974), p. 317.
3. *Eça de Queirós and European Realism* (New York and London: New York University Press, 1980), p. 116 (cited as 'Coleman' in subsequent references). What Coleman terms 'the apparent correspondences' between the two novels are discussed on pp. 114–20.
4. See Coleman, pp. 93–4.
5. Quoted in Coleman, p. 34.
6. *Cousin Bazilio*, trans. by Roy Campbell (London: Max Reinhardt, 1953; repr. Manchester: Carcanet Press, 1992); *Obra Completa*, 2 vols, ed. by João Gaspar Simões and others (Rio de Janeiro: Companhia José Aguilar Editõra, 1970), I, 551–840. The Campbell translation, the only one available in English, is both incomplete, cutting many short passages and some of considerable length, and extremely unreliable. Chapter numbers are indicated for both texts because Campbell's numbering is incorrect from Chapter VII onwards; where I have modified the translation, this is indicated by the abbreviation 'TM'. There is a nineteenth-century American translation by Mary J.

Serrano inappropriately entitled *Dragon's Teeth* (Boston: Ticknor, 1889). Although this is more complete than Campbell's, and generally more accurate, it is explicitly a bowdlerized version of Eça's text and it introduces further chapter divisions.

7. Coleman, pp. 78–9.
8. See Coleman, pp. 45–6 and 124–8.
9. Coleman, pp. 14–15 and 95–7.
10. See Coleman, pp. 89–93.
11. This is Machado's word, quoted in Coleman, p. 46.
12. Coleman, p. 45.
13. See, for example, *The Dialogic Imagination: Four Essays by M. M. Bakhtin*, trans. and ed. by Michael Holquist, University of Texas Press Slavic Series, 1 (Austin: University of Texas Press, 1981); and *Problems of Dostoevsky's Poetics*, trans. and ed. by Caryl Emerson, Theory and History of Literature, 8 (Manchester: Manchester University Press, 1984).
14. *The Lady of the Camélias* is the only one of these allusions to be represented in Campbell's translation (e.g. I.7 and 9–10; I.556 and 559–60). For the other four see *Obra Completa*, I, IX.739–40 (*Clémenceau*), I.559 (*Camors*), VI.680–1 (Proudhon and others), and IV.635 (*Eugénie Grandet*).
15. Quoted in Coleman, p. 5.
16. Coleman, p. 88.
17. Trans. by Alec Brown (London: Elek, 1957; repr. 1970). Coleman, p. 104, points out that Eça is indebted to Zola in at least two descriptive passages in the second version of *The Sin of Father Amaro*, but, as he says, 'these are minor matters'.
18. *The Sin of Father Amaro*, trans. by Nan Flanagan (London: Max Reinhardt, 1962; repr. Manchester: Carcanet Press, 1994).
19. Coleman, p. 187.
20. *Émile Zola* (Boston: G. K. Hall, 1966), p. 75.
21. Harmondsworth: Penguin; New York: Viking Penguin, 1984, p. 7. Alas is often also known by his pen-name, Clarín.
22. *Leopoldo Alas: La Regenta*, Critical Guides to Spanish Texts, 9 (London: Grant & Cutler, 1974), p. 40. The exception is the passage in which Don Víctor Quintanar, Ana's husband, finds out about her adultery.
23. Introduction to *La Regenta*, p. 16.
24. *The Craft of Fiction* (London and Toronto: Jonathan Cape, 1921; repr. 1939), p. 246.
25. *A Social History of Modern Spain* (London and Cambridge, MA: Unwin Hyman, 1990), pp. 32–3.
26. 'On Monstrous Birth: Leopoldo Alas's *La Regenta*', in *Naturalism in the European Novel: New Critical Perspectives*, ed. by Brian Nelson (New York and Oxford: Berg, 1992), pp. 191–209 (pp. 198–9).
27. 'Mysticism and Hysteria in *La Regenta*: The Problem of Female Identity', in *Feminist Readings on Spanish and Latin-American Literature*, ed. by L. P. Condé and S. M. Hart (Lewiston, NY, Queenston, Ont., and Lampeter, Wales: Edwin Mellen Press, 1991), pp. 37–46 (p. 41).
28. *The Deceived Husband*, p. 213, note 38; as Sinclair indicates, the point is

masked in Rutherford's translation, which renders '*la Regenta*' as 'Ana'.

29. See Raymond Carr, *Spain: 1808–1939* (Oxford: Clarendon Press, 1966; repr. 1975), pp. 320 and 355–379.
30. *Leopoldo Alas: La Regenta*, p. 53.
31. 'Kiss and Tell: The Toad in *La Regenta*', in *"Malevolent Insemination" and other essays on Clarín*, ed. by Noël Valis, *Michigan Romance Studies*, 10 (1990), pp. 87–100 (p. 97).
32. '*La Regenta* and Contemporary History', *Revista de Estudios Hispánicos*, 11 (1977), 287–302 (p. 300).
33. '*La Regenta* and Contemporary History', 300.
34. *The Decadent Vision in Leopoldo Alas: A Study of La Regenta and Su único hijo* (Baton Rouge and London: Louisiana State University Press, 1981), pp. 23–4; 'City, Country and Adultery in *La Regenta*', *Bulletin of Hispanic Studies*, 63 (1986), 53–66 (p. 53).
35. Trans. by Paul O'Prey (Harmondsworth: Penguin, 1990); and by Roser Caminals-Heath (Athens and London: University of Georgia Press, 1992).
36. See 'Emilia Pardo Bazán: *Un viaje de novios* and Romantic Fiction', in *Feminist Readings on Spanish and Latin-American Literature*, pp. 63–76; and Chapter 1, above, p. 11.
37. See Maryellen Bieder, 'Between Genre and Gender: Emilia Pardo Bazán and *Los Pazos de Ulloa*', in *In the Feminine Mode: Essays on Hispanic Women Writers*, ed. by Noël Valis and Carol Maier (London and Toronto: Associated University Presses, 1990), pp. 131–45.
38. See Lisa P. Condé, *Stages in the Development of a Feminist Consciousness in Pérez Galdós (1843–1920): A Biographical Sketch*, Hispanic Literature, 7 (Lewiston, NY, Queenston, Ont., and Lampeter, Wales: Edwin Mellen Press, 1990), pp. 150–1, 159–60, 171–2, and 182.
39. '*La Regenta* and Contemporary History', p. 288.
40. See *Galdós's Novel of the Historical Imagination: A Study of the Contemporary Novels*, Liverpool Monographs in Hispanic Studies, 2 (Liverpool: Francis Cairns, 1983). This is a very detailed reading of the contemporary novels in their political and historical contexts.
41. *Pérez Galdós: La de Bringas*, Critical Guides to Spanish Texts, 30 (London: Grant & Cutler, 1981), p. 59.
42. *The Spendthrifts*, trans. by Gamel Woolsey (London: Weidenfeld and Nicolson, 1951; repr. for Readers Union, 1953); *La de Bringas*, ed. by Ricardo Gullón (Englewood Cliffs, NJ: Prentice-Hall, 1967). Woolsey's translation is neither complete nor always accurate; and after Chapter VI it fails to follow Galdós's chapter divisions. References are therefore to the Spanish edition as well as to the translation, with chapter numbers included for both.
43. See *Gender and Representation: Women in Spanish Realist Fiction* (Amsterdam and Philadelphia: John Benjamins, 1990), pp. 125–35 (p. 126).
44. *Galdós's Novel of the Historical Imagination*, pp. 64–5.
45. 'Narrative Ambiguity and Situational Ethics in *La de Bringas*', in *Galdós' House of Fiction: Papers Given at the Birmingham Galdós*

Colloquium, ed. by A. H. Clarke and E. J. Rodgers (Llangrannog, Wales: Dolphin, 1991), p. 19.

46. In her study *The Adulteress's Child*, Naomi Segal does not discuss *Fortunata and Jacinta*.

47. Harriet S. Turner argues that it is the marriage that is sterile rather than Jacinta. See 'Family Ties and Tyrannies: A Reassessment of Jacinta', *Hispanic Review*, 51 (1983), 1–22; and *Benito Pérez Galdós: Fortunata and Jacinta* (Cambridge and New York: Cambridge University Press, 1992), pp. 62–70.

48. *Fortunata and Jacinta: Two Stories of Married Women*, trans. by Agnes Moncy Gullón (Athens: University of Georgia Press, 1986; repr. Harmondsworth: Penguin, 1988).

49. For a discussion of organicism in nineteenth-century thought, see Sally Shuttleworth, *George Eliot and Nineteenth-Century Science: The Make-Believe of a Beginning* (Cambridge and New York: Cambridge University Press, 1984), especially Chapter 1, 'Science and social thought: The rise of organic theory'.

50. For discussion of the historical parallels, see Geoffrey Ribbans, 'Contemporary History in the Structure and Characterization of "Fortunata y Jacinta"', in *Galdós Studies*, ed. by J. E. Varey (London: Támesis Books, 1970), pp. 90–113; and Peter A. Bly, *Galdós's Novel of the Historical Imagination*, pp. 85–115.

51. *Galdós's Novel of the Historical Imagination*, p. 106.

52. As Lisa P. Condé suggests in *Stages in the Development of a Feminist Consciousness in Pérez Galdós*, p. 142.

53. 'Individual, Class and Society in *Fortunata and Jacinta*', in *Galdós Studies*, II, ed. by Robert J. Weber (London: Támesis Books, 1974), pp. 49–68; repr. in *Galdós*, ed. by Jo Labanyi (London and New York: Longman, 1993), pp. 116–39 (p. 124).

54. See *The Dialogic Imagination: Four Essays by M. M. Bakhtin*; and *Galdós and the Art of the European Novel: 1867–1887* (Princeton, NJ: Princeton University Press, 1981), pp. 248–90.

55. 'The Subversive Angel in *Fortunata y Jacinta*', *Anales Galdosianos*, 24 (1989), 79–91.

56. 'Individual, Class and Society', pp. 118 and 135.

57. *Galdós's Novel of the Historical Imagination*, pp. 111–15 and 111.

58. 'The Sexual Representation of Politics in Contemporary Hispanic Feminist Narrative', in *Feminist Readings on Spanish and Latin-American Literature*, pp. 107–19 (p. 107).

59. Quoted by Peter B. Goldman in 'Galdós and the Nineteenth-Century Novel: The Need for an Interdisciplinary Approach', *Anales Galdosianas*, 10 (1975), 5–18; repr. in *Galdós*, ed. by Jo Labanyi, pp. 140–56 (p. 144). The ellipsis marks in the quotation are Goldman's.

60. 'The Subversive Angel in *Fortunata y Jacinta*', 90; and *Stages in the Development of a Feminist Consciousness in Pérez Galdós*, passim. See also Lisa P. Condé, *Women in the Theatre of Galdós: From Realidad (1892) to Voluntad (1895)*, Hispanic Literature, 6 (Lewiston, NY, Queenston, Ont., and Lampeter, Wales: Edwin Mellen Press, 1990).

Bibliography

PRIMARY SOURCES

Agoult, Marie d' ('Daniel Stern'), *Valentia; Hervé; Julien; La Boîte aux lettres; Ninon au couvent* (Paris: Calmann Lévy, 1896)

Alas, Leopoldo ('Clarín'), *La Regenta*, trans. by John Rutherford (Harmondsworth: Penguin; New York: Viking Penguin, 1984)

——, *La Regenta*, 7th edn, 2 vols, ed. by Juan Oleza (Madrid: Catedra, 1993)

Andersen, Hans Christian, *The Complete Fairy Tales and Stories*, trans. by Erik Christian Haugaard (New York: Doubleday, 1974)

Balzac, Honoré de, *Conjugal Life: Pinpricks of Married Life and The Physiology of Marriage*, trans. by Geoffrey Tickell (London: Neville Spearman, 1957)

——, *La Grande Bretèche and other stories*, trans. by Clara Bell, in *La Comédie Humaine*, 40 vols, ed. by George Saintsbury, XVII (London: Dent; New York: Macmillan, 1896)

——, *History of the Thirteen*, trans. by Herbert J. Hunt (Harmondsworth: Penguin, 1974)

——, *The Lily of the Valley*, trans. by James Waring, in *La Comédie Humaine*, ed. by George Saintsbury, XXI (1897)

——, *The Muse of the Department*, trans. by James Waring, in *La Comédie Humaine*, ed. by George Saintsbury, XXVIII, *Parisians in the Country* (1898)

——, *The Physiology of Marriage*, trans. by Francis Macnamara (London: Casanova Society, 1925)

——, *Selected Short Stories*, trans. by Sylvia Raphael (Harmondsworth: Penguin, 1977)

——, *A Woman of Thirty*, trans. by Ellen Marriage, in *La Comédie Humaine*, ed. by George Saintsbury, XL (1897); also includes *A Forsaken Lady, La Grenadière, Gobseck*, and *The Message*

——, *La Comédie humaine*, 12 vols, ed. by Pierre-Georges Castex and others (Paris: Gallimard, 1976–81); includes *Le Conseil*, II, 1365–73, and 'La Femme de province', IV, 1378–87

Baudelaire, Charles, *The Poems in Prose with La Fanfarlo*, trans. by Francis Scarfe (London: Anvil Press Poetry, 1989)

——, *The Prose Poems and La Fanfarlo*, trans. by Rosemary Lloyd (Oxford and New York: Oxford University Press, 1991)

——, *Oeuvres complètes*, ed. by Claude Pichois, 2 vols (Paris: Gallimard, 1975–6)

Bernanos, Georges, *The Diary of a Country Priest*, trans. by Pamela Morris (London: Boriswood, 1937)

Blicher, Steen Steensen, *Twelve Stories by Steen Steensen Blicher*, trans. by Hanna Astrup Larsen (Princeton, NJ: Princeton University Press, 1945)

Champfleury (pseudonym of Jules-Husson Fleury), *Les Bourgeois de Molinchart*, 2nd edn (Paris: Librairie nouvelle, 1855)

Chateaubriand, *Atala and René*, trans. by Rayner Heppenstall (London and New York: Oxford University Press, 1963)

——, *Oeuvres romanesques et voyages*, ed. by Maurice Regard, 2 vols, I (Paris: Gallimard, 1969)

Chekhov, Anton Pavlovich, *Lady with Lapdog and Other Stories*, trans. by David Magarshack (Harmondsworth: Penguin, 1964)

——, *Letters on the Short Story, the Drama and Other Literary Topics*, ed. by Louis S. Friedland (New York: Minton, Balch, 1924; repr. Dover, 1966)

——, *The Oxford Chekhov*, 9 vols, trans. by Ronald Hingley (Oxford and New York: Oxford University Press, 1965–80)

——, *Tales from Tchehov*, 13 vols, trans. by Constance Garnett (London: Chatto & Windus; New York: Macmillan, 1917–23)

Chernyshevsky, Nikolai, *What Is to Be Done?*, trans. by Michael R. Katz (Ithaca, NY, and London: Cornell University Press, 1989)

——, *What Is to Be Done?*, trans. by N. Dole and S. S. Skidelsky (New York: T. Y. Crowell, 1886; repr. Ann Arbor, MI: Ardis, 1986)

Colet, Louise, *Lui: A View of Him*, trans. by Marilyn Gaddis Rose (Athens and London: University of Georgia Press, 1986)

Constant, Benjamin, *Adolphe*, trans. by Leonard Tancock (Harmondsworth: Penguin, 1964)

——, *Oeuvres*, ed. by Alfred Roulin (Paris: Gallimard, 1957)

Dostoyevsky, Fyodor, *A Writer's Diary*, trans. by Kenneth Lantz, 2 vols (Evanston, IL: Northwestern University Press, 1993–4; London: Quartet, 1994–5)

Dumas, Alexandre *fils*, *La Dame aux Camélias*, trans. by David Coward (Oxford: Oxford University Press, 1986)

Eça de Queirós, José Maria de, *Cousin Bazilio*, trans. by Roy Campbell (London: Max Reinhardt, 1953; repr. Manchester: Carcanet Press, 1992)

——, *Dragon's Teeth*, tr. and abr. by Mary J. Serrano (Boston: Ticknor, 1889)

——, *The Sin of Father Amaro*, trans. by Nan Flanagan (London: Max Reinhardt, 1962; repr. Manchester: Carcanet Press, 1994)

——, *Obra Completa*, ed. by João Gaspar Simões and others, 2 vols (Rio de Janeiro: Companhia José Aguilar Editõra, 1970)

Feydeau, Ernest, *Fanny: or the Revelations of a Woman's Heart*, trans. anon (London: George Vickers, 1860)

——, *Fanny: Étude*, 4th edn (Paris: Amyot, 1858)

Flaubert, Gustave, *Madame Bovary: Provincial Lives*, trans. by Geoffrey Wall (Harmondsworth: Penguin, 1992)

——, *Madame Bovary*, Norton Critical Edition, ed. by Paul de Man (New York: Norton, 1965)

——, *November*, trans. by Frank Jellinek (London: Michael Joseph, 1966)

——, *Sentimental Education*, trans. by Robert Baldick (Harmondsworth, Penguin: 1964)

——, *Correspondance*, 3 vols, ed. by Jean Bruneau (Paris: Gallimard, 1973–)

——, *Madame Bovary: Moeurs de Province*, ed. by Claudine Gothot-Mersch (Paris: Garnier, 1971)

—— and George Sand, *Flaubert–Sand: The Correspondence*, trans. by Francis Steegmuller and Barbara Bray (London: HarperCollins, 1993)

Fontane, Theodor, *L'Adultera*, trans. by Lynn R. Eliason (New York: Peter Lang, 1990)

——, *Two Novellas: The Woman Taken in Adultery and The Poggenpuhl Family*, trans. by Gabriele Annan (Chicago and London: University of Chicago Press, 1979; repr. Harmondsworth: Penguin, 1995)

——, *Before the Storm*, trans. by R. J. Hollingdale (Oxford and New York: Oxford University Press, 1985)

——, *Beyond Recall*, trans. by Douglas Parmée (London and New York: Oxford University Press, 1964)

——, *Effi Briest*, trans. by Douglas Parmée (Harmondsworth: Penguin, 1967)

——, *Effi Briest*, trans. by Hugh Rorrison and Helen Chambers (London: Angel Books, 1995)

——, *Entanglements: An Everyday Berlin Story*, trans. by Derek Bowman (Bampton, Oxfordshire: Three Rivers Books, 1986)

——, *L'Adultera*, in *Werke und Schriften*, 54 vols, ed. by Walter Keitel and Helmuth Nürnberger, VII (Carl Hanser: Munich, 1971; repr. in Fontane Bibliothek, Frankfurt-am-Main, Berlin, Vienna: Ullstein, 1991)

——, *Effi Briest*, in *Werke und Schriften*, XVII (1974; 1979)

——, *Unwiederbringlich*, in *Werke und Schriften*, XV (1971; 1991)

Fromentin, Eugene, *Dominique*, trans. by Sir Edward Marsh (London: Cresset Press, 1948; repr. Soho Book Company, 1986)

——, *Dominique*, ed. by S. de Sacy (Paris: Gallimard, 1966; repr. 1974)

——, *Dominique*, ed. by Barbara Wright (Oxford: Basil Blackwell, 1965)

Gautier, Théophile, *Mademoiselle de Maupin*, trans. by Joanna Richardson (Harmondsworth: Penguin, 1981)

Gide, André, *Strait is the Gate*, trans. by Dorothy Bussy (London: Martin Secker & Warburg, 1924; repr. Harmondsworth: Penguin, 1969)

Goethe, Johann Wolfgang von, *Elective Affinities: A Novel*, trans. by David Constantine (Oxford and New York: Oxford University Press, 1994)

Grand dictionnaire universel du dix-neuvième siècle, 17 vols (Paris: Larousse et Boyer, 1866–86)

Huysmans, Joris-Karl, *Against the Grain* [trans. by John Howard, pseud.] (New York: Three Sirens Press, 1931; repr. Dover, 1969)

——, *À Rebours*, in *Oeuvres Complètes de J.-K. Huysmans*, ed. by Charles Grolleau, 18 vols (Paris: Crès, 1928–34), VII

Jacobsen, Jens-Peter, *Marie Grubbe: A Lady of the Seventeenth Century*, trans. by Hanna Astrup Larsen (New York: American-Scandinavian Foundation; London: Oxford University Press, 1917); 2nd edn, rev. by Robert Raphael, The Library of Scandinavian Literature, 30 (Boston: G. K. Hall, 1975)

——, *Mogens and other stories*, trans. by Tiina Nunnally (Seattle: Fjord Press, 1994)

——, *Niels Lyhne*, trans. by Tiina Nunnally (Seattle: Fjord Press, 1990)

Lucas, Hippolyte, 'La Femme Adultère', in *Les Français peints par eux-mêmes: encyclopédie morale du dix-neuvième siècle*, 8 vols (Paris: Curmer, 1840–2), III, 265–72

Mérimée, Prosper, *Carmen and Other Stories*, trans. by Nicholas Jotcham (Oxford and New York: Oxford University Press, 1989)
——, *A Slight Misunderstanding*, trans. by Douglas Parmée (London: John Calder, 1959)
——, *Théâtre de Clara Gazul, Romans et nouvelles*, ed. by Jean Mallion and Pierre Salomon (Paris: Gallimard, 1978)
Montégut, Émile, 'Le roman intime de la littérature réaliste', *Revue des Deux Mondes*, 18 (1858), 196–213
Musset, Alfred de, *A Modern Man's Confession*, trans. by G. F. Monkshood, pseudonym of W. J. Clarke (London: Greening, 1907)
——, *La Confession d'un enfant du siècle* in *Oeuvres complètes en prose*, ed. by Maurice Allem and Paul-Courant (Paris: Gallimard, 1960)
Nerval, Gérard [Labrunie] de, *Daughters of Fire: Sylvie – Emilie – Octavie*, trans. by James Whitall (London: Heinemann, 1923)
Pardo Bazán, Emilia, *The House of Ulloa*, trans. by Paul O'Prey (Harmondsworth: Penguin, 1990)
——, *The House of Ulloa*, trans. by Roser Caminals-Heath (Athens and London: University of Georgia Press, 1992)
——, *A Wedding Trip*, trans. by Mary J. Serrano (New York: Cassell, 1891)
Pérez Galdós, Benito, *Fortunata and Jacinta: Two Stories of Married Women*, trans. by Agnes Moncy Gullón (Athens: University of Georgia Press, 1986; repr. Harmondsworth: Penguin, 1988)
——, *The Spendthrifts*, trans. by Gamel Woolsey (London: Weidenfeld and Nicolson, 1951; repr. for Readers Union, 1953)
——, *Fortunata y Jacinta: Dos historias de casadas*, ed. by Francisco Caudet, 2 vols, 4th edn (Madrid: Catedra, 1994)
——, *La de Bringas*, ed. by Ricardo Gullón (Englewood Cliffs, NJ: Prentice-Hall, 1967)
Prévost, Abbé, *Manon Lescaut*, trans. by L. W. Tancock, 2nd edn, introd. by Jean Sgard (Harmondsworth: Penguin, 1991)
——, *Manon Lescaut*, ed. by Frédéric Deloffre and Raymond Picard (Paris: Bordas, 1990)
Sainte-Beuve, Charles-Augustin, *Causeries du lundi*, 4th edn, 16 vols (Paris: Garnier, n. d.)
Sand, George (pseudonym of Aurore Dudevant), *Indiana*, trans. by Sylvia Raphael (Oxford and New York: Oxford University Press, 1994)
——, *Jacques*, trans. by Anna Blackwell, 2 vols (New York: J. S. Redfield, 1847)
——, *Lélia*, trans. by Maria Espinosa (Bloomington and London: Indiana University Press, 1978)
——, *Leone Leoni*, trans. by George Burnham Ives (Philadelphia: G. Barrie, 1900; repr. Chicago: Academy Press, 1978)
——, *Lettres d'un Voyageur*, trans. by Sacha Rabinovitch and Patricia Thomson (Harmondsworth: Penguin, 1987)
——, *Valentine*, trans. by George Burnham Ives (Philadelphia: G. Barrie, 1902; repr. Chicago: Academy Press, 1978)
——, *Le Compagnon du tour de France* (Paris: Perrotin, 1843; repr. Éditions d'Aujourd'hui, 1976)
——, *Correspondance de George Sand*, ed. by Georges Lubin, 24 vols (Paris:

Garnier, 1964–90)

——, *Le Dernier amour* (Paris: Michel Lévy, 1867; repr. Éditions des femmes, 1991)

——, *Indiana*, ed. by Pierre Salomon (Paris: Garnier, 1962)

——, *Jacques* (Paris: Perrotin, 1842; repr. Éditions d'Aujourd'hui, 1976)

——, *Oeuvres autobiographiques*, ed. by Georges Lubin, 2 vols (Paris: Gallimard, 1970–1)

——, *Valentine* (Paris: Perrotin, 1843; repr. Éditions d'Aujourd'hui, 1976)

—— and Gustave Flaubert, *Flaubert–Sand: The Correspondence*, trans. by Francis Steegmuller and Barbara Bray (London: HarperCollins, 1993)

Stendhal (pseudonym of Henri Marie Beyle), *The Red and the Black*, trans. by Catherine Slater (Oxford: Oxford University Press, 1991)

Tolstoy, Leo Nikolayevich, *Anna Karenin*, trans. by Rosemary Edmonds, rev. edn (Harmondsworth: Penguin, 1978)

——, *Anna Karenina*, trans. by Louise and Aylmer Maude (Oxford: Oxford University Press, 1918; repr. Oxford and New York, 1980)

——, *The Cossacks, Happy Ever After, The Death of Ivan Ilyich*, trans. by Rosemary Edmonds (Harmondsworth: Penguin, 1960)

——, *The Kreutzer Sonata and Other Stories*, trans. by David McDuff (Harmondsworth: Penguin, 1983)

——, *Resurrection*, trans. by Rosemary Edmonds, rev. edn (Harmondsworth: Penguin, 1966)

——, *Tolstoy's Diaries*, 2 vols, trans. and ed. by R. F. Christian (London: Athlone Press, 1985)

——, *Tolstoy's Letters*, 2 vols, trans. and ed. by R. F. Christian (London: Athlone Press, 1978)

——, *What Is Art? and Essays on Art*, trans. by Aylmer Maude (London: Oxford University Press, 1930)

Tristan, Flora, *Méphis*, 2 vols (Paris: Ladvocat, 1838)

Turgenev, Ivan Sergeyevich, *On the Eve*, trans. by Gilbert Gardiner (Harmondsworth: Penguin, 1950)

Zola, Émile, *The Abbé Mouret's Sin*, trans. by Alec Brown (London: Elek, 1957; repr. 1970)

——, *Thérèse Raquin*, trans. by Leonard Tancock (Harmondsworth: Penguin, 1962)

SECONDARY SOURCES

Aldaraca, Bridget, 'The Revolution of 1868 and the Rebellion of Rosalía Bringas', *Anales Galdosianos*, 18 (1983), 49–60

Andrew, Joe, *Women in Russian Literature, 1780–1863* (London: Macmillan, 1988)

Armstrong, Judith, *The Novel of Adultery* (London: Macmillan, 1976)

——, *The Unsaid Anna Karenina* (London: Macmillan, 1988)

Atkinson, Dorothy, Alexander Dallin and Gail Warshofsky Lapidus (eds), *Women in Russia* (Stanford, CA: Stanford University Press, 1977; Brighton, Sussex: Harvester, 1978)

Auerbach, Erich, *Mimesis: The Representation of Reality in Western Literature,* trans. by Willard Trask (Princeton, NJ: Princeton University Press, 1953)

Bakhtin, Mikhail, *The Dialogic Imagination: Four Essays by M. M. Bakhtin*, trans. and ed. by Michael Holquist, University of Texas Press Slavic Series, 1 (Austin: University of Texas Press, 1981)

——, *Problems of Dostoevsky's Poetics*, trans. and ed. by Caryl Emerson, Theory and History of Literature, 8 (Manchester: Manchester University Press, 1984)

Bance, Alan, *Theodor Fontane: The Major Novels* (Cambridge and New York: Cambridge University Press, 1982)

Basch, Françoise, *Relative Creatures: Victorian Women in Society and the Novel, 1837–67*, trans. by Anthony Rudolf (London: Allen Lane, 1974)

Beauvoir, Simone de, *The Second Sex*, trans. and ed. by H. M. Parshley (London: Jonathan Cape, 1953; repr. Harmondsworth: Penguin, 1972)

——, *Le Deuxième Sexe*, 2 vols (Paris: Gallimard, 1949)

Berghahn, Volker R., *Imperial Germany 1871–1914: Economy, Society, Culture and Politics* (Providence, RI, and Oxford: Berghahn Books, 1994)

Bernheimer, Charles, *Figures of Ill Repute: Representing Prostitution in Nineteenth-Century France* (Cambridge, MA, and London: Harvard University Press, 1989)

Bersani, Leo, *A Future for Astyanax: Character and Desire in Literature* (Boston: Little, Brown, 1976; London: Marion Boyars, 1978)

Besant, Walter, 'Candour in English Fiction: I', *The New Review*, 2 (1890), 6–9

Bieder, Maryellen, 'Between Genre and Gender: Emilia Pardo Bazán and *Los Pazos de Ulloa*', in *In the Feminine Mode: Essays on Hispanic Women Writers*, ed. by Noël Valis and Carol Maier (London and Toronto: Associated University Presses, 1990), pp. 131–45

Billy, André, *Mérimée* (Paris: Flammarion, 1959)

Black, Michael, *The Literature of Fidelity* (London: Chatto and Windus, 1975)

Blackbourn, David, and Richard J. Evans (eds), *The German Bourgeoisie: Essays on the social history of the German middle class from the late eighteenth to the early twentieth century* (London and New York: Routledge, 1991)

—— and Geoff Eley (eds), *The Peculiarities of German History: Bourgeois Society and Politics in Nineteenth-Century Germany* (Oxford and New York: Oxford University Press, 1984)

Bly, Peter A., *Pérez Galdós: La de Bringas*, Critical Guides to Spanish Texts, 30 (London: Grant & Cutler, 1981)

——, *Galdós's Novel of the Historical Imagination: A Study of the Contemporary Novels*, Liverpool Monographs in Hispanic Studies, 2 (Liverpool: Francis Cairns, 1983)

——, 'The Use of Distance in Galdós's *La de Bringas*', *Modern Language Review*, 69 (1974), 88–97; repr. in *Galdós*, ed. by Jo Labanyi (London and New York: Longman, 1993), pp. 103–15

Bredsdorff, Elias, 'Moralists *versus* Immoralists: The Great Battle in Scandinavian Literature in the 1880's', *Scandinavica*, 8 (1969), 91–111

Brooks, Peter, *Reading for the Plot: Design and Intention in Narrative* (Oxford: Clarendon Press, 1984)

——, *The Novel of Worldliness: Crébillon, Marivaux, Laclos, Stendhal* (Princeton, NJ: Princeton University Press, 1969)

——, 'Virtue-tripping: Notes on *Le Lys dans la vallée*', in *Intoxication and Literature, Yale French Studies*, 50 (1974), 150–62

Camp, Wesley D., *Marriage and the Family in France Since the Revolution: An Essay in the History of Population* (New York: Bookman Associates, 1961)

Carr, Raymond, *Spain: 1808–1939* (Oxford: Clarendon Press, 1966; repr. 1975)

Cate, Curtis, *George Sand: A Biography* (Boston: Houghton Mifflin; London: Hamish Hamilton, 1975)

Charnon-Deutsch, Lou, *Gender and Representation: Women in Spanish Realist Fiction* (Amsterdam and Philadelphia: John Benjamins, 1990)

——, *Narratives of Desire: Nineteenth-Century Spanish Fiction by Women* (University Park: Pennsylvania State University Press, 1994)

Christian, R. F., *Tolstoy: A Critical Introduction* (Cambridge: Cambridge University Press, 1969)

Clarke, A. H., and E. J. Rodgers (eds), *Galdós' House of Fiction: Papers Given at the Birmingham Galdós Colloquium* (Llangrannog, Wales: Dolphin, 1991)

Clyman, Toby W. (ed.), *A Chekhov Companion* (Westport, CT, and London: Greenwood Press, 1985)

Coleman, Alexander, *Eça de Queirós and European Realism* (New York and London: New York University Press, 1980)

Cominos, Peter T., 'Late-Victorian Sexual Respectability and the Social System', *International Review of Social History*, 8 (1963), 2 parts (18–48 and 216–50)

Condé, Lisa P., *Stages in the Development of a Feminist Consciousness in Pérez Galdós (1843–1920): A Biographical Sketch*, Hispanic Literature, 7 (Lewiston, NY, Queenston, Ont., and Lampeter, Wales: Edwin Mellen Press, 1990)

——, *Women in the Theatre of Galdós: From Realidad (1892) to Voluntad (1895)*, Hispanic Literature, 6 (Lewiston, NY, Queenston, Ont., and Lampeter, Wales: Edwin Mellen Press, 1990)

—— and S. M. Hart (eds), *Feminist Readings on Spanish and Latin-American Literature* (Lewiston, NY, Queenston, Ont., and Lampeter, Wales: Edwin Mellen Press, 1991)

Copley, Antony, *Sexual Moralities in France 1780–1980: New Ideas on the Family, Divorce and Homosexuality* (London and New York: Routledge, 1989)

Cox, Don Richard (ed.), *Sexuality and Victorian Literature*, Tennessee Studies in Literature, 27 (Knoxville: University of Tennessee Press, 1984)

Crecelius, Kathryn J., *Family Romances: George Sand's Early Novels* (Bloomington and Indianapolis: Indiana University Press, 1987)

Crisp, Olga, and Edmondson, Linda (eds), *Civil Rights in Imperial Russia* (Oxford: Clarendon Press, 1989)

Culler, Jonathan, *Flaubert: The Uses of Uncertainty* (London: Paul Elek, 1974; rev. edn, 1985)

Datlof, Natalie, Jeanne Fuchs, and David A. Powell (eds), *The World of*

George Sand (New York and London: Greenwood Press, 1991)

Davies, Catherine, 'The Sexual Representation of Politics in Contemporary Hispanic Feminist Narrative', in L. P. Condé and S. M. Hart (eds), *Feminist Readings on Spanish and Latin-American Literature* (Lewiston, NY, Queenston, Ont., and Lampeter, Wales: Edwin Mellen Press, 1991), pp. 107–19

Desanti, Dominique, *Daniel, ou le visage secret d'une comtesse romantique: Marie d'Agoult* (Paris: Stock, 1980)

Dijkstra, Sandra, *Flora Tristan: Feminism in the Age of George Sand* (London: Pluto Press, 1992)

Donzelot, Jacques, *The Policing of Families*, trans. by Robert Hurley (London: Hutchinson, 1979)

Drinkwater, Judith, 'Emilia Pardo Bazán: *Un viaje de novios* and Romantic Fiction', in L. P. Condé and S. M. Hart (eds), *Feminist Readings on Spanish and Latin-American Literature* (Lewiston, NY, Queenston, Ont., and Lampeter, Wales: Edwin Mellen Press, 1991), pp. 63–76

Dupêchez, Charles F., *Marie d'Agoult*, Collection Terres des Femmes (Paris: Perrin, 1989)

Durand, Frank, 'Leopoldo Alas, "Clarín": Consistency of Outlook as Critic and Novelist', *Romanic Review*, 56 (1965), 37–49

Eidelman, Dawn D., *George Sand and the Nineteenth-Century Russian Love-Triangle Novels* (London and Toronto: Associated University Presses, 1994)

Eikhenbaum, Boris, 'Chekhov at Large', in *Chekhov: A Collection of Critical Essays*, ed. by Robert Louis Jackson (Englewood Cliffs, NJ: Prentice-Hall, 1967), pp. 21–31

——, *Tolstoi in the Sixties*, trans. by Duffield White (Ann Arbor, MI: Ardis, 1982)

——, *Tolstoi in the Seventies*, trans. by Albert Kaspin (Ann Arbor, MI: Ardis, 1982)

Ellis, Havelock, *The Task of Social Hygiene* (London: Constable, 1912; repr. 1927)

Engel, Barbara Alpern, *Mothers and Daughters: Women of the Intelligentsia in Nineteenth-century Russia* (Cambridge: Cambridge University Press, 1983)

Evans, Mary, *Reflecting on Anna Karenina* (London and New York: Routledge, 1989)

Evans, Richard J., and W. R. Lee, *The German Family: Essays on the Social History of the Family in Nineteenth- and Twentieth-Century Germany* (London: Croom Helm; Totowa, NJ: Barnes and Noble, 1981)

Fahnestock, Jeanne, 'Bigamy: The Rise and Fall of a Convention', *Nineteenth-Century Fiction*, 36 (1981), 47–71

Fairlie, Alison, 'Constant's *Adolphe* read by Balzac and Nerval', in D. G. Charlton, Jean Gaudon, and Anthony R. Pugh (eds), *Balzac and the Nineteenth Century* (Leicester: Leicester University Press; New York: Humanities Press, 1972), pp. 209–224

——, *Flaubert: Madame Bovary*, Studies in French Literature, 8 (London: Arnold, 1962)

Felman, Shoshana, *What Does a Woman Want? Reading and Sexual Difference*

(Baltimore and London: Johns Hopkins University Press, 1993)

Festa-McCormick, Diana, *Honoré de Balzac* (Boston: G. K. Hall, 1979)

Flandrin, Jean-Louis, *Families in former times: Kinship, household and sexuality* (Cambridge and New York: Cambridge University Press, 1979)

Fout, John C. (ed.), *German Women in the Nineteenth Century: A Social History* (New York and London: Holmes and Meier, 1984)

Frappier-Mazur, Lucienne, 'Marginal Canons: Rewriting the Erotic', in *The Politics of Tradition: Placing Women in French Literature*, Yale French Studies, 75 (1988), 112–28

Freud, Sigmund, *Introductory Lectures on Psycho-Analysis*, in *The Standard Edition of the Complete Psychological Works*, trans. by James Strachey, 24 vols (London: Hogarth Press, 1953), XV–XVI

Frevert, Ute, *Women in German History: From Bourgeois Emancipation to Sexual Liberation*, trans. by Stuart McKinnon-Evans in association with Terry Bond and Barbara Norden (Oxford and Hamburg: Berg; New York: St Martin's Press, 1989)

Fuchs, Jeanne, 'George Sand and Alfred de Musset: Absolution Through Art in *La Confession d'un enfant du siècle*', in *The World of George Sand*, ed. by Natalie Datlof, Jeanne Fuchs, and David A. Powell (New York and London: Greenwood Press, 1991)

Furst, Lilian R., '*Madame Bovary* and *Effi Briest*', *Romanistisches Jahrbuch*, 12 (1961), 124–35

Garland, Henry, *The Berlin Novels of Theodor Fontane* (Oxford: Clarendon Press, 1980)

Gilman, Stephen, *Galdós and the Art of the European Novel: 1867–1887* (Princeton, NJ: Princeton University Press, 1981)

Girard, René, *Deceit, Desire, and the Novel: Self and Other in Literary Structure*, trans. by Yvonne Freccero (Baltimore: Johns Hopkins University Press, 1965)

Glasgow, Janis, 'George Sand's Multiple Appearances in Balzac's *La Muse du département*', in *The World of George Sand*, ed. by Natalie Datlof, Jeanne Fuchs, and David A. Powell (New York and London: Greenwood Press, 1991), pp. 217–25

Goldman, Peter B., 'Galdós and the Nineteenth-Century Novel: The Need for an Interdisciplinary Approach', *Anales Galdosianos*, 10 (1975), 5–18; repr. in Jo Labanyi (ed.), *Galdós* (London and New York: Longman, 1993), pp. 140–56

—— (ed.), *Conflicting Realities: Four Readings of a Chapter by Pérez Galdós* (London: Támesis Books, 1984)

Goody, Jack, 'A Comparative Approach to Incest and Adultery', in *Comparative Studies in Kinship* (London: Routledge and Kegan Paul, 1969), pp. 13–38

Gothot-Mersch, Claudine, *La Genèse de 'Madame Bovary'* (Paris: Corti, 1966)

Grant, Elliott, *Émile Zola* (Boston: G. K. Hall, 1966)

Gray, Francine du Plessix, *Rage and Fire: A Life of Louise Colet* (London: Hamish Hamilton; New York: Simon and Schuster, 1994)

Griest, Guinevere L., *Mudie's Circulating Library and the Victorian Novel* (Bloomington and Indianapolis: Indiana University Press; Newton Abbot, Devon: David and Charles, 1970)

Grønbech, Bo, *Hans Christian Andersen* (Boston: G. K. Hall, 1980)

Gutwirth, Madelyn, 'The Engulfed Beloved: Representations of Dead and Dying Women in the Art and Literature of the Revolutionary Era', in *Rebel Daughters: Women and the French Revolution*, ed. by Sara E. Melzer and Leslie W. Rabine (New York and Oxford: Oxford University Press, 1992), pp. 198–227

Guyon, Bernard, '*Adolphe, Béatrix* et *La Muse du département*', *L'Année balzacienne*, 1963, 149–75

Hahn, Beverly, *Chekhov: A study of the major stories and plays* (Cambridge and New York: Cambridge University Press, 1977)

Hardwick, Elizabeth, *Seduction and Betrayal: Women and Literature* (London: Weidenfeld and Nicolson, 1974

Harsin, Jill, *Policing Prostitution in Nineteenth-Century Paris* (Princeton, NJ, and Guildford: Princeton University Press, 1985)

Heath, Stephen, *Gustave Flaubert: Madame Bovary* (Cambridge and New York: Cambridge University Press, 1992)

Heldt, Barbara, *Terrible Perfection: Women and Russian Literature* (Bloomington and Indianapolis: Indiana University Press, 1987; repr. Midland Books, 1992)

Hellerstein, Erna Olafson, Leslie Parker Hume, and Karen M. Offen (eds), *Victorian Women: A Documentary Account of Women's Lives in Nineteenth-Century England, France and the United States* (Stanford, CA: Stanford University Press, 1981)

Hemingway, Maurice, *Emilia Pardo Bazán: The Making of a Novelist* (Cambridge: Cambridge University Press, 1983)

——, 'Narrative Ambiguity and Situational Ethics in *La de Bringas*', in A. H. Clarke and E. J. Rodgers (eds), *Galdós' House of Fiction: Papers Given at the Birmingham Galdós Colloquium* (Llangrannog, Wales: Dolphin, 1991), pp. 15–27

Hemmings, F. W. J. (ed.), *The Age of Realism* (Harmondsworth: Penguin, 1974)

Henn, David, *The Early Pardo Bazán: Theme and Narrative Technique in the Novels of 1879–89*, Liverpool Monographs in Hispanic Studies, 8 (Liverpool and Wolfeboro, NH: Francis Cairns, 1988)

Hingley, Ronald, *A New Life of Anton Chekhov* (London: Oxford University Press, 1976)

Hirsch, Marianne, *The Mother/Daughter Plot: Narrative, Psychoanalysis, Feminism* (Bloomington and Indianapolis: Indiana University Press, 1989)

Hobsbawm, Eric, *The Age of Revolution: Europe 1789–1848* (London: Weidenfeld and Nicolson, 1962; repr. 1969)

——, *The Age of Capital: 1848–1875* (London: Weidenfeld and Nicolson, 1975)

Hollier, Denis (ed.), *A New History of French Literature* (Cambridge, MA, and London: Harvard University Press, 1989)

Hunt, Herbert J., *Balzac's Comédie Humaine* (London: Athlone Press, 1959)

——, *Honoré de Balzac: A Biography* (London: Athlone Press, 1957)

Ingwersen, Niels, 'Problematic Protagonists: *Marie Grubbe* and *Niels Lyhne*', in *The Hero in Scandinavian Literature*, ed. by John M. Weinstock and Robert T. Rovisky (Austin and London: University of Texas Press,

1975), pp. 39–61

Jackson, Robert Louis (ed.), *Chekhov: A Collection of Critical Essays* (Englewood Cliffs, NJ: Prentice-Hall, 1967)

——, 'On the Ambivalent Beginning of *Anna Karenina*', in *Semantic Analysis of Literary Texts*, ed. by Eric de Haard, Thomas Langerak, and Willem G. Weststeijn (Amsterdam and New York: Elsevier, 1990), pp. 345–52

Jackson, Robert M., '"Cervantismo" in the Creative Process of Clarín's *La Regenta*', *Modern Language Notes*, 84 (1969), 208–27

——, '*La Regenta* and Contemporary History', *Revista de Estudios Hispánicos*, 11 (1977), 287–302

Jagoe, Catherine, 'The Subversive Angel in *Fortunata y Jacinta*', *Anales Galdosianos*, 24 (1989), 79–91

Jardin, André, and André-Jean Tudesq, *Restoration and Reaction, 1815–1848*, trans. by Elborg Forster, Cambridge History of Modern France, I (Cambridge and New York: Cambridge University Press; Paris: Editions de la Maison de l'Homme, 1983)

Jauss, Hans Robert, *Toward an Aesthetic of Reception*, trans. by Timothy Bahti (Brighton, Sussex: Harvester, 1982)

Jefferson, Ann, *Reading Realism in Stendhal* (Cambridge: Cambridge University Press, 1988)

Jensen, Niels Lyhne, *Jens Peter Jacobsen* (Boston: G. K. Hall, 1980)

Joeres, Ruth-Ellen B. and Mary Jo Maynes, *German Women in the Eighteenth and Nineteenth Centuries: A Social and Literary History* (Bloomington: Indiana University Press, 1986)

John, Nicholas (ed.), *Violetta and her Sisters: The Lady of the Camellias, Responses to the Myth* (London and Boston: Faber and Faber, 1994)

Koc, Richard A., *The German Gesellschaftsroman at the Turn of the Century: A Comparison of the Works of Theodor Fontane and Eduard von Keyserling* (Berne and Frankfurt-am-Main: Peter Lang, 1982)

Kocka, Jürgen and Allen Mitchell (eds), *Bourgeois Society in Nineteenth-Century Europe* (Oxford and Providence, RI: Berg, 1993)

Kuhn, Anna K. 'Modes of Alienation in Fassbinder's *Effi Briest*', in Sandra Frieden and others (eds), *Gender and German Cinema: Feminist Interventions*, 2 vols, I, *Gender and Representation in New German Cinema* (Providence, RI, and Oxford: Berg, 1993), pp. 35–50

Labanyi, Jo, 'City, Country and Adultery in *La Regenta*', *Bulletin of Hispanic Studies*, 63 (1986), 53–66

—— (ed.), *Galdós* (London and New York: Longman, 1993)

——, 'Mysticism and Hysteria in *La Regenta*: The Problem of Female Identity', in L. P. Condé and S. M. Hart (eds), *Feminist Readings on Spanish and Latin-American Literature* (Lewiston, NY, Queenston, Ont., and Lampeter, Wales: Edwin Mellen Press, 1991), pp. 37–46

——, 'The Problem of Framing in *La de Bringas*', *Anales Galdosianas*, 25 (1990), 25–34

LaCapra, Dominick, '*Madame Bovary' on Trial* (Ithaca, NY, and London: Cornell University Press, 1982)

Lampert, E[vgeny], *Sons against Fathers: Studies in Russian Radicalism and Revolution* (Oxford: Clarendon Press, 1965)

Landes, Joan B., *Women and the Public Sphere in the Age of the French Revolution* (Ithaca, NY, and London: Cornell University Press, 1988)
Lawrence, D. H., *Study of Thomas Hardy and Other Essays*, ed. by Bruce Steele (London: Grafton, 1986)
Lawson, Annette, *Adultery: An Analysis of Love and Betrayal* (New York: Basic Books, 1988; repr. Oxford: Oxford University Press, 1990)
Levine, Linda Gould, Ellen Engelson Marson and Gloria Feiman Waldman (eds), *Spanish Women Writers: A Bio-Bibliographical Source Book* (Westport, CT, and London: Greenwood Press, 1993)
Lloyd, Rosemary, *Madame Bovary*, Unwin Critical Library (London: Unwin Hyman, 1990)
Lock, Peter W., 'Point of View in Balzac's Short Stories', in D. G. Charlton, Jean Gaudon, and Anthony R. Pugh (eds), *Balzac and the Nineteenth Century* (Leicester: Leicester University Press; New York: Humanities Press, 1972), pp. 57–69
Lubbock, Percy, *The Craft of Fiction* (London and Toronto: Jonathan Cape, 1921; repr. 1939)
Lukács, Georg, *The Historical Novel*, trans. by Hannah and Stanley Mitchell (London: Merlin Press, 1962)
MacDonogh, Giles, *Prussia: The Perversion of an Idea* (London and Auckland: Sinclair-Stevenson, 1994)
McPhee, Peter, *A Social History of France, 1780–1880* (London and New York: Routledge, 1992)
MacPike, Loralee, 'The Fallen Woman's Sexuality: Childbirth and Censure', in *Sexuality and Victorian Literature*, ed. by Don Richard Cox, Tennessee Studies in Literature, 27 (Knoxville: University of Tennessee Press, 1984), pp. 54–71
Magd-Soëp, Carolina De, *Chekhov and Women: Women in the Life and Work of Chekhov* (Columbus, Ohio: Slavica, 1987)
Mandrell, James, 'Realism in Spain: Galdós, Pardo Bazán, Clarín and the European Context', *Neohelicon*, 15 (1988), 83–112
Mathewson, Rufus W., Jr., *The Positive Hero in Russian Literature*, 2nd edn (Stanford, CA: Stanford University Press, 1975)
Meister, Charles W., *Chekhov Criticism: 1880 Through 1986* (Jefferson, NC, and London: McFarland, 1988)
Melzer, Sara E., and Leslie W. Rabine (eds), *Rebel Daughters: Women and the French Revolution* (New York and Oxford: Oxford University Press, 1992)
Meyer, Alfred G., 'The Radicalization of Lily Braun', in *German Women in the Nineteenth Century: A Social History*, ed. by John C. Fout (New York and London: Holmes and Meier, 1984)
Mickel, Emanuel J., Jr., *Eugène Fromentin* (Boston: G. K. Hall, 1981)
Miller, Nancy K., 'Emphasis Added: Plots and Plausibilities in Women's Fiction', *PMLA*, 96 (1981), 36–48; repr. in *The New Feminist Criticism: Essays on women, literature and theory*, ed. by Elaine Showalter (New York: Pantheon, 1985; repr. London: Virago, 1986), pp. 339–60
——, *The Heroine's Text: Readings in the French and English Novel, 1722–1782* (New York: Columbia University Press, 1980)
——, 'Men's Reading, Women's Writing: Gender and the Rise of the Novel',

in *The Politics of Tradition: Placing Women in French Literature*, Yale French Studies, 75 (1988), 40–55

——, 'Novels of Innocence: Fictions of Loss', *Eighteenth-Century Studies*, 11:3 (1977–78), 325–39

——, *Subject to Change: Reading Feminist Writing* (New York: Columbia University Press, 1988)

——, '"Tristes Triangles": *Le Lys dans la vallée* and Its Intertext', in *Pre-Text, Text, Context: Essays on Nineteenth-Century French Literature*, ed. by Robert L. Mitchell (Columbus: Ohio State University Press, 1980), pp. 67–77

Minden, Michael, '"Effi Briest" and "Die Historische Stunde des Takts"', *Modern Language Review*, 76 (1981), 869–79

Mitterauer, Michael, and Reinhard Seider, *The European Family: Patriarchy to Partnership from the Middle Ages to the Present*, trans. by Karla Oosterveen and Manfred Hörzinger (Oxford: Basil Blackwell, 1982)

Montégut, Émile, 'Le roman intime de la littérature réaliste', *Revue des Deux Mondes*, 18 (1858), 196–213

Morrow, Nancy, 'Willa Cather's *A Lost Lady* and the Nineteenth Century Novel of Adultery', *Women's Studies*, 11 (1984), 287–303

Morson, Gary Saul, *The Boundaries of Genre: Dostoyevsky's Diary of a Writer and the Traditions of Literary Utopia* (Austin: University of Texas Press, 1981)

Moser, Charles A., *Antinihilism in the Russian Novel of the 1860's*, Slavistic Printings and Reprintings (The Hague, London, Paris: Mouton, 1964)

——, *Pisemsky: A Provincial Realist* (Cambridge, MA: Harvard University Press, 1969)

Moses, Claire Goldberg, *French Feminism in the Nineteenth Century* (Albany: State University of New York Press, 1984)

—— and Leslie Wahl Rabine, *Feminism, Socialism, and French Romanticism* (Bloomington and Indianapolis: Indiana University Press, 1993)

Naginski, Isabelle Hoog, *George Sand: Writing for Her Life* (New Brunswick, NJ, and London: Rutgers University Press, 1991)

Nead, Lynda, *Myths of Sexuality: Representations of Women in Victorian Britain* (Oxford and New York: Basil Blackwell, 1988)

Nelson, Brian (ed.), *Naturalism in the European Novel: New Critical Perspectives* (Oxford: Berg, 1992)

Nimetz, Michael, 'Eros and Ecclesia in Clarín's Vetusta', *Modern Language Notes*, 86 (1971), 242–53

Norberg, Kathryn, '"Love and Patriotism": Gender and Politics in the Life and Work of Louvet de Couvrai', in *Rebel Daughters: Women and the French Revolution*, ed. by Sara E. Melzer and Leslie W. Rabine (New York and Oxford: Oxford University Press, 1992), pp. 38–53

Orr, John, *Tragic Realism and Modern Society: Studies in the Sociology of the Modern Novel* (London: Macmillan, 1977; Pittsburgh, PA: University of Pittsburgh Press, 1978)

Pallucchini, Rodolfo, and Paola Rossi, *Tintoretto: Le opere sacre e profane*, 2 vols (Milan: Gruppo Editoriale Electa, 1982)

Pascal, Roy, *The German Novel: Studies* (Manchester: Manchester University Press, 1956)

Pattison, Walter T., *Emilia Pardo Bazán* (New York: Twayne, 1971)

Percival, Anthony, *Galdós and his critics* (Toronto, Buffalo, and London: University of Toronto Press, 1985)

Petrey, Sandy, *Realism and Revolution: Balzac, Stendhal, Zola and the Performances of History* (Ithaca, NY, and London: Cornell University Press, 1988)

Phillips, Roderick, *Putting asunder: A history of divorce in Western society* (Cambridge and New York: Cambridge University Press, 1988)

Planche, Gustave, 'Essai sur Adolphe', in Benjamin Constant, *Adolphe* (Paris: Charpentier, 1839), pp. 371–87

Pommier, Jean, '*La Muse du département* et le thème de la femme mal mariée chez Balzac, Mérimée et Flaubert', *L'Année balzacienne*, 1961, pp. 191–221

Porter, Laurence M. (ed.), *Critical Essays on Gustave Flaubert*, Critical Essays on World Literature (Boston: G. K. Hall, 1986)

Powell, David A., *George Sand* (Boston: G. K. Hall, 1990)

Prendergast, Christopher, *Balzac: Fiction and Melodrama* (London: Edward Arnold; New York: Holmes and Meier, 1978)

——, *The Order of Mimesis: Balzac, Stendhal, Nerval, Flaubert* (Cambridge: Cambridge University Press, 1986)

Rabine, Leslie, 'Feminist Writers in French Romanticism', *Studies in Romanticism*, 16 (1977), 491–507

——, 'George Sand and the Myth of Femininity', *Women and Literature*, 4 (1976), 2–17

——, *Reading the Romantic Heroine: Text, History, Ideology* (Ann Arbor: University of Michigan Press, 1985)

Radcliffe, Stanley, *Fontane: Effi Briest*, Critical Guides to German Texts, 6 (London and Wolfeboro, NH: Grant & Cutler, 1986)

Raitt, A. W., *Prosper Merimée* (London: Eyre & Spottiswoode, 1970)

Rayfield, Donald, 'Chekhov and the Literary Tradition', in *A Chekhov Companion*, ed. by Toby W. Clyman (Westport, CT, and London: Greenwood Press, 1985), pp. 35–51

Remak, Joachim, *The Gentle Critic: Theodor Fontane and German Politics, 1848–1898* (Syracuse, NY: Syracuse University Press, 1964)

Riasanovsky, Nicholas V., *A History of Russia*, 4th edn (New York and Oxford: Oxford University Press, 1984)

Ribbans, Geoffrey, 'Contemporary History in the Structure and Characterization of "Fortunata y Jacinta"', in *Galdós Studies*, ed. by J. E. Varey (London: Támesis Books, 1970), pp. 90–113

——, *Pérez Galdós: Fortunata y Jacinta*, Critical Guides to Spanish Texts, 21 (London: Grant & Cutler, 1977)

——, *Reality Plain or Fancy? Some Reflections on Galdós's Concept of Realism* (Liverpool: Liverpool University Press, 1986)

Riechel, Donald C., '*Effi Briest* and the Calendar of Fate', *Germanic Review*, 48 (1973), 189–211

Riffaterre, Michael, 'Flaubert's Presuppositions', *Diacritics*, 11 (1981), 2–11; repr. in *Flaubert and Postmodernism*, ed. by Naomi Schor and Henry F. Majewski (Lincoln and London: University of Nebraska Press, 1984), pp. 177–91

——, 'Relevance of Theory/ Theory of Relevance', *Yale Journal of Criticism*, 1 (1988), 163–76

Robb, Graham, *Balzac: A Biography* (London: Picador, 1994)

Robinson, A. R., *Theodor Fontane: An Introduction to the Man and his Work* (Cardiff: University of Wales Press, 1976)

Rossel, Sven H. (ed.), *A History of Danish Literature*, A History of Scandinavian Literatures, I (Lincoln and London: University of Nebraska Press, 1992)

Rowe, William W., *Leo Tolstoy* (Boston: G. K. Hall, 1986)

Rubin, Gayle, 'The Traffic in Women: Notes on the "Political Economy" of Sex', in Rayna R. Reiter (ed.), *Toward an Anthropology of Women* (New York and London: Monthly Review Press, 1975), pp. 157–210

Rutherford, John, *Leopoldo Alas: La Regenta*, Critical Guides to Spanish Texts, 9 (London: Grant & Cutler, 1974)

——, 'On Translating *La Regenta*: Sameness and Otherness', in '*Malevolent Insemination' and other essays on Clarín*, ed. by Noël Valis, *Michigan Romance Studies*, 10 (1990), pp. 47–66

Sagarra, Eda, *A social history of Germany, 1648–1914* (London: Methuen, 1977)

Sainte-Beuve, Charles-Augustin, *Causeries du lundi*, 4th edn, 16 vols (Paris: Garnier, n. d.)

Sartori, Eva Martin, and Dorothy Wynne Zimmerman (eds), *French Women Writers: A Bio-Bibliographical Source Book* (Westport, CT, and London: Greenwood Press, 1991)

Sartre, Jean-Paul, *L'Idiot de la famille*, 3 vols (Paris: Gallimard, 1971–2; rev. edn, 1988)

Schor, Naomi, *Breaking the Chain: Women, Theory, and French Realist Fiction* (New York: Columbia University Press, 1985)

——, 'Female Fetishism: The Case of George Sand', *Poetics Today*, 6 (1985), 301–10; repr. in *The Female Body in Western Culture: Contemporary Approaches*, ed. by Susan Suleiman (Cambridge, MA: Harvard University Press, 1986), pp. 363–72

——, *George Sand and Idealism* (New York and Chichester, West Sussex: Columbia University Press, 1993)

——, 'Triste Amérique: Atala and the Postrevolutionary Construction of Woman', in *Rebel Daughters: Women and the French Revolution*, ed. by Sara E. Melzer and Leslie W. Rabine (New York and Oxford: Oxford University Press, 1992), pp. 138–56

—— and Majewski, Henry F. (eds), *Flaubert and Postmodernism* (Lincoln and London: University of Nebraska Press, 1984)

Segal, Naomi, *The Adulteress's Child: Authorship and Desire in the Nineteenth-Century Novel* (Oxford and Cambridge, MA: Polity Press, 1992)

——, *Narcissus and Echo* (Manchester University Press: Manchester, 1988)

——, 'Our Lady of the Flowers', in Nicholas John (ed.), *Violetta and her Sisters: The Lady of the Camellias, Responses to the Myth* (London and Boston: Faber and Faber, 1994)

Sheridan, Susan (ed.), *Grafts: Feminist Cultural Criticism* (London and New York: Verso, 1988)

Shires, Linda M., 'Of maenads, mothers, and feminized males: Victorian Readings of the French Revolution', *Rewriting the Victorians: Theory, history, and the politics of gender*, ed. by Linda M. Shires (London: Routledge, 1992), pp. 147–65

Shubert, Adrian, *A Social History of Modern Spain* (London and Cambridge, MA: Unwin Hyman, 1990)

Shuttleworth, Sally, *George Eliot and Nineteenth-Century Science: The Make-Believe of a Beginning* (Cambridge and New York: Cambridge University Press, 1984)

Sieburth, Stephanie, 'Interpreting *La Regenta*: Coherence vs. Entropy', *Modern Language Notes*, 102 (1987), 274–91

——, 'Kiss and Tell: The Toad in *La Regenta*' in *'Malevolent Insemination' and other essays on Clarín*, ed. by Nöel Valis, *Michigan Romance Studies*, 10 (1990), pp. 87–100

Sinclair, Alison, *The Deceived Husband: A Kleinian Approach to the Literature of Infidelity* (Oxford: Clarendon Press, 1993)

Sinnigen, John H., 'Individual, Class and Society in *Fortunata and Jacinta*', in *Galdós Studies*, II, ed. by Robert J. Weber (London: Támesis Books, 1974), pp. 49–68; repr. in *Galdós*, ed. by Jo Labanyi (London and New York: Longman, 1993), pp. 116–39

Sivert, Eileen Boyd, '*Lélia* and Feminism', in *Feminist readings: French texts/American contexts*, *Yale French Studies*, 62 (1981), 45–66

Smith, Bonnie, *Ladies of the Leisure Class: The Bourgeoises of Northern France in the Nineteenth Century* (Princeton, NJ, and Guildford: Princeton University Press, 1981)

Smith, Maxwell A., *Prosper Merimée* (New York: Twayne, 1972)

Smith, Virginia Llewellyn, *Anton Chekhov and the Lady with the Dog* (London and New York: Oxford University Press, 1973)

Sourian, Eve, 'The Important, Little-Known Friendship of George Sand and Alexandre Dumas fils', in *The World of George Sand*, ed. by Natalie Datlof, Jeanne Fuchs, and David A. Powell (New York and London: Greenwood Press, 1991), pp. 243–53

Stavrou, Theofanis George, *Art and Culture in Nineteenth-Century Russia* (Bloomington: Indiana University Press, 1983)

Stenbock-Fermor, Elisabeth, *The Architecture of Anna Karenina: A History of its Writing, Structure, and Message* (Lisse, Neth.: Peter de Ridder Press, 1975)

Stern, J. P., *Re-Interpretations: Seven Studies in Nineteenth-Century German Literature* (London: Thames and Hudson, 1964; repr. Cambridge and New York: Cambridge University Press, 1981)

Still, Judith and Worton, Michael (eds), *Textuality and Sexuality: Reading theories and practices* (Manchester and New York: Manchester University Press, 1993)

Stites, Richard, *The Women's Liberation Movement in Russia: Feminism, Nihilism, and Bolshevism 1860–1930* (Princeton, NJ: Princeton University Press, 1978)

——, 'Women and the Russian Intelligentsia: Three Perspectives', in *Women in Russia*, ed. by Dorothy Atkinson, Alexander Dallin and Gail Warshofsky Lapidus (Stanford, CA: Stanford University Press, 1977; Brighton, Sussex: Harvester, 1978)

Stone, Lawrence, *The Family, Sex and Marriage in England 1500–1800*

(London: Weidenfeld and Nicolson, 1977)

Subiotto, Frances M., 'The Function of Letters in Fontane's "Unwiederbringlich"', *Modern Language Review*, 65 (1970), 306–18

Sutherland, John, *The Longman Companion to Victorian Fiction* (Harlow, Essex: Longman, 1988)

Swales, Erika, 'Private Mythologies and Public Unease: On Fontane's "Effi Briest"', *Modern Language Review*, 75 (1980), 114–23

Tanner, Tony, *Adultery in the Novel: Contract and Transgression* (Baltimore and London: Johns Hopkins University Press, 1979)

Terdiman, Richard, *Discourse/Counter-Discourse: The Theory and Practice of Symbolic Resistance in Nineteenth-Century France* (Ithaca, NY, and London: Cornell University Press, 1985)

Terras, Victor, 'Chekhov at Home: Russian Criticism', in *A Chekhov Companion*, ed. by Toby W. Clyman (Westport, CT, and London: Greenwood Press, 1985), pp. 167–83

Thomas, Donald, *A Long Time Burning: The History of Literary Censorship in England* (London: Routledge and Kegan Paul, 1969)

Thomas, Keith, 'The Double Standard', *Journal of the History of Ideas*, 20 (1959), 195–216

Thomson, Patricia, *George Sand and the Victorians: Her Influence and Reputation in Nineteenth-Century England* (Macmillan: London, 1977)

Thorlby, Anthony, *Leo Tolstoy: Anna Karenina* (Cambridge: Cambridge University Press, 1987)

Troyat, Henri, *Tolstoy*, trans. by Nancy Amphoux (New York: Doubleday, 1967; London: W. H. Allen, 1968; repr. Harmondsworth: Penguin, 1970)

Turner, C. J. G., 'Divorce and *Anna Karenina*', *Forum for Modern Language Studies*, 23 (1987), 97–116

——, *A Karenina Companion* (Waterloo, Ont.: Wilfrid Laurier University Press, 1993)

Turner, Harriet S., 'Family Ties and Tyrannies: A Reassessment of Jacinta', *Hispanic Review*, 51 (1983), pp. 1–22

——, *Benito Pérez Galdós: Fortunata and Jacinta* (Cambridge and New York: Cambridge University Press, 1992)

Valis, Noël Maureen, *The Decadent Vision in Leopoldo Alas: A Study of La Regenta and Su único hijo* (Baton Rouge and London: Louisiana State University Press, 1981)

—— (ed.), *'Malevolent Insemination' and other essays on Clarín*, Michigan Romance Studies, 10 (1990)

——, 'On Monstrous Birth: Leopoldo Alas's *La Regenta*', in Brian Nelson (ed.), *Naturalism in the European Novel: New Critical Perspectives* (Oxford and New York: Berg, 1992), pp. 191–209

——, 'Order and Meaning in Clarín's *La Regenta*', *Novel: A Forum on Fiction*, 16 (1983), 246–58

—— and Carol Maier (eds), *In the Feminine Mode: Essays on Hispanic Women Writers* (London and Toronto: Associated University Presses, 1990)

Varey, J. E. (ed.), *Galdós Studies* (London: Támesis Books, 1970)

Vargas Llosa, Mario, *The Perpetual Orgy* (London and Boston: Faber, 1987; first published in Spanish, 1975)

Velardi, Carol Hawkes, *Techniques of Compression and Prefiguration in the Beginnings of Theodor Fontane's Novels* (Berne and New York: Peter Lang, 1992)

Waller, Margaret, 'Being René, Buying Atala: Alienated Subjects and Decorative Objects in Postrevolutionary France', in *Rebel Daughters: Women and the French Revolution*, ed. by Sara E. Melzer and Leslie W. Rabine (New York and Oxford: Oxford University Press, 1992), pp. 157–77

——, *The Male Malady: Fictions of Impotence in the French Romantic Novel* (New Brunswick, NJ: Rutgers University Press, 1993)

Watt, George, *The Fallen Woman in the Nineteenth Century English Novel* (London and Canberra: Croom Helm; Totowa, NJ: Barnes and Noble, 1984)

Weber, Robert J. (ed.), *Galdós Studies*, II (London: Támesis Books, 1974)

Weeks, Jeffrey, *Sexuality and its Discontents: Meanings, Myths and Modern Sexualities* (London: Routledge and Kegan Paul, 1985)

Wesseling, Pieter, 'Structure and its Implications in Leopoldo Alas' *La Regenta*', *Hispanic Review*, 51 (1983), 393–408

Wightman, A. R., 'A Socialist "Ehebruchsroman": Günter de Bruyn's *Buridans Esel*', *New German Studies*, 13 (1985), 71–94

Williams, D. A., *Psychological Determinism in 'Madame Bovary'*, University of Hull Occasional Papers in Modern Languages, 9 (Hull: University of Hull, 1973)

Williams, Raymond, *Culture* (Glasgow: Fontana, 1981)

——, *Modern Tragedy* (London: Chatto and Windus, 1966; repr. Stanford, CA: Stanford University Press, 1987)

Williams, Tony, 'Champfleury, Flaubert and the Novel of Adultery', *Nineteenth-Century French Studies* 20 (1991–2), 145–57

Wilson, A. N., *Tolstoy: A Biography* (London: Hamish Hamilton, 1988)

Wing, Nathaniel, *The Limits of Narrative: Essays on Baudelaire, Flaubert, Rimbaud and Mallarmé* (Cambridge: Cambridge University Press, 1986)

Winner, Thomas, *Chekhov and his prose* (New York: Holt, Rinehart and Winston, 1966)

Winnifrith, Tom, *Fallen Women in the Nineteenth-Century Novel* (London: Macmillan; New York: St Martin's Press, 1994)

Wright, Barbara, and David H. T. Scott, *La Fanfarlo and Le Spleen de Paris*, Critical Guides to French Texts, 30 (London: Grant & Cutler, 1984)

Zeldin, Theodore, *France 1848–1945*, 2 vols (Oxford: Clarendon Press, 1973–7)

Index

28 D

GAYLORD

PRINTED IN U.S.A.